Dæmons Are Forever

James A. Millward, Series Editor

The Silk Roads series is made possible by the generous support of the Henry Luce Foundation's Asia Program. Founded in 1936, the Luce Foundation is a not-for-profit philanthropic organization devoted to promoting innovation in academic, policy, religious, and art communities. The Asia Program aims to foster cultural and intellectual exchange between the United States and the countries of East and Southeast Asia, and to create scholarly and public resources for improved understanding of Asia in the United States.

The Compensations of Plunder: How China Lost Its Treasures
Justin M. Jacobs

PUBLISHED 2020

Geocultural Power: China's Quest to Revive the Silk Roads for the Twenty-First Century
Tim Winter

PUBLISHED 2019

Islam and World History: The Ventures of Marshall Hodgson
Edited by Edmund Burke III and Robert J. Mankin

PUBLISHED 2018

Sacred Mandates: Asian International Relations since Chinggis Khan
Edited by Timothy Brook, Michael van Walt van Praag, and Miek Boltjes

PUBLISHED 2018

Dæmons Are Forever

Contacts and Exchanges in the Eurasian Pandemonium

DAVID GORDON WHITE

The University of Chicago Press
Chicago and London

The University of Chicago Press, Chicago 60637
The University of Chicago Press, Ltd., London

Published 2021
Printed in the United States of America

30 29 28 27 26 25 24 23 22 21 1 2 3 4 5

ISBN-13: 978-0-226-69240-1 (cloth)
ISBN-13: 978-0-226-71490-5 (paper)
ISBN-13: 978-0-226-71506-3 (e-book)
DOI: https://doi.org/10.7208/chicago/9780226715063.001.0001

Library of Congress Cataloging-in-Publication Data

Names: White, David Gordon, author.
Title: Daemons are forever : contacts and exchanges in the Eurasian pandemonium / David Gordon White.
Other titles: Silk roads (Chicago, Ill.)
Description: Chicago : The University of Chicago Press, 2021. | Series: Silk roads | Includes bibliographical references and index.
Identifiers: LCCN 2020026851 | ISBN 9780226692401 (cloth) | ISBN 9780226714905 (paperback) | ISBN 9780226715063 (ebook)
Subjects: LCSH: Demonology—History. | Mythology, Indo-European.
Classification: LCC BL660 .W49 2020 | DDC 133.4/209—dc23
LC record available at https://lccn.loc.gov/2020026851

♾ This paper meets the requirements of ANSI/NISO Z39.48-1992 (Permanence of Paper).

For my father,
Gordon Robens White (d. 2017),
a gentle man

Contents

Abbreviations

AV	*Atharva Veda*
CS	*Caraka Saṃhitā*
CST	*Cakrasaṃvara Tantra*
DJ	*Devadhamma Jātaka*
KGB	Kashmir-Gandhara-Bactria
KS	*Kauśika Sūtra*
KSS	*Kathāsaritsāgara*
MBH	*Mahābhārata*
MMVS	*Mahāmāyūrīvidyārājñī-sūtra*
MV	*Mahāvamsa*
NT	*Netra Tantra*
PMG	"Greek Magical Papyri"
QC	"Quaestiones Conviviales" of Plutarch
RA	*Rasārṇava*
ṚV	*Ṛg Veda*
ŚK	*Śānti Kalpa*
SPS	*Saddharmapuṇḍarīka Sūtra*
SS	*Suśruta Saṃhitā*
TSBH	*Tantrasadbhāva*
WGDR	"Wedding of Sir Gawain and Dame Ragnelle"
ZY	*Zamyād Yašt*

Note on Translations

Unless otherwise indicated, all translations from the French, Old French, Danish, Hindi, Pali, Prakrit, and Sanskrit are my own. Except where indicated, none of the translations from other languages are my own.

1

Dæmon-ology

Night: and once again, the nightly grapple with death, the room shaking with daemonic orchestras . . .

MALCOLM LOWRY, *Under the Volcano*

1

In a contrarian 1934 publication,[1] Paul Mus challenged several scholarly commonplaces concerning medieval Indian civilization by viewing its religious productions through the lens of cognate Southeast Asian traditions. Suddenly, phenomena that had appeared to be specific to South Asia ("phallic" *liṅgam* worship and so forth) were shown to be but Indian instantiations of a broader (South)east Asian palette of traditions. For the past decade or so, I have been engaged in a similar project, viewing the ancient and medieval dæmon-ology of Europe as the Western extension of an aggregate of traditions spanning the entire Eurasian landmass.

Many if not most of the world's religions have situated a protean grouping of spirit beings somewhere between their generally benevolent high gods and their generally malevolent demons. Known to the ancient Greeks as *daimōn*s and to the ancient Romans as *dæmon*s, their most distinguishing feature has been their ambiguity. By turns benign and malign, powerful and vulnerable, innate and remote, earthbound and aerial, inert and evanescent, dæmons often constitute a nameless horde whose members morph between human, mammalian, and avian forms of often indeterminate gender. Historically, this ambiguity, this indeterminacy, has afforded dæmons a remarkable mobility. Dæmons have always traveled more lightly than gods. Here I am not speaking of agency and mobility on the part of the dæmons themselves, but rather of the movements and activities of the humans seeking congress with or relief from them. Dæmonology, the "science of dæmons," is a religious vernacular that, unbound by exclusivist theological and institutional strictures, has been shared across every non-modern and modern culture and incorporated into their respective scriptural and literary traditions, ritual observances, material cultures, and iconographic programs. For the most part, it is a vernacular for which no hieratic intervention is required. Manipulating or transacting with dæmons does not require a sophisticated belief system or sacerdotal institution: what is essential is that the techniques employed be effective. Ritual gestures, speech acts without semantic content (i.e., spells), mute power substances, and man-made devices are what human specialists have been offering their clientele for millennia. Like the dæmons themselves, these human agents have generally been an ambiguous group, with the borderline between a sorcerer and a counter-sorcerer or a black and a white magician often being situational if not reversible.[2]

This book is about dæmon-ology in the sense that it is principally a study of the dissemination of myths and ritual technologies proper to the pan-dæmonium that preceded the advent of Christianity in the West, Islam in Western and Inner Asia, Buddhism and theistic Hinduism in South Asia, and Buddhism in Inner and East Asia. It is also a book about demon-ology inasmuch as some of those dæmons were malign and properly speaking, demonic; but also because it concerns the transformations that the various dæmons underwent at the hands of their respective culture brokers—the Catholic clergy, Hindu brahmins, Buddhist monks, Zoroastrian high priests, and so forth—who by turns demonized, domesticated, and appropriated their local dæmons, transforming them into local or regional demons, or, with surprising frequency, into Catholic saints, Hindu gods, Buddhist bodhisattvas, and the like.

In spite of my use of the term in an earlier article on the subject, there never has been a demonological "cosmopolis."[3] I say this because, unlike the Sanskrit language in South and East Asia, transactions with these spirit beings have never been linked to a *polis*, to a hegemonic political formation.[4] To the contrary, as Jonathan Z. Smith demonstrated with respect to Near Eastern late antiquity, a hallmark of demonology has been its apolitical if not subversive quality, and the capacity of its specialists to survive and even thrive in situations of anomie.[5] (In this respect, the snake oil salesmen of the old Far West had a venerable pedigree.) However, the wearing of a demonifuge amulet need not require the intervention of a specialist, and common folk have had unmediated interactions with dæmons and demons for millennia.

Demonological techniques as well as dæmons themselves have drifted across the Eurasian expanse on the ebb and flow of trade, travel, migration, political expansion, and warfare, a tantalizing piece of evidence for this being a three-inch-tall statuette (plate 1) unearthed at Urgench (Turkmenistan) in the middle of the twentieth century. The modern Urgench sits atop the ruins of Gurganj, a city that Cingghis Khan's army laid waste in 1220 CE, and this bronze statuette, cast in Bengal, represents Śītalā, a goddess (many would say, a demoness) long associated with smallpox in northern India.[6] Jeannine Auboyer and Marie-Thérèse de Mallmann paint a vivid tableau of the troubled period in which the statuette made its 2,500-mile journey, hypothesizing that it was either carried west by one or more soldiers "as a talisman, rightly fearing the ravages caused by deadly epidemics in times of invasion," or that it made its way to Gurganj in the saddlebags of a merchant caravan.[7] Nine centuries earlier, the city of Antioch, that "gravitational center of the eastern Mediterranean world in antiquity" which drew merchants from as far away as China, was a halting place for another type of traveler. As Dayna Kalleres relates in her study of the Christian bishop John Chrysostom's demonization of the city's pagan dæmons, "itinerant *goētes*, *magoi*, divinatory experts (Gk. *manteis*), theurgic practitioners, and *Chaldaei* from the farthest reaches of both the Roman and Persian empires continually move[d] through the city, introducing new forms of ritual practices. . . . In the end, it [was] a competitive, charismatic market fed continuously by trade routes and energized by urban demand."[8] The intervening centuries saw all manner of exchanges in dæmonological and allied traditions and technologies, including the spread of magic squares from China into India, the Islamic world, and Europe; the dissemination of astrological science from the Hellenistic world into Persia and India; and the transmission of ayurvedic demonology from India into Inner, East, and Southeast Asia and the Arab world.[9] Well before the "signed" accounts of Marco Polo, Ibn Battuta, and other illustrious travelers, a treasury of wondrous tales would also overspread the Eurasian ecumene, carried by unknown voices and unknown hands. Here, I am not speaking of folktales, which I will address later in this introductory chapter, but rather massive corpora whose contents overflow and challenge the modern-day categories of history, legend, myth, religion, and science. By the sixteenth century, the "Alexander Romance," a fourth-century Greek mythologization of the life of the historical world-conqueror, had been translated into over a dozen languages, ranging from Arabic to Malay to French. In its many retellings, the young Macedonian general would be transformed into the son of an Egyptian pharaoh; identified with the mysterious Dhû-l-Qarnayn ("Two-Horns") of Qur'anic tradition; elevated as a defender of the bastions of Christendom (and Islam) against the Biblical armies of Gog and Magog; and made out to be a soothsayer, a dragon-slayer, and an explorer of underwater depths in a prototype bathyscaphe.[10]

The same period saw the transmission and translation—from India to the Christian West via Arabic, Armenian, and Slavonic adaptations—of Sanskrit-language accounts of the life of the Buddha. Extant in over sixty versions in Europe, the Christian East, and Africa, the collection of tales known as the

"Legend of Barlaam and Josaphat" would not only spur the emergence of an essential medieval European literary convention, but also define the ideal of the spiritual life in medieval Christendom.[11] The legend of another Christian "saint," in this case a martyred greyhound, which also had its origin in India, will be discussed below in chapter 4.[12] So too, an Inner Asian ethnogenic myth was the likely source of a body of medieval tradition which, spanning much of Eurasia, concerned the mating practices of "races" of Amazon women and Cynocephalic men.[13] This latter group would be added to a broader class of "monstrous races" that, featured in medieval European "ethnography" and iconography for well over a millennium, had their origins in India's great epic, the *Mahābhārata* (MBh).[14] Pan-Eurasian traditions such as these—oral and literary, iconographic, ethnological, mythological, ritual, and technological—will form the subject matter of the interlaced dæmonological studies that comprise this book.

2

The seeds for this project were first planted in my mind during a 1999 research tour that took me out of the urban environments of the Gangetic plain and into India's western hinterlands and the Kathmandu Valley of Nepal. There, it became clear to me that the selective scripture-based metanarrative that had colonized my vision of South Asian religions was at variance with the ethnographic and historical record. That metanarrative maintained that "classical Hinduism" had, in magnificent isolation from the other great religions of the subcontinent and the outside world, evolved directly out of the speculative hymns of the *Ṛg Veda*, the philosophical teachings of the Upaniṣads, and the monotheistic gospel of the *Bhagavad Gītā* to culminate in the devotional cults of the supreme beings championed in the mythology of the *Rāmāyaṇa* and the Purāṇas. Over the past several decades, that tortured schema, which continues to inform many a university-level introduction to Hinduism, has remained largely unchallenged.

However, since the 1970s, a growing body of scholarship has shown that Tantra, that bugbear of the colonial era, was, for well over a thousand years, South Asia's predominant religious idiom, permeating every one of the subcontinent's official religions. The medieval and early modern religious civilization of South Asia,[15] as well as of much of Southeast, Inner, and East Asia, was tantric, with a hallmark of Tantra being its incorporation of the "fierce gods,"[16] the male and female dæmons and demons of the South Asian pandemonium, into a highly elastic pantheon. India's intelligentsia and priesthood (the two were often the same) and their royal and aristocratic patrons were, for the most part, tantric practitioners, with royal devotion to tantric deities the rule rather than the exception. Even today, the ritual programs of India's great temples, as sanctioned in the Purāṇas themselves, bear the mark of a strong tantric legacy.

Scripture-based *bhakti*, the "official Hinduism" of India's modern-day urban society, is an epiphenomenon.[17] Historical latecomers to the South Asian scene,[18] the devotional cults of the Vaiṣṇava, Śaiva, and Śākta high gods have always comprised the minority religion of South Asia. This remains the case down to the present day in village India, which is still home to some three-quarters of the population. There, in spite of efforts going back to colonial-period Hindu reform movements to root out the "superstitions" of their benighted coreligionists, religion has always been local, grounded in the ancestral and landscape-specific deities of household and village,[19] commonly known as *devatā*s, the Indic equivalents of the Greco-Roman dæmons.[20] Furthermore, Hindu elites themselves have perennially reverted to "vernacular" practices under specific circumstances and pivotal moments in their lives, with the interplay between local, regional, and translocal traditions being complex and multifaceted.[21] Even as many of the subcontinent's ancient dæmons have been demonized in one way or another in Sanskrit scripture, the religious practices of the South Asian masses have always been dæmonological.

In many respects, the policies of Hindu reformers and nationalists have reprised those of the Catholic Church, which constantly strove with mixed success to impose its normative vision of the true Christian faith upon a diverse populace. Like the proponents of *hindutva*, the great majority of the medieval Catholic hierarchy were urbanites isolated from and contemptuous of rural culture and society. That contempt translated into two terms that, first coined in postclassical Latin, made their way into several Romance and Germanic vernaculars in the twelfth century. These are "pagan" and "peasant," both derived from the classical Latin *pagus*, "rural district."[22] Peasant religion was pagan religion. As Jean-Claude Schmitt has observed,

> while grounded to a certain extent in objective reality, the clerical denunciation of "survivals" of paganism—itself a blanket category that conflated traditions whose various strands the clergy were incapable of untangling—was also a reflection of pre-established ideological categories. By virtue of their classical training, the bishops were well familiar with the names of the pagan gods. However, in their eyes these were so many demons whose virulence only increased as one distanced oneself from the bastions of civilization that were, in their view, the cathedral cities.[23]

An essential distinction between the missionary efforts of the medieval Church and those of modern-day Hindu nationalists concerns the village religion that the latter are currently seeking to supplant (together with Islam and Christianity) in favor of their vision of the true Hindu faith. In Europe, the old pagan religions—Greco-Roman, Celtic, Germanic, and so forth—did not share a common confessional heritage with the Catholic Church. Such is not the case in India. As I will argue in the next chapter, many elements of popular Hindu practice are more ancient and authentically "vedic" than those deemed normative by India's urban elites. Unbeknownst to its practitioners, many aspects of South Asia's village religion carry forward traditions found in the ancient scriptural canons; and generally unbeknownst to ethnographers of "village studies," the content and dynamics of these traditions bear a remarkable uniformity across time and territory.[24]

One of the strategies of the medieval Church in its battle against the enduring cults of Europe's old pagan gods was to identify them as malign demons. In some cases this was an accurate assessment, but the actual situation was generally more complex. Catholic theologians were fully cognizant of the fact that Christendom's demons were survivals of the supernatural beings known as dæmons in pagan late antiquity.[25] These were, for the most part, tutelary deities, ranging from the guardian angels of individual humans like Plato to spirits of the dead and the *genii locorum* of ancient Roman landscapes.[26] Long before humans' first contact with them, the groves, forest clearings, spring-fed pools, and hilltops of ancient Europe belonged to these spirit deities: nymphs, fairies, dryads, elves, trolls, and so forth. So, for example, the "land spirits" (*landvættir*) of pagan Scandinavia were tutelary deities, often identified as giants (*bergbúi*), denizens of sylvan groves, earthen mounds, stone outcroppings, and waterfalls. These were assimilated with another group, the *landáss* ("Aesir of the Land"), a class of deities immediately subordinate to the Aesir, that is, to the high gods Odin, Freyr, and Njordr. With the Christianization of Scandinavia, the Church quickly demonized the *landvættir* and prohibited all forms of worship at their ancient sanctuaries.[27]

Occasionally, the ancient Greeks employed *daimōn* interchangeably with *theos*, the word for an Olympian god; in other cases the term denoted an aerial demigod, a celestial spirit situated between the high gods and the world of men.[28] In these roles, ancient Greek and Etruscan iconography frequently depicted them as fine-featured anthropomorphic beings with magnificent wings. This aspect of the pagan world's auspicious dæmons accounts for the iconography and certain elements of the angelology of the three Western monotheisms. So it was that, according to the third-century Christian theologian Origen, the bodies of dæmons, angels, and the invisible gods were all

FIGURE 1.1. The "Chinese" god Vitek or Ninifo. Image from Picart, *Cérémonies et coutumes religieuses* (1728), vol. 3, following p. 222.

composed of the same immaterial "substance."[29] Similarly, late antique and early medieval Christian art portrayed the fallen angel Lucifer or Satan with birdlike wings as feathered as those of the cherubim and seraphim; it was not until the middle of the thirteenth century that the Lord of Darkness and his minions would come to be represented with the sinister wings of bats (plate 2), a transformation likely inspired by exposure to the Buddhist art of Central Asia.[30] Like the Scandinavian *landvættir*, the dæmons of pagan antiquity would quickly be repudiated by Jewish, Christian, and Muslim theologians as the demonic minions of Satan himself, with all positive aspects of their original divine natures expunged. These are the Biblical demons exorcised by Jesus Christ, demons that in medieval art are shown emerging, often bat-winged, from the mouths of their erstwhile victims (plate 3). A few centuries later, in one of the earliest European representations of Asian iconography, bat-winged demons would reappear, in the role of attendant deities to a certain "Chinese" god named "Vitek or Ninifo" (fig. 1.1).[31]

A parallel case of demonization occurred in Sasanian Persia, for whereas in the Old Iranian Avesta, the term *daēva* referred to a divinity of pre-Zoroastrian polytheism, with the hardening of Zoroastrian orthodoxy under the Sasanians, the Middle Iranian (Pahlavi) cognate term *dēw* came to denote malign demons alone.[32] Of interest in this regard is a Parthian-language text inscribed on a circa sixth-century Manichean amulet, probably written in the Balkh region of modern-day northern Afghanistan. In addition to reproducing several names from a fourth-century Buddhist catalog of the South Asian *genii locorum* known as *yakṣa*s, this document also speaks of routing "demons, *yakṣa*s, *peri*s, *druj*s, *rākṣasa*s, idols of darkness and spirits of evil." Before being exported with Buddhism into Central and East Asia in the early centuries of the Common Era, the yakṣas and rākṣasas evoked here figured prominently (often as auspicious dæmons) in the Vedas as well as in ancient Buddhist and Jain scripture; however, these spirit beings would also be demoted to malign demonic status in later Indic literature.[33] As for the *peri*s and *druj*s, these were, like the *dēw*s, evil demons from the Zoroastrian pandemonium. Through the power of Lord Jesus Christ, Mar Mani (the Manichean savior), the angels Michael, Sera'el, Raphael, Gabriel, and others, the amulet text concludes, these demons and their ilk would be made to "flee . . . vanish, take fright, [and] pass away . . . to a far place."[34]

These examples notwithstanding, the malevolence of these ancient dæmons was not a pure fabrication on the part of religious officialdom. Long before the advent of the three monotheisms and the great religions of the eastern world, the ancient Eurasian lifeworld had been populated by a pandemonium of evil dæmons that, either foreign, intrinsically evil, or fallen through some transgressive act,[35] were notorious for plaguing humans with every sort of affliction, both physical and spiritual.[36] So, for example, as I will discuss in chapter 3, the Greco-Roman world had always considered the "evil eye demon" (*baskanos daimōn*) to be a malign spirit, and was in no need of Christian or Jewish theologians to pronounce it so.

By the same token, demonology, the body of doctrines concerning malign demons and the techniques for combating them, predated the advent of the three monotheisms by centuries, if not millennia. Such was also the case in both ancient Persia and India, whose venerable vedic corpus, the *Atharva Veda* (AV) in particular, was heavily demonological in content. Here as well, India's modern-day demonological traditions have remained faithful to their archaic sources, in the light of which I find it appropriate to speak of a South Asian demonological substratum. This substratum—a demonic pantheon, demonological nomenclature, and a body of demonifuge techniques—informed the later ancillary Atharvan literature, the ayurvedic corpus, Buddhist demonological literature, and Hindu, Buddhist, and Jain Tantra, just as it informs modern-day practice. While only a small cohort of modern-day malign demons can claim textual pedigrees extending back to the *Ṛg Veda* (ṚV) itself, their numbers have swelled exponentially over time, through the incorporation of demons from indigenous and foreign sources and the invention or discovery of "new" demons as agents of the infinite panoply of human afflictions.[37] Furthermore, demonology (*bhūtavidyā*) was in many respects the bedrock of Tantra—that mainstream religion of medieval and early modern India—which, in its early phases, enshrined voluntary possession by demonic beings as the sine qua non of initiation and other essential elements of practice.[38]

However, like the West, India has also had its complement of benign dæmons whose latter-day fate bears comparison with that of their pagan homologues at the hands of the Catholic Church. From the vedic period down to the present day, the most widely employed generic Sanskrit terms for these supernatural beings have been *yakṣa* (female *yakṣī* or *yakṣiṇī*) and *devatā*.[39] Like their Greco-Roman homologues, these were cast in early Hindu, Buddhist, and Jain literature as the primordial inhabitants and *genii locorum* of both sublime and terrible features of the natural landscape. The current efforts of the Hindu nationalists notwithstanding, these popular deities and their cults have been tolerated for centuries by Hindu, Buddhist, and Jain communities, which have sought to assimilate them through two interrelated strategies. The first of these may be termed *subordination*: the yakṣas and devatās have been accorded secondary status, supporting roles in the Hindu, Buddhist, and Jain pantheons. The second strategy is *adaptation*: as Charlotte Vaudeville and others have demonstrated for Kṛṣṇa and Balarāma, the puranic mythology of these avatars of Viṣṇu owes much to the local yakṣa traditions of the Mathura region of north central India dating back to the early centuries of the Common Era.[40] Similarly, Śiva's aniconic manifestation, the liṅgam, is an adaptation of yakṣa iconography from the same time and place.[41] So it is that the region's yakṣas of yore live on in the village worship of a divinity named Jakhaiyā ("yakṣa" in the local vernacular), alongside or in the shadow of the high gods that have supplanted them by appropriating many of their features and prerogatives. One finds similar developments in Buddhism and Jainism, into whose pantheons a number of named yakṣas and yakṣīs, as well as the converted demoness Hāritī, came to be revered as bodhisattvas and gods in the medieval period.[42]

This second strategy was also adopted by the medieval and modern Catholic Church. When it became clear that, in spite of centuries of prohibitions by Rome, the European peasantry showed no sign of relinquishing the archaic practice of taking the waters of "pagan" wells and springs for a variety of ills, the Church sanctified these places of healing into Christian sanctuaries, now ascribing their powers to the miracles of this or that canonized saint or virgin. As I will describe in chapter 4, this dæmonological substratum has persisted across a half-dozen coastal regions of western Europe, where the waters of "Our Lady of Sorrows" and other shrines are renowned for easing the sufferings of the faithful. All of which should caution scholars against "evolutionary and teleological models, in which primitive polytheism inevitably led to ritualistic monotheism."[43]

3

"Global" cross-cultural studies of myth and religion have been out of vogue for a few decades now, more or less since the time I wrote a monograph on the cynocephalic "race" of ancient and medieval Eurasia.[44] My PhD thesis, of which a revised version appeared as *Myths of the Dog-Man* in 1991, was a historical reconstruction of the origins and dissemination of the mythology of the Cynocephali out of Inner Asia and into Europe, India, and China. When I wrote my dissertation, I was a student in the History of Religions program at the University of Chicago's Divinity School. However, in contrast to the program in Church History at that institution, students in the History of Religions were not trained in the craft of writing history. There, History of Religions so-called was something more akin to Comparative Religion, rather pompously referred to in those days as the Phenomenology of Religion. In the early 1980s, its model was Mircea Eliade's 1958 *Patterns in Comparative Religion*,[45] even if Eliade was then hard at work composing his *History of Religious Ideas* during those same years.

It was in the course of writing my dissertation that I came to realize that identifying recurrent patterns in myths and symbols synchronically was a vain pursuit, in spite of the theoretical justifications that were in the air at the time. The most prominent among these were Eliade's idealized subject, termed *homo religiosus*, whose enchanted experience of the "sacred" was, as he claimed, one and the same across the world's archaic and traditional (i.e., non-modern) religions; and Claude Lévi-Strauss's stance that the meaning of myths was to be found not in their content but rather in their structure, which was identical across world cultures because the workings of the human mind were identical the world over. Like all the totalizing theories that had preceded theirs, Eliade's and Lévi-Strauss's eventually collapsed under the weight of their own reductionist assumptions.

That decline was hastened by developments both from within and outside of the History of Religions field. Primary among the latter was the meteoric rise in the 1970s of the congeries of cultural theory labeled postmodernism. Originally a rejection of modernist historiography, its purview quickly expanded to comprise a critique of all positivist methodologies, essentialized categories, discursive regimes of power, and the validity of Eurocentric hegemonic discourse. Here, the deconstruction of modernist metanarratives was held up as the necessary precondition for allowing the voices of "historically muted" non-modern, non-Western actors to emerge. While the postmodernists' first move, of applying a hermeneutics of suspicion to modernist categories and discourse, has had a salutary, even cathartic, effect on academic discourse, the other shoe has yet to fall. In South Asia, the Subaltern School's widely announced hermeneutics of retrieval, in their case the championing of minority or "subaltern histories,"[46] has never truly lived up to its promise. Quickly abandoning its extraordinary project of writing carefully researched case studies of peasants, workers, and other of India's "little people" in favor of discourse analysis of the elite groups that dominated them,[47] its proponents went on to exoticize and essentialize a theoretical subaltern subject as an ahistorical creature, asserting without supporting documentation that her lifeworld "of gods and spirits" was incompatible with, because not encompassed by, a Eurocentric "frame of a single historical time that envelops all other kinds of time."[48] In this respect, their essentialized subject came to differ but little from Eliade's *homo religiosus*.

In a highly influential essay, Gayatri Spivak took matters a step further, contending that because the historically muted subaltern subject was unable to speak for herself, any attempt to represent her subjectivity, however well-meaning, would actually contribute to her further repression.[49] Furthermore, because a "hyperreal Europe"[50] was always the basis for comparison, no non-Western or minority tradition could ever be evaluated on its own terms or according to its own values and aspirations. From this perspective, philological and textualist approaches to South Asian cultures, the legacy of dead white males, would stand especially guilty by association. As Stephanie Jamison delicately put it, "The Subaltern has Spoken, and the general view is that he doesn't speak Sanskrit."[51] These polemics have had a corrosive effect on humanities and social sciences scholarship, in the United States in particular.[52] By ignoring or rejecting historical connections outright, we not only close ourselves off from constructive engagement with others but also isolate ourselves from the outside world, and by the same token, contribute to the perceived irrelevance of the humanities and social sciences as legitimate academic disciplines. Not only do we impoverish ourselves, but we also leave the way open for religious ideologues, bigots, dilettantes, and journalists to define critical discourse and appropriate or invent selected mythic narratives as "histories" in order to further their own agendas. In India, where Hindu nationalists have been employing just such a strategy for the past decades, members of the Subaltern School writing "in the interests of social justice"[53] have largely remained silent, with only courageous objective historians like Romila Thapar raising their voices to challenge them.

The post–World War II programmatic focus on Area Studies in the humanities and social sciences has further exacerbated matters, contributing to a general neglect of networks of contact and exchange between world areas. In the field of South Asian religions, this has translated into a paucity of research on connections between the Indian subcontinent and other parts of the Asian and European world that, united politically, economically, and culturally in earlier times, have become separated (at least in our mental maps) by contemporary political boundaries. Treating the Indian subcontinent as a geographical and cultural isolate, the parochialism of the Area Studies approach has also tacitly comforted the claims of Hindu nationalists for whom Hinduism and people of Aryan blood rose up out of the Land of the Āryas (*āryāvarta*) shortly after the beginning of time.[54]

The purview of the field of classical Indology also dovetails with the Hindu nationalist worldview. For both, the borders of India—geographical in the case of the Hindu nationalists and textual in the case of the Indologists—define the horizon of discourse. And for both, when they have looked beyond those boundaries, their nearly exclusive focus has been the contributions of India's magnificent Sanskritic civilization to the wider world, rather than what India has imported from the outside. This is particularly ironic in the case of Hindu Tantra, much of whose canon was compiled in medieval Kashmir, a region that, although a part of the "Sanskrit cosmopolis," had cultural ties to Inner Asia that were as strong as those it maintained with the subcontinent. Now, it is true that colonial historiography erroneously painted "India"—including the culturally Indianized regions of ancient Gandhara, Bactria, and Sogdiana—as the passive recipient of Western art, culture, and science; or, as Hegel argued, as a land entirely outside of History itself prior to its introduction onto the stage of History through European colonization.[55] These modernist prejudices notwithstanding, much may be gained by looking beyond arbitrary boundaries to examine the flow of goods, ideas, technologies—and dæmons—as multidirectional and unbounded by modern geographical borders.

The methodological positions of the two leading theoreticians of the Religious Studies field have also contributed to the narrowing of its horizons. In a 1965 essay titled "Crisis and Renewal in History of Religions," Eliade considered the declining fortunes of the discipline and proposed a road map to the recovery of its former greatness.[56] Such was not to be. Twenty years later, Eliade's own legacy was in crisis as revelations concerning his dark political past began to surface. But well before this, in fact only three years after the publication of his 1965 essay, the metaphysical foundations of Eliade's grand theoretical edifice were already coming under critical scrutiny. At a lecture presented at Chicago's Divinity School in the winter of 1968, a young scholar challenged Eliade's pivotal category of sacred space.[57] In the decades that followed, that scholar, a certain Jonathan Z. Smith, would continue to dismantle Eliade's theoretical constructs, and with them, the foundations—even the legitimacy—of our discipline as it had been previously constituted. As is well known, a primary focus of Smith's project has been comparison.[58] In his view, comparison in the Eliadean mode has had more to do with "magical thinking" than scholarship, with the history of the discipline's comparative adventures one of "an enterprise undertaken in bad faith." If we are to take him at his word, the very "possibility of the study of religion" cannot be realized unless and until an appropriate method for comparison is articulated, and a certain number of preconditions fulfilled. As recently as 2004, Smith was still awaiting those developments.[59]

It was in his 1971 article "*Adde Parvum Parvo Magnus Acervus Erit*" that Smith laid the groundwork for theorizing the limitations and potential of Religious Studies comparison, and it was here that he took a position that he never satisfactorily explained concerning the writing of history. In that study, Smith cast historiography as one of four broad methods or styles of comparison, ranging the "genetic" or "diffusionist" type of comparison under the general heading of the "evolutionary" style. In later writing, he would nuance his position, speaking in terms of "genealogical" assumptions with respect to influence and borrowing, contrasting these unfavorably to an approach based on "*analogous processes*, responding to parallel kinds of religious situations."[60]

At bottom, Smith was advocating for what is commonly referred to as "comparative history." Pioneered by Marx and Weber, the perennial foci of this approach have been the political economies of nation-states, the emergence of "modernity," the socioeconomic conditions underlying the rise of capitalism and so forth.[61] Here, the working assumption is that nations, societies, and cultures that find themselves in analogous political, social, and existential situations may be taken as objects of comparison. When Smith's objects of comparison were the various religions of late antiquity, he was alert to change over time with respect, for example, to the shift from a "locative" to a "utopian" worldview, or the rise of the itinerant magician at the expense of the temple priest.[62] When, however, he stepped outside of his area of expertise, for example comparing ancient Babylonian New Year rites to the "cargo situation" of an early twentieth-century Indonesian people,[63] he presented his comparanda as ahistorical cameos, frozen in time but comparable to one another in the mind of the scholar. He did so not because he was uninterested in history, but rather because writing history was for him less interesting than theorizing or "imagining religion." In his classic formulation, a comparison was "a disciplined exaggeration in the service of knowledge . . . provid[ing] the means by which *we* 're-vision' phenomena as *our* data in order to solve *our* theoretical problems."[64] Left unexplained throughout, however, is the ground on which Smith saw fit to reduce historiography to a type of comparison.

For the past three decades, Bruce Lincoln has generally followed Smith's lead in these matters. Also like Smith, he has rejected the option of writing objective history, in his case on the basis of an expanding set of ideological positions.[65] Over time, these have hardened into a sort of methodological scholasticism,[66] which has forced him to narrow his hermeneutical horizon to what he has termed, of late, "weak comparison."[67] Comparative history in everything but name, Lincoln's project is to compare texts from diverse historical periods and contexts (often, *pace* Smith, a pair comprised by one ancient and one modern source) generated under analogous social or cultural circumstances. Lincoln draws the data he has "stipulated as exemplary"[68] from mythological texts, broadly construed, composed either by representatives of "official religion" or by its oppressed victims. With few exceptions, these are marshaled to prove his axiomatic position that myths are always already narrative expressions of ideology, most often that of an oppressor "authority," with religion constituting the most ancient and extreme form of ideology.[69]

Over the past decades, Lincoln has also injected postmodernist idioms into his discourse, most (in)famously in his characterization of scholarship as "mythology with footnotes," for which he offers two rationales. The first, constructive, maintains that footnotes are recognitions of an ongoing engagement with both the data at hand and the broader scholarly community. The second, deconstructive, asserts that footnotes "provide opportunities for misrepresentation, mystification, sycophancy, character assassination, skillful bluff, and downright fraud." It is on the basis of this latter position that he concludes his 1999 collection of essays by rejecting projects of "reconstruction" in favor of those of criticism.[70] He would have us do the same.

4

When in the mid-1980s I set about writing my dissertation, my original impulse was to follow the normative "History of Religions" model in comparing the ways in which the idea of a hybrid "monster," half-human and half-animal, had been articulated across a half-dozen distinct mythological traditions. As I originally conceived my project, I would, in a second move, orient my comparative data toward a deeper set of reflections on the meaning of those myths, both for those distinct cultures of old and for we moderns in the here and now. That meaning, as I saw it, would concern the concept of alterity, the "othering of the Other" that was very much in the air in those days; and it was for that reason that the title of my dissertation was "The Other Gives Rise to Self." In other words, mine was to be an exercise in the "phenomenology of religion" in the parlance of the time—that is to say, in "comparative history." Which it was, to a certain extent, and traces of that original project may still be found in the first and final chapters of *Myths of the Dog-Man*.

However, as mentioned above, when I began to organize and analyze the data I had been culling from Eurasian mythology, I realized that there was another way to approach my subject, that way being the historical approach. Here, I was fortunate to have been exposed, during my student years in Paris in the late 1970s, to the work of several scholars whose histories of medieval Europe had captivated and inspired me to emulate them in my own way. Here I am speaking of the past century's leading French historians of *mentalités*, microhistory, and historical anthropology: Marc Bloch, Jacques Le Goff, Georges Duby, Emmanuel Le Roy Ladurie, and, most recently, Jean-Claude Schmitt. While these historians have generally limited their focus to medieval western and central Europe,[71] I considered that my data lent itself to the wider scope of ancient and medieval Eurasian history. And so it was that my project became one of drawing out patterns of influence and identifying the networks of contacts and exchanges between Europe and South and East Asia that generated a shared body of myth. That historical detective work, which led me back to the hypothetical origins of the myths of the dog-man in a set of Inner Asian ethnogenic accounts, proved to be far more rewarding than an ahistorical comparative study in alterity.[72]

While there is a place for imagining religion and for theorizing myth, these pursuits should not replace historical inquiry. Like the lore of monstrous races, that of dæmons—whether demonized or not—commends itself to historical analysis across cultural, geographical, and linguistic boundaries, because dæmons travel lightly and because dæmons are forever. A year after *Myths of the Dog-Man* appeared, Walter Burkert theorized this approach in his introduction to a monograph on the influence of the Near Eastern cultural sphere upon ancient Greek religion and culture when he wrote that "the modest aim of this book is to serve as a messenger across boundaries. . . . If in certain cases the materials themselves do not provide incontrovertible evidence of cultural transfer, the establishment of similarities will still be of value, as it serves to free both the Greek and the oriental phenomena from their isolation and to create an arena of possible comparisons."[73] There are, in fact, two approaches to history embedded in this statement, the one focusing on what I have been calling comparative history, and the other on "cultural transfer," that is, historical contacts and exchanges. In 1997, this latter approach was theorized by Sanjay Subrahmanyam for early modern and modern Eurasia, under the rubric of "connected histories," a theme he has expanded upon in much of his later writing.[74] In the conclusion to his original manifesto, he encapsulated the argument against comparative history in the following terms:

> Let me end, therefore, with the plea, once more, that we not only compare from within our boxes, but spend some time and effort to transcend them, not by comparison alone but by seeking out the at times fragile threads that connected the globe. . . . This is not to deny voice to those who were somehow "fixed" by social and cultural coordinates, who inhabited "localities" in the early modern period and nothing else, and whom we might seek out with our intrepid analytical machetes. But if we ever get to "them" by means other than archaeology, the chances are that it is because they are already plugged into some network, some process of circulation.[75]

Here, we must not confuse connected histories with diffusionism, whose assumptions and disastrous track record have rightly consigned it to the dustbin of humanities scholarship. Once again, the insights of Walter Burkert are helpful, inasmuch as he analogizes diffusionism with etymology (the two sharing a preoccupation with origins), and transmission with metaphor: "More pertinent than 'etymology' would be the analogy of metaphor. . . . To understand a true metaphor one must know the primary meaning, else one does not get the point of the secondary application; to understand myth, similar knowledge of historical levels is required."[76] In this book, I will follow Burkert's and Subrahmanyam's leads as I chase down the traces left across Eurasia by historical actors transacting in dæmonological and demonological narrative, theory, and practice. Here, I find myself in the good company of an expanding number of "Silk Road Studies" programs, the online "Sino-Platonic Papers" monograph series, and the efforts of scholars who view a connected approach to history as a necessary corrective to the isolating effects of much of postmodern, Area Studies–based, and traditional Indological scholarship.

In his writing, Subrahmanyam limits his time frame to the early modern and modern periods, which he dates from the late fourteenth century, the time of the Mongol conqueror Tamerlane.[77] It was in the same decades that European maps began to incorporate elements of the geographical knowledge of Asia that had been reported by Marco Polo a century earlier.[78] Subrahmanyam's choice of the early modern period as his point of departure for a connected histories approach to Eurasian studies is based on his position that it was only then that people living in different parts of the world were able to imagine for the first time, however unevenly, "the existence of processes on a truly global scale."[79] As he argues contra both religious nationalist and Subaltern School ideologies, cultures have always been open-ended systems, with each "formed in the crucible of processes of acculturation, whether defined by circuits that had their limits within the Indian subcontinent, or extending outside of it."[80] In spite of his early modern focus, Subrahmanyam acknowledges that there existed "long-distance commercial flows" within Asia from as early as the late first millennium CE;[81] and it is a fact that robust exchange networks, both commercial and cultural, had been in place from a far earlier time in the "Afro-Eurasian ecumene," comprising regions of South, East, and Southeast Asia, as well as the east coast of Africa, the Arabian peninsula, and the eastern Mediterranean (plate 4). Working from archeological, epigraphical, and textual sources, scholars have generated detailed accounts of these ancient maritime and overland trading networks, a number of which will be discussed in later chapters.[82] Furthermore, although the early modern European nation-states were among the last to enter into these networks, there did exist "world systems" well before the early modern period,[83] to say nothing of instances of indirect trade dating from the third millennium BCE.[84]

Earlier in this chapter, I discussed pan-Eurasian cultural exchanges dating from the first centuries of the Common Era: the Alexander Romance and so forth.[85] In a recent study, Philippe Beaujard has tracked the expansion and contraction of four successive Afro-Eurasian world systems that predated the early modern period, providing detailed maps of the shifting networks linking the nodes of the various systems. In order, these date (1) from between the first and third centuries CE; (2) the seventh and ninth centuries CE; (3) the eleventh and thirteenth centuries CE; and (4) the thirteenth and fourteenth centuries CE. These networks were subject to the vicissitudes of changing political formations, trading cartels, and so forth, with the collapse of each successive world system resulting from a variety of disrupting factors: invasion, imperial overextension, epidemic, social upheaval, economic recession, and climate change.[86] Whenever, however, the conduits of exchange were open, the political and economic actors of the day were in constant search of information about their distant trading partners, both for strategic reasons and out of simple curiosity.[87] These, then, are the contacts and exchanges upon whose warp and weft the tapestry of Eurasian dæmonology has been woven since the beginning of the Common Era, a tapestry that justifies the writing of its connected histories.

5

For certain of these histories, however, I will adduce contacts from a far earlier time. Here as well, my reconstructions find support in world system theory, in this case that of Andre Gunder Frank and Barry K. Gills, who have argued for world systems extending back five thousand years to the Early Bronze Age.[88] In these cases, I will tether my hypothetical reconstructions to the early period of what have been termed the Indo-European migrations. Here, the presence of common mythic structures and themes will be interpreted as the effect of monogenesis: the dissemination of cognate data, embedded in disparate languages, societies, and cultures, from a common source.[89] Based on archeological, philological, and most recently, DNA analysis, it has been shown that the speakers of the "Proto-Indo-European" (*PIE) language that generated the classical and modern languages of the Indo-European language family began to migrate eastward and westward out of their Anatolian "homeland" sometime between 7500 and 6000 BCE,[90] with *PIE diversifying into the five major Indo-European subfamilies—Celtic, Germanic, Italic, Balto-Slavic, and Indo-Iranian—between 4000 and 2000 BCE.

Launched by a famous suggestion made in 1786 by Sir William Jones,[91] the field of Indo-European philology has reached a high level of precision in both recovering the archaic root forms, vocabulary, and grammatical structures of the *PIE language and mapping, even predicting, their transformations across the ancient and modern languages of Indo-European family. Founded in 1938 by Georges Dumézil, the sister field of Indo-European mythology has never achieved the same level of precision.[92] The reasons are simple: mythemes have more moving parts than do phonemes, and there are far fewer myths than words in the Indo-European compendium. Over the past decades, both Dumézil and his theories have come under harsh scrutiny, some of it justified, by postmodernists and historians of various stripes who have interpreted his writings through the lens of twentieth-century European racial and political ideologies. These have ranged from *procès d'intention* by his former epigones Daniel Dubuisson and Bruce Lincoln[93] to the more abstract musings of Jacques Derrida, who characterized metaphysics as "the white mythology which resembles and reflects the culture of the West; the white man takes his own mythology, Indo-European mythology, his own *logos*, that is, the *mythos* of his idiom, for the universal form of what he must still wish to call Reason. Which does not go uncontested."[94]

Independent of its real or imagined links to his early political affiliations and agendas, the quality of Dumézil's scholarship has also been criticized on a number of other counts. While Indo-European philologists have judged certain of his etymological analyses to be overly speculative, a number of literary historians have branded his analyses as euhemerist and essentialist.[95] Elsewhere, he has been criticized for forcing Indo-European mythemes into preformated tripartite or "trifunctional" categories, and for assuming that in the image of their divine pantheons, ancient Indo-European societies were organized around the three ideal functions of sovereignty, martial strength, and fertility.[96]

6

It is these elements of the Indo-European hypothesis that have provided theoretical cover for some of the poisoned rhetoric and early primate chest-thumping proper to religion- and race-based nationalisms. However, as I will show in chapters 5 and 6, the tools of Indo-European mythology can be used to great advantage if we uncouple our interpretations from Dumézil's overriding focus on social hierarchy and the theme of sovereignty, and rather consider the myths and rituals proper to the dæmons that have populated, even defined, Eurasian lifeworlds for the past several thousand years. Apposite here is a recent observation made by Régis Boyer concerning the problematic nature of the category of "Germanic religion." Because the medieval authors of the Eddas and Sagas were also immensely cultivated scholars with a thorough knowledge of classical mythology, and because virtually all medieval European literature combined *interpretatio* with *imitatio*, the mythic profile of the Germanic Odin, for example, could not but have been "contaminated" by those of the Roman Mercury and the Greek Zeus and Proteus. For Boyer, the exception to this rule was "what is conveniently and all too readily referred to as 'lower mythology,' that is, the study of supposedly secondary supernatural beings or myths, [which] . . . probably less 'contaminated' by non-indigenous models . . . might allow us to come a bit closer to the way things were."[97] For Boyer, this means that Germanic traditions surrounding such dæmons as the Valkyries would have been more purely "Germanic" than those regarding Odin, whose equivalents from classical mythology were known to and appropriated by the medieval *sagnamenn*. Yet, as Boyer notes in an aside, Valkyrie mythology may itself have been influenced in some way by the vedic *apsaras* or by some notion of a guardian angel. It is this insight that I will take as my point of departure for my treatment of the Indo-European foundations of certain of the dæmonological traditions under study in this volume. These creatures of the "lower mythologies" of various Indo-European traditions are a vast untapped resource for the wider historical study of Indo-European myth, ritual, and doctrine. Borrowing a page from the great contrarian paleontologist Stephen Jay Gould, I would suggest that, like the anomalous fossils of the Burgess Shale that defied all preformated evolutionist categories, dæmons resemble the "grubby little creatures of the sea floor . . . [that] we greet . . . with awe because they are the Old Ones, and they are trying to tell us something."[98]

Rather than the sea floor, the abodes of many of the "Old Ones" are what the ancient Greeks termed *temenoi* and the Romans *luci*. As John Scheid has shown contra Eliade, these salient elements of the natural landscape were not worshiped as gods themselves, but rather were venerated as settings whose exceptional nature was indicative of a deity's presence or direct intervention. While *lucus* primarily denoted a sacred "clearing,"[99] or a domesticated space in the wild forest (chapter 4), the ancient Romans also applied the term to extraordinary bodies of water: natural springs (chapter 5), boiling or sulfurous pools (chapter 6), and so forth.[100]

My studies of the dæmons of these three types of Indo-European *luci* constitute a relatively unexplored realm of Indo-European mythology, ritual, and ideology. And, in the light of recent breakthroughs, they find themselves in good company. Using computational and statistical methods originally developed by evolutionary biologists to infer family trees, anthropologists have shown that of the two thousand folktales classified in the Aarne Thompson Uther catalog of "international tale types," as many as seventy-six can be traced back to the splitting off of the eastern and western branches of the Indo-European language family.[101] Here, a focus on the lesser deities of Indo-European "vernacular" traditions opens up new horizons for History of Religions research, for which the five interlaced studies that follow are an *entrée en matière*. This being said, I do not wish to imply that these traditions are or were specifically "Indo-European." Such was manifestly not the case, because, once again, these were not, contra Dumézil, linked to a social structure or ideology. An example is the body of data that will be discussed in chapter 6 concerning a complex Indo-European protomyth that was adapted into three non-Indo-European languages and traditions—in these cases alchemical—in the first and second millennia of the Common Era. In other words, Indo-European monogenesis has never precluded the possibility of contacts and exchanges across language (-family) barriers. Now, to those who would say that the monogenesis argument is simply the old discredited diffusionist hypothesis by another name, I offer the following responses. On the one hand, the empirical data of the field of Indo-European philology can only be explained through monogenesis. The shared vocabulary of the Indo-European languages points to a common origin, the reconstructed *PIE language. On the other, the fact of monogenesis does not preclude a constellation of multidirectional contacts and exchanges—the topic of this book—across time and space. In other words, it is possible to engage with the monogenesis hypothesis while keeping one's focus on transformations rather than origins.

A final word on the scope of the studies that make up this book. While I have limited my purview to the Eurasian landmass, I am aware that certain of the complex narratives, rituals, and doctrines treated in this book may have existed and may continue to exist in other parts of the world. In some cases, such would be due to the fact that they were carried abroad through trans-Atlantic or trans-Pacific movements of populations, for example by migrations across a former land bridge joining Siberia to modern-day Alaska, or by European conquests of the Americas.

7

This book is divided into two parts, devoted broadly speaking to ritual and myth. In each chapter, I argue that common myths as well as ritual theories and technologies from across Eurasia may be explained on the basis of verifiable—or at the very least, inferable—contacts and exchanges. Common or shared mythological and ritual complexes are so many traces of the activities of historical actors, and each chapter is devoted to plotting the paths over which those actors carried them across the Eurasian expanse. Much of my academic career has been devoted to the study of South Asian religions, cultures, and systems of knowledge, and so it is that each of the studies contained in this book grew out of an encounter I had with that world, either on the ground or through images and texts. From there, my investigations spiraled outward into the wider Eurasian world, and into the present set of connected histories.

That process began modestly, with field-based research carried out in Rajasthan and Kathmandu in 1999 on the topic of nearly identical practices involving the fabrication and use of protective amulets or phylacteries.[102] Chapter 2 is devoted to tracing the origins, transformations, and dissemination of these practices, which were carried north out of India by itinerant ascetics. During that same research tour in Rajasthan I photographed a *sāl* tree, there associated with the Hindu god Bhairava, which was hung with pieces of infant clothing. Recalling a passage from a book I had read concerning a similar phenomenon documented in thirteenth-century France, I began in 2016 to investigate cognate practices across Europe and Asia. These led me to identify a complex body of rituals, observed in coastal western Europe and western India alone, whose goal it is to recover infants (and in some cases, fetuses) that have been abducted by spirit beings. The remarkable parallels between the two are the subject of chapter 4. Based on primary source data from several demonological traditions as well as ethnographic research carried out in sub-Himalayan India, chapter 3 explores the dissemination, out of the Mediterranean world and into much of Eurasia, of an elaborate theory concerning the mechanics of the casting of the evil eye, and of a set of ritual technologies designed to identify and combat the demonic agents of malevolent sorcery. Prominent among these are mirror divination and the fabrication of incanted weapons to counter the demons and demonic devices mobilized or created by black magicians.

The first of two essays on the dissemination of myths via maritime and overland trade routes, chapter 5 examines a dozen cognate myths that describe a set of encounters between humans and the dæmons of remote, sylvan *luci*, most often spring-fed pools and water sources. This mythological complex points to an archaic ritual situation in which human trespassers were required to respond to a set of interrogations posed by the *genius loci* of a given site, often at the peril of their lives. As with chapter 5, my interest in the complex body of myth treated in chapter 6 dates back to the 1990s, and was announced in an earlier publication.[103] In over a dozen accounts, dæmons inhabiting and controlling sites of geothermal activity explode through the surface of the earth to pursue and punish trespassers and, more generally, any evildoer who would come into their presence. Like the mythic corpus discussed in chapter 5, these traditions appear to be grounded in a ritual complex, which in this instance involves real or metaphorical horses.

2

Of Filth and Phylacteries

1

In March 1999 I had the occasion to observe an apotropaic ritual performed at a temple located on the outskirts of Ghatiyali, a village in southeastern Rajasthan.[1] Locally known as the Līlāḍ ("Gods' Play") Mandir, the temple houses several groups of deities, including the sixty-four Yoginīs, the fifty-two Bherūṃ-jīs (the Marwari equivalent of the Sanskrit Bhairava, and the Hindi Bhairav), another group known as the eight Bherūṃ-jīs (Aṣṭabhairava), as well as individual deities named Bāla-jī, and Kāl and Gor ("Black" and "White") Bherūṃ-jī. Built on a cement slab with a low surrounding wall, the Līlāḍ Temple conforms to the tantric Yoginī temple plan on one count alone: it is hypaethral, that is, roofless and open to the sky (fig. 2.1). Within it, however, the principal shrine—to Black and White Bherūṃ-jī—is roofed but open on three sides; and a shed situated on its southeast corner is also covered. None of the images in the temple are iconic. Rather, all are simply stones smeared with a mixture of vermilion paint and sesame oil (*tel-sindūr*), and covered with silver foil, a combination called *māḷīpanā* throughout much of Rajasthan.[2] The most rudimentary of these are the images of the sixty-four Yoginīs and fifty-two Bherūṃ-jīs, most of which are small rounded stones placed in niches located in the temple's eastern and western walls, respectively. In addition, the eight Bherūṃ-jīs as well as a number of Yoginīs are made up of clusters of vermilion-smeared and foil-covered stones rooted in the ground, situated both inside and outside of the walled compound (fig. 2.2). One other stone, located a few feet to the south of the temple entrance, is also identified as a Bherūṃ-jī. This, the sole Bherūṃ-jī to be located outside the temple compound, is nonetheless important inasmuch as this is the sole deity of the Līlāḍ Mandir complex to receive blood offerings. This was evident at the time of my visit, which fell shortly after the conclusion of the

FIGURE 2.1. Līlāḍ Temple, Ghatiyali, Rajasthan. Photo by author.

FIGURE 2.2. Yoginīs, Līlāḍ Temple, Ghatiyali, Rajasthan. Photo by author.

spring Nine Nights (*navarātri*),[3] a festival closely associated with India's goddess cults: hanging from the branches of the *ḍhok* (Anogeissus pendulla) tree above this Bherūṃ-jī were the fetlocks of six goats that had recently been sacrificed to him. The reason that this Bherūṃ-jī was the recipient of blood offerings to the exclusion of all the Bherūṃ-jīs and Yoginīs located within was, I was told, the presence inside of the strictly vegetarian Bāla-jī (a deity also called Vīr and identified by some with Hanuman).[4]

The ritual that I observed took place at the base of the images of Black and White Bherūṃ-jī, a divine pair frequently encountered in both iconic and aniconic form throughout Rajasthan.[5] Here, the two are present in stones that are slightly larger than those embodying the other Bherūṃ-jīs, stones upon which the iconography is also more detailed. In addition to the usual *māḷīpanā*, these have inset pairs of glass eyes, as well as "mouths" stenciled into the foil with which they are coated. The pair is also surrounded by a small entourage of lesser, unnamed stones, many of which also bear similar rudimentary facial features (plate 5). Like many of the Bherūṃ-jīs of Rajasthan, the principal offering made to Black and White Bherūṃ-jī is the *māḷīpanā* itself. On the spring and fall Nine Nights festivals as well as in the course of wedding processions (*jāts*) and children's hair-cutting rites, the Bherūṃ-jīs of Rajasthan demand such tributes (*bali*),[6] which are undoubtedly substitutes for blood offerings received in earlier times.

Over time, repeated applications of this mixture have literally increased the size of these images, as is most strikingly evident at Baḍalī ka Bherūṃ-jī ("Banyan-Tree Village Bhairava"), an open-air shrine located at the foot of a massive banyan (*baḍ*) in the village of Barali ("Banyan Tree"), some eight miles to the west of Jodhpur, the seat of the former kingdom of Marwar and a modern-day district capital in western Rajasthan. Here, six imposing conical figures that rise up to over four feet in height are fused together at their base to form a single massive image, which devotees identify as Devī (the image to the far right) and Bherūṃ-jī (the five figures to her left, who collectively constitute her "son") (plate 6). In spite of the fact that the Gosain priest of the shrine insisted to me that these images had simply risen out of the ground at the place,[7] it would rather appear that at some time in the distant past six separate stones or truncated prop roots had been worshiped beneath the banyan tree there. Over time, these became fused at their base, conical in shape, and of ever-increasing height through the repeated application of layers of *māḷīpanā*. One may observe a parallel development in the worship image of the goddess named Bījāsan Devī, a goddess propitiated for cases of polio and other forms of childhood paralysis,[8] whose hilltop shrine is located in western Madhya Pradesh. Originally a fist-sized stone, it has grown to over three feet in height and breadth through the repeated application of *tel-sindūr*.

At the Līlāḍ Temple in Ghatiyali, each time a new layer of *māḷīpanā* is applied to the surfaces of the Black and White Bherūṃ-jī stones, drops of red *tel-sindūr* fall down to accumulate at their base. It was in front of their images that the ritual I observed was performed (plate 7). This began with the measuring out by a Bhopā priest of bundles of red and yellow thread,[9] which he then twisted into phylacteries: small string bracelets or belts (called *māḷī*).[10] Before he presented a bracelet to one of the assembled devotees, the priest held it over the smoke of a clarified butter lamp and burning joss sticks, and smeared it with the mixture of the *tel-sindūr* and other detritus that had dripped down from the lower edge of the "faces" of the two gods. It should be noted here that this unctuous mass was called neither *tel-sindūr* nor *māḷīpanā* in this case; rather, it was *mail*—a term signifying "impurity," "filth," or "excrement"—that was employed.[11] These phylacteries were destined for children, who wear them in order to ward off the assaults of the spirit beings (usually called *bhūt-pret*) considered to be the prime causes of childhood diseases. Worn either apotropaically or therapeutically, they are, at the end of their use, removed and wound around the trunk of a tree or hung from a wall within the temple compound. Here, as in other parts of Rajasthan, Bhopās will optionally apply the same *mail* directly onto the hair or as a bodily unguent, rather than onto the mediating phylacteries.[12]

What is the logic behind this rite? In answer to this question, I begin by relating two local myths, one from western Rajasthan and the other from coastal Gujarat, in which divine bodily secretions, again called *mail*, play a crucial role. The first of these is a story that was told to me by Pyārī Lāl, a devotee at Rikyāṃ ("Blood") Bherūṃ-jī, the principal Bherūṃ-jī temple of Jodhpur.[13] In a story reminiscent of the puranic account of the creation of Gaṇeśa by Pārvatī, the dark god Śiva and the fair god Viṣṇu, quarreling over their relative powers, both rub *mail* from their bodies, which they enliven with *śakti* to create Black and White Bherūṃ-jī, respectively. These two then battle as surrogates for their creators, and no one knows or remembers who emerged victorious: the point of the story is to explain how the divine pair came into being. At bottom, these, the two most widely worshiped Bherūṃ-jīs of Rajasthan, were created from the filth of their fathers to serve them—originally as fighters, but subsequently to simply stand in for the two otiose high gods.

The term *mail* is a cognate of the Sanskrit *malam*, "filth, impurity,"[14] and it is divine filth, smeared from the epidermis of a god, that accounts both for the creation of the Bherūṃ-jīs themselves as well as for a body of practice that involves the smearing of *their* filth for the protection and healing of their devotees. At the Līlāḍ Temple in Ghatiyali, the term *māḷī* was employed to signify the string bracelets upon which the *mail* of Black and White Bherūṃ-jī was smeared. The first member of the compound *māḷīpanā*, *māḷī* is related to the Rajasthani *m(ah)āḷiyo*, a term whose semantic range is more or less coterminus with that of *prasāda*, the divine grace transmitted by gods when they return offerings of food, flowers, and so forth, to their devotees at the conclusion of the act of worship.[15] Pyārī Lāl, however, had a variant

FIGURE 2.3. Melaḍī Mātā, polychrome, ca. 1965.

explanation, an example of what philologists like to call a "folk etymology": for him, the term *māḷīpanā* was itself identifiable with *mail*, the filth exuded from the bodies of these gods.

The second myth, recorded by David Pocock in the Gujarati village of Sundarana in the 1970s, concerns a western Indian regional goddess named Melaḍī Mātā ("Mother of Impurities") (fig. 2.3):[16]

> Once the gods were fighting with a *zan* (sorcerer), fearful and disgusting just like a member of the *Bhangi* caste, scavengers, or a *Vāghari*. They fought three long days and did not win. Indeed, they were so tired that the *zan* nearly conquered them. At night they sat down to consider the situation and one of them said "Brothers, let's make a goddess from our faeces." This they did. Their new goddess was so powerful that she fought the *zan* and killed him. Once she had achieved her purposes the gods ran off because they had made the goddess from filth. However, the goddess ran ahead and, by taking a short cut, outdistanced them and, by her magic, made a garden in the road along which they should pass. The gods came, saw the garden, and sat down to drink from the well in the middle of it. As soon as they had drunk the water, the goddess appeared before them and said, "Well, brothers, you have drunk my water and what are you going to do about that now?" They were in danger of becoming

> Untouchable and begged the goddess for mercy. She said, "Well, I will release you on condition that you give me a name and worship me." After thinking about it they decided to call her Melaḍī Mātā because she was made from filth, *mel.* And that is how she has always been known.[17]

It would appear that a type of homeopathic magic is operative here. Like Melaḍī Mātā, Black and White Bherūṃ-jī are created from the bodily secretions (*mail*) of transcendent gods, in order to fight on their behalf. Their bodies are composed of *mail.* In the case of the Black and White Bherūṃ-jīs of Ghatiyali, it is the *mail* that these two lesser but nonetheless powerful deities exude from their skin that becomes the *prasāda*, the counter-prestation they make to devotees who feed and cause them to grow by applying *māḷīpanā* to their bodies. Their *mail* is in turn worn against the skin (a principal site of invasion by demons and other malefic entities who would otherwise corrupt their bodies from within through possession) of their human clients, through the *mail*-smeared phylacteries they receive at the temple. Now, both Ghatiyali in southeastern Rajasthan and Sundarana in coastal Gujarat are villages, and the devotees of Black and White Bherūṃ-jī and Melāḍī Mātā are generally low-caste individuals. This being the case, one might be tempted to interpret these two myths with their attendant ritual practices as so many strategies on the part of subalterns to valorize what McKim Marriott has referred to as "pessimal substance-code."[18] Because their low status prohibits them from transacting in the purer substance-codes of social elites, low-status individuals, the "scum of the earth," replace the edible grace of temple *prasāda* with the bodily secretions of gods who are themselves laborers in the service of the high gods of the Hindu pantheon.

Such an interpretation proves to be hasty and unfounded in the light of the fact that a nearly identical practice is observed at a Bhairava temple that, located in an urban center, pulls in a relatively high-caste clientele and is served by priests belonging to the high status Śreṣṭha subcaste. This is the shrine of Ānand Bhairab, which is situated in the Gyaneshwor-Mahādev temple compound in central Kathmandu. Here, what was originally a great multi-armed iconic image of the god has been so covered with layer upon layer of offertory matter as to become a nearly amorphous reddish mass, with only the dark stone mouth of the underlying image being left uncovered (fig. 2.4). If anything, the technique of smearing is more visible here than in Rajasthan. On his worship days, Ānand Bhairab's devotees (or the Śreṣṭha priest) will use their entire right hand to smear as much as a pint of *tel-sindūr* over the entire image. Following this, they will prostrate themselves before the god, transferring the mixture (and whatever else has been poured or smeared over the image, including rice,

FIGURE 2.4. Ānand Bhairab, Gyaneshwor-Mahādev Temple, Kathmandu. Photo by author.

flower parts, and animal blood)[19] directly onto their foreheads—as well, quite often, as onto their forearms, hair, and clothing![20] (Plate 8.)

Ānand Bhairab plays the same specialized role in Nepal as do Black and White Bherūṃ-jī in Rajasthan: he is a god to whom people bring their children for protection against, or for the healing of diseases caused by, spirit beings or other demonic agents of possession. What is most remarkable is the near identity of both the practice and its underlying logic at these two sites. Unlike Black and White Bherūṃ-jī (but like Baḍalī kā Bherūṃ-jī, according to that god's priest), Ānand Bhairab was not created from the filth, the *mail*, of a high god but simply "rose up out of the ground" at his present site. However, as in the case of Black and White Bherūṃ-jī, devotees of Ānand Bhairab employ the same term, *mail*, to describe the "active ingredient" of their god's healing power. It is his *mail*, collected at the base of his image, which is gathered up and tied into small bundles of red cloth, called *būṭīs*.[21] These are then closed off with red, white, or black pieces of thread and fastened about children's necks, where they remain, either until the child has been healed or until a new *būṭī* is tied on in its place.

2

What links these two rituals that are identical in nearly every respect, in spite of their diverse social and geographic contexts? How is it that we find an identical rite—using identical techniques (smearing) and terminology (*mail*) and involving the same god (Bhairava)—at two sites located a thousand miles apart, the one rural and the other urban, and involving low- and high-status priesthoods and clienteles respectively? The most obvious explanation involves cultic transmission through the agency of itinerant members of various Śaiva religious orders. The cult in question is that of Bhairava, who has remained the principal male deity of South Asian Tantra from the eighth century down to the present day. While the names of the itinerant Śaiva orders have changed over the centuries, the behaviors, dress, and regalia of their adherents have generally remained constant. Over the past three to five centuries, the two terms most commonly applied to these sectarians in northern South Asia have been "Gosain" and "Yogi." While the former term has, since the early nineteenth century, come to signify a broad range of actors—including members of the Vaiṣṇava Rāmānandī and Bairāgī orders, householder Vaiṣṇavas, a western Indian subcaste, or virtually any type of holy man—it was originally applied specifically to the warrior Śaiva ascetics known as Dasnāmi Nāgas.[22] At the time of its foundation in 1146 CE, one of the most illustrious of the Nāga suborders, the Jūna Akhāḍa ("Ancient Regiment"), was called the Bhairava Akhāḍa;[23] and Bhairava continues to be widely venerated among the Nāgas. As such, an early twentieth-century notice of "Gosain" devotion to Bhairava was likely referring to a Dasnāmi Nāga practice: "The Gosains of the Central Provinces . . . who worship Bhairon make a round mark with vermilion between the eyes, taking it from beneath the god's feet."[24] This is a description of the application of the god's *mail*, without the intermediary of a phylactery or pouch amulet.

As has already been noted, the priest of the Bherūṃ-jī temple in Barali, Rajasthan, is a Gosain. So too are the *pujārī*s of three of the principal Bhairava temples in the city of Benares, the god's most important cult center in all of South Asia: Bhūt Bhairav, Ās Bhairav, and Saṃhār Bhairav. Throughout the western Deccan plateau, the term *Gosāvī* covers the same range of actors as does its northern cognate Gosain, and is applied to both a subcaste and a religious order. In the latter case, however, the term *Kānphaṭa* ("Split-Eared") is appended to the name: *Kānphaṭa Gosāvī* is the term employed in Maharashtra for the itinerant monks of the Nāth or Kānphaṭa Yogi order.[25] Long based at Sonari in southwestern Maharashtra, one of the most important cult sites of Kāl Bhairav in the entire state, the Kānphaṭa Gosāvīs have been responsible for the spread of the cults of both Kāl Bhairav and the Aṣṭabhairav throughout the region.[26] According to Günther-Dietz Sontheimer's analysis,

> [the cult of] Bhairav [was] spread mainly by the Kānphaṭa Gosāvīs. Bhairav is a god who invades the forest, conquers demons, and often takes on the defilement arising from Śiva's deeds. Through him, the new area becomes a *kṣetra*, and he protects it as Kālbhairav, the *koṭvāl* [chief constable] of Benares. . . . The Gosāvī who penetrates the forest and identifies himself with his god has also surely contributed to the iconography; indeed, one can assume that the iconographic representation of the god had as its model the figure of the Gosāvī who identifies himself with Kālbhairav.[27]

Along with the Dasnāmi Nāgas cum Gosains, the Nāth or Kānphaṭa Yogis (also simply known as Yogis) have, since the fourteenth century at least, been the primary agents for the dissemination of Bhairava's cult in South Asia. Images of Bhairava figure prominently in their monasteries and shrines across the northern Indian subcontinent, only rivaled in number by images of the order's founder Gorakhnāth himself.[28] Although their numbers have greatly declined over the past century, the Nāth Yogis remain a significant group, most especially in western India and Nepal. Although a small village, Ghatiyali has an active Nāth monastery; there are also several in the Kathmandu Valley, the most important being located at Mrigsthali, on a hilltop across the Bagmati River from the national shrine of Paśupatināth.

Between the fourteenth and nineteenth centuries, the Nāth Yogis enjoyed great success in aligning and allying themselves with South Asian kings from Maharashtra to Nepal. Royal chronicles and hagiographies alike portray charismatic, wonder-working warrior Nāth Yogis raising untested princes to the thrones of the kingdoms of Marwar in Rajasthan (of which Jodhpur was the capital), Nepal (Kathmandu), as well as the lesser sub-Himalayan kingdoms of Chaṃbā, Ṭiharī, Devalgaḍh, Champāwat, Kumaon, Almora, Ḍoṭi, Jumla, Ḍāng, and Gorkha.[29] As Véronique Bouillier and Günter Unbescheid have noted, the kings so elevated by their Nāth Yogi stratèges were often Rajputs who, driven from their Rajasthani homelands, sought refuge in the Himalayan foothills of Uttarakhand and Himachal Pradesh in India, and eventually western Nepal and the Kathmandu Valley.[30] In the modern-day Kumaon region of Uttarakhand, it is claimed that Yogis are able to ward off the evil eye through the use of amulets and other magical devices.[31] Similarly, in the Kangra Valley of Himachal Pradesh, Bāba Bālak Nāth, a deified Nāth Yogi loosely identified with Śiva, is said to protect children from the attacks of spirit beings through amulets called *singhi*.[32] It is with these groups that we find the most plausible link between the *mail*-related rites of Ghatiyali and Kathmandu: they were brought from western India to the Kathmandu Valley by the Nāth Yogis, power brokers to Rajput princes and devotees of Bhairava.

3

While the activities of itinerant ascetics may account for the near identity of these two Bhairava-related rituals, they are not sufficient to explain the presence of *mail* in the mythology of Melāḍī Mātā in Gujarat. In this myth, the goddess is created from the animated feces of unnamed higher gods in order to combat a sorcerer with low-caste connections, whom she alone is able to slay. In spite of its erasure from the normative discourse of Indian analytical thought, sorcery is a ubiquitous component of South Asian religious practice. Primarily used to manipulate spirit beings and turn them against one's victims, sorcery functions in the same way as the apotropaic and healing rituals observed at the two Bhairava temples, with one obvious difference: the object of the *mail*-smearing rites is to protect against the very demonic agents of possession that the sorcerer would unleash.

These are the two faces of South Asian demonology (*bhūtavidyā*), a body of practice that is remarkably uniform across the entire subcontinent, and which finds scriptural sanction in vedic, ayurvedic, epic, puranic, and tantric literature. Certain types of human affliction—especially mental illness, pathologies related to pregnancy, and childhood diseases—are attributed to the activities of malign spirit beings often identified with the unhappy dead. These *bhūt-pret* are predisposed to evil, invading the minds and bodies of living family members or fellow villagers out of revenge for their own miserable condition—of hunger, thirst, homelessness, oblivion—which they blame on the living. At the same time, they are relatively weak, and therefore easily manipulated by stronger beings, including not only sorcerers but also more powerful supernatural entities. These may be either male or female, with the former often being termed "Lords of Spirit Beings" (*bhūtanāthas*, *bhūteśas*, *bhūteśvaras*, *bhūtapatis*, etc.) and the latter identified with goddesses like Melāḍī Mātā and Bayasāb Mātā, who control families or clans of less powerful beings. These male and female types are discussed in the nineteenth chapter of the *Netra Tantra* (NT, "Tantra of the Eye"), a circa 825–850 CE Śaiva scripture from Kashmir:[33]

> The seven [Mothers] are praised as the leaders of all the [lesser] mothers. After one has worshiped [them] with white, red, yellow and black flowers of various sorts . . . [the condition] of children immediately improves. It is therefore through an offering to [their] leaders that subordinate divinities become satiated in every situation [and that the child's] health immediately improves. . . . If a man has become possessed by terrible Spirit Beings (*bhūtas*) and Seizers (*grahas*),[34] then a Lord of Spirit Beings (*bhūteśvara*) is to be worshiped with tribute offerings (*bali*). . . . When the eight types of goddesses are hostile in any place whatsoever, one shall gain complete relief after making an offering to Bhairava.[35]

It is in this context—of combating the demonic agents of human affliction through the propitiation of a Lord (or Mistress) of Spirit Beings—that a wide array of tantric rituals involving both binding and smearing, witnessed since the medieval period, are to be analyzed. Such treatments are prescribed in the NT:

> When evil beings behold a fortunate child who is well praised and marked with every auspicious attribute, they will vigorously seek to fatally wound the happy infant. Therefore, [such] a child, [and] especially a royal prince is to be ceaselessly protected in every way possible, with the enclosing spell or with various [other] auspicious spells (*mantras*) that have been written or deployed on a device (*yantra*) . . . and with threads that, steeped in incense and so forth, have been closely wrapped around his throat; and likewise with amulets (*maṇi*) worn [on his body]; or with demon-slaying marks (*tilakas*) placed on the forehead, together with lustrations.[36]

A similar technique, involving a *yantra* in the form of a diagram enclosed by an amulet, is described in the *Jayākhya Saṃhitā*, a Vaiṣṇava Tantra from the

FIGURE 2.5. Two Yoginīs with male victim, Chinnamastā Temple, Patan, Kathmandu. Photo by author.

same period: "One should wrap this *yantra* with a five-coloured thread [and] put it into a golden casket. . . . Child-Seizers (*bāla-graha*), etc. leave the child and go far away if this *yantra* is present on its body. A pregnant woman bears easily on account of wearing [this *yantra*]. A barren woman [and] a woman whose new-born children die will have children."[37]

Jain sources refer to similar precautions taken for none other than the heroic founders of the faith, the *tīrthaṃkara*s themselves: protective amulets (*rakkāpoṭṭalika*s) wrapped in string were tied to the wrists of the newborn Ṛṣabha, Parśvanātha, and Mahāvīra. Another type of protective technique, referred to in medieval Jain sources as *bhūtikaraṇa*, involved smearing the body with holy ashes and binding it with threads.[38] Practices of this sort are also documented in narrative and iconography. A number of tales from the eleventh-century Kashmiri *Kathāsaritsāgara* (KSS: "Ocean of Rivers of Story") portray Yoginīs literally transforming men into beasts by tying mantra-incanted threads or ropes around their throats.[39] An undated mural from the hypaethral Chinnamastā temple in Patan, Kathmandu, depicts just such a situation: an old crone leads a young woman who is holding a rope tied around the neck of a naked man walking on all fours (fig. 2.5). A regional narrative from the Kāl Bhairav temple in Sonari, Maharashtra, tells a similar story in a way that highlights that god's role as a Lord of Spirit Beings. Here, a thaumaturge named Siddhanāth, who is said to be Kāl Bhairav incarnate, descends to the underworld to bring the malign goddess Yogeśvarī under his control. He hangs a garland on her, and she is forced to obey all his commands. Another account has Siddhanāth subduing one of the seven tree goddesses of the region by cutting her tree down, seizing her by the braids, boring a hole through her nose and tying her to a bullock cart.[40]

On the basis of scriptural and literary data, then, we may conclude that the *mail*-related practices of smearing and binding as observed at the Līlāḍ Temple in Ghatiyali and the Ānand Bhairab shrine in Kathmandu have a history and a place in the medieval Sanskrit- and Prakrit-language record. This being the case, one is obliged to question the frequent assumption that these rites are mere examples of "popular religion." Like the "folk etymologies" rejected by philologists on the basis of the rules of historical linguistics, such traditions tend to be dismissed by normative Indian analytical discourse as mere superstition or at best, sympathetic magic—beyond the pale of true religion or scientific medical practice. This sort of dichotomization—between religion and superstition, or between official and folk religious practice, great and little tradition, or scriptural and vernacular traditions—is the legacy both of modernity and of India's colonial experience, and as such it is freighted with all manner of Eurocentric assumptions internalized by India's urban society. It is not my intention here to rehearse, for the thousandth time, the infernal dynamic of the colonial constructions of South Asian categories. In the balance of this chapter, I will rather attempt to trace the genealogy of this specific body of apotropaic ritual and to suggest that it has been sanctioned by the same sorts of scriptural sources as the "scientific" procedures of the Indian medical tradition and the "religious" practices of so-called mainstream devotional Hinduism.

I have already surveyed a number of medieval tantric sources for these practices. Given the fact, however, that most modern-day Hindus consider Tantra to have been a marginal aberration—an unfortunate short-lived deviation from the vedic or *bhakti* norm, which only survives today among benighted populations of the rural hinterlands manipulated by criminally insane *tāntrika*s—an examination of earlier, less contested sources becomes necessary. Whereas the tantric and ayurvedic canons generally link the creation of the Seizers (*graha*s) to an act of Śiva,[41] the earliest etiological account of these dire beings traces their origins to the birth of Skanda-Kumāra, the divine son of both Agni and Rudra-Śiva. This myth, which first appears in the *Mahābhārata* (MBh),[42] explains the origin of the *skanda-graha*s, "Skanda-Seizers," a general term employed in several ayurvedic sources to denote the

FIGURE 2.6. Skanda wearing demonifuge amulets, Benares, fifth century CE. Courtesy of Bharat Kala Bhavan, Benares Hindu University, Varanasi.

demonic agents of childhood diseases. In this epic narrative, the newborn god is first a potential victim of the Seizers before he is made to be their leader. Later in this account, a bride is chosen for Skanda. One of her names, Ṣaṣṭhī ("the Sixth"), refers to the protective rites offered on the sixth day after childbirth. In modern-day Bengal, her annual festival day is marked by the tying of "ceremonial threads" colored yellow with turmeric and curds to the wrists of children.[43] A number of early sculpted images of Skanda portray him with the distinctive sort of phylactery typically worn by children for protection from the Female Seizers and other spirit beings. Fifth- and ninth-century images of Skanda-Kumāra, from Benares and Kathmandu respectively, feature nearly identical phylacteries combining clay medallions, tiger claws, and oddly shaped stones and beads (fig. 2.6).[44]

These traditions resurface in the literature of classical Āyurveda, which diverges most significantly from its normative humor-based explanations for disease pathologies in the subfields of pediatrics (*kaumara-bhṛtya*) and demonology (*bhūtavidyā*). For pathologies related to complications arising in pregnancy and childbirth, childhood diseases, and mental disorders, it is demonic agents of possession, rather than humoral imbalances, that are identified as the exogenous causes of the affliction.[45] While the ayurvedic sources wax eloquent on the symptomologies of possession by various types of demonic agents,[46] they have relatively little to say about clinical procedures for the same. The treatments that they do describe, both preventative and therapeutic, appear to anticipate those found in the later tantric literature and the *mail*-related rituals observed at our Bhairava temples. So it is that the *Caraka Saṃhitā* (CS, "Caraka's System")[47] makes the following general statement concerning treatments for insanity: "One should worship, offer tribute, make offerings of food, apply ointments incanted with spells, and perform pacification rituals. . . . Propitiating the god Īśvara, the lord of the universe, the Lord of Bhūtas (*bhūtānām adhipa*), continually and zealously . . . and offering worship to the minions of Rudra called the Tormenters (*pramathas*), a person is released from the various forms of insanity. . . . Exogenous possession becomes pacified through . . . wearing medicinal plants [as phylacteries] . . . and through the employment of perfected mantras and medicines."[48] This identification of Śiva—here called Īśvara—as the Lord of Spirit Beings is documented in coinage from the same period. Kushan coins dating from the middle of the second century CE depict a four-armed god bearing a trident and a two-headed drum in two of his hands. These bear the legend OHþO, which, as Adalbert Gail has shown, may be read as a Middle Indic form of Bhūteśa (fig. 2.7).[49] A first-century Śiva liṅgam named Bhūteśvara from Mathura, the Kushans' southern "capital," further attests to this identification.[50]

In its enumeration of the specific phylacteries to be worn by children, the CS prescribes materials similar to those represented on images of the child-god Skanda: the tips of the right horns of rhinoceroses, antelopes, *gayal*s, or bulls, as well as a variety of medicinal herbs or "whatever is deemed appropriate by Brahmins versed in the *Atharva Veda* (AV)."[51] The *Suśruta Saṃhitā* (SS, "Suśruta's System") prescribes the wearing of phylacteries by infants that have been afflicted by the demoness Revatī: the affected child is made to wear a charm necklace (*rucaka*), in this case made of beads from the wood of various trees, including the *varaṇa* (Crataeva Roxburgii).[52] A more elaborate ritual is described in the circa seventh-century *Aṣṭāṅgasaṃgraha* ("Compendium of the Eight Branches") of Vāgbhaṭa: "An area one hand's breadth in size is purified and smeared with cow dung. . . . Then the physician . . . should take a white or a three-colored goddess-phylactery (*pratisarā*)[53] in his hand and wind it around a leaf of the birch tree on which the *aparajita* spell has been

FIGURE 2.7. OHþO, Kushan coin, second century CE. Image courtesy of the British Museum.

written in ox-gall (*gorocana*).... This is to be fastened around the neck of the child."[54] As the phylactery is tied on the child, the physician intones a long hymn of praise to various protector gods and their minions, which concludes: "This bound phylactery is a destroyer of sin for thee. Thou who art enclosed [by it], mayest thou live happily and without fear for one hundred years."[55] Then follows the description of a tribute offering made to the spirit beings upon a round or square diagram upon which [?the name of] the Healing Lord of the Spirit Beings (*bhiṣag-bhūtapati*) has been inscribed, surrounded by "all of the boy-god's wet-nurses" (*dhātryaḥ sarvāḥ kumārasya*). These are invited to accept the offering, before being exhorted to depart immediately and permanently to the distant Gandhamādana peak, where their leader Skanda dwells.[56]

Later ayurvedic texts, such as the mid-eleventh century *Cikitsāsaṃgraha* ("Compendium of Therapeutics") of Cakrapāṇidatta, the late sixteenth-century *Āyurveda Saukhyam* ("Health through Āyurveda") attributed to Ṭoḍarānanda, and the eighteenth-century *Yogaratnākara* ("Jewel-Mine of

Applications") prescribe similar therapies, including salves and the tying of mantra-incanted phylacteries (*bandhanas*) for insanity of exogenous origin (*āgantūnmāda*), as well as for the treatment of pathologies caused by spirit beings (*bhūta cikitsā*) and childhood diseases (*bālarogacikitsā*).[57]

4

As the ayurvedic texts themselves repeatedly proclaim, the medical canon is but an extension of practices revealed in the AV itself. And in fact, the AV and its ancillary literature abound in preventative and therapeutic treatments against demonic possession. Several AV passages evoke amulets fashioned from gold, silver, copper, lead, and wooden beads; splinters of wood cut from a variety of trees or from a plowshare or the rim of a chariot wheel; *darbha* grass, red-colored string, and so forth. When incanted with mantras, these are to be worn both for protection against *viṣkandhas* (identified by commentators as demonic Guardians [*rākṣasas*] and Flesh-Eaters [*piśācas*]), demons, sorcerers, and other human enemies; and for the attainment of victory, prosperity, longevity, virility, strength, good health, safe childbirth, etc.[58] As a general rule, the mantras associated with these phylacteries are identified with deities whose power is thereby made to reside in them. While many of these are, like the malign beings they combat, "personified" with individual names—and even identified as men or heroes (*vīras*) that go on the attack against various forms of sorcery—common terms include *sūtra* ("thread"), *maṇi* ("necklace"),[59] and *pratisara*. According to Indian etymologies and commentaries, this final term is to be understood in a twofold sense, relative to its form and function. On the one hand, any necklace or bracelet turns around (*prati-√sṛ*) on itself to form a loop. On the other, a phylactery's magical power, as a countercharm, is to hoist by their own petard the human or superhuman enemies of its wearer by turning their sorcery and magical devices back on themselves.[60]

Mainly devoted to healing, exorcism, and sorcery, the AV's ancillary literature—the *Kauśika Sūtra* (KS, "Kauśika's Manual"), the circa 500 CE *Śānti Kalpa* (ŚK, "Rules for Expiation"), and the Atharvan *Pariśiṣṭas* ("Appendices")—are late vedic sources that weave the mantras of the AV into the liturgies of their "pacification" (*śānti*) rites.[61] Among these the KS, a text that has been called "the oldest system of Indian medical science,"[62] stands out as the quintessential Atharvanic compendium of ritual magic. In the explanatory rules (*paribhāṣās*) to the seventh chapter of this work, we find instructions for the preparation and tying on of phylacteries. Here, the phylactery is first to be steeped for three days in a mixture of curds and honey, following which an oblation of clarified butter is made. The residue of the oblation is placed on the phylactery, which is then fastened, most often around the neck, to the ritual patron.[63] The twenty-fifth chapter of this work, which, devoted to rites for protection against disease, the exorcism of demons, conception of sons, and safe childbirth, comprises multiple references to the use of phylacteries made from medicinal herbs, barley, rice, shells, horn and ivory.[64] In the treatment it proposes for *rápas*, a type of demonic affliction,[65] the KS states: "With [mantras from] AV 5.9 and 6.91, [the healer] pours four [portions] of the dregs (*sampātān*) of clarified butter into a water jar; two [portions are poured] on the earth; having recovered these two, he washes [the patient with them]; and [putting the dregs] in [a cup] with barley, he binds [to the patient that] barley [as an amulet], while reciting the latter [hymn, i.e., AV 6.91]."[66]

This practice, of pouring the dregs or residue of offertory material from a previous rite onto an amulet or phylactery to be worn by a person afflicted by a demonically induced infirmity, bears a structural similarity to the *mail*-smearing rites I observed at Bhairava temples in 1999. A more detailed rite of the same sort is enjoined in the ŚK, which adheres closely to the KS's ritual program.[67] Embedded in the conclusion of its *amṛtā-mahāśānti* pacification rite is the description of a ceremony in which an offering of clarified butter is poured onto a fire, with the residue of the same being used to besmear the requisites for the ritual. These include a *pratisara*, a staff of *tumbara* wood, various plants, and ten stones.[68] The sacrificer covers all of these objects with the residue of the oblation, placing the plant matter and stones at the ten directions of the dwelling that is to be protected. As for the staff, it is placed above the door.[69] The phylactery in question is brought into play at the conclusion of the ritual:

> There must be an oblation of bdellium [made] in silence, and he [the offering priest] must get a gift for the Protectors (*rakṣas*) [saying], "Obeisance to the Rakṣas, obeisance to the great Rakṣas, obeisance to the Leader of Rakṣas (*rakṣo 'dhipati*). Obeisance to the Host (*gaṇas*), obeisance to the . . . Leader of the Great Host (*mahāgaṇādhipati*)." After making an oblation with the Ayuṣya chant, he puts the leavings (*sampātān*) on himself. After making an oblation with the Patnīvanta chant, he puts the leavings on the [sacrificer's] wife. . . . With the Prāṇa hymn (AV 11.4.1–26)[70] he puts the leavings of the oblation on the rice and barley that is to be tied on as a necklace (*maṇi*). After adorning and praising them, he should have him [the sacrificer] put on the two [necklaces].[71]

Yet another rite of the same sort is enjoined in the *Sāmavidhāna Brāhmaṇa* ("Explanation of Doctrines Concerning the Use of Chants") for a woman whose children have died in their infancy. An amulet made from the sheaths of the buds of the banyan tree is to be worn by the woman on her girdle until she bears a son. This is then placed around the child's neck. The leavings of the butter of earlier saved oblations are given to the child to eat and are rubbed each day on all of his body orifices. As a result, it is promised that the child shall live for one hundred years, without suffering the infirmities of old age.[72]

5

The most salient parallel between the *mail*-smearing rituals performed at modern-day Bhairava temples and these Atharvanic rites of pacification is the smearing of the residue of a food offering onto a phylactery worn for protection against spirit beings and demons. There are significant differences, however: the *mail*-smearing rituals are undertaken for the protection of children rather than adults; the ŚK makes no reference to the dregs of the butter oblation as "filth" or "excrement"; the butter oblation is "cooked" whereas the *mail* or *māḷīpanā* of the Bhairava temple images is "raw"; and the dynamics of vedic fire offerings differs greatly from that of feeding gods in a temple shrine.[73] Furthermore, whereas the *mail*-smearing practices are undertaken without mantras, Atharvan and ayurvedic rituals involving the smearing or tying of phylacteries are always accompanied by the intoning of mantras.

In spite of these data, however, it is not inappropriate to speak of structural parallels, if not historical continuities, between protective rituals found in the Atharvanic, ayurvedic, and tantric scriptures, on the one hand, and, on the other, the "vernacular" practices observed at Bhairava temples in Rajasthan and Kathmandu. Indian demonology, with its hierarchy of supernatural beings, rites, mythology, and nosology has remained virtually unchanged since the beginning of the Common Era. Bhairava has played his role as the *bhūtanātha* of this hierarchy since the time of the NT, a role that he clearly inherited from Īśvara-Śiva, the Lord of the Demonic Dead (*bhūtānām adhipa*) of the CS and the Bhūteśa of Kushan coinage.

The modern-day South Asian use of phylacteries closely resembles ancient traditions whose origins are traceable to the original vedic revelation (*śruti*). In fact, the sole point on which the practices we have reviewed contradict the doctrines of Hindu orthodoxy is their use of the term *mail*, which is a cognate of the Sanskrit *malam*. Now, according to orthodox Śaiva soteriology, it is *malam*,[74] precisely, which is, as the "fundamental impurity," the principal fetter (*pāśa*) to the liberation of mortal creatures (*paśus*). Because it is a substance (*dravyam*), this *malam* can only be expunged through ritual practice.[75]

Once this fetter has been removed, a *paśu* ("creature, victim") accedes to the status of a *pati*, that is, of Śiva as the "lord." According to Śaiva orthodoxy, this is tantamount to liberation: one becomes a "second Śiva," victorious over disease, death, or any other affliction proper to the human condition. This being the case, the use of the term *mail* in Bhairava temples to signify the divine impurity that frees devotees from the ills associated with the assaults of spirit beings would appear to be in flagrant contradiction with orthodox usages. Which begs the following question: what is orthodox about this orthodoxy? The post-700 CE Śaivasiddhānta scriptures do not form a portion of the original revelation (*śruti*), but rather fall under the heading of later tradition (*smṛti*). The use of amulets, with or without the adjunction of the residue of offerings, is sanctioned by the AV—that is, by vedic revelation—while the CS, a foundational ayurvedic text, refers to the customs of "Brahmins versed in the *Atharva Veda*" in its selection of raw materials for the fabrication of these objects. As has been noted, the same text contains instructions for fashioning a birch bark phylactery inscribed with letters written in ox-gall and tied with colored threads, to be used for ensuring conception and an easy childbirth, instructions reprised in the *Jayākhya Saṃhitā* and the *Kādambarī* of Bāṇabhaṭṭa.[76] Nearly identical instructions are found in a collection of demonological traditions written in 1849 by a Gujarati exorcist under the title of *Bhut Nibandh: An Essay Descriptive of Demonology and Other Popular Superstitions of Guzerat*. Concerning a charm of Ghaṇṭakarṇ Mahāvīr,[77] a highly popular *bhūtanātha* among the Jains of western India, this text explains that "if a person [should] . . . write this diagram [containing the mantra of Ghaṇṭakarṇ Mahāvīr] on Bhoj-patra [birch bark], place it in a locket and give it to a pregnant woman, her delivery is effected. If the same locket be given to a barren woman, she will conceive."[78]

How, then, is one to determine what is orthodox and what is heterodox or eccentric with respect to this orthodoxy? Since the end of the nineteenth century, Hindu reformers, seeking to distance themselves from the "kitchen rituals" of the masses while embracing a Hinduism grounded in a refined spirituality redolent of that of Protestantism as well as rational and scientific doctrine, have chosen to define orthodoxy according to their proper modernist conceptions of "true" religion. This tendency was further fueled in the latter half of the twentieth century by scholarly theories of "Sanskritization" and of the so-called "great" and "little traditions" of Indian religion, according to which the Sanskritic scriptural traditions of brahmin orthodoxy were held to be normative, over and against vernacular, popular practice.[79] Over thirty years ago, Chris Fuller dismantled these theories as so many expressions of tautological reasoning.[80] More relevant to our interests here are observations made by Fred Smith in his remarkable study of the history of possession in South Asia:

> One of the chief characteristics of this history has been a flow of ideas . . . from educated elites who control texts into the popular imaginaire and, conversely, from popular, non-Brahman, culture into texts. The juxtaposition of and exchange between classical and folk is, in fact, nowhere more evident than in the area of *bhūtavidyā*. It appears . . . that the banishment of the subaltern from much of classical discourse is a thin and tenuous construction or, perhaps more generously, an artifact of orthodox conditioning within the minds of both classical Indian and modern Western-trained scholars.[81]

Writing on the topic of *longue durée* global history, Jerry Bentley has identified this conditioning as "modernocentrism . . . an enchantment with the modern world that has blinded scholars and the general public alike to continuities between premodern and modern times."[82] Two-tiered models—of great versus little traditions, elite versus vernacular, literate versus nonliterate, modern versus non-modern—presuppose that individuals, including members of socioreligious elites, are not constantly engaged in an inner dialogue regarding what is normative in terms of their personal experience. As the folklorist Leonard Primiano argued in his seminal 1995 study, the elite or official is always already circumscribed by the vernacular. No individual—whether a pope, a high priest, or a patriarch—inhabits the world of his (or her) "official" religion at all times. The vernacular is always the default mode of being, including for members of religious elites. "Even while representing the most institutionally normative aspects of their religious tradition, there is always some passive accommodation, some intriguing survival, some active creation, some dissenting impulse, some reflection on lived experience that influences how these individuals direct their religious lives."[83]

These inner acts of reflection and interpretation have often taken the form of negotiations between individual subjects, social classes, cultures, and polities. Toward the beginning of the second millennium CE, brahmins posted to the hinterlands of eastern Indian kingdoms found themselves confronted with the task of revitalizing the old vedic social order by converting rural populations there, an endeavor documented in the Sanskrit-language corpus of the Bengal "regional Purāṇas." The people who were the object of these missionary endeavors being ignorant of Sanskrit, one might assume that these would have been chronicles of one-sided oppression, of the submission of local custom to the universal claims of official Hindu religion. This was not the case. Strangers in a strange land, these immigrant brahmins were vulnerable to and dependent on the cooperation of local populations for their survival. And so it is that a leitmotiv of these works is the recognition, even the insistence, that local custom should take precedence over Hindu *dharma*.[84] As Kunal Chakrabarti has observed, "The Bengal *Purāṇas* naturalize the speech of several others and in the process display inner tensions, collaborations and negotiations, which are more than mere authoritative statements, but are comparable to dialogues. The plurality of voices makes the *Purāṇas* truly polyphonic in character . . . The Puranic texts were constituted through this complex process of negotiation."[85] Such was also the case in western Europe, where down into the thirteenth century, the rural nobility remained immersed in the culture of their rustic subjects. Raised on popular tales told to them by their wet nurses, they in their castles enjoyed the poetry of the same wandering minstrels as did the *vulgi* in their villages. "Vernacular poetry was a sort of cultural binder that, crossing social barriers, even found its way into monasteries in spite of the expressed scorn of the Church hierarchy."[86] It is in lifeworlds such as these that we must situate the sources of much of the written documentation upon which this book relies. Representatives of socioreligious authority, our scribes inhabited two cultures from birth, shuttling between two (or more) languages and navigating between oral and written forms of expression.

If in this chapter we have challenged several of the artificial binaries of both neotraditionalist theories of "true" religion and postmodernist theories of culture, our purview has remained limited to the Indian subcontinent, with the itinerant members of the mendicant orders the principal agents for the dissemination of a specific body of ritual theory and practice. In the next chapter, we will see those horizons expand to cover many of the ancient and medieval world's paths of overland and maritime travel, trade, migration, and warfare, paths trodden by a host of historical actors including Buddhist merchants cum missionary monks, Catholic clerics, a Zoroastrian high priest, an Apollo temple officiant, and a gaggle of unnamed magicians.

3

The Demons Are in the Details: Demonological Sciences and Technologies, East and West

1

The 100 BCE–150 CE *Saddharmapuṇḍarīka Sūtra* (SPS, "Manual of the Lotus of the True Law") provides the following list of demons prohibited from "mounting onto the head to bring harm to one who proclaims the Dharma": yakṣas, rākṣasas, pretas, piśācas, pūtanas, kṛtyas, vetāḍas, kumbhāṇḍas, *stabdhas*, *omārakas*, *ostārakas*, and apasmārakas.[1] With the exception of the italicized names, these are garden variety demons found in Hindu, Buddhist, and Jain demonological and dæmonological nomenclature from the late vedic period down to the historical present of the SPS. These names recur time and again across the scriptures of the three great religions as well as in medical and secular literature. But then, in a group of Mahāyāna works from India's great northwest—loosely corresponding to the regions of Kashmir, Gandhara, and Bactria (hereafter KGB)—as well as from the Tarim Basin of Chinese Turkestan, a new set of names came to be appended to lists of the usual suspects. A precious source for this supplementary data is the *Mahāmāyūrīvidyārājñīsūtra* (MMVS, "Teaching of the Great Pea-Hen, the Queen of Spells"), Buddhism's earliest comprehensive compendium of demonological lore. While the MMVS's earliest extant redaction dates from the early fourth century CE, its traditions may be traced back to the first centuries of the Common Era.[2] The work contains extensive geographical references to the KGB region, especially in its renowned "catalogue of yakṣas" section, which also attests to the important presence of yakṣa shrines strung along the principal trade routes of the day, as well as in various urban settings.[3]

A sixth-century codex recovered near Kuqa on the northern edge of the Tarim Basin in 1890, the Bower Manuscript contains substantial portions of the MMVS.[4] But this is but one of several works recovered from the Chinese Turkestan with significant demonological content. Another trove of

Mahāyāna manuscripts, also containing extensive demonological material and dating from the third century CE, was uncovered at Gilgit in 1931. Situated in the northwestern corner of modern-day Pakistan, the Gilgit Valley lies midway between the Tarim Basin and the Indus River Valley, and was an important pivot for overland trade between Inner Asia and the Indian subcontinent.[5] Given this distribution of these early Buddhist manuscripts as well as other data that I will discuss below, I would suggest that it was in Inner Asia rather than in the lower Indian subcontinent itself that these new names found their way into the Sanskrit-language demonological lexicon.

The KGB region lay astride the three east-west trade corridors that funneled through the mountain passes of Inner Asia to converge at the western rim of the Tarim Basin, a region dotted with trading towns harboring highly cosmopolitan populations.[6] As such, this Inner Asian region was pivotal not only to trade along the so-called Silk Road, but also to the intermingling of the peoples, languages, and religions of South Asia, East Asia, Persia, and the Mediterranean world. For about a thousand years, down into the eighth century of the Common Era, Silk Road trade would be dominated, more or less in succession, by Bactrians, Parthians, Kushans, Sogdians, and Sasanians.[7]

Between 206 BCE and the first decades of the Common Era, the Indo-Greeks would play a leading role in commercial and cultural exchanges in the region. The expatriate Greek populations of the "Indo-Greek States," including Bactria, were a heterogeneous group comprised of captives exiled there by the Persian Achaemenids, soldiers who had settled in the garrison towns founded by Alexander's generals, and émigrés from Mediterranean Greece itself. Some of these intermarried with the indigenous populations, forming a Hellenized aristocracy that assimilated with the region's Indic warrior class, forming a distinctive culture that blended Persian, Indic, and Greek elements. Trade with China began in this period, with silks transiting through the region to Indian Ocean ports.[8] The Bactrians were major players in both overland and maritime trade with Rome, with a circa 65 CE source reporting sightings of Bactrians, Scythians, Persians, and Indians among the public at the Roman theater in Alexandria as well as in Rome itself.[9] The sole urban center constructed by the Indo-Greeks, Ai Khanum in northern Afghanistan boasted a Greek theater and archive; and bilingual scholars are known to have translated Aśoka's edicts into literary Greek in the middle of the third century BCE.[10]

Following the Bactrians, trade with Rome and China would be dominated by the Kushans, whose empire at its height extended across the territories of the modern-day nation-states of Pakistan, Afghanistan, Uzbekistan, and Tajikstan, as well as much of northern India; and whose powerful armies protected and controlled trade routes linking Bactria to Kashmir, the Karakorum mountain range, China, the Punjab, the Ganges basin, and ports at the mouth of the Indus.[11] The Kushan emperors were the earliest Indic kings to refer to themselves as *devaputras*, "sons of god" in the Sanskrit, a title they adapted, as Sylvain Lévi convincingly argued in his last published article, from the Chinese *tiānzǐ* ("son of heaven") via the Middle Iranian *baypuhr*.[12] Their cosmopolitanism in religious matters is prominently displayed in their coinage, which featured Greek, Zoroastrian, and Hindu gods, as well as images of the Buddha himself.[13] The same cosmopolitanism appears in Gandharan Buddhist *stūpa* reliefs of the period, on whose lower registers Zoroastrian fire stands frequently appear.[14] It was also during the Kushan age that Greek astronomy, as well as, perhaps, Greek demonology, made their way into India's great northwest: I will return to this point later in this chapter.[15] Elsewhere, a Kushan-period Śiva temple at the site of Surkh Kotal (northeastern Afghanistan) attests to the short-lived presence of a Śaiva community there, which apparently fell victim to the suppression of heretical practices by the third century CE Sasanian high priest Kirdēr, about whom more shortly. As David Scott has suggested, Śaiva "refugees" from his persecutions may have made their way northward into Sogdiana, where a profusion of Śaiva images begin to appear between the sixth and eighth centuries CE, the period in which Śaiva Tantra emerged in Kashmir.[16] Even after losing their Indian territories in the early third century CE, Kushan nobles remained a powerful force west of the Indus down into the fifth century, as vassals of the Persian Sasanids.[17]

Situated at the northwestern limit of the former Kushan Empire, the cluster of principalities known as Sogdiana arched over the north of Bactria, their territories roughly corresponding to those of the modern nation-states of Uzbekistan and Tajikstan. Its people were Zoroastrians,[18] whose language—like Parthian, Bactrian, and the Pahlavi language of the Sasanians—belonged to the Middle Iranian family.[19] Between the fifth and eighth centuries, the Sogdians would dominate Silk Road commerce, with their trading networks extending from China, Southeast Asia, and India to Byzantium.[20] Like their Bactrian and Kushan predecessors, a significant number of Sogdian merchants converted to Buddhism; like their predecessors, many settled in the Tarim Basin, which served as their base for trade with China; and like their predecessors, many in their expatriate communities played a pivotal role in the transmission and translation of Buddhist texts. Indeed, it was via the trade corridors linking India to Inner Asia that Buddhism began to spread into the wider world in the first centuries of the Common Era; horses, the prime weapon of war, would transit in the opposite direction, down into the eighteenth century.[21] As already noted, the Bower Manuscript, whose sixth and seventh "books" contain portions of the MMVS, was found at a site on the northern edge of the Tarim Basin. The Gilgit Valley, the site of another important cache of demonological works, was, between the fourth and sixth centuries CE, a trans-Himalayan trade corridor for Sogdian and Indian merchants.[22] It was during this period of robust economic, cultural, and religious exchange that the MMVS reached its definitive form, as attested in three sixth- to eighth-century Chinese translations.[23]

By way of demonstrating the universal effectiveness of the great peacock spell, the MMVS provides extensive catalogs of the supernatural beings against which it affords protection.[24] Several of these, which rank them according to their relative benevolence or malevolence, comprise the following collective names, always given in the same order: "Devas, Nāgas, Asuras, Marutas, Garuḍas, Kinnaras, Mahoragas, Yakṣas, Rākṣasas, Pretas, Piśācas, Bhūtas, Kumbhāṇḍas, Pūtanas, Kaṭapūtanas, Skandas, Unmādas, *Chāyās*, Apasmāras, and *Ostāras*."[25] Apart from this source and the SPS, the Ostāras (also written Ostārakas) appear nowhere else in the Sanskrit record.[26] As for the Chāyās, first introduced here, these reappear time and again in both Sanskrit and vernacular forms from the medieval period down to the present day. A second recurring list found in the MMVS's demonological catalogs is less systematic and more idiosyncratic. Noteworthy is the fact that the word *chāya*/*chāyā* is the sole term to appear twice in this second set of lists, the first time as a class of demons, and the second time as . . . something else. The longest of these passages reads as follows:

> Slain are the Kṛtyās, slain the emaciators,[27] slain the Kākhordas, the Kiraṇas, the Vetāḍas, the Ciccas, [and] the Preṣakas;[28] slain are the Skandas, the Unmādas, the Chāyas, the Apasmāras, [and] the Ostārakas; slain are fears, deadly philtres, [and] poisons; slain [the demons of] consumption; [the demons of] things poorly digested; [the demons of] things vomited, [and] the evil [C]hāyā(s) (*duśchāyā[ḥ]*);[29] slain those that are beheld with evil intent, those [whose names are] written with evil intent, those that are trodden upon with evil intent; slain are those that have been shaken off.[30]

Given the fact that few of these names or terms are found in either classical or Buddhist Hybrid Sanskrit, my translation here is tentative.[31] In any case, I am offering it (1) to underscore the redundant use of the term *chāya*/*chāyā*,[32] the first time in the company of the same demonic beings as found in the MMVS's first set of lists mentioned above, and the second time in the midst of a heterogeneous catalog of pathologies, toxins, and acts of sorcery; and (2) to introduce three other terms, one vedic and two not found in earlier Sanskrit sources: *kṛtyā*, *kākhorda*, and *vetāḍa*. The final section of this chapter will be devoted to a discussion of these three terms within the Sanskrit literary record as well as in the broader context of contacts and exchanges between the KGB region, India, Iran, and the Mediterranean world.

Chāyā is a feminine Sanskrit noun attested since the time of the Vedas. In classical Sanskrit, its primary sense is "shadow," "shade," or "a reflected image"; it can also denote "luster," "light," and "complexion." In rare cases, the masculine form, *chāya*, is also employed.[33] While the MMVS's default use of the term retains the feminine ending, in one passage we find both masculine and feminine forms employed to denote a wide range of kinship and courtly relationships: male Chāyas, female Chāyās, Chāya sons, Chāyā daughters, Chāya chamberlains, Chāyā ladies-in-waiting, male Chāya retainers, and female Chāyā retainers.[34] However, in the passage just translated, the expression "the evil *chāyā*" (*duśchāyā*) is a feminine singular noun embedded in a series of terms denoting acts of sorcery rather than names of demons. This second use of the term, which would appear to be intentional on the part of the MMVS's compilers, will be the focus of the next section of this chapter. Here, however, I wish to concentrate on Chāy(ā)s as demons. It is precisely in vernaculars from the north and west of the Indian subcontinent that cognate terms for Chāya unambiguously denote a type of demon. These, however, retain the feminine ending: Chāyā. In Nepali, *chāyā* can, in addition to "shadow" or "shade," also mean "phantom."[35] In several Indo-Aryan languages, *chāyā-puruṣa* has the sense of "dead person appearing as his shadow."[36] In the Marwari and Mewari languages of Rajasthan, the expression *chāyā ānā* denotes the onslaught of a state of possession, often induced, in which a spirit medium's body is racked by contortions and his or her power of speech taken over by the possessing spirit being.[37] In modern Hindi, both *chāyā* and its alloform *sāyā* denote a spirit being (*bhūt*, *pret*, *jinn*, and *parī*),[38] with the expressions *sāyā honā*, meaning "possessed by a spirit being," and *sāyā meṃ ānā*, "to fall under the power of a spirit being." In the same vein, *sāyā utarnā* means "to lift away the influence of a spirit being."[39]

When one turns, however, to languages not employing the Devanagari script and less attentive to standard Sanskrit usage, the masculine short-a ending resurfaces. So, for example, the Hindustani expression *sāya honā* has the same meaning as does *sāyā honā* in modern Hindi, the sole difference being in the orthography.[40] The Urdu *sāya* likewise has the sense of "influence of an evil spirit,"[41] with *parī kā sāya* meaning "possession by an evil spirit."[42] In Pashto, *sāya'h* has the same range as *chāyā* in Nepali: "shade, apparition, specter."[43] So too, in modern Persian, *sāya* denotes "shade, shadow; an apparition; a wicked spirit," as well as the name of a specific demon. Regardless of their endings, all of these terms have "shade" or "shadow" as their primary sense, with "a (type of) demon" a secondary usage. Here, one might think to look to Middle Iranian sources for the origins of the use of *chāya* to denote a type of demon. This is not the case: in Sogdian, Pahlavi, and Manichean Middle Iranian; the cognate terms *sy'k(h)*, *sāyag*, and *s'yg* simply denote a shade or shadow, and are therefore synonymous with the primary sense of the Sanskrit *chāyā*.[44]

Now, the MMVS's lost archetype manuscript was a Sanskrit work from India, with its closest witnesses being three early Chinese translations dating from between 350 and 450 CE. However, it is only in the work's three later Chinese translations, dating from the sixth to eighth centuries, that the "catalogue of yakṣas" with its geographical focus on the KGB region and long lists of spirit beings, including the Chāyas, appears, together with the *duśchāyā*(s) and its/their ilk. Due to the close similarity between these three, Marc DesJardins has suggested that all three translators were working from a common fifth-century Sanskrit hyparchetype.[45] Both types of (C)hāy(ā) also appear in the sixth-century Bower Manuscript. Based on these data, we may conclude that these spirit beings were incorporated into the MMVS at a time when the Sanskrit hyparchetype manuscript was circulating in Inner and East Asia. Given the close similarity between its demonological passages and those found in these three Chinese translations, I would surmise that the Bower Manuscript's sixth and seventh books drew upon that same source.[46] If this was the case, I would further suggest that the Chāya/Sāya was a demon type circulating in the Inner Asian region that produced the MMVS's fifth-century archetype as well as other manuscript versions of early Buddhist demonological works.

A modern-day ethnographic study of a Dalit community conducted by William Sax provides a wealth of complementary data. For nearly four decades, Sax's field of research has been the northern Indian state of Uttarakhand. Sharing borders with Nepal, Tibet, and Himachal Pradesh, and encompassing the medieval polities of Garhwal and Kumaon, this sub-Himalayan region lies on the southern fringe of the ancient and medieval KGB cultural zone. Here, demons or spirit beings named Chāyās are often paired with two other types of spirit beings, called Chaḷs and Chidras.[47] In the state's Chamoli district, the most widely performed healing ritual, undergone by 95 percent of women living there, is called *chaḷ pūjā*. In several Indo-Aryan languages, the primary sense of the term *chaḷ* (Sanskrit *chalam*) is "deceit" or "trickery," leading Sax to surmise that "in this context, 'guile' is personified as a set of demons who afflict people, especially recently married women. Hence," he continues, "I have translated *c[h]hal* as 'crafty demons.' "[48] *Chaḷ*s are said to become attached (*lag jānā*) to their victims while they are in desolate places, such as forests, mountains, and ravines. As is the case throughout South Asia, young women are especially vulnerable to demonic possession of this type, particularly if they have experienced a sudden fright or a shock of some kind.[49] In a case described by Sax as typical, a girl suffering from various physical and mental disorders was diagnosed as being "afflicted by a Chāyā; specifically the ghost of a woman who had been murdered in the mid-1990s in a wild area above the village. . . . In this case, it had attached itself to the victim one day when she was cutting grass in the forest."[50] Note here that *Chāyā* is the term employed for the afflicting "ghost" or "shade"; yet, the first two of three rituals that are performed to exorcise the Chāyā are in fact called *chaḷ pūjā*s.

Every *chaḷ* exorcism involves a demon named Masan (from the Sanskrit *śmaśāna*, "cremation-ground"), who can take on any one of six forms: four are fearsome male figures (Sayyid, Pathan, Mongol, Masan) and two are malevolent female sprites associated with high places, named Eḍī and Āccharī.[51] Here, the throngs of *chaḷ*s are identified as forms or minions of Masan that dwell in both the afflicted female's body and in the wild, uninhabited spaces of Garhwal.[52] As for Masan's six named forms, these appear to function in the same way as the *bhūtanātha*s of South Asian demonology, as intermediaries between the pandemonium of the spirit world and one or another form of Śiva or the great Goddess.

The series of rites Sax describes made use of typical demonifuge strategies: demon-subduing mantras, the sweeping away of the *chaḷ* demons from the body of the afflicted onto an image of the *bhūtanātha* (named Masan, in this case), auspicious food offerings made in the domestic space of the village, and a goat sacrificed in the wilderness. Also present were the combination of cajoling and threats that one so often finds in South Asian exorcisms.[53] The culminating moment of the second *chaḷ pūjā* was the sacrifice of a goat performed in the wild, uninhabited space where the Chāyā was said to have originally attached itself to the girl. In this rite, the Chaḷs[54] were swept not onto the image of Masan but rather onto the goat itself. Then, speaking to the goat, the exorcist said, "All these evil things, *chaḷ*, *chidra*, ghost, Masan, and so forth . . . all of them are satisfied by your sacrifice, and they will not afflict the girl anymore."[55] This is not where the exorcism ended, however. The *chaḷ pūjā*s now completed, the *chāyā pūjā* immediately followed, its most dramatic moment occurring after the girl was made to gaze into a tin of heated oil to behold the face of the Chāyā, superimposed on her own. The reflecting oil was then dashed into a fire, and with it, the girl was released from the Chāyā's thrall.[56] Following this, the ritual cycle from the earlier *chaḷ pūjā* was completed with the eating of the sacrificial goat, resulting in a "kind of recycling of the *chaḷ*—from their original location [in the wilds] into the body of the victim, and later back to the place where they belonged, via the bodies of the sacrificial animal and the local men [who eat the goat] . . . eventually passing into the earth through their feces."[57] As I will discuss at length later in this chapter, the most dramatic moment of Sax's *chāyā pūjā* is nothing other than a modern South Asian instantiation of a complex ritual technology that likely had its origins in Egypt in the first centuries of the Common Era.

2

In his 1828 "statistical sketch" of Kumaon, George William Traill referred to the *Acherí* (Sax's Āccharī) as "the ghosts of young female children; these reside at the top of the mountains, but descend at dusk. . . . When female children are taken suddenly ill, it is immediately concluded that the Acherí have cast their spell or shadow (*chāyā*) on the child, with the view of adding her ghost to their numbers."[58] William Crooke made a similar observation with respect to Masan: children afflicted by him are said to be "under his shadow" and waste away by a sort of consumption.[59] At first blush, it would appear that in these cases the term *chāyā* is being employed in its primary sense, as a simple shadow. However, these accounts also appear to accord agency and power to these demonic shadows in a process through which innocent girls fall sick, sometimes fatally. This dynamic has a textual precedent, which furthermore brings together the Chāyās, Chidras, and Chaḷs of Sax's Garhwal-based ethnography. This usage, which would also correspond to the MMVS's "evil *chāyā*" (*duśchāyā*), is brought to the fore in the most extensive discussion of the term found anywhere in the Hindu tantric canon. This is the circa 825 CE *Netra Tantra*, the "Tantra of the Eye," whose nineteenth chapter, devoted to demonology, opens with an account of the workings of the evil eye, here called the "casting of the gaze" (*dṛṣṭi-pāta*).[60]

The NT was composed in the Vale of Kashmir, some 150 miles due south of the Gilgit Valley, that pivot of Silk Road trade where fifth-century codices containing early Mahāyāna demonological works were uncovered in the last century.[61] This is a composite work, with two well-defined layers of redaction.[62] The first of these is the demonological stratum, which comprises unadorned descriptions of demons, symptoms of demonological possession, and techniques for countering the same. This stratum comprises a pragmatic, technical guide to certain types of ritual as practiced by *sādhaka*s, tantric "white magicians" working for the protection of the king and society at large. Prominently featured are votive rites, including practices of protection, pacification, exorcism, and the cultivation of prosperity (the "six acts" of tantric sorcery). The second layer of redaction, which attempts to structure the text into a coherent and unified thesis, is devoted to the form of Śiva known as the "Lord of Immortality" (Amṛteśa), and more importantly, to his all-powerful "Death Conquering" (*mṛtyuñjaya*) mantra, which controls, routs, and destroys demons with total efficacy (in this, it resembles the MMVS's Great Peacock Spell).

Abrupt shifts in content and style mark this later redaction. One finds such a shift, for example, in the middle of the eighty-first verse of chapter 19—where, following a long discussion of symptomologies of possession, of the clans of the demonic Seizers, and of the ritual means for parrying their assaults—Śiva, the narrator of the text, abruptly launches into a praise of the universal applicability of the "Death Conquering" mantra, which he had never divulged before. As is so often the case in these Kashmirian traditions, the earlier, demonological stratum of the NT is overtly dualistic in its metaphysics, and in this respect very much in line with orthodox Śaivasiddhānta doctrine. Its later layer of redaction, however, is nondualist after the Trika fashion, casting even the demons and demonesses of childhood possession as internal to Śiva and the universe he embodies.

This trend is further pronounced in the detailed eleventh-century commentary of Kṣemarāja, the illustrious Abhinavagupta's highly erudite disciple who seldom misses an occasion to champion the nondualist exegesis. This sometimes makes for forced readings, if not outright misinterpretations on his part, of certain data. His learned commentary is nonetheless a helpful guide, both for a number of its insights and for its extensive quotations from several probable South Asian sources for the NT's demonology, including such "Bhūta Tantras"[63] as the eleventh-century *Kriyākālaguṇottara* ("Full of Virtues for the Time of Treatment") and the *Totula Tantra*.[64]

The first seventy-five verses of the NT's nineteenth chapter comprise what is to my knowledge the sole comprehensive treatment of the evil eye in the entire tantric corpus. As is typical in these works, the discussion opens with the great Goddess requesting clarification from Śiva concerning something he had revealed to her previously:

> Now I wish to hear this. There is a doubt in my heart [concerning] the evil eye that the Mothers always cast upon people. Those [Mother] goddesses are innumerable [and] their power immeasurable, [but] the Yoginīs [who] afflict [their victims] by means of the "*chāyā* opening" (*chāyā-cchidreṇa*) are more powerful still. They are horribly filthy. They are violent, merciless, fearless, mighty, and injurious to all creatures, especially children. Their number is incalculable. This being the case, tell me the strategy [for combating them]. They constantly engage in trickery (*chalam*) that takes the form of the *chāyā*,

> and likewise the trickery that consists of the casting of the gaze. O God! [Concerning] the *chāyā*: how manifold is it thought to be? What is the peril of the evil eye? How does one divert it?[65]

Replying that he will provide a comprehensive account of the *chāyā*, Śiva launches into a demonological foundation myth in which we see him creating innumerable hosts of demonic beings for the destruction of the Daityas, the perennial archenemies of the gods. Once the Daityas have been destroyed, however, these demonic beings—here called Mothers (*mātṛ*s), Spirit Beings (*bhūta*s), and Seizers (*graha*s)—request from Śiva the boon of invincibility, which he grants.[66] Now invincible, these begin to oppress the gods themselves, who in turn appeal to Śiva to destroy them. To this end, Śiva creates tens of millions of Mantras ("male spell-beings") and Vidyās ("female spell-beings"), and the terrified Mothers and Seizers who have not been destroyed by these animated spells are cast by Śiva into various desolate regions of the sky, earth, and the waters, the correlates of the lonely mountains, forests, and ravines that are the haunts of the Chāyās of Uttarakhand.[67]

While Śiva does not address the matter here, these demonesses' "trickery in the form of the *chāyā*" may also refer to the invisibility that empowers them to approach and possess their victims unawares. This appears to be the sense of a passage from the alchemical *Rasārṇava* (RA: "Ocean of Essential Elements"). Referring to Nandikeśvara and Kumāra, this work states that because their *chāyā*s are invisible (*naṣṭa-chāyā*), these dæmons are not seen by alchemists when they enter into their bodies to steal away the precious mercury they have ingested.[68] This scenario is dramatized in an episode of the coeval KSS, in which we see a young brahmin alchemist stymied in his efforts to produce alchemical gold because each time he attempts to project his transmuting powder onto a piece of copper, an invisible yakṣa steals it away in midair.[69]

This NT account appears to draw upon an earlier version of the myth, attested in the *Kāśyapa Saṃhitā* ("Kaśyapa's System"), a seventh-century ayurvedic work devoted mainly to pediatrics that was apparently unknown to Kṣemarāja, who does not cite or quote it in his commentary. Unlike the NT version—which introduces three types of beings: the Daityas; the Mothers, Spirit Beings, and Seizers who defeat them; and the male spell-beings and female spell-beings who in turn control these—this myth mentions only the first two: the Asuras (in the role of the Daityas) and the Jātahāriṇīs ("Child Abductresses") who destroy them.[70] This explanation for the origin of the demons of possession clearly takes its inspiration from the MBh account of the birth of Skanda and his granting of various powers to the Mothers and

Female Seizers.[71] According to the *Kāśyapa Saṃhitā*, the Jātahāriṇīs were created by Skanda in order to destroy a demoness named "Long-Tongue" (Dīrghajihvī).[72] Following their victory, these Child Abductresses, taking the form of she-wolves, female hyenas (*śālāvṛkī*), and birds of evil omen (*śākunī*), began to plague children with all manner of affliction.[73]

In the verses that follow in the NT myth, Śiva describes the ways in which the Mothers, Spirit Beings, and Seizers—his own creations—are able to torment their victims. Here, a palette of sinful and impure acts or dispositions opens the wicked-souled (*durātmānam*) human evildoer (*durācāram*) to possession and corruption by these demonic entities;[74] and it is in his description of their modus operandi that Śiva fully explains the term *chāyā-cchidram*.

> A vile woman or likewise a man, having not bathed,[75] may cast a shadow on children and kings, their queens [and] ascetics. By [means of] that very *chāyā* opening (*chāyācchidreṇa*), those Spirit Beings—as well as the Mothers who are more powerful still—that have found their opening (*labdhacchidrāḥ*) effect the casting of their evil gaze. [It is] out of a wish to destroy [them that] the injurious ones [i.e., the Spirit Beings and the Mothers] cast [their] wild gaze on children, whilst those supremely sinful evildoers [i.e., humans possessed of, or by, the *chāyā*] are likewise tormented [or "consumed": *grastāḥ*] by the Spirit Beings, [i.e.,] the Fevers, etc. . . . If when conjointly casting (*sampātya*) their fearsome gaze, these [human evildoers, Spirit Beings and Mothers] and many others [should then] look collectively at children as well as at the aforementioned [king, queen or ascetic], then, knowing that the evil eye has manifested, one should act for their welfare.[76]

As with the NT, the *Kāśyapa Saṃhitā*'s account of the workings of the evil eye also involves evil or impure human intermediaries whose gaze becomes a conduit for Child Abductresses to penetrate the bodies of their victims (fig. 3.1).[77] Here, a Child Abductress is said to latch onto (*sajjate*) the openings (*chidreṣu*) or doors of unrighteousness (*adharmadvāreṣu*) opened in evil persons through their sinful acts. When such an evil person fixes his or her gaze on a pregnant woman for whom protective rites have not been performed, the Child Abductress latches onto her.[78] However, the *Kāśyapa Saṃhitā* account makes no mention of either *chāyā*s or *chalam*s.

To this point, I have translated *chidram* as "opening." Is this a correct translation? In other medieval sources, it is the primary classical Sanskrit sense of the term that is attested: a person's weak point, a chink in their bodily defenses, a gap or discontinuity in their psychosomatic Gestalt. According to South Asian understandings of human physiology, the opportunities for spirit beings to penetrate these defenses are limitless. In the words

FIGURE 3.1. Demon, Hadda, Afghanistan, third/fourth century CE. Musée des Arts Asiatiques-Guimet, Paris. Image © RMN Grand Palais / Art Resource, NY.

of a Kerala-based ayurvedic physician "Every hair on the body grows out of a hole [and] these holes run deep into the body."[79] Such concepts can be traced back to at least the time of the *Harivaṃśa*, a work dating from the first centuries of the Common Era. There, we are told that following the gods' victory over the demon Kālanemi, Brahmā warned them to never let down their guard because "the despicable Dānavas always force their way into the openings (*chidreṣu*)."[80] The ayurvedic CS and *Aṣṭāṅgasaṃgraha* make similar statements with respect to *grahas*, who attack persons in whom they notice a *chidram* on certain lunar dates.[81] The term also appears in a number of Trika works,[82] with Abhinavagupta employing the verbal form *chidrayanti* ("crack open") to speak of the dangers of witches (*śākinīs*) brought under a practitioner's power, by force, through the use of a Bhairava mantra: if they are not released immediately after his use of them, they will crack their way into a practitioner through his weak points.[83] Merutuṅga uses the term in a similar way in his 1304 *Prabandhacintāmaṇi* ("Wishing Stone of Narratives") to describe how the Jain scholar Hemacandra contracted a skin disease, perhaps leprosy: "Owing to [a] curse . . . the disease of leprosy entered into the sage through that opening (*tacchidreṇa*)."[84] Kṣemarāja notes a similar usage in his commentary on NT 19.71, where he quotes the *Tantrasadbhāva* (TSBh, "True Meaning of the Tantras") on the subject of a Śabarī demoness that "does not kill, but rather relishes blood through an opening (*chidreṇa*)."

Yet, another gloss by our commentator gives pause. In his commentary on NT 19.3, Kṣemarāja writes that "*chidram* [means] wailing in the wilderness, and so forth."[85] What are we to make of this cryptic statement? Later in this same chapter, the NT lists wailing as one of the behaviors that specifically render women vulnerable to possession, and this is the probable basis for his interpretation.[86] However, the qualifier "in the wilderness" opens up other possibilities that align with the demonic Chidras, Chaḷs, ghosts, and Masans of Uttarakhand.[87] On the one hand, desolate wilderness settings are the places where these demons are known to latch onto their female victims: in its list of the *chidrams* exploited by the Seizers, the *Aṣṭāṅgahṛdayasūtra* ("Manual for the Heart of the Eight Branches") lists "abiding nocturnally in desolate places or on cremation grounds, etc."[88] On the other, this trope has a vedic precedent. A hymn from the ṚV's tenth book, offered to the wilderness goddess Araṇyāṇī, observes that "he who spends the night in the wilderness hears the voice of someone crying."[89]

Are we to read both this passage and Kṣemarāja's gloss as allusions to nocturnal products of over-active imaginations? The human-like cries of hyenas?[90] The activities of witches and foolish women?[91] Or, was Kṣemarāja actually referring to a demonic being?[92] Perhaps the answer is "both," because, as Sax informs me, a modern-day Garhwali might well understand *chāyācchidr*(*ā*) as "the Yoginīs who afflict their victims by means of little female demons."[93] The same is clearly the case with *chāyā*, which I have generally left untranslated in these passages. After all, the data from the MMVS, Sax's ethnography, and Indo-Aryan philology are ambiguous. Not simply a shadow cast by a polluted and evil person, it is also a demonic being. Furthermore, in his opening invocation to the NT's nineteenth chapter, Kṣemarāja presents *chāyā-cchidrāṇi* as a dvandva compound, and not as a tatpuruṣa, in which case he too may have viewed these as names for different classes of demons.[94] Of the fifteen mentions of the word *chāyā* in the NT's nineteenth chapter and Kṣemarāja's commentary, only two clearly employ the term in the sense of "shadow,"[95] whereas in seven, Chāyā unambiguously refers to a demonic being.[96]

With his explanation of *chāyā-cchidram* complete, Śiva has also completed his response to the Goddess's original query concerning the two types of *chalam*.[97] The two are linked. The first *chalam*, which takes the form of the Chāyā, a demon-cum-shadow, is instrumental to the second *chalam*, the evil eye, which the dread Mothers, Yoginīs, and Spirit Beings cast through the eyes of a malignant human whose shadow has fallen upon a vulnerable victim—a person with a *chidram*. Apart from the NT, the sole Sanskrit-language use of *chalam* in such a technical sense is a verse from the circa-eighth-century TSBh, which Kṣemarāja quotes in his commentary on NT 19.71.[98] Here we read that "a female being who, for the purpose of shape-shifting, continually drinks the fluids of living beings after attracting [them] through trickery (*chalena*)—and who after obtaining [their fluids] slaughters [her] victims—shall be known as a *śākinī*, ever delighting in dreadful places."[99] In the vernacular context, the term *chaḷ* denotes, as we have seen, a type of demon in Uttarakhand, with its cognate *ċhaw* meaning "goblin" in the Gaṅgoi dialect of Kumaoni.[100]

With this, the NT turns to the techniques for releasing children and other persons who have now fallen prey to the conjoined gaze of their superhuman and human tormentors. These techniques include the combination of cajoling and threats directed at the possessing demons (also seen in Sax's ethnography and found in exorcisms across South Asia),[101] fully bathing or anointing the head of the potential victim with mantra-incanted water,[102] and making offerings to the alpha males and females of the various families or clans of Spirit Beings, Mothers, Seizers, and so forth.[103] Here, the nature of the spirit being determines the type of the offering as well as the setting in which it is to be made.[104] When buffalo or goats are to be sacrificed, these take place in the regions to which the Spirit Beings were exiled by Śiva: the wild forest, desolate spaces, cremation grounds, Yoginī temples (called "circles of mothers"), and so forth.[105]

In his commentary on these verses, Kṣemarāja provides an extended discussion of the various types and activities of Yoginīs—the Clan-Born, Mound-Born, and Field-Born—fully quoting long descriptive passages from the TSBh. This he does because, as he states in his conclusion to his excursus, "Bhairava [is] the lord of the circle of all the Śaktis."[106] Kṣemarāja's analysis encapsulates the hermeneutic of the Trika school, and indeed of much of Hindu tantric commentary. South Asian demonology, whose Atharvanic origins predate the advent of Tantra by well over a millennium, and whose traditions have remained intact and often unchanged across the entire subcontinent down to the present day, views the universe as a pandemonium of noxious beings that prey on vulnerable humans, making them sick, driving them insane, and eventually killing them. Then as now, such beings can only be controlled by placating the masters of their respective hosts: that is, one of the Seven Mothers, or *bhūtanāthas* like Bhairava, Gaṇapati, Vīrabhadra, or Hanumān. Already attested in the ayurvedic literature,[107] these Lords of Spirit Beings came to be incorporated into early demonological pantheons. However, through processes that we see at work in the NT itself, later tantric traditions came to subordinate these divinities and their demonic minions to the divine person of a more exalted deity. Through what Alexis Sanderson has termed the strategy of "superenthronement,"[108] these were "stacked" to form a hierarchy dominated by the supreme being of a given tantric system (Amṛteśa in the case of the NT), who occupied the raised center of its worship mandala. The dominion and energy of this deity streamed downward and outward to the mandala's dark fringe, where the *bhūtanāthas*, now reduced to the status of guardians at the gates, were mobilized to wall out the demonic horde.[109]

3

Several late Middle Iranian (Pahlavi) Zoroastrian scriptures were composed under Sasanid (226–642 CE) patronage, even if this canon was not closed until the ninth and tenth centuries.[110] In its twenty-seventh chapter, which comprises a catalog of demons (*dēws*), the *Greater Bundahišn* ("Creation") employs the Pahlavi term *sāyag* ("shadow"). Here, following an evocation of the avestan evil eye demons Agaš and Rashk,[111] this work identifies the "bone destroyer" Astwihād with the demon Vāyu, "Evil Wind," who, "when (his) hand strokes a man, it is lethargy; when he casts his shadow (*sāyag*), it is fever; when he sees with his eye (*čašm*), he slays the breath-soul—and this they call death."[112]

While in the first portion of this passage, *sāyag* may simply denote "shadow" in a nonspecialized sense, this does not exhaust the Zoroastrian data on the evil eye. In a recent article, Shai Secunda showed that Middle Iranian Zoroastrian works conceptualized the transmission of the evil eye in two different ways, with the chronologically earlier accounts appearing to anticipate the NT's model. The specificity of these Zoroastrian accounts lies in the source of the gaze, which is that of a menstruant woman. Emblematic of this earlier Zoroastrian model is a passage from the circa 632 CE *Šāyest nē šāyest* ("Allowed and Not Allowed"), which explains that menstrual impurity is disseminated through the activity of an especially violent demon unique in its ability to strike objects with the evil eye (*aš*).[113] A passage from the coeval *Zand ī fragard ī jud-dēw-dād* ("The Commentary on the Chapters of the *Vidēvdād*") takes a similar position, attributing the menstrual demon's nearly unparalleled destructive powers to the fact that "it always strikes with the evil eye." Cast as the adversary of the menstruant woman herself, it controls her and then acts to destroy the material world through her gaze.[114]

While the combined action of the menstruant woman's gaze and the menstruation demon continue to be a source of defilement in later Pahlavi sources, these make no mention of the evil eye. Furthermore, in these later sources the internal dynamics of the casting of the gaze has changed. So, for example, the *Dēnkard* ("Works of the Tradition") states that the menstruant woman is "infected" as it were by the highly polluting corpse demonesses known as the *druz ī nasuš*. These "scurry onto the menstruant woman as a living thing. Through the *nasuš*-containing gaze of that woman," the *nasuš* swarm over ritually cleansed objects, befouling them as if by the stench of a fart.[115]

In the earlier model in particular, whose textual witnesses predate the seventh century,[116] we appear to be in the presence of a dynamic anticipating that of the NT's *chāyā-cchidrāṇi*, with the menstruant woman playing an intermediary role. Kṣemarāja states this in his commentary on NT 19.3, where he expressly identifies menstruant women as sources of the *chāyā*. If these were not independent innovations, the existence of what appears to be a cognate phenomenon leaves open the question of influence. Were these Zoroastrian traditions a source of the NT's treatment of the evil eye? Or might both have been influenced by some other prior source?

In India, the planets are called "Seizers" (*grahas*), the same term as that employed for a class of spirit beings in South Asian demonology. As I have argued previously, it is likely that the astronomical grouping called the *navagraha* (Nine Seizers, comprised by the sun, moon, five visible planets, and two eclipse nodes) was a transposition of a group of nine Seizers, already known to earlier epic mythology, from the realm of demonology to that of astrology.[117] Furthermore, the planets are described in Indian astrological literature as personified powers, with human characteristics, emotions, and powers—including, as the circa 600–800 CE *Bṛhatparāśarahorāśāstra* ("Parāśara's Great Teaching on Horoscopy") indicates, "evil gaze" (*pāpadṛṣṭi*).[118] As Caterina Guenzi notes, "malevolent planets afflict humans with their 'rage' (*prakop*), their 'wrath' (*krodh*) and their 'gaze' (*dṛṣṭi*). . . . A planet's influence is said to attach itself to (*lagnā*), and the planets to seize (*pakarṇā*) their prey, these two [Hindi] verbs also being widely employed to describe the assaults of the spirits of the dead (*bhūt-pret*)."[119] The darkest and most malign of the planetary seizers is Śani (Saturn), whose dread influence is magnified by the great duration of his revolution around the sun, a full thirty years. His gaze is thought to both imprint his characteristics on those he views and brand them with his own undesirable physical features.[120] The introduction to a 2001 Hindi-language astrological guide encapsulates Saturn's perils: "The power of Śani's cruel gaze (*krūr dṛṣṭi*) is well known to everyone: the afflicted person is bound by a chain of curses. . . . When Śani becomes fully enraged, no one is able to put a halt to his total devastation."[121]

The ancient Greeks held a similar view. Linked to the optics of extramission, for them, "the heavenly bodies that 'shoot enflamed rays from their eyes' see the world at the same time as they illuminate it, because their luminous rays are also rays of vision that strike and touch the objects that they illuminate."[122] In the centuries prior to the beginning of the Common Era, the introduction of Babylonian and Greek astral sciences profoundly transformed Indic astronomy and astrology. By the beginning of the Common Era, India had adopted the Greek system in naming its days of the week after the planetary deities Sun, Moon, Mars, Jupiter, Mercury, Venus, and Saturn, respectively;[123] and many other features of Indian astrology, including the system of the decans and the names of the zodiacal signs were also borrowed more or less directly from Greco-Roman systems. Pivotal works in the history of India's hybridized system of horoscopic astrology are Sphujidhvaja's *Yavanajātaka* ("Ionian Astrological Calculation of Nativity") and Yavanādhirāja Mīnarāja's *Vṛddhayavanajātaka* ("Ancient Ionian Astrological Calculation of Nativity"), titles that bespeak the prestige of the "Ionians" (Yavanas) in the field.[124] In the light of this, a statement concerning Saturn's wrath, embedded in a fourth-century CE Greek novel, the *Aethopica* of Heliodorus of Emesa, bears comparison with the wrath of the South Asian Śani: "A few years later, the fatal course of the celestial bodies upset my destiny: the eye of Saturn (*omma kronion*) struck my house and changed its fortunes for the worse."[125]

In his novel, Heliodorus links the eye of Saturn to those of Rhodopis, a courtesan of irresistible charm. As Calasiris, an Egyptian priest who plays a leading role in the novel, relates, she is Saturn's agent or persona, simply a mask worn by the planetary deity: "I perceived that this woman was the inception of those evils of which I was divinely forewarned; I understood that she was a personification of fate and that the deity (*daimōn*) who governed my lot had clothed himself with her as with an actor's mask (*prosōpeion*)."[126] Greek actors' masks being faces perforated at the eyes and mouth (fig. 3.2), what Calasiris is saying is that a *daimōn* was now casting the harsh gaze of its eye (*omma*) through those of the seductress Rhodopis, eyes that she used like a dragnet to draw men inexorably into her clutches.[127] A short time later, Calasiris commends himself as an expert in the evil eye, the workings of which

FIGURE 3.2. Actor's mask, ancient Greece. Image courtesy of Mark Cartwright of Ancient History Encyclopedia (www.ancient.eu).

are already implicit in the language of this passage, workings that appear to reassemble the trio of actors present in both the NT's and Sasanian-era Zoroastrian accounts of the evil eye: a malign supernatural being casting its gaze through the eyes of an impure or sinful (usually) female human upon a human victim. Also essential to this process is extramission, the model of visual perception undergirding both Indic and Greek articulations of the dynamics of the evil eye.[128] In what follows I will argue that it is this specific constellation of factors that sets these three specific traditions—Kashmirian, Iranian, and Hellenistic—apart from the dozens of instantiations of this cultural phenomenon from the world over.[129]

Since the time of the ancients, the West has entertained two opposing models of visual perception.[130] The extramission theory, first promulgated by Empedocles in the fifth century BCE, was treated systematically in Plato's *Timaeus*,[131] then followed by Galen, Ptolemy, Saint Augustine, al-Kindi, William of Conches, and many others. The countertheory of intromission, first formulated by Democritus, was refined by Aristotle,[132] then significantly elaborated by Avicenna (Ibn Sina) and Alhazen (Ibn al-Haytham).[133] The intromission theory, which laid the foundation for modern optics, maintained that visual perception is initiated on the surface of the retina in response to light received from the environment. Contrariwise, the extramission model of perception posited that vision occurs when a ray of light, emitted by the eye, conforms to the surface of an object of perception. As such, the locus of perception was not the eye, but rather the surface of an object external to the body; this model also implied that the act of perception created a sort of hard connection between the viewing eye and the viewed object, with vision a form of touching.

The extramission model, which also grounded Indic optical theory from the beginning of the Common Era down into the modern period, is encapsulated in an aphorism from Gautama's first- to second-century CE *Nyāya Sutra* ("Manual of Logic"): "Perception is the consequence of contact between a ray and an object."[134] Here, the ray's source was none other than the luminous mind or soul (*antaḥkaraṇa*), whose effulgence streamed outward through the eyes.[135] An important corollary to this theory, developed in later commentarial literature, was the concept of an enhanced type of ocular perception by which powerful beings could penetrate and possess the bodies and minds of other, weaker beings through their rays of perception. This power, shared by gods, enlightened Buddhas, powerful demons, and yogis, was variously termed yogi perception (*yogipratyakṣa*), the divine eye, the Buddha eye—and, in the case of a yogi's possession (*āveśa*) or takeover of other bodies, subtle yoga (*sūkṣma yoga*).[136]

While the intromission model has generally held the field of Western optics since the eleventh century, the extramission model has remained operative in other realms of discourse down to the present day.[137] Prominent among these has been the articulation of the workings of the evil eye, which links the strong emotions of love and envy to an internal power emitted through the eyes onto and into a human victim. As Thomas Rakoczy has shown, hundreds of ancient Greek works by over 150 authors contain thousands of references to the evil eye (*baskanos ophthalmos*) and the dread power of the envious gaze, both human and divine (and, by extension, planetary).[138] The ancient Greek *baskanos* ("sorcerer, one who bewitches") has for its Latin cognate *fascinus* ("evil spell, bewitchment"), with both terms related to the casting of the evil eye as well as to the amulets, often phallic, worn around the neck to ward off the same.[139] I have already mentioned one of the Hellenistic works that treat of the evil eye: Heliodorus's *Aethiopica*. As Matthew Dickie has argued, however, this work's account of the evil eye is intentionally sensationalized, a device for Heliodorus to lampoon the mystagogy of fraudulent Egyptian priests and holy men in general. While Dickie's interpretation has been contested, there is general agreement that Calasiris's discussion of the evil eye is a pastiche of a number of theories that were in the air at the time.[140] One of these is attributed to Alexander of Aphrodisias, an early third-century CE Aristotelian:

> Why do certain persons cast an evil eye and especially against children? Because their [the children's] nature is sensitive and variable. What transpires is as follows. There are certain persons who, due to the wickedness of their souls (*kakias psuchēs*), have a nature that is bitten by what is beautiful. When their wickedness is awakened by limitless envy, it [this wickedness] shoots forth from the pupils [of the eyes] like a poisonous destructive beam (*aktis*). When it penetrates the envied person through the eyes, it changes soul and nature into an insalubrious mixture, decomposes the bodily fluids, and leads the bodies of these persons to illness.[141]

Here, Alexander's language concerning persons with wicked souls anticipates that of the NT's discussion of wicked-souled evildoers.[142] His destructive "beam" is the homologue of the ocular rays by means of which powerful malign beings, demonic and human, possess and overcome the weak in numerous Indic accounts, albeit not according to NT 19 itself. In his discussion of the late Pahlavi-language accounts of the dire effects of a menstruant woman's gaze, Secunda suggests that these sources combined preexisting Zoroastrian misogynist speculations about menstruation with "a 'naturalistic' frame of mind interested in the workings of causality."[143] According to Secunda, the source of this latter approach would have been ancient Greek science, as epitomized in Aristotle's well-known statement concerning the dulling effects of a menstruant woman's gaze upon the polished surface of a mirror. For Aristotle, menstruation altered the physiology of a woman's eyes, "and the eyes set up a movement in the air. This imparts a certain quality to the layer of air extending over the mirror, and assimilates it to itself; and this layer affects the surface of the mirror."[144]

Here I fully concur with Secunda with respect to Greek influence; however, I believe the source of this late Zoroastrian scientific turn was substantially later than Aristotle (or Pliny, who quotes him).[145] In fact, the most extended and coherent late antique account of the workings of the evil eye is embedded in the circa 100 CE *Moralia* of Plutarch,[146] an officiant at the renowned oracle of Apollo at Delphi,[147] who presents the evil eye in terms of "the 'scientific' knowledge of upper class, educated elites" who regarded the evil eye "not as a superstition . . . but as a natural phenomenon explainable in the conventional scientific terms of that time."[148] Cast as a symposium with five discussants, Plutarch's language in the *Moralia* anticipates that of Alexander as he refers to the effulgent streams of particles emitted by the eye: "Odor, voice, and breathing are all emanations of some kind, streams of particles from living bodies. . . . Living bodies are, because of their warmth and motion, far more likely in reason to give off these particles than are inanimate bodies. . . . The most active stream of such emanations is that which passes out through the eye. For vision, being of an enormous swiftness and carried by an essence that gives off a flame-like brilliance, diffuses a wondrous influence."[149]

Identifying love and envy as the emotions that produce the most powerful streams of such emanations, he explains that "when those possessed by envy . . . let their glance fall upon a person, their eyes, which are close to the mind [or soul: *psuchē*] and draw from it the evil influence of their passion, then assail that person as if with poisoned arrows."[150] Then, invoking the fifth-century BCE Democritus, perhaps abusively, Plutarch's dinner guest Gaius explains the optics of the evil eye: "That man [Democritus] says that envious people emit these [*eidōla*], which are not entirely separate from either sense perception or intent, and are quite full of the wickedness and envy [emanating] from those sending them forth. These [*eidōla*], being molded with them [i.e., with wickedness and envy], and remaining and cohabiting with those being bewitched by the evil eye (*baskainomenois*), do trouble and harm those wretches' bodies and minds."[151] The semantic field of the term *eidōlon* is significant inasmuch as it, more than any other, lends to a comparison with the NT's accounts of the workings of the evil eye. While it primarily denotes "phantom" or reflected "image," translators of this passage from Plutarch have also read *eidōlon* as "simulacrum," "effulgence," and "shade."[152] More than this, for the ancient Greeks *eidōlon* also connoted a certain order of deception. As Gérard Simon has noted, an *eidōlon* is something one sees "as if it were the thing itself, whereas it is actually its double: shades of the dead in Hades (*Odyssey* 11.476), the replica of Helen created by Hera (Euripedes, *Helen* 33), an effigy or portrait that offers to the gaze persons who are absent, or finally that which appears in a mirror but which in fact is not there. In short, the *eídōlon* is the visual bearer of an illusion."[153] As we have seen, the Sanskrit *chāyā* has same range of connotations: shadow, likeness, reflected or deceptive image, with *chāyā* and the evil eye constituting the two types of trickery (*chalam*) resorted to by the dire Mothers and Yoginīs. Two sources, one ayurvedic and the other alchemical, link *chāyā* in the sense of "reflection" to the invisible movements of the Seizers and their ilk.[154]

A few words on Democritus's theory of visual impressions, as well as on its (mis)appropriation by others, is in order here. Democritus's was, in fact, the earliest theory of *intromission*, albeit an incoherent one. Such was the considered opinion of Theophrastus, in whose writings we find the most complete documentation of Democritus's optics.[155] Furthermore, Democritus may never have used the vocabulary of the *eidōla* in his primary explanation of vision.[156] This being the case, Plutarch's evocation of Democritus for the *extramission*-based optics of the evil eye he and his dinner guests have been discussing appears to have been misplaced.[157] However, Plutarch's parting words to his invitees leave open the possibility that Democritus's *eidōla* were altogether relevant to his discussion of the evil eye: "I wonder how it escaped you that the only things I denied to the emanations were life and free will. Don't think that I want to make your flesh creep and throw you into a panic late at night like this by bringing on sentient *eidōla* and apparitions (*phasmata*)."[158]

As Colin Webster has observed, a number of ancient writers, some of them citing Democritus, linked these *eidōla* to paranormal experience rather than, or in addition, to the mechanics of visual perception.[159] In Homer, the *eidōla* were "phantoms," objective dream images that carried with them the effects of the waking mental activities of the dreamers themselves.[160] Noting that such images would necessarily have been perceived as dæmons by those who were affected by them, Jean Salem cites another passage from Plutarch, where that author explicitly equates *daimonas* with *eidōla*.[161] Here, in a discussion of the role of dæmons as oracles, he muses that "Democritus, by his prayer that we may meet with 'propitious spirits' (*eulogchōn eidōlōn*), clearly recognized that there exists another class of these [beings] that is perverse and possessed of vicious predilections and impulses."[162] As such, these evil *eidōla* would have been the Greek cognates of the MMVS's *duśchāyās*.

With this, we may surmise that Plutarch may well have understood the *eidōla* projected in the casting of the evil eye to have been not only "images," "shades," "reflections" or "simulacra," but also demonic beings—bringing his account of the workings of the evil eye still closer to those of the later Pahlavi sources and the NT.[163] Furthermore, throughout the Greco-Roman world there was a widely held belief in the "evil eye demon" (*baskanos daimōn*), which was regarded not only as an intermediary in the workings of the evil eye cast by humans, but also as a malevolent, autonomous being whose evil gaze was particularly noxious to its victims. These demons, already attested in Democritus's day, would become fixtures of later Greek literature as well as of funerary and apotropaic inscriptions, where they were portrayed as afflicting the virtuous, the young, and the fortunate with dishonor, sickness, and death.[164] A final witness, in this case a Christian writer, rejects the extramission model proposed by Plutarch, while presenting a theory that hews closer than any other to that found in both Pahlavi sources and the NT. This is the fourth-century CE Basil of Caesarea (Cappadocia) who, in his homily on envy, suggests that when they observe the close similarity between themselves and human emotion of envy, demons appropriate the eyes of sorcerers or malicious persons (*baskanoi*) as their "servants," so many agents for spreading their evil.[165]

This ambiguity or redundancy—of the evil eye as cast by wicked humans and the evil eye cast by evil eye demons—is reproduced in the NT in two ways: (1) in the ambiguity of the term *chāyā*—as well, perhaps, of *chidram*—at once a demon and a mechanism in the casting of the evil eye; and (2) in the redundancy of the NT's two types of *chalam*, whose conjoined evil gaze penetrates and sickens their human victims.[166] Furthermore, like Plutarch, the NT's ninth-century compilers also assumed (3) that transmission of the evil eye was quickened by the connection between the eye and the mind/soul/inner organ; and (4) that ocular perception occurred through extramission. (5) Finally, common to Greek (Aristotle), Iranian, and Indic (Kṣemarāja) traditions, the gaze of a menstruant woman, serving as a conduit for a demon's gaze, was particularly destructive. These parallels are tabulated in table 3.1. This complex model, for which Plutarch is our earliest extant witness, and which persisted in the West for well over a millennium,[167] is nowhere articulated in the Indic canon before or after the NT.

Long before Plutarch, Democritus, and the earliest Greek attestations, the evil eye was already known to ancient India, Iran, and the Semitic world. While the Indic ṚV and AV both speak of the "terrible eye" (*ghoram cakṣus*) of flesh-eating fiends and enemy sorcerers,[168] the Old Avesta's references to the evil eye always involve demonic agents.[169] Similarly, ancient Mesopotamian documents speak of the evil eye in general terms or in connection with various demons. As for ritual and magical protections and precautions against the evil eye, techniques for conjuring the evil eye, and the human targets of the evil eye, these are the subject of ancient, medieval, and modern traditions from the world over. Similarities abound, in such usages as the wearing of protective amulets and the combined employment of incense, unguents, and spells as evil-eye demonifuges.[170] However, these types of data lack the specificity, complexity, and sophistication of the parallel Hellenistic, Iranian, and Indic models I have been comparing here. In this regard, we may

TABLE 3.1 The workings of the evil eye

Hellenistic traditions	*Tantric traditions*	*Iranian traditions*
The *eidōlon* is a shadow and a spirit being.	The *chāyā* is a shadow and a spirit being.	
The *eidōlon* is cast by the gaze of envious persons.	The *chāyā* is cast by the gaze of sinful or impure persons.	
Menstruation alters the physiology of a woman's eyes.	A menstruant woman's gaze is a source of the *chāyā*.	
A more powerful dæmon (Saturn, the *baskanos daimōn*) casts the evil eye through the eyes of envious persons.	A more powerful demon (a Mother, Yoginī, or Bhūta) casts the evil eye through the eyes of sinful/impure persons.	An evil eye demon disseminates destructive menstrual impurity by casting the evil eye (*aš*) through the gaze of a menstruant woman.
This dynamic presupposes the extramission model of visual perception.	This dynamic presupposes the extramission model of visual perception.	This dynamic presupposes the extramission model of visual perception.
The power of the gaze is linked to the eye's proximity to the *psyche*.	The power of the gaze is linked to the eye's proximity to the *antaḥkaraṇa*.	

take modern-day Sri Lankan lore of the evil eye as an illustrative counterexample. There—in spite of numerous features that replicate those encountered in medieval and modern KGB and north India, with the penetrating gaze (*diṣṭiya*) of malign yakṣas (called *yakku*) playing a role analogous to that of the Mothers and Yoginīs of the NT—the *chāyā-chalam-chidram* dynamic is absent.[171] What I am suggesting is that some time before the ninth century CE, a model similar to that found in Plutarch's *Moralia* reached both Iran and KGB, where Chāy(ā)s (as well, perhaps as Chalams and Chidrams) already figured in that region's pandemonium. Through their innovative use of these three terms, the compilers of the NT adapted Plutarch's "*eidōlon* model" into Sanskritic idioms even as they fused it with specific local cultural paradigms.

4

Four decades ago, in the rural Bocage region of northwestern France, Jeanne Favret-Saada documented a practice wherein magicians revealed the face of a witchcraft target's tormenter *au grand miroir*, on the surface of a water-filled basin.[172] We have already seen a similar dynamic in Sax's ethnography of the exorcism of a Chāyā demon in Uttarakhand, in which the *chāyā pūjā* reached its climax when

> [a] small fire was lit, and over it was placed an old round tin, filled with oil. The girl was directed to stand over the hot oil and look into it. At that

> moment, she was supposed to see the Chāyā, superimposed on her own face. She was directed to kick over the tin of oil with her foot, and when she did so it spilled into the fire and a huge tongue of flame shot up. . . . If the ritual was done properly and if she followed these instructions, the Chāyā would be left behind and would not afflict her any more.[173]

A similar body of practice, also involving a type of *chāyā*, is observed in modern-day Benares by persons suffering from the influence of the dire eclipse demons Rāhu and Ketu, as well as the planet Saturn. These heavenly bodies are the source of a debilitating black shadow (*kālī chāyā*) that hovers around its human target. In order to repel it, an "offering to the Chāyā" is to be made in the following way: "The person should look at her own face as reflected in a bowl containing oil, and offer that oil to a poor brahmin in the street. This procedure should be repeated every Saturday for several weeks (between four and sixteen) and the size of the bowl and the quantity of oil are to be proportional to the dimension of the face. . . . By so doing, a person is thought to free herself from the evil influence of the shadow planets (*chāyā-grahas*)."[174] This astrological usage is significant for two reasons. The first is that, as discussed at the beginning of this chapter, the compound *chāyā-graha* also appears in two of the MMVS's catalogs of demons. As with Chāyās (given in the feminine in this list), the names of all of the demon-types found in these two lists are compounded with the word *graha*, "seizer": *bhūta-graha*, *kumbhāṇḍa-graha*, etc.[175] In modern-day Benares, *chāyā-graha*s no longer denote demonic seizers, but rather dire planets, although as mentioned earlier, the planetary usage is derived from a demonological prototype. Secondly, the astrological "offering of the *chāyā*" is significant for the same reason as its Uttarakhand homologue: in both cases, a person gazes into the reflective surface of a film of oil in order to be released from evil or demonic influences. This type of practice has an ancient pedigree, and although its goal in the two cases noted here diverges from the original model, its procedures and actors reproduce it precisely. This is particularly the case with Sax's account, in which three actors—the ritual priest, the possessed girl, and the Chāyā—are brought together when the girl sees the Chāyā's face superimposed upon her own in the reflective oil.

In its earliest iterations, this practice was divinatory. Divination by gazing into a reflective surface, often oil, is known as lecanomancy; closely related is catoptromancy, divination by gazing into a mirror. Several other types of reflective surfaces are also used: an oil-smeared fingernail, the blade of a sword, and so forth; in many cases, a lighted lamp or torch is the divination support. Hereafter, I will refer to the general practice as "mirror divination."[176]

All of these forms of the practice are attested in medieval and modern South Asian works, some of them from Kashmir, and many of them tantric. I will return to these shortly. However, the earliest documentation for mirror divination involving three actors—a human child medium, an adult magician or priest, and a divinity or dæmon—appears in a set of late antique magical papyri from Egypt, the great bulk of which date from the third century CE.[177] Discovered at Luxor (the ancient Thebes), these papyri form a subset of the massive collection generally known as the "Greek Magical Papyri." As it happens, the most detailed prescriptions for mirror divination contained in this collection are written in Egyptian (Demotic), rather than Greek. Nearly all of these are found in two manuscripts, written by and for the personal use of the same scribe.[178] The divination rituals recorded in these works were not invented from whole cloth. Rather, they were innovations based on archaic rituals known to the practitioners who copied and improvised on the techniques described in these papyri. Documents of "late pagan syncretism," they contain material from not only Greek and Egyptian, but also Jewish, Assyrian, Babylonian, and Sumerian sources.[179] As for the ingredients of the potions employed in these papyri's ritual instructions, nearly all come from India. As Elizabeth Ann Pollard has noted, two to three centuries earlier these were luxury condiments used in Roman recipes, but by the third century, "when contact with India is waning, these spices have clearly taken on a more mystical flavor."[180] As such, Indian spices formed a part of the material culture of late antique demonology.

The Demotic papyri contain eleven sets of complete or partial accounts of divination involving three actors (child medium, adult specialist, dæmon), and employing either reflective surfaces or lamps.[181] A series of stunning pictorial representations of the practice are found in a fifteenth-century late Byzantine manuscript (plates 9 and 10). All of the salient elements of the rite appear in the following passage:

> You bring a copper cup; you engrave a figure of Anubis on it; you fill it with settled water guarded (*sic*) which the sun cannot find; you fill the top [of the water] with true oil; you place it on [three] new bricks, whose undersides are spread with sand; you put another four bricks under the youth; you make the youth lie down on his stomach; you make him put his chin on the bricks of the vessel; you make him look into the oil, while a cloth is stretched over him and while a lighted lamp is in his right hand and a burning censer in his left hand; you put a lobe of Anubis plant on the lamp; you put this incense up [on the censer]; and you recite these writings which are above to the vessel seven times. . . . When you have finished, you should make the youth open his eyes and you should ask him, "Is the god (*nouthe*) coming in?" If he says, "The god

> has already come in," you should recite before him. . . . And you should ask him concerning that which you [desire]; when you have finished your inquiry about which you are asking, you should recite to him seven times and you should dismiss [the god] to his home. . . . You should take the lamp from the child, you should take the vessel containing the water, you should take the cloth off him. You can also do it alone, by vessel inquiry. It is very good, tested nine times.[182]

Nowhere does one find an account of a procedure containing all of these elements prior to those recorded in these magical papyri, and so one might conclude that the "complete" version of the practice had its origin in this late antique Egyptian context.[183] One must bear in mind, however, that the religious specialists who made use of these guides were independent, itinerant magicians who had no institutional constraints against improvisation, and who made use of whatever resources were available to them.

As has been noted, the ritual described by Sax is a demonic exorcism rather than a divinatory practice involving a dæmon: in it, the oil on whose surface the young Garhwali woman sees the Chāyā is kicked into the fire, effectively ending her possession. These sorts of variations occur frequently outside the ambit of the Egyptian magical papyri. The earliest western European reference to the practice also features a demon, sans reference to divination. This is an eighth-century work of Irish canon law, which speaks of persons who would accuse a woman of sorcery on the grounds of having seen a *lamia* in a mirror,[184] a scenario reproduced in modern-day witchcraft-conjuring divination in the Bocage.

It is worthy of note that no datable European account of the full-blown practice of mirror divination appears prior to a circa 1159 CE work, the *Policraticus* of John of Salisbury, who identifies its practitioners as "specularies" (*specularii*), "those who, practicing divination on such polished and shining objects as weapon blades, basins, chalices, and various sorts of mirrors, answer curious people's questions."[185] What makes John's account most fascinating is that it is autobiographical. The child in the "sacrilegious" ritual he describes is none other than himself, and the diviner a member of the Catholic clergy. In it, he and an older child had been made to sit at the priest's feet and called upon to reveal to him the demon(s) they perceived on the surface of his fingernail or the polished surface of a basin that had been rubbed with holy oil or chrism. Whereas his older companion claimed to see the pale reflection of this or that demon, John, through the grace of god, saw nothing.[186] In Jewish traditions dating from Talmudic times, the polished surfaces employed in lecanomancy and catoptromancy were referred to as the "princes of oil," "princes of the thumb-nail," and so forth. An account of the practice recovered from the Cairo Geniza brings together the diviner, a "lad or a virgin girl," a mirror, and a demon named Apulis.[187]

The history of the dissemination of mirror divination into western Europe, the Byzantine Empire, China, and India has been richly documented by Armand Delatte, Michel Strickmann, and Fred Smith.[188] In what follows, I will supplement their findings with additional material from South Asia and also incorporate Martin Schwartz's recent reinterpretation of a Sasanian source that was the likely bridge between the Near East and South Asia. Schwartz's "text" is a set of rock-cut inscriptions left by Kirdēr, the imperial high priest of the Zoroastrian faith during the early years of the Sasanian Empire.[189] In these inscriptions, Kirdēr reports a premonitory vision relating to his anticipated favorable reception in the afterlife. However, as Schwartz indicates, Kirdēr does not claim to have seen these things directly; rather, he has induced seated or squatting boys to have the vision for him while remaining in conversational contact with them throughout their clairvoyant trance, into which they have entered by gazing into a reflective surface.[190] Since Kirdēr indicates that this was an unusual form of divination, one might surmise that it was not indigenous to his late third-century CE Persian world.[191] As Schwartz has demonstrated through a virtuoso piece of etymological reconstruction, Kirdēr calls the divination procedure in question a "rite of the mirror," or a "formula of/for mirroring/reflection." Through this rite of mirror divination, as Kirdēr reports, the children beheld an image or double of himself accompanied by a "dæmon," Kirdēr's female psychopomp (*daēnā*) in the Zoroastrian afterlife.[192] Given the textual data at our disposal, we cannot know with any degree of certainty whether Kirdēr's "unusual" rite originated in the Near East, whose Demotic-language papyri date from the same period as his own rock-cut inscriptions. It may be that both the Egyptian and the Persian techniques derived from an earlier lost tradition, perhaps proper to the Jews who were so renowned as magicians in the Sasanian Empire.[193] While the matter of origins remains unresolved, both Kirdēr's and John of Salisbury's accounts make it clear that the practice was known to, if not the prerogative of, the official priesthood: in John's case, none but a Catholic cleric would have had access to the holy oil employed by the *specularii*.[194]

In India, mirror divination is first attested in the *Dīgha Nikaya* (DN, "Collection of Long Discourses"), a second-century BCE Buddhist source that prohibited monks from practicing divination by using either mirrors or maidens. However, this elliptical reference omits to bring together the ritual actors or ritual sequences found in the aforementioned Demotic and Pahlavi sources, and it is telling that in his fifth-century commentary on this work, Buddhaghosa treats these as separate practices.[195] Then, in about the seventh century, accounts of the complex ritual begin to appear in a small number of Jain, Hindu, and Buddhist works. In these, the procedure and actors are the same as in the Demotic and Pahlavi accounts, with two important differences. First, the divinity's entrance into the reflective surface is generally referred to as a "descent," an *avatāraṇa*. Second, the divinity that so descends is often given a name: this is Prasenā/Praśnā, a goddess whose appellation, as Sanderson has convincingly argued, is the feminine form of *praśna*, "question," a Sanskrit back formation generated from the Middle Indo-Aryan *pasiṇa*. A seventh-century Jain commentary glosses *pasiṇa* as "calling a deity into a mirror," and evokes the questioning of the goddess named *pasiṇā* "who has entered into one's thumbnail . . . a mirror, a sword blade, water . . ."[196] As Smith observes in his exhaustive study of the topic, "after *pasiṇa/praśna* had become widely employed to denote 'divinatory practice,' the term was subsequently feminized as *pasiṇā* or *praśnā* and identified as a spirit or minor deity that could be invited into the body of the practitioner, child, or an inanimate object to reveal answers to questions about the past, present and future."[197]

Between the seventh and twelfth centuries, this terminology and the practice of using child clairvoyants in mirror divination would be documented in a handful of tantric Hindu, tantric Buddhist, and Taoist[198] texts from Kashmir, northeast India, China, Japan, and Tibet. The earliest of these, dating from the seventh and eighth centuries, are the Hindu *Niḥśvāsaguhya* ("Secret [Manual] of [Śiva's Yogic] Outbreath"),[199] TSBh,[200] and *Jayadrathayāmalatantra* ("Jayadratha's Union Tantra");[201] the Buddhist *Cakrasaṃvara Tantra* (CST)[202] and *Subahuparipṛcchā* ("Manifold Inquiries"); as well as two Chinese translations or adaptations of lost Sanskrit works: Vajrabodhi's *Pu-ting shih-che t'o-lo-ni pi-mi-fa* ("Secret Rites of the Spells of the Divine Emissary, the Immovable One") and the *Suji liyan Moxishouluo tian sho aweishe fa* ("The [Garuḍa] Áveśa Rite Explained by the God Maheśvara Which Swiftly Establishes its Efficacy").[203] The most complete, albeit somewhat garbled, South Asian account of the practice appears in the eleventh-century RA's chapter on alchemical initiation. Here, the alchemist is instructed that

> in order to bring about the descent of Praśnā, he shall, with mind composed, meditate on . . . Mercurial Bhairava. Let him then practice mental absorption on that [god]. [Then, after placing a variety of tantric protector divinities on the corners of a hexagonal diagram and his own body, and after repeating the "garland" and "root" mantras] he should place a [water-]filled pot over the center [of the diagram, and] a platter [whose surface is scattered] with grains of rice. On top of that [he should place] an oil lamp [and] a wick, and incant [that lamp] with mantras. Having brought together a girl and a handsome boy, he should assemble one, two, three, four or five [male or female

> children]—according to however many are available—and he should venerate [them] with offerings of fragrant flowers, incense, oil lamps and edibles. He should deposit the mantra divinities, beginning with [the divinity of] the heart, on each of those girls. Then, having stared into that lamp, all of the girls there [will] behold dæmons (*devatāḥ*) in its flame, and the boys [will behold] both good and evil. The girls [will] declare either success or failure [in the alchemical Work]. Knowing this to be the descent of Praśnā, [the alchemist may now] undertake [all] the alchemical procedures.[204]

As Smith has observed, there are very few Sanskrit-language texts that describe mirror divination in isolation from another far more widely disseminated form of South Asian oracular divination. Known as *svasthāveśa* (literally "possession of [a] healthy [person]"), this is a type of voluntary possession through which a divinity descends into the body of a child or adult medium to prophesy directly through their mouths. The earliest work to combine—or juxtapose—the two practices is Vajrabodhi's Chinese-language "Secret Rites." Translated from the Sanskrit by him between 719 and 732,[205] the work is an early window onto the gradual shift from *prasenā* to *svasthāveśa*.

> In front of an icon of the Immoveable One, [let the officiant] cleanse the ground and burn Parthian incense (gum guggul). Then take a mirror, place it over the heart [presumably the heart of the painted image], and continue reciting the spell. Have a young boy or girl look into the mirror. When you ask what they see, the child will immediately tell you all you want to know. You should then summon a dragon-spirit; once you have its name in mind, stand the young boy or girl in a purified place and recite the spell over him or her. The spirit will then enter the child's heart, and when the officiant discusses matters pertaining to the past, present, or future, all questions will be answered.[206]

There are clearly two distinct forms of divination described here, the first a form of mirror divination and the second a form of controlled possession. Whereas the former quickly disappeared from Hindu South Asia, it has persisted, in some cases down to the present day, in Buddhist and Taoist Inner and East Asia.[207] As for the latter, it became the sole form of divination involving child mediums preserved in Hindu Tantra, and the dominant form of the same in Buddhist Tantra. While there can be no question that *svasthāveśa* was an Indic innovation that was subsequently exported, together with Tantra, into Inner and East Asia, the same cannot be said for mirror divination, which, given the data reviewed above, reached KGB and western India via trade routes from the Mediterranean world that passed through Sasanian Persia. In the end, the original inspiration for the complete practice—Egyptian mirror divination involving children—came to be supplanted in the Hindu world by a Sanskritized Indic variant.[208] With one important exception: the exorcistic variant documented by Sax in his account of *chāyā pūjā* in Uttarakhand.

Over twenty years ago, Strickmann laconically observed that mirror divination, attested in a simplified form in Greece as early as the fifth century BCE, "was undoubtedly known to Indian Buddhists three hundred years later, since monks were prohibited from its practice."[209] In the intervening decades, no scholar of Tantra or South Asian religions has explored this possibility in significant depth, further evidence, if such be needed, for the shuttered state of these academic fields.

5

First appearing together in the MMVS, the terms *kṛtya*, *kākhorda*, and *vetāla* resurface in the NT, to which I now return. All three are found together in Kṣemarāja's commentary on NT 18.1–4, where he writes that "the things relating to Kṛtyās and *khārkhodas* that are used by others are destroyed [through techniques of countersorcery]. A Kṛtyā is a female zombie (Vetālī) that has been introduced into a woman's corpse for the destruction of one's enemies. A *khārkhoda* is a device (*yantra*)[210] causing death, expulsion (*uccāṭana*), and so forth."[211] Here, the passage that Kṣemarāja is interpreting in his commentary is one treating of "spells . . . by means of which (1) practitioners gain mastery; (2) *kṛtyā-khārkhoda*-type objects and so forth, which are hurled by others, are destroyed; and by means of which (3) practitioners repeatedly slay evildoers by hurling the counter-device cum spell goddess Pratyaṅgirā [back at them]."[212]

Attested in the AV's ancillary literature, Pratyaṅgirā is a female spell being (*vidyā*) that is the embodiment of the practice of countersorcery. The *Ṛgvidhāna*, a medieval work of uncertain date, explains its terminology as follows: "The man over whom the experts cast a charm by means of rituals taught by Aṅgiras [i.e., Atharvanic spells], wards them off by practice of the Pratyaṅgirasa or defensive rituals."[213] While Pratyaṅgirā appears once in the Buddhist *Sādhanamālā* ("Garland of Perfections"),[214] the most powerful Buddhist spell deity was Mahāpratisarā, the goddess cum counterdevice of the widely disseminated *Mahāpratisarā-Mahāvidyārājñī* ("Great Queen of Spells of the Goddess of the Great Phylactery").[215] The leader of a widely venerated set of five divinized Buddhist protective spells (*pañcarakṣās*)—a grouping that also included Mahāmāyūrī—Mahāpratisarā's anthropomorphic images are scattered across the medieval and modern Buddhist world.[216] Many of her painted images portray the goddess encircled by her spell, her *dhāraṇī*, the speech act that activated the countersorcery device. Here, we see form following function, given the etymology of the term *pratisara*: "that which turns back, reverts." This was in fact their shape: like the *paritta*s, the spell-binding threads of Mahāyāna Buddhism, these were loops—in this case, loops of graphemes written on paper and sometimes encased in ring-shaped amulets.[217]

The earliest attestation of *pratisara*s as counterdevices is found in the AV, which refers to them as "heroes" (*vīra*s) that "drive the Kṛtyās back."[218] The term *kṛtyā* appears with some frequency in the *Atharva*, but not in the *Ṛg Veda*. In the AV, it signifies both a female being manufactured through witchcraft and the witchcraft used to create her. So, for example, an Atharvanic hymn belonging to the class of "hymns that repel sorceries" (*kṛtyāpratiharaṇāni*) describes a Kṛtyā and her expulsion in the following terms:

> She whom the wise ones fashion out, as a bride at a wedding, the multiform (Kṛtyā), fashioned by hand, shall go to a distance: we drive her away. The Kṛtyā that has been brought forward by the fashioner of the Kṛtyā, that is endowed with head, endowed with nose, endowed with ears, and multiform, shall go to a distance; we drive her away. The (Kṛtyā) that has been prepared by a Śūdra, prepared by a king, prepared by a woman, prepared by Brāhmaṇas, as a wife rejected by her husband, shall recoil upon her fabricator and his kin![219]

Returning to Kṣemarāja's commentary, we can see that while he chose to read *khārkhoda* as a device, he viewed Kṛtyās as female zombies (Vetālīs). What he did not clarify was whether a female zombie was capable of acting autonomously,[220] or rather constituted an animated tool or device created in order to be "hurled by others," as stated in the text. Varāhamihira's fifth- to sixth-century *Bṛhatsaṃhitā* ("Great System") describes black magicians as being "addicted to spells and ritual acts concerning Kṛtyās, Vetālas, etc." In his ninth- to tenth-century reading of this passage, the Kashmiri commentator Bhaṭṭotpala glosses these terms in ways that anticipate Kṣemarāja: a Kṛtyā is "a woman conjured up from the midst of a fire in order to slaughter one's enemies," and *vetālam* the "resurrection of an excellent corpse using spells."[221] Here, he also appears to be reprising the language of the fifth-century Buddhist commentator Buddhaghosa, who, in his commentary on a verse from the DN, glosses *vetālam* as "banging a gong; [while] some [say it means] 'the raising of a dead body with a mantra.'" This passage, which is likely the earliest attestation of the term in the scriptural record, lists *vetālam* among a long list of performances—including dancing, singing, drum playing, acrobatic and conjuring tricks, cockfighting, military reviews, etc.—that Buddhist monks were to adjure.[222] That being the case, it would appear that the latter portion of Buddhaghosa's gloss is incorrect, and informed by a later tradition of sorcery and black magic. We will encounter a "conjured" Kṛtyā in chapter 5, where I translate the term as "female humanoid simulacrum."[223] As for *khārkhoda*, this is a Hindu tantric variant of the MMVS's *kākhorda*. It also resembles a range of terms found in other sources, many of them Buddhist, from both KGB and other parts of Inner Asia. Before examining these, I first wish to return to the NT, which mentions *kṛtyā-khārkhoda* in two other contexts.

Deep into its nineteenth chapter, the NT unambiguously identifies the Khārkhodas as demons, classing them together with the Seizers, Śākinīs, yakṣas, Flesh Eaters, and Guardians.[224] However, in the NT's eighteenth chapter, we read that

> a person [may be] suffering from a hundred cuts, or afflicted with the pangs of sorrow, or saddled with every [sort of] misfortune. [He may be] tormented by the Kṛtyā-Khārkhodas, by [another person's] spells, magical devices, visualization practices, practices involving chanting and fire offerings, and [the uses of] powders, pastes, and unguents—as well as by the tricks (*kuhakāni*) that enemies will play: [but] wherever She [here, the Goddess Śrī] is honored in this way by either a man or a woman, She shall become their Pratyaṅgirā.[225]

Here, the Sanskrit of this passage appears to be a paraphrase of that of the opening verses of the NT's nineteenth chapter quoted above: both describe "the tricks that [enemies] will play"—or, perhaps, "the witchcraft that [enemies] will practice" or "the witchcraft devices that enemies will fashion."[226] Recall, however, that in NT 19.5–6, two types of *chalam* were mentioned, the one involving the Chāyā and the other the casting of the gaze (*dṛṣṭi-pāta*).[227] Later, after evoking the "injurious ones who have found their opening [and] effect[ed] the casting of their evil gaze," that source went on to say that "enemies who are puffed up with [their own] intelligence, [and] who are mad, evil-minded, sinful, greatly depressed, power-hungry, [or] envious" are capable of doing the same.[228] By juxtaposing these two references, we can see that many of the enemies against which tantric *sādhaka*s did battle were human: they were evil sorcerers. But whereas in NT 19 these enemies' "tricks" or "witchcraft" involved the evil eye, here in NT 18 they bring various sorts of devices into play. As we saw earlier, NT 19 offered no specific countermeasures against the evil eye cast by human enemies. Their particular case was subsumed under the general rule, that is, that the Mothers and Spirit Beings that possessed their victims through the casting of the evil eye could be countered through offerings to one or another sort of *bhūtanātha*. At two points in NT 18, however, we find references to counterdevices to be used against the devices of enemy sorcerers.[229] Here as well, Kṣemarāja's commentary is instructive: "'Tricks'

[are] the devices, the *kṛtyā*s and so forth, that enemies will make. . . . [There is] the person against whom the device, etc. is fashioned. By means of that [uttered spell] 'the counter-device goddess Pratyaṅgirā shall come into being.' Like a badly hurled missile, it [the enemy's device] shall become a destroyer of the enemy's own cohort."[230] The first mention in the NT of counter-devices appears two chapters earlier, in NT 16.31–32, in the context of a discussion of protective measures to be taken against "others in the world who are viewed as injurious to *siddhis*"—that is, against enemy sorcerers who would seek to disrupt the initiations of the very *sādhaka*s who, by virtue of said initiations, would become empowered to do battle against their sorcery. The text then continues with a list of dark arts practiced by wicked spell-binders (*duṣṭamantribhiḥ*) that includes nailing, cleaving, pounding, and *pratyaṅgiratvam*, which Kṣemarāja glosses as "the counter-measure taken against the wielder of a spell, used for controlling Spirit Beings and so forth."[231]

This brings us back to the problem raised by Kṣemarāja's just-cited commentary to NT 18.89–90. In it, he made the *kṛtyā* out to be one of the devices held in an enemy sorcerer's bag of tricks (or repertory of spells). In his commentary on NT 18.4, however, he identified a Kṛtyā as "a female zombie (Vetālī) introduced into a woman's corpse for the destruction of one's enemies,"[232] seemingly in distinction to a *khārkhoda*, which he simply called a "device" (*yantra*). Interestingly, he made the same observation in his commentary on NT 19.132, which clearly identified the Khārkhodas as malign spirit beings and not fabricated instruments of sorcery. Which is the correct reading? Is there a qualitative difference between a Kṛtyā and a Khārkoda, the two members of this dvandva compound? Why do they form a compound? Other Kashmirian sources are equally ambiguous. The twelfth-century *Haracaritacintāmaṇi* ("Wishing Stone of the Acts of [Śiva] the Destroyer") includes the compound *kṛtyā-khārkhoṭa-vetālā* in a list of the afflictions routed by Time.[233] Kalhaṇa's twelfth-century *Rājataraṃgiṇī* ("River of Kings") mentions *khārkhoda-vidyā*, and speaks of a regicide whose perpetrator, "a *khārkhoda* expert" (*khārkoda-vedin*), used sorcery to cause a king to die of fever.[234] Several passages from the *Jayadrathayāmalatantra* also employ the term in this way. In his extensive discussion of *khārkhoda*, Sanderson provides several quotations from this work, as well as from the *Tridaśāḍāmara-pratyaṅgirākalpa* ("Rules for Counterdevices Causing Tumult among the Thirty [Gods]") and a number of the Buddhist works cited in what follows.[235]

When we turn to Buddhist documentation on the subject, we find that, as was the case with the Chāya demons, its discussions of Kṛtyas and Kākhordas predate all Indic (and Hindu) sources by a few hundred years. These early works all hail from KGB and the Tarim Basin. Among the earliest of these is the second-century CE *Nagaropamasūtra* ("Manual of the Exalted City"), a work from Turfan that lists *kṛtyakākhordamantravetāḍa* at the end of an enumeration of the baneful forces or beings that "scatter back [to the place from which they came] (*prativigamiṣyanti*)" whenever that text is recited.[236] It should be noted that, like *chāya*, *kṛtya* is declined in these Buddhist sources as a masculine noun, rather than the feminine form found in Hindu works.

Four Buddhist works embedded in the Gilgit Manuscript offer similar data. The *Āryaśrīmahādevīvyākaraṇa* ("Prophecy of the Noble and Venerable Great Goddess") praises a goddess as the "destroyer of every Kṛtya and Kākhorda."[237] The *Bhaiṣajyagurusūtra* ("Manual of the Medicine Buddha") evokes persons who, "by enlisting a Kākhorda or Vetāla . . . desire to bring about an obstacle to [the target's] life or to destroy his body."[238] Reprising language found in the MMVS, the *Mahāpratisarā-Mahāvidyārājñī* lists (K)ākhordas together with a series of pathologies, toxins, and acts of sorcery.[239] Finally, a version of the *Pañcaviṃśati* ("The Twenty-Five") from Gilgit contains the expression *kākhorda . . . kuryāt*, which could either be read as "one who would practice *kākhorda*" or "one who would fashion a Kākhorda."[240] "Asiloma's Protective Spell," a fragmentary work also embedded in a manuscript from Turfan, speaks of "protection from the practice of *kṛtya*, and from seizure relating to *kākhorda*s (or Kākhordas) and *vetāḍa* (or Vetāḍas)."[241] Here, the compound *kākhorda-vaitāḍa* may be compared to the NT's *kṛtyā-khārkhodakādayaḥ*, "things relating to *kṛtyā*, *khārkhoda*, and so forth." In both cases, the abstraction of the two members of the dvandva compound renders the meaning ambiguous: they could be demonic beings or they could be the dark arts or spells that generate such beings. The same ambiguity obtains in northern traditions of the *Gaṇḍavyūhasūtra* ("Manual of the Excellent Manifestation"), a "proto-tantric" Mahāyāna work from South India. In its sole extant Sanskrit recension, which dates from the eighth century,[242] mention is made of "*vetāla* mantras and *kākhorda*(s) used for the purpose of killing. Their enemies become stiff."[243]

Chinese and Tibetan translations from the Sanskrit betray the same ambiguity and imprecision. In his remarks on the use of these terms in the various recensions and translations of the Sanskrit-language *Suvarṇaprabhāsottamasūtra* ("Manual of the Golden Light") Johannes Nobel indicates that both the Chinese ideograms for and Tibetan translations of *kākhorda* and *vetāḍa* vary from one source to another, that they appear to denote both demons and magical practices, that they often occur as dvandva-type compounds, and that they at times are undifferentiated from one another.[244] The most common Tibetan translation for *vetāḍa* is *ro laṅs*,[245] commonly translated as a "zombie" or "revenant," while the Chinese ideogram employed in

Yijing's translation denotes the practice of "making corpses stand up."[246] As for *kākhorda*, Yijing translates the term as "evil, adversarial demon," with the further implication that said demon, when animated by curses, generates poisonous serpents that beset their targets with various afflictions.[247] *Byad*, the Tibetan translation for *kākhorda*, denotes an "imprecation, malediction, combined with sorcery, the name of an enemy being written on a slip of paper and hid in the ground, under various conjurations."[248] *Gśed byed*, the Tibetan translation for Kṛtya, commonly denotes an "evil spirit."[249]

Several other works, nearly all from the same period and the same KGB–Tarim Basin cultural region, reproduce the same data with respect to Buddhist usages of these terms: (1) *kṛtya*, *kākhorda*, and *vetāḍa* may be read as either classes of demonic beings or the dark arts that generate such beings; (2) the terms are often listed together with names of various classes of malign demons from South and perhaps Inner Asian demonology; and (3) these beings or the practices responsible for creating them can either be destroyed, immobilized, or dispersed back to their source (*prati-vi-gam*) by conjuration. Commenting on the use of this verb in the *Nagaropamasūtra*, Siglinde Dietz notes that in Buddhist texts, it "mainly occurs in conjunction with abstract words or mental objects and never with persons," concluding that the compound *kṛtya-kākhorda-mantra-vetāḍa* denotes "sorceries, magics [*sic*], charms and demonic arts."[250] However, a third-century CE document discovered by Sir Aurel Stein in the vicinity of Niya on the southern edge of the Tarim Basin, challenges her interpretation: "Lṕipeya says that there they brought out three witch-women (*khakhorni stri*). They only killed his woman; the other women they let go. Concerning this you received an order from Apǵeya, saying that Lṕipeya's woman was to be compensated for." Another fragment treats of the same issue of compensation for the wrongful execution of this *khakhorni*:[251] "They have killed her. . . . If she has not been seen or heard of [because she has been put to death] and if . . . [she] is not a witch, that woman is to be made recompense for to her full value and [this recompense] is to be taken by Puǵo and Lṕipeya. A decision is to be made according to law. The property they took from her Puǵo and Lṕipeya are to receive along with her person [?her remains]."[252]

On the basis of this datum, as well as the alternate spellings of the word *kākhorda/khakhorn(a)/khārkhoda*, the obvious conclusion is that this is a loan word—and so it is, from Old Iranian via Pahlavi. The unjust end of Lṕipeya's woman, who was put to death as a witch when two of her alleged accomplices were spared, is an indication that in certain contexts the term clearly denoted a human being. And so it originally was in the language of the Avesta, whose term *kax*^{w}*arəδa* has been identified as the source of the Sanskrit *kākhorda* in its variant spellings. *Kax^{w}arəδa* appears together with its feminine form *kax^{w}arəiδī* in a *Yasna* (61.2–3) from the Younger Avesta, which catalogs these together with several other types of human sorcerers and witches: "for the discomfiture and removal of the Evil Spirit [Angra Mainyu], with [his] creations . . . for the discomfiture and removal of the *kax^{w}arəδa*s and *kax^{w}arəiδī*s . . . of thieves and violators . . . of the *zanda*s and the *yātumant*s."[253]

Another hymn from the same collection links *yātumant*s ("sorcerers, black magicians") to an adjectival form of *kax^{w}arəδa*.[254] *Yātumant* is one among a number of terms found in both vedic and avestan scripture, signaling a common Indo-Iranian heritage.[255] An ancient loan word from a non-Indo-European Inner Asian language, *yātu* denoted "sorcery" or "black magic" in both traditions.[256] It was, however, in the Sasanian and later periods that many Pahlavi and modern Persian demonological terms (including *sāya*) were incorporated into the languages of north India as loan words. These included *jādug* (from the avestan *yātu*), the source of the term *jādū*, which means "conjuration" or "magic" in both modern Persian as well as a wide range of modern Indo-Aryan languages. This shared terminology extends to a number of malign spirit beings. The term *pairikā* (Pahlavi *parīg*; modern Persian *parī*) originally denoted a shape-changing "witch" in avestan sources.[257] As we have seen, *parī* means "evil spirit" in Urdu; in Kashmiri and several other north Indian languages, it carries the sense of "imp" or even "fairy." The *jaini*s, a class of malicious female spirit beings named in the Avesta, became the *jinn*s of later Islamic tradition.[258] The *zanda*, an evil being associated with sorcerers in the Avesta and with Manichean heretics in later Persian sources, may be the source of the Gujarati *zān* ("low-caste sorcerer") discussed in chapter 2.[259] On the basis of these data, we may surmise that the avestan *kax^{w}arəδa* was transformed, in its KGB and Indic contexts, from a sorcerer or "speech actor" into a "speech act" or form of sorcery.

The term *kax^{w}arəδa* has survived, in two vernacular forms, near the two geographical limits of the Sasanian Empire:[260] in modern Kashmiri, *khokhu* denotes a "bogey-man," while in modern Armenian *kaxard* signifies a "witch" or "warlock."[261] *Kerėtoja*, an ancient Lithuanian word still employed today for a witch, sorceress, or enchantress, may also be a cognate term.[262] Likely derived from the Iranian root √*x^{w}arδ*, the Old Iranian *kax^{w}arəδa* is also attested in the Khwarezmian √*xurδ* ("flee"), of which the causative root √*xurziy* means "to drive out, expel." According to Schwartz, this would be "an allusion to the wizard's expulsion of evil spirits," with the *ka-* prefix having a pejorative sense, like the *ku-* of Indo-Aryan languages.[263] This would align with Kṣemarāja's definition of the *khārkhoda* as a "device for expulsion" (*uccāṭanam yantram*) and the frequency of the verb *prati-vi-gam* ("disperse back to the source") in the context of *kākhorda*-related practices in the Buddhist works reviewed above.

With this, let us return to the compounds in which the term *khārkhoda/kākhorda* is most frequently encountered: *kṛtyā-khārkhoda* in the Hindu NT; and some combination of *kṛtya* (m.), *kākhorda*, *mantra*, and *vetāḍa* in several earlier Buddhist sources. Here, let us recall Kṣemarāja's commentary on NT 18.4: "A Kṛtyā is a female zombie (Vetālī) that has penetrated into the corpses of women for the destruction of one's enemies." A similar ambiguity is found in the Buddhist *Laṅkāvatārasūtra*'s ("Manual on the Descent into Laṅka") treatment of the *vetāla*, which may be read as denoting a device.[264] As is well known, it is a tantric (if not a vedic) commonplace to identify a being or deity with a mantra, that is, with the acoustic ground or correlate of that entity, which can be used to create, manipulate, or identify with it.[265] Beings and the mantras that create or denote them are virtually indistinguishable, and the same is the case for the practice or manipulation of a mantra or device (*yantra* may also be translated as "charm"). So it is that when, in the NT, Śiva has to find a solution to the hordes of Mothers, Spirit Beings, and Seizers to which he has granted invulnerability, he creates a new class of beings, simply called Mantras ("male spell-beings") and Vidyās ("female spell-beings"), to destroy and drive them away. As the most powerful being in the NT's universe, the Amṛteśa form of Śiva himself is nothing less than the divinization of his all-powerful "Death Conquering" mantra. The vedic goddess Vāc, the mother of all speech and thereby of all mantras and all the beings that mantras create and control, is herself a divinized speech act. In the NT, the form that she is said to take as the consort of Mṛtyujit-Amṛteśa is Śrī, who herself becomes the counterdevice goddess Pratyaṅgirā in order to rescue persons afflicted by the Kṛtyā-Khārkhodas (or by *kṛtyā-khārkhoda*-type devices).[266]

These data allow us to suggest that it is this virtual identification—of cause (the sorcery of the sorcerer) and effect (the Kṛtya and Khārkhoda as creatures of sorcery)—that makes for the ambiguity of this terminology. Similarly, the pairing of *kṛtya* with *kākhorda* in Buddhist sources from KGB and Inner Asia simply bears witness to the two ancient traditions that informed these practices. The compilers of the many KGB sources that employed these terms in a compound may or may not have been aware that they were the issue of two different traditions; what was essential was that both belonged to the same category of speech acts/devices/beings employed in sorcery and countersorcery across much of Inner, South, and East Asia.

In his analysis of the Old Iranian *kax^{w}arəδa*, Schwartz suggests a second possible etymology of the term based on an expression found in the Sogdian martyrology of Saint Tarbo, where the Sogdian *syxwrdnt* translates as "they shouted." On the basis of this reading, together with the possibility that the Sanskrit √*svar* ("make a sound, be loud") is a cognate term, he suggests that "*kax^{w}arəδa* may be the pejorative 'shouter' or 'howler,' or the like, from the sorcerer's most obviously derisible trait: one may compare the Greek *góēs* 'sorcerer,' from *goân* 'to wail,' [and] *góos* 'wailing.'"[267] This resonates, if I may use the expression, with Buddhaghosa's identification of *vetālam* with the banging of gongs. *Ḍākinī*, a common name for a fearsome class of tantric goddesses, may be generated from the root √*ḍam* ("sound") and translate as "noisemaker." With this, Kṣemarāja's gloss of the term *chidram* as "wailing in the forest, and so forth" also makes a certain sense.

In this chapter, we have surveyed a constellation of data surrounding the theory and practice of the evil eye, the practice of mirror divination, and the fabrication of sorcerers' devices and counterdevices. These data have indicated that these demonological theories, practices, and categories first surfaced in Buddhist texts from the KGB region before appearing in the Kashmirian NT in the first half of the ninth century. In nearly all of these cases, we can trace likely origins of these theories, practices—and, in certain cases, terminology—to Sasanian Iran and the Hellenistic world. All of which should spur scholars of Hindu Tantra to reflect upon a certain number of common presuppositions. First, while it remains useful to speak of regional or local traditions (Bengali Tantra, for example), it is totally inappropriate to assume that translocal traditions conform to modern geopolitical maps of the Indian subcontinent. Hindu Tantra is "Indic" only to the extent that KGB, Nepal, and the Tarim Basin of Chinese Turkestan are parts of India, which they are not. Second, in matters of tantric demonology—which is the foundation upon which all of the magnificent tantric systems and pantheons that Hindu Tantra specialists study are grounded—both substratal (in the sense of vedic and ayurvedic textual traditions as well as local or regional cults of yakṣas, devatās, bhūtas, and the like), adstratal (Iranian, Chinese, European), and even superstratal (Indo-European) traditions have to be taken into account in our reckoning of origins and influences.[268]

In his massive tome on the Sanskrit cosmopolis,[269] Sheldon Pollock argued that Sanskrit did not become the common language of expression of much of South and Inner Asia until it had been freed from its self-imposed strictures, as an exclusively hieratic language, by non-Hindu rulers who were simply looking for a common language through which they, their vassals, neighbors, enemies, priests, and subjects could communicate. Similarly, the language of demonology—less a language of words than of gestures and speech acts without semantic content (i.e., spells)—was highly cosmopolitan, part of a broader phenomenon of late antiquity identified by Jonathan Z. Smith as the anthropologization of the cosmos, in which "the new center and chief means of access to divinity [became] a divine man, a magician . . . an entrepreneur without fixed office . . . related to 'protean deities' of relatively unfixed form whose major characteristic [was] their sudden and dramatic autophanies."[270] More than this, as Walter Burkert has observed for the ancient and Hellenistic world, "successful charismatic specialists became, as they can today, widely sought-after personalities; they could cross frontiers more easily and more often than other craftsmen with simpler skills. Being the mobile bearers of cross-cultural knowledge, the migrant charismatics deserve particular attention as to cultural contacts."[271] Finally, as Michel Strickmann has noted with specific reference to divinatory and healing techniques, "it is quite possible to conceive of these readily transportable arts and artifacts as spreading from one culture to another even without the mediation of a major religion."[272] From Bengal to Gurganj, for example.

As the historical record makes plain, the ports and halting places of the so-called Silk Road were informational changing-houses where soldiers, merchants, monks, and magicians transacted in demonological services, devices, and expertise. On a broader scale, the demonology that became a commodity along ancient and medieval trade and invasion routes was itself a translocal tradition, greater in its range and depth than the various tantric traditions that it spawned. Sanjay Subrahmanyam's characterization of culture as "formed in the crucible of processes of acculturation" is once again applicable here.[273] If one limits one's purview of Tantra to South Asian philosophical schools or sects, scriptural canons, or authorized pantheons, one does so at the cost of missing a far broader and truer picture.

4

Medieval and Modern Child Abductions

> Rock-a-bye baby,
> on the tree top
> When the wind blows,
> the cradle will rock
>
> EIGHTEENTH-CENTURY ENGLISH LULLABY

1

Not without irony, it would appear, the Catholic Church deemed that Saint Lawrence's saintly attribute should be the man-sized gridiron upon which he was roasted to death, a heavy cross to bear (fig. 4.1). The de facto patron saint of pre-Reformation Denmark,[1] Sankt Lars's third-century martyrdom is depicted on the frescoes (*kalkmalerier*) of dozens of medieval Danish country churches. Among these however, only two—the Undløse[2] and Skamstrup[3] churches in southern Sjælland—also portray his infancy. These may well be the sole surviving images for this period in the future saint's *Vita* in the entire Christian world.[4] The earlier of the two, found on the apse of the Undløse church, is the most evocative. Dating from the second quarter of the fifteenth century, it depicts a particular episode from Lawrence's early infancy in three successive tableaus. In the first, we see his mother lying asleep on her bed, with the tiny outline of a baby's head on the pillow next to her (fig. 4.2). The second and most interesting for our purposes shows a horned faun or dæmon handing the tightly swaddled baby up to another imp in a laurel tree. The gangly legs and tail of the latter are twined around the trunk of the tree so as to closely mimic its branches (fig. 4.3). The final scene shows the face and torso of a humanoid figure in the same tree, remitting the infant, its head now encircled by a halo, into the hands of a person in ecclesiastical dress. Here as well, the body of this figure appears to blend into the ramifications of the tree itself (fig. 4.4).

The Skamstrup church's fresco of Lawrence's birth, which dates from between 1460 and 1480, adds a significant detail. In its second scene, in addition to the dæmon holding the infant in the upper branches of the tree, one sees a woman leaning over a cradle in which there lies a second child with deformed facial features (fig. 4.5).[5] This detail provides us the key to the saint's

FIGURE 4.1. Saint Lawrence, Auning Church, Denmark, ca. 1510 CE. Image courtesy of Denmark National Museum.

FIGURE 4.2. Birth of Saint Lawrence, Undløse Church, Denmark, 1425–1450 CE. Photo by author.

FIGURE 4.3. Detail, Birth of Saint Lawrence, Undløse Church, Denmark. Photo by author.

legend: Lawrence was a changeling, an infant taken at birth by a supernatural or demonic being and exchanged for a "demon child" before being recovered, in this case by a representative of the Church. The earliest extant version of Lawrence's birth legend as illustrated by these frescoes dates from less than a century before they were painted. This, the *Gesta Romanorum*,[6] relates that Lawrence was born to a pagan king and queen of Spain who had vowed to convert to Christianity if God would grant them a son. Shortly after the child's birth (but prior to his baptism), the Devil transformed himself into the likeness of the newborn babe, and taking the real Lawrence to a forest in "Rome," abandoned him there in a basket (*sporta*) hanging from a bay laurel tree. There he was discovered by Pope Sixtus II (d. 258 CE), who, hearing the child crying in his basket, took him down, baptized him, and named him Lawrence after the tree in which he had been suspended.[7]

FIGURE 4.4. Detail, Birth of Saint Lawrence, Undløse Church, Denmark. Photo by author.

Lawrence was not the first Catholic saint and martyr to have had a changeling episode as a prelude to his legendary life. That distinction falls to Saint Stephen, whose changeling narrative is first attested in the tenth- to eleventh-century *Vita Fabulosa*.[8] His story spawned a number of artistic representations, of which the most stunning example is a polyptych attributed to Martino di Bartolomeo (1389–1434).[9] Here, the second of seven panels shows the child, deposited by the Devil outside the door to a bishop's residence, being suckled by a white doe (plate 11). This incongruous transposition, of a creature of the forest into the midst of an urban setting, was not a painterly invention. A fourteenth- to fifteenth-century manuscript account of the saint's birth tells just such a story,[10] which nonetheless does not ring true. A doe's natural habitat is the forest,[11] like the *silva* in which the Devil had abandoned Saint Lawrence in that saint's recorded legend, as well as in representations of the same on the ceilings of two Danish churches. But Martino's inspiration was likely a literary or folkloric one. White hinds or stags were a common fixture of fairyland, and it was often in pursuit of such exotic creatures that the heroes of courtly romance were drawn into the enchanted lands of fairy princesses.[12]

Less than a century after the Skamstrup ceiling was painted, Martin Luther identified a changeling as a soulless mass of flesh, the Devil's spawn that "he places in cradles, carrying off the real child." Given his druthers, Luther said he would drown the little devils.[13] Of course, Luther's diatribe was but a late chapter in the demonization of the dæmons of pagan Europe, a phenomenon as old as Christendom itself.[14] The leading architect of this strategy was Saint Augustine, who, in drawing up an inventory of superstitions that it was the Church's task to repudiate and eradicate, officialized the entrance of the fairies (*fata*) of pagan traditions into the Christian lexicon and imagination.[15] It was also Augustine who first described how such creatures reproduced, explaining in his *City of God* that "sylvans" and "fauns" were demonic

FIGURE 4.5. Birth of Saint Lawrence, Skamstrup Church, Denmark, 1460–1480 CE (1909 photograph). Image courtesy of Denmark National Museum.

incubi that copulated with human women.[16] That these were the same sorts of forest-dwelling creatures as those pictured on our fifteenth-century Danish church ceilings is attested a century after Augustine by Martianus Capella, who explained that

> Where the earth is inaccessible to men it is crowded with the ancient beings who inhabit the woods and forests (*silvas nemora*), groves (*lucos*),[17] lakes, springs and rivers—the beings called Pans, Fauns, Fones, Satyrs, Silvani, Nymphs, Fatui and Fatuae or Fantuae or even Fanae; Fanes are named after these, whose custom it is to prophesy. All of these beings die, just like men, after an extended lifespan; but they have extraordinary powers of foreknowledge, aggression, and injury.[18]

Nearly all the terms in "F" here derive from *fatas*, the Latin term for the Fates, three ancient goddesses who meted out and cut off the lives of mortals. From their name is derived the Old French *fae* and modern French *fée* ("fairy"), from which *faerie* ("fairyland"), the source of the medieval and modern English "fairy."[19] However, the words "changeling" and "fairy" have long been used interchangeably in Great Britain,[20] and folk traditions across western European identify changelings as the offspring of shape-changing fairies, fauns, elves, dwarves, trolls, evil spirits, underworld folk, water sprites, and the like.[21] No less a figure than Merlin, King Arthur's wizardly mentor, was said to have been a changeling.[22] The passing of that enchanted world is lamented in the opening verses of the "Wife of Bath's Tale" by Chaucer, who sarcastically links the demons of Augustinian doctrine to the churchmen of his day:

> In th'olde dayes of the King Arthour,
> Of which that Britons speken greet honour,
> Al was this land fulfild of faierye.
> The elf-queene with hir joly compaignye
> Daunced ful ofte in many a grene mede . . .
> But now kan no man se none elves mo,
> For now the grete charitee and prayeres
> Of limitours and othere holy freres,
> That serchen every lond and every streem
> As thick as moters in the sonne-beem . . .
> This maketh that ther been no faieryes.
> For ther as wont to walken was an elf,
> Ther walketh now the limitour himself . . .
> Wommen may go saufly up and doun.
> In every bussh or under every tree
> Ther is noon oother incubus but he,
> And he ne wol doon [t]hem but dishonour.[23]

Counter to Church doctrine and legend,[24] the medieval fairies of popular tradition were nearly always female, and their motives for abducting human infants generally benign. As Jakob Grimm explains, "elves are anxious to improve their breed by means of the human child, which they design to keep among them, and for which they give up one of their own."[25] Regardless of the fairies' motives, the inhuman nature of their children—betrayed by their unusual appearance, behavior, muteness, and, especially, their poor health—would become quickly apparent to their surrogate human parents. This was a leitmotiv of the rich lore surrounding the changelings: chronically sickly children were diagnosed as fairy substitutes, and so the sole way for a child to "recover" was to recover the real child from its fairy abductors. This was a risky process, and so the prime strategy was a preventive one: once baptized, the infant would be protected from the demons, fairies, or elves that might otherwise attempt to exchange it for one of their own. This of course was an acknowledgment of the power of the Church and its sacraments. However, as the legend of Saint Lawrence indicated, the period between birth and baptism was a window of opportunity for these spirit beings.

2

While there were a number of strategies for recovering one's child once the changeling had been found out,[26] the most detailed documentation of medieval rituals to this end is a report made by the Dominican inquisitor Stephen of Bourbon (1190?–1261) regarding the "superstitions" surrounding the worship of a certain Saint Guinefort in the Dombes region of southeastern France. Working from Stephen's report, Jean-Claude Schmitt brilliantly analyzed this tradition in a groundbreaking work of historical anthropology,[27] whose findings I follow here. The salient portions of Stephen's report are as follows:

> Above all, though, it was women with sick or weak children who took them to this place. They would go and seek out an old woman in a fortified town a league distant, and she taught them the rituals they should enact in order to make offerings to demons, and in order to invoke them, and she led them to the place. When they arrived, they would make offerings of salt and other things; they would hang their babies' swaddling clothes (*panniculos*) on the bushes roundabout; they would drive nails into the trees which had grown in this place; they would pass the naked babies between the trunks of two trees: the mother, on one side, held the baby and threw it nine times to the old woman, who was on the other side.[28] Invoking the demons, they called upon the fauns (*faunos*) in the forest of Rimite to take the sick, feeble child, which,

> they said, was theirs, and to return their child that the fauns had taken away, fat and well, safe and sound.[29]

As Stephen relates, a mother would then expose her infant, leaving it naked and alone "on straw from the cradle" (*super stramina cunabili*) at the foot of Guinefort's tree for the time it took for one-inch candles, placed around the baby's head or in the trunk of the tree above, to burn down. Following which, she plunged the infant nine times into the waters of the nearby Chalaronne River.[30] If, after this, it survived, as Stephen remarks, it was only by virtue of a strong constitution. The Dominican monk concludes his report by saying that he exhumed the body of the uncanonized saint (who was in fact a greyhound) and cut down the trees around his shrine, burning them together with the dog's bones.[31]

How a greyhound came to be abusively viewed (at least in the eyes of the Church) as a saint in this medieval backwater is a story in itself. Guinefort's "exemplum"—which has him unjustly put to death by his master for the death of an infant child that he had in fact attempted to protect from a deadly serpent—is a version of a folktale recorded in some forty languages, classified in the Aarne-Thompson-Uther folktale type index under the heading "The Innocent Dog."[32] The earliest extant version of Guinefort's "martyrdom" is found in the *Pañcatantra* ("Five Treatises"),[33] a classic collection of animal fables from India thought to date from the third century CE. In that work, it is a mongoose rather than a greyhound that, after saving a child in its cradle, is rashly put to death by its master before the true culprit (a cobra) is discovered. The *Pañcatantra* was translated into Pahlavi in the sixth century, following which it made its way west via Arabic, Hebrew, and Greek adaptations, appearing in Latin and French versions by the thirteenth century.[34] Whether the story known to the peasants of the Dombes region of thirteenth-century France came to them via this chain of transmitted texts, or whether, as Schmitt suggests, "it belonged to oral traditions proper to the local peasantry, stemming from an ancient Indo-European source,"[35] is a question to which I will return at the end of this chapter.

A similar set of questions may be asked about the rites surrounding the holy greyhound's rustic shrine. How local were they, and if they belonged to a wider network of practice, did that network extend beyond the borders of the Dombes region? of France? of medieval Europe? The ritual as Stephen presents it was divided into three parts or sequences, performed at two different sites.[36] The first comprised a set of preliminaries: offerings of salt and other substances, a nail driven into the saint's tree, and swaddling clothes hung on surrounding bushes. It was the presence of Guinefort's remains there that made these practices effective, with his saintly "charisma," transmitted through the vegetation growing above his tomb, imparting its healing powers to the sickly infant. Those powers are referenced in the oft-repeated formula, attested in a half-dozen languages: "Saint Guinefort, for life or for death."[37]

The logic of the rite's second sequence was entirely different. The saint had no role here; this was a ritual transaction, an exchange between two mothers involving exposure, an integral component of changeling rites across all of Europe.[38] The naked child, laid out on the straw of its cradle, was abandoned to the elements, fire, and wild beasts, including, as Stephen relates, the Devil in the shape of a wolf. The third portion of the rite brought another sort of exposure into play, the plunging of the infant into the freezing waters of a nearby river.[39] This ordeal was the means by which to verify that the fairies had in fact exchanged the two infants, an exchange that the mother was not permitted to witness directly.[40]

The goal of the exchange ritual, as stated in Stephen's account itself, was of a piece with broader changeling traditions: to compel the spirits of the forest (*faunos*) to take back the fairy child they had earlier placed in the human child's cradle, and return the human child to its birth mother via a ritual cradle, the tiny bed of straw on the shrine's forest floor. Here, as with all changeling rituals, the ritual actors were exclusively female, and so we should assume that these traditions were passed down from generation to generation by women.[41] Underlying these practices was the assumption that maternal affection was an emotion common to all creatures: exposing the changeling infant to the elements, even whipping it with young tree branches, was unproblematic because it was understood that the fairy mother, refusing to allow *her* infant's life to be placed at risk, would feel compelled by her maternal instincts to rescue the child and make the exchange.[42]

A question to which I will return later in this chapter concerns Stephen's reliability as an "ethnographer" of these rites. To be sure, as an inquisitor, he had demonstrated experience in carrying out investigations into the beliefs and practices of the *rustici*, the rustic peasants of southeastern France. As a representative of the Church whose mission it was to uproot—here, in the literal sense of the term—superstition, Stephen would have been a priori hostile to the practices he reports here. But his hostility and scorn for them would also have been grounded in deeper social and ideological divisions between the urban aristocrats who filled the upper echelons of the Church hierarchy and a peasantry that, largely left to its own devices after the collapse of the old structures of Gallo-Roman rural society, had returned to its pre-Roman, mainly Celtic, ways. The words *urbani* and *rustici* attest to these stubborn ideological divides, as did the evolution of the term *pagus*, discussed in chapter 1.[43] Under such circumstances, one might ask whether a Latin-speaking aristocrat "parachuted" into a rural backwater would have been sufficiently interested in the superstitions he was charged with eradicating to distinguish between them. Since he states in his report that his findings are based on the testimony of the women themselves,[44] did the practices at Guinefort's rustic shrine actually comprise three sequences of a ritual ensemble, or were they three discrete procedures that he conflated in his report into a single rite? For the time being, I will respect Stephen's ordering; later in this chapter, however, I will treat them as three separate rituals.

Elements of the first sequence of the thirteenth-century rite are widely attested across much of Europe and Asia, albeit with highest concentrations in western, mainly coastal, regions of both India and western Europe. Let us begin by noting the role of trees in the changeling recovery ritual, some of which appear to inform the portrayals of Saint Lawrence's changeling narrative on our two Danish churches. In these, the child is suspended in the bay laurel tree by gangly fauns—who, blending into the trees, are themselves very much "of the forest"—and then returned from the tree by another, fatter and healthier figure with a human face. It is as if the qualities of the child himself (who is furthermore depicted with a halo in the final panel, even if, according to his written legend, he had not yet been baptized) are being expressed by the intermediary figures involved in the exchange. Furthermore, as his legend explicitly states, he is named Lawrence (Laurencius) after the bay laurel (*laurus*) into which he had been abducted before being remitted to the hands of the pope. As Schmitt notes with respect to the changeling recovery ritual at Saint Guinefort's shrine, a direct link was created, via the intermediary of the clothing, the nail, and the branches and roots of the bushes and trees of his shrine, between the child's sickly body and that of the martyred saint.[45] While a relatively small number of modern-day practices target children specifically (such is the case at approximately 20 percent of healing shrines in France),[46] many medieval and modern European sources contain references to healing rites involving the passing of children between trees, through holes in trees and stones, as well as through openings in the altars or tombs of Christian saints.[47]

In spite of Stephen's destruction of the place, the medieval practices chronicled by him continued for several centuries at Guinefort's shrine, as noted in an 1879 report penned by Augustin Vayssière:

> We . . . came to a clearing or circle whose center was occupied by the stump of an oak tree from which some frail shoots were growing. This is the sacred spot where the curious rites I mentioned earlier were carried out, with this clump

> of stunted oaks possibly descending from those trees through which the mothers handed their infants. The first thing that catches one's eye in approaching this clump is the presence of a multitude of pieces of clothing hung from its branches. I note a little undershirt, some tiny slippers, and wee stockings. . . . Those who have come and left these various traces of their visit do so in order to invoke Saint Guinefort on the behalf of weak or sickly infants. According to them, Saint Guinefort has the power to restore these children to health. When the infirmity is in a leg, they bring the britches of the lame child; when the foot alone is deficient, they only bring a slipper; when the back is weak, one is to hang the entire upper garment in the bush's branches.[48]

Seconding Stephen's original description and Vayssière's interpretation of the ritual use of these objects of clothing, Schmitt notes that "often interpreted as *ex votos* because they are recovered at pilgrimage sites following such rites, the swaddling clothes, wraps and slippers left at them are in fact preliminaries to the 'cure' and not signs of thanksgiving."[49]

This is by far the most common modern-day survival of the medieval rite, with the faithful continuing to drape articles of clothing at arboreal and freshwater shrines for the purpose of healing the ills of children and adults alike. This practice is attested across several continents. Documented by nineteenth- and early twentieth-century folklorists from across western Europe,[50] the practices of hanging rags and articles of clothing in bushes (particularly in the vicinity of healing wells and springs),[51] and of driving nails into trees has persisted down to the present day in several coastal regions of Celtic Europe: Scotland, Ireland, Wales,[52] France, and Belgium. The highest concentrations of these "rag trees" are found at sites in the rural Landes region of southwestern France (fig. 4.6 and plate 12)[53] and along the northern coasts of France and Belgium (fig. 4.7 and plate 13),[54] while several others are located in Ireland, Wales, and Scotland.[55] My own findings in Flanders, Picardy, and the Landes, as well as recent ethnographies from the same regions all point to an alternative, emic, explanation for the efficacity of these practices. That explanation, attested at every one of these European sites, is the following: sufferers transfer their ailments or afflictions onto rags—pieces of clothing that have been in contact with their bodies—which they affix to trees or bushes. In barren regions without vegetation, one encounters "rag wells" at which clothing is strewn or draped over surrounding rocks or—as is the case at the Fountain of Saint Girons, located near the village of Suzan in the Landes—on the posts and wires of fences erected around the spring (plate 14). So too, the earliest British documentation of these practices, from seventeenth- and eighteenth-century Scotland, concern "rag wells."[56] While in the wake of their Christianization, these sanctuaries came to be identified with the saints of the Church,

FIGURE 4.6. Fontaine Sainte Luce, Escource, Landes, France. Photo by author.

it is reasonable to assume, as most historians and ethnographers have done, that before these became venues for Christian miracles, they were remarkable sanctuaries whose healings were attributed to the power of the place itself, if not that of the pagan dæmon whose *lucus* it originally was.

In an 1893 study, Sidney Hartland characterized the logic behind such transfers as "sympathetic magic,"[57] a term that is perhaps appropriate here, given the universally attested corollary to the practice, to wit, that its effects may be reversed if, upon leaving the site, one were to touch the rag a second time. Whether through the efforts of evangelizing clergy or because they were so classified prior to their Christianization, most of these watered shrines are specialized, with the cure at each corresponding to a specific ailment and its saint,[58] and with a particular act by that saint adduced as the spring's origin. In some cases, the spring suddenly erupted at the site of the saint's martyrdom; in others, the act of driving his staff into the ground would have had the same effect. So, for example, at Saint Godeleine's Fountain in the French village of Wierre-Effroy (Nord-Pas-de-Calais), the transformative implement was that female saint's spindle, which figures in her iconography (fig. 4.8).[59] Often, the saint's name is indicative of the affliction to be healed: Saint Eutrope for lameness and other problems of motricity;[60] Saint Claire or Saint Luce for problems of vision; Saint Cô (*cœur*) for heart problems, and so forth. A touching example of this type of specialization is Saint Martin's Fountain in the village of Sanghen in Nord-Pas-de-Calais, where one finds baby shoes and stockings hanging over the mouth of the grotto that encloses the miraculous spring (fig. 4.9).

FIGURE 4.7. Chapelle de Saint Vast, Woirel, Picardy, France. Photo by author.

FIGURE 4.8. Sainte Godeleine with spindle, Wierre-Effroy, Nord-Pas-de-Calais, France. Photo by author.

In the decades following World War II, many of the traditions specific to these healing groves and springs died out. One of these would have been the protocol for determining which spring and which saint were to be visited for a given condition. In the Landes, people consulted women specialists, known in the regional patois as "recommandaïres," who were also known for their powers of healing: as was the case in the medieval Dombes region, these practices were female prerogatives.[61] Because "the saints vie with one another to occupy a spring,"[62] these shrines could change saintly hands from one day to the next, and in order to determine which spring was inhabited by which saint, the Landes recommandaïre employed a type of divination using candles (*candelous*) called "drawing saints" (as in "drawing lots"). Each candle signifying a particular saint and his or her spring, she would burn several funerary tapers simultaneously. The first (or last) of these to burn out indicated the healing shrine to be visited.[63]

When and where did these practices originate? Prior to Stephen of Bourbon's report concerning the shrine of Saint Guinefort, there is no extant documentation for changeling-related rituals or the hanging of articles of clothing at any sylvan or freshwater shrine in Europe.[64] In the ancient Roman world, people offered prayers to the gods of the sylvan *luci* by binding ribbons, threads, and *vittae* to their branches.[65] Archeological and textual evidence indicates that trees also played an important role in ancient Celtic and Germanic cultic practice, which, in spite of the debasing of the Druids and the "official" abandonment of the old sacred groves, persisted through the Roman period.[66] Here, we should also note that the rare Roman references to *nemetons*, Gaulish sanctuaries, tended to designate them as *luci* (as opposed to *templa*, etc.): the same term, also employed to denote Italic worship sites from pre-Roman times, denoted a shrine characterized by its vegetation rather than by its architecture.[67] This has been borne out by recent palynological

FIGURE 4.9. Fontaine Saint Martin, Sanghen, Nord-Pas-de-Calais, France. Photo by author.

analyses of important Gaulish settlements such as Ribemont-sur-Ancre in the Somme region of northeastern France.[68] As a wealth of documents of the medieval Church attest, attempts to eradicate the pagan veneration of trees, groves, and springs in northern and western Europe were largely unsuccessful.[69] Although all forms of veneration at these pagan shrines were banned by the fourth-century Theodosian Code,[70] banned again by Pope Gregory in the 590s, and condemned by monks and priests from across the Christian world over the centuries that followed, it has never died out entirely. As the data reviewed above indicate, identifying these sites with its own saints and martyrs became a rearguard strategy for converting the peasantry to Christianity.[71] Stephen's is, however, the sole extant medieval record to link such practices to the healing of children, or to their recovery from fairy abductors.

3

An eighth-century narrative portrayed on two eleventh- to twelfth-century manuscript illuminations not only attests to the medieval survival of "tree worship" in the Flanders region of France and Belgium, but also lends to a formal comparison between western European and South Asian iconographies of tree shrines. In an eighth-century *Vita* of the seventh-century Saint Amandus, we read that that future bishop of Maastricht once visited the home of an old woman who, seeking to cure her blindness, had been worshiping a tree consecrated to a demon. Condemning her pagan practice, Amandus had the tree cut down and healed her through the power of Christ.[72] Also mentioned in the narrative is the demon's image (*idolus*), which appears in one of two manuscript illuminations from Valenciennes depicting this miracle (plate 15). Here, the representation of the *idolus*—as a head in profile atop a cubical base at the foot of a tree—bears comparison with a first-century CE image from the Mathura region of northern India (fig. 4.10).[73] The subject of the right half of this bas-relief has generally been interpreted as a one-faced (*ekamukha*) Śiva *liṅgam*, that face being shown in profile atop a cubical brick base at the foot of a tree. On the left half, two dwarflike beings are shown facing a (badly damaged) human figure holding a basket.[74] I will return to this second grouping shortly, in the context of what appears to be a modern-day survival of this practice. A second manuscript folio, also from Valenciennes, depicts Saint Amandus's ordering of the destruction of the tree shrine. Here, a woman is shown taking an ax to the trunk of the tree, out of the foliage of which two faces emerge (plate 16). This representation of a tree dæmon (or dæmons) bears a striking resemblance to that found on a late eighteenth-century fresco from Degaldoruva in central Sri Lanka (fig. 4.11).

FIGURE 4.10. Tree shrine with local devatās, Mathura region, first century CE. Image courtesy of Sonya Rhie Mace.

FIGURE 4.11. Tree yakkhiṇī, Degaldoruva, Sri Lanka, late eighteenth century.

Ethnographers and folklorists have noted the practice of decorating trees, for a variety of purposes, in other regions of the world, including Greece, Ukraine, and parts of north and west Africa.[75] In the Muslim world, tombs of Sufi saints from the Balkans to northeastern India, but most especially in Central Asia, have long featured *tughs*, votive offerings comprising strips of cloth, pieces of clothing, flags and cloth tassels affixed to poles, tree trunks, branches, or prayer screens.[76] Here, each piece of cloth (*latta*) corresponds to a votive prayer, and in Xinjiang in western China, the flapping of cloth flags in the wind is thought to drive away evil spirits.[77] This apotropaic function notwithstanding, Alexander Papas has strongly argued that the symbolism of the *tugh*s was originally martial: a battlefield standard, the *tugh* was an early modern emblem of the Sufi saint's role as sovereign defender of the Muslim faith. However, as Papas further notes, the Muslim *tugh*s of Central Asia also resemble prayer flags and other Buddhist cultic paraphernalia that predated Islam's penetration into the region by nearly a millennium.[78]

As I will argue in what follows, these Buddhist practices are the legacy of a body of millennial traditions that has persisted down to the present day in rural western India. Since the beginning of the Common Era, trees in Hindu, Jain, and Buddhist South and Southeast Asia have been festooned with ribbons, tassels, bolts of cloth, and articles of clothing. Widely documented in the ancient and medieval textual and iconographic record, this phenomenon was a signal feature of South Asia's cults of yakṣas or devatās, spirit beings of water sources and forest groves. As we will see in the next chapter, many of the earliest monumental sculptures of South Asia were representations of yakṣas and yakṣīs. These early images were largely "nondenominational," because they predated the appropriation and subordination of these deities and their cults by the emerging dominant religions of the subcontinent. That appropriation took the form of the incorporation of yakṣas into early Hindu, Buddhist, and Jain mythology, with yakṣa shrines figuring prominently in early Buddhist sculpture.[79]

By far the richest early textual description of a great yakṣa shrine is that found in the *Aupapatika Sutra* ("Manual on Spontaneous Arising"), a circa first-century CE Jain work. Here, the yakṣa Pūrṇabhadra's *ceie* (Skt. *caitya*) is situated in the midst of a lush forest to the northeast of the city of Campa. In a clearing at the center of that forest stands an *aśoka* tree, and beneath that tree is a great stone block that "resembles a throne." A crowded place of worship, its groves of trees are heavily hung with canopies, garlands, pennants, banners, bells, and yak-tail-topped standards. Slab altars and plastered walls and gates are also mentioned, as are flocks of calling birds and elaborate water gardens.[80] Similar descriptions of such shrines are found in the MBh[81] and several *Jātaka*s ("Stories of the [Buddha's Prior] Births"). A number of these, which will be discussed in the next chapter, alternate between the terms "yakṣa" and "devatā" to denote these figures. There nonetheless appears to be some distinction between the two, with lesser, sylvan figures being more often termed "devatās," and the dæmons of major and/or urban shrines called "yakṣas."

FIGURE 4.12. Votive cloth offering to a tree yakṣī/Birth of the Buddha, Amaravati, Andhra Pradesh, first century CE. Image courtesy of the British Museum.

Although many of these came to be urbanized, with their images or slab altars being placed at the gates or crossroads of ancient cities and towns,[82] yakṣa iconography generally situated them in their native element, which was nearly exclusively sylvan. Even when, as we will see in the next chapter, they were cast as guardians of lotus ponds, yakṣas were also tree dwellers,[83] and their propitiation often involved the placing of offerings at the base of said trees, or in their branches. Dozens of sculptures from Buddhist reliquary monuments (*stūpas*) depict their tree-shrine complexes (*caitya-vṛkṣas*) as trees heavily draped with flower garlands and, in some cases, lengths of cloth.[84] A number of early sculptures portray devotees approaching these shrines with great bolts of cloth—a luxury item for the time—in one case so long as to be borne by four persons standing in a line. The lower right panel of a bas-relief from the site of Amaravati (Andhra Pradesh) in southeastern India, which depicts the birth of the Buddha, shows such a group approaching the Buddha's mother, Māyāvatī, with what are thought to be the child's swaddling clothes. However, on the basis of her pose and the stone "throne" at her feet, one might just as readily identify her as a simple tree yakṣī (fig. 4.12). The left side of the same panel, which depicts Māyāvatī's presentation of the infant Buddha to a local devatā, also features a bolt of cloth, which doubles as the

FIGURE 4.13. Parinirvāṇa of the Buddha with tree yakṣīs, Mathura region, ca. 15 CE. Image courtesy of the Norton Simon Museum.

child's swaddling clothes and a tribute offering (see below, fig. 4.14).[85] When they were represented anthropomorphically, the dress of male yakṣas was often limited to just this: a great cloth wrap worn loosely about the shoulders with its ends hanging down below the knees (plate 17).

Taken together, these images bear witness to the close identification between yakṣas or devatās and the offerings made at their arboreal dwellings. As their cults came to be gradually supplanted by those of the emergent high gods of Hindu theism, the latter appropriated certain of their attributes. One of the most illustrious episodes of Kṛṣṇa's youth has the blue god in his customary cowherd disguise, stealing the clothing of the village cowherdesses as they bathe. One of India's most exquisite miniature paintings brings this episode to life as it depicts the *gopīs*, in a state of undress, beseeching the blue-skinned lothario in the *kadamba* tree to return them their saris (plate 18). Surrounded by colorful pieces of clothing amid the tree's boughs and foliage, there is little to differentiate the Kṛṣṇa of this image from depictions of yakṣas or yakṣīs of yore in their arboreal settings (fig. 4.13). Bordering the shores of the Yamuna River, the forest in which Kṛṣṇa sported had long been home to the great "Parkham Yakṣa," one of the god's yakṣa forebears.[86] He will reappear in all his glory in the next chapter.

In their role as fertility deities, yakṣas/devatās were called upon to grant children to barren couples,[87] who would, as a story from the Buddhist *Aṭṭhakathā* relates, subsequently honor them:

> [A childless householder named "Much Gold"] seeing on the roadside a branching leafy "Lord of the Forest" (i.e., a great tree) [thought to himself], "This [tree] must be haunted by a powerful devatā." So he had the area underneath the tree purified, a surrounding fence erected, [and] sand spread out; and having hoisted up and adorned the Lord of the Forest with flags and banners, he joined his hands together [and vowed]: "If I should receive a son or a daughter, I will pay you great honor." So saying, he went on his way.[88]

When the wishes of such petitioners were granted, the gratified parents would then present the newborn child to the yakṣa at its shrine. The newborn Buddha was himself presented in just this way by his mother to a forest devatā, as attested in sculptures dating from the beginning of the Common Era at Amaravati, Chandavaram, Nagarjunikonda, and Kanganhalli. In these, we see the devatā emerging from the altar at the foot of his tree to bow before the newborn child (fig. 4.14).[89] Trees continue to be wrapped and hung with votive bolts of cloth, from the Bodhi Tree in Bodhgaya to Buddhist sites throughout Southeast Asia (fig. 4.15).[90]

FIGURE 4.14. Presentation of Buddha to forest devatā, Amaravati, Andhra Pradesh, first century CE. Image courtesy of the British Museum.

FIGURE 4.15. Ficus draped with bolts of cloth, Tiger Caves Monastery, Krabi, Thailand. Photo by author.

4

According to Buddhist sources, yakṣas and yakṣīs were not strictly vegetarian, and so the tribute offerings (*bali*) made to them could include the flesh of animals,[91] often presented together with a request for children. We also see this in the "Dummedha Jātaka" description of the worship of a devatā, which, after evoking the "slaughter of many sheep, goats, cocks, swine, and the like," speaks of people making tribute offerings (*bali-kamma*) with flowers and fragrances as well as flesh and blood. The same source states that the people of Benares worshiped just such a devatā at the foot of a banyan tree, praying to him to grant them sons and daughters.[92] The "Sutasoma Jātaka" attests to similar appetites, this time on the part of a yakkhī. The bodhisattva, here reborn as a prince named Sutasoma, is the companion of a "prince of Benares" who begins to suffer from a sort of gustatory "flashback": a yakkha anthropophage in a previous life, he has recently experienced a flare-up of his old addiction to human flesh. As the supply of human victims in a neighboring forest dwindles, he makes a vow to its tree-dwelling yakkhī to sacrifice one hundred princes of India to her in exchange for her assistance in feeding his habit. He manages to round up ninety-nine of the princes, hanging them by their hands in the yakkhī's tree (plate 19), but when he captures the one-hundredth—Sutasoma—the bodhisattva skillfully defuses the situation. All lives are spared and the prince of Benares returns to his throne and proper vegetarian ways.[93]

A passage from the MBh brings together both of these themes: "Women known by the name of 'crones' (*vṛddhikās*)[94] are eaters of human flesh. These goddesses, who are born in trees, are to be worshiped by persons desiring children."[95] This statement comes at the close of the epic's longest, and likely earliest, disquisition on ancient Indian demonology, discussed in chapter 2. Here, we read that the "great Seizers called the Youths and Maidens are all fetus-eaters"; that "Saramā . . . the divine Mother of Dogs . . . is constantly snatching away human fetuses"; that persons wishing to have sons bow to the Mother of Plants who dwells in the *karañja* tree; that "when [the serpent-demoness named] Kadru, taking on a subtle form, enters a pregnant woman, she eats the embryo inside, and the mother gives birth to a snake"; and finally, that "she who is the Mother of the Gandharvas seizes the fetus and goes off. That woman is then viewed on earth as one whose fetus has melted away."[96]

Which brings us back in a circuitous way to the changeling traditions of western Europe. There are no changeling narratives in South Asia;[97] however, as narrativized in the birth myth of Kṛṣṇa, in utero exchanges of human and demonic embryos were not extrinsic to classical Indic systems of knowledge.[98] Here, the malevolent spirit beings that steal away human infants invariably do so fatally, either in the womb or during the first days, weeks, or months of life. Nearly all of these beings are female, and they are collectively known by a range of by now familiar names: "Mothers" (*mātṛs*), Female Seizers (*grahaṇīs*), yakṣīs and Yoginīs.[99] These demonesses usually possess their victims, entering into their bodies and feeding on them from within. Identified with such fatal childhood diseases as smallpox and wasting fevers, they are also notorious agents of miscarriage, stillbirth, and various childbirth complications. Revenge is a dish relished cold here, since, as the MBh's treatise on demonology clearly states, these *jātahāriṇīs* ("Child Abductresses," "Female Baby Snatchers") are often cast as the ravening spirits of women who had died in childbirth in a previous life. Denied their biological destiny of maternity, they now feel authorized to abduct, kill, and eat the babies of living human mothers.[100] Unlike the European fairies, these are Mothers with no offspring of their own to exchange, and so their vengeance results in the death of their tiny human victims, either in their biological mothers' wombs or shortly after birth.

In South Asia, there are two principal strategies for combating the *jātahāriṇīs*, strategies that we may call the "carrot" and "stick" approaches. In the first of these, when worshiped, these dread beings quickly become the guardians of the very infants that had been their erstwhile victims. This too is addressed in the MBh's demonological chapters. When the "Mothers of the World" petition the child-god Skanda to grant them leave to eat human babies, he assents with the caveat that "when you are well honored . . . protect the children."[101] The most notorious of all the baby snatchers of South Asia was the Buddhist "Queen of the Yakṣas," Hāritī, whose name may also be translated as the "Abductress." According to a well-known legend, a woman quite advanced in pregnancy was forced to dance at a festive gathering, aborting the fetus she was carrying. Reborn as a vengeful yakṣī named Abhiratī, she became notorious for devouring hundreds of infant children. However, once converted by the Buddha, she became a renowned guardian of infants, and so has been represented across Buddhist Asia with babes in her arms and lap, on her hips and at her feet (fig. 4.16). Here, a Kushan-period Gandharan sculpture of Hāritī from Yusufzai in northeastern Pakistan may be viewed as a case study in Silk Road dæmonological cosmopolitanism. In a recent article, Naman Ahuja has shown that the iconography of the eight children sculpted together with that goddess represents no fewer than five distinct religious traditions: "the Ptolemaic world of Egypt, Phoenician Lebanon or Cyprus, Zoroastrian Iran, Hellenistic Greece, Hindu India, and . . . Buddhism." On the basis of their distinctive hairstyles, clothing, and other significant features, Ahuja has identified these children as the Buddhist Priyaṃkara, the Egyptian Harpocrates (son of Isis), Kārttikeya (son of Śiva), the Greek Dioscuri, a "Phoenician temple boy," as well as, perhaps, the avestan Ameretat and Haurvatat (fig. 4.17).[102] Hāritī is also represented in an auspicious, protective mode on a seventh-century mural from Khotan in Chinese Turkestan that will be discussed at the beginning of chapter 6.[103] Her ambiguous status, as a supernatural being both protective and destructive of human life, is of a piece

FIGURE 4.16. Hāritī, Candi Mendut, Java, Indonesia, ninth century CE.

with that of yakṣīs in general, as also attested in the mythology of a yakkhī/devatā named Kuvaṇṇā, who was a man-eater before becoming the superhuman lover and mother of the children of a prince named Vijaya. Their story will be told in the next chapter.

Another Child Abductress is cast in a decisive role in the birth of a king named Jarāsandha. A story from the MBh tells how the future king, through a piece of magic gone awry, has been born in two halves from the wombs of two queens. Exposed outside the royal palace, the two semi-babies are snatched up by a Child Abductress named Jarā ("Decrepitude"), the better to eat them. In order to heft the two little monsters more easily, she fuses the halves into one, and so the infant is named Jarāsandha, "Fused by Jarā." The newborn prince, now a complete human, is recovered by the king, to whom the demoness addresses the following soliloquy: "I am a Female Guardian (*rākṣasī*) who dwells eternally in every human home. 'House-Goddess' (*gṛhadevī*) is my name. Verily, I was created by the Self-Generated [god Śiva]. Possessed of a divine form, I have been established [here] for the destruction of demons. Prosperity dwells in the home of him who draws on the wall [of his house an image of] me and my son, accompanied by [his entourage of demonic] Youths. Otherwise, he suffers loss. Dwelling in your house, my Lord, I am worshiped perpetually."[104]

Some of the data included in Jarā's speech are also evocative of the common modern-day South Asian assumption that spirits of the dead, including children, often do not depart to the world of the ancestors but rather take up residence as household deities in their former homes. These potentially

FIGURE 4.17. Hārītī, Yusufzai, Pakistan, second/third century CE. Photo by John C. Huntington, courtesy of the John C. and Susan L. Huntington Photographic Archive of Buddhist and Asian Art.

malevolent bairns impose their whims on their families, which in their case are satisfied through feeding and coddling, in return for which they provide advice and grant blessings.[105] Interestingly, in southern Rajasthan, such children are referred to as *pattar*, the cognate of *pitṛ*, the blanket Sanskrit term for "forefather" or "adult ancestor." As Ann Grodzins Gold explains, according to widespread Hindu understandings of reincarnation, great-grandfathers reincarnate as great-grandsons. This being the case, there is an identity between ancestors and the lingering spirits of the juvenile dead.[106] A similar dynamic appears to be at play in coastal Andhra Pradesh, where the spirits of children and young adults who have died premature deaths are called *vīrulu* (heroes), a term generally reserved for the spirits of adult warriors who died gloriously in battle. Deified beings of limited power, these young dead "heroes" return to haunt their families, which they only harm if they are not offered the respect they feel to be their due.[107]

We may compare this relationship—between human parents and household deities that either protect or abduct the children born there or else *are* the spirits of children previously born there—with a motif found in a number of western European changeling narratives.[108] In a nineteenth-century account from upper Brittany, when a woman discovers that her child has been replaced by a changeling (*faiteau*), she cries out "Nasty little witch, I'm gonna kill you!" *But the fairy who was in the attic* called to her, "Don't kill mine and I'll bring yours back, don't kill mine and I'll bring yours back!"[109] Here, once again, fairies are understood to be the mothers of changelings, who are none other than fairy infants.[110] As for the fairies themselves, many specialists of medieval literature and modern folklore concur that the fairies that seduced and spirited away errant knights of courtly romance were none other than the ancestral dead of pagan Europe. Fairyland was a survival, a memory of pre-Christian worlds of the dead, with fairies playing the role of psychopomps and spirit beings.[111] As such, abduction by alluring fairy maidens was tantamount to a temporary or permanent relocation to the world of the dead.[112] As we have seen, these characterizations ran counter to Church doctrine.

In his exhaustive study of western European changeling traditions, Jean-Paul Doulet has drawn similar conclusions, bringing to light the popular links between changelings and the spirits of unbaptized dead children.[113] Yet, as is the case in India, these infant dead also end up melting into the faceless throng of the ancestral dead, including spirits who have long been dead. We see this in a leitmotiv of European changeling narratives, which describe the changeling as a ravenous yet sickly infant with the wrinkled and decrepit features of a centenarian. Congenitally mute, the changeling is made to abruptly reveal its greatly advanced age through a subterfuge on the part of the abducted infant's mother.[114] This motif has the woman of the house setting about to boiling water using eggshells as cooking pots, brewing beer in nutshells, or engaging in some other absurd form of cuisine. Nonplussed at such an incongruous sight, the changeling utters a stock phrase, which recurs in hundreds of local and regional variants, as exemplified in a nineteenth-century folktale from Picardy: "I may be a shade over nine hundred years old, but I've never seen so many little pots!" Following which, the changeling-fairy returns the mother's biological child to its place in the cradle.[115]

As has been noted, Christian clerics who knew their classics explained *fata*, the Latin word for the fairies, in terms of the goddesses known as the Fates of Greco-Roman mythology.[116] However, another set of beings from that same mythological tradition would come to have a greater impact on the medieval imagination. These were the nymphs, seductive denizens of sylvan pools and streams similar in so many ways to the yakṣīs of Indic mythology. While "fairy lovers" (*fées amantes*) were a staple of courtly romance literature,[117] it was another sort of medieval fairy, which Doulet has termed the "obstetric fairy," that is most relevant here.[118] In both the pagan world and the *imaginaire* of medieval romance, the birth of a child was attended by two sets of fairies, the "womb fairies" (*fées ventrières*) that assisted or interfered in childbirth and the "fairy godmothers" (*fées marraines*) that determined the newborn's future.[119] Heiresses to both the Matronae—ancient mother goddesses known throughout the medieval West—and the Greco-Roman Parcæ and Fates,[120] these intervened at two levels, both aiding infants to come into the world and endowing them with whatever qualities they chose, both negative and positive. In return for these gifts, they expected the newborn's parents to offer them a feast—but woe to those who would disrespect them in any way, however slight, for these petulant goddesses were notorious for avenging themselves on the child, afflicting it with defects that it would carry to its (often early) grave. This theme, attested in medieval literature as early as the fourteenth century, remained a fixture of western European folklore down into the last century.[121] The resemblances between the Matronae and "womb fairies" of western Europe and the Mothers, Child Abductresses, and yakṣīs of South Asia are worth noting: both groups determined the life or death of infants coming into the world, and both could be moved to clemency when venerated and propitiated with a tribute offering or "feast."

5

As we have seen, the prototype of the Guinefort legend was a tale first attested in an Indian work, Viṣṇuśarman's third-century CE *Pañcatantra*. Also found in India are the three components or sequences of the changeling ritual as described by Stephen of Bourbon, with some dating from before the time of the *Pañcatantra* and others observed in modern-day Rajasthan and Maharashtra, states situated in the western part of the subcontinent. In the light of what follows, however, we must ask whether the three principal sequences of the French changeling ritual were not three *independent* practices, brought together by the "old woman" and peasants in a piece of ritual *bricolage*, or by Stephen of Bourbon himself in his inquisitor's report.

A moment ago, I identified a medieval myth of the young cowherd Kṛṣṇa as an appropriation of ancient yakṣa traditions. Another Hindu god, closely identified with Śiva, also bears the stamp of the yakṣa cults. This is Bhairava, who is the object of a number of rituals that recall those surrounding Saint Guinefort and the fairies of western Europe. Nowhere in South Asia does one encounter Bhairava with such frequency as in Rajasthan, a religiously conservative state where many traditions that have long since disappeared from much of the subcontinent have persisted down to the present day. As I discussed at length in chapter 2, multitudes of Bherūṃ-jīs are found in virtually every village, town, and urban neighborhood of Rajasthan. Most often worshiped as a stone or group of stones at the base of a tree, their usually aniconic images are also found in dwellings, alongside step-wells, on street corners, and in wayside shrines. In this, they carry forward the legacy of the yakṣas/devatās, whose shrines were located both in the wilds and at the crossroads of villages, towns, and marketplaces.[122]

A

In an 1861 article, the Irish antiquarian William Hackett made the following comparative observation:

> Various minor charms and superstitions of our [Irish] peasantry have their counterparts, if not prototypes, in India. As to the religious rites which are identical with those of India, one is, that of affixing rags to trees at holy wells. This is generally regarded in the light of votive offering, but it is of a character altogether different. We read of a Hindoo Rajah performing his devotions, on the occasion of a pilgrimage to a celebrated temple, which he enriched with a variety of offerings of diamonds, and other valuable treasures: one of his gifts being a golden statue of a cow of full size, all solid. Having performed all the ceremonies and rites, he ended his devotions by attaching a *rag* to an adjacent tree. The intent with which this is done in India, is identical with the notions of our peasantry, namely, that all spiritual and corporeal ailments of the votaries are deposited in the rag. The words used on such occasions by the Irish votary clearly express this object: *Air impidh an Tiarna, mo chuid tinnis do fhiagint air an àit so*: that is to say, "invoking the Lord, my ailments are deposited in this place."

In a footnote to this passage, Hackett indicates that he had come across this description in *Asiatic Researches*, that venerable flagship serial of British

Orientalism, without referencing the specific volume of that journal. As for the Hindoo Rajah's intent, he says he relied on "the statement of a non-commissioned officer, for many years employed in India as a writer."[123] While Hackett's mystery source's explanation for the aim of the practice will be nuanced in the pages that follow, a royal connection may be adduced at Mandore, the site of the ancient capital of the once-powerful Rathore dynasty of western Rajasthan. Here, in the old palace's park-like setting, one finds several royal cenotaphs as well as an eighteenth-century "Hall of Heroes" flanking the shrines of five gods that include Black and White Bherūṃ-jī. When I visited the site in March of 1999 there was a small *sāl* (*Shorea robusta*) tree that, set into an adjacent masonry plaza, was marked by a painted sign identifying it as "Bherūṃ-jī's Sāl Tree" (plate 20). Hanging from the branches of that tree were a profusion of infants' garments and swaddling clothes offered by women petitioning the god for the birth of children. According to Buddhist tradition, the *sāl* is revered as the tree to which Māyāvatī, the future Buddha's mother, clung when she gave birth to the holy child. Ancient and medieval images of this Buddhist Madonna clinging to her *sāl* are virtually indistinguishable from those of the yakṣīs (plate 21; see also above fig. 4.12), and so we may see in "Bherūṃ-jī's Sāl Tree" the persistence of an ancient association between tree dæmons, childbirth, and this particular tree.[124]

Now, the *sāl* is a tree that grows to great heights in the semi-tropical, sub-Himalayan regions of India and Nepal that are its natural habitat, but here in the Rajasthani desert, "Bherūṃ-jī's Sāl Tree" was, in 1999, a mere ten feet in height. When my Rajasthani colleague Bhoju Ram Gujar visited the site in July of 2016, the tree was all but dead, with a single piece of cloth hanging from a withered lower bough. A pile of baby clothes, lying in the corner of the masonry plaza behind it, had the look of a rubbish heap. No doubt the practice will die out shortly at the site, with the inevitable demise of the tree. However, cognate practices continue to be observed throughout the region at other of the god's Rajasthani shrines, including that of Baḍalī ka Bherūṃ-jī, already visited in chapter 2, where lengths of cloth, rope, and thread are offered for the healing of ailing children;[125] and the shrine of Khulkhulya Bherūṃ-jī, where the clothing of children suffering from chronic cough are offered to the god on the branches of the thorny *vilāyatī babūl* (*Prosopis juliflora*) bush (figs. 4.18 and 4.19).[126] In Kathmandu, a pipal (*Ficus religiosa*) tree adjacent to the shrine of Pacali Bhairab is also hung with the clothing of sickly children. There I was informed that that tree, inhabited by the dire goddess Alakṣmī, was petitioned to transmit its vital sap and energy to the child. Offertory practices at this arboreal shrine are virtually identical both to those portrayed in Buddhist sculpture from the beginning of the Common Era (plate 22, fig. 4.20)

FIGURE 4.18. Votive cloth offerings, Baḍalī ka Bherūṃ-jī, Barali, Rajasthan. Photo by author.

and to those documented in medieval western Europe. So too are the roles played by the healing saints of the European shrines and the Indian *bhūtanāthas*, with both communicating their power through the shoots and branches of their trees. Khulkhulya Bherūṃ-jī's shrine is situated on the outskirts of Shahpura (Bhilwara District, Rajasthan), a town some thirty miles southwest of Ghatiyali, the scene of the "filthy phylacteries" rituals discussed in chapter 2. As was also noted in that chapter, Ghatiyali is home to well over a dozen Bherūṃ-jī shrines, and it is in the proximity of one of these that another, far more elaborate set of practices evocative of European changeling traditions is regularly performed.

B

While the actors involved in the European changeling rituals were human and fairy mothers, the site of their transaction, that is, the ritual support for the exchange of infants, was invariably the cradle. The human infant, stolen from its cradle and replaced with a changeling, was—if all went well—restored to the same cradle (or onto straw from the cradle on the forest floor) by its fairy abductors. In a small number of changeling narratives, including that concerning Saint Stephen,[127] the Devil would leave a simulacrum of the abductee, most often in the form of a log, wax figure, bundle of straw, or roughly hewn block of wood. While it was most often the infant itself that was replaced by the

FIGURE 4.19. Votive cloth offerings, Khulkhulya Bherūṃ-jī, Shahpura, Rajasthan. Image courtesy of Bhoju Ram Gujar.

simulacrum, the abductees could also be young or mature women carried off for the purpose of childrearing in the fairies' world. In these cases, the otherworldly fairies were sometimes conflated with demonesses, or with the witches with whom these came to be associated during Europe's early modern witch craze.[128]

PLATE 1. Śītalā, bronze, Bengal via Urgench (Turkmenistan), ca. 1200 CE. Musée des Arts Asiatiques-Guimet, Paris. Image © RMN Grand Palais / Art Resource, NY. Photo by Thierry Olivier.

PLATE 2. Angel and demon, Angers Apocalypse, late fourteenth century. Image © Antoine Ruais / Centre des Monuments Nationaux.

PLATE 3. Christ exorcising a demon, *Les Très Riches Heures du Duc de Berry*, France, fifteenth century. Très Grandes Heures, fol. 166r.

PLATE 4. Al-Hârith departs with an Indian crew for an Indian Ocean voyage, Iraq, 1237. Bibliothèque Nationale de France, Département des Manuscrits arabes 5847, f. 119v.

PLATE 5. Black and White Bherūṃ-jī, Līlāḍ Temple, Ghatiyali, Rajasthan. Photo by author.

PLATE 6. Baḍalī ka Bherūṃ-jī, Barali, Rajasthan. Photo by author.

PLATE 7. *Mail*-smearing rite, Līlāḍ Temple, Ghatiyali, Rajasthan. Photo by author.

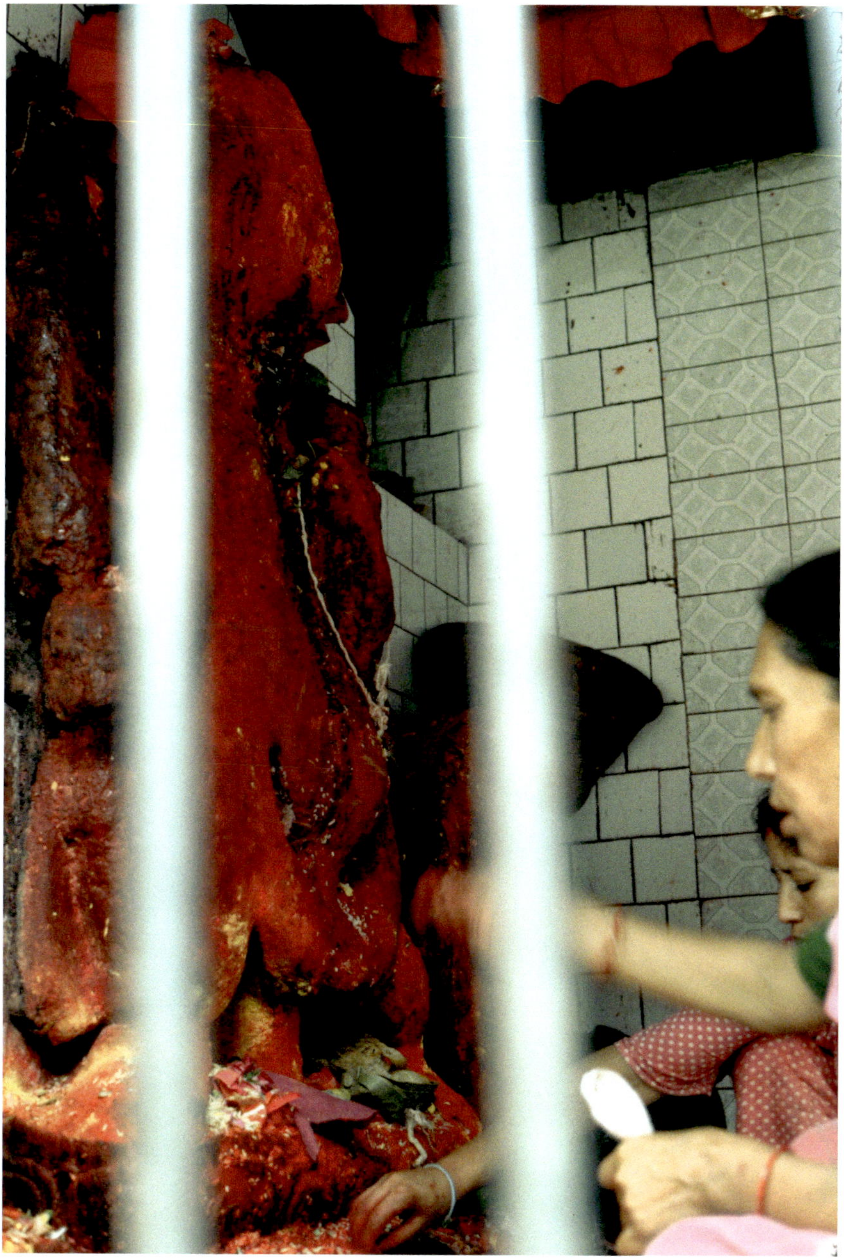

PLATE 8. Collection of *mail*, Ānand Bhairab, Gyaneshwor-Mahādev Temple, Kathmandu. Photo by author.

PLATE 9. Catoptromancy, Byzantine, fifteenth century. University of Bologna, MSS 3632, fol. 348v.

PLATE 10. Lecanomancy, Byzantine, fifteenth century. University of Bologna, MSS 3632, fol. 349r.

PLATE 11. Saint Stephen suckled by white doe, Martino di Bartolomeo, ca. 1425 CE. Image © Städel Museum—U. Edelmann—ARTOTHEK.

PLATE 12. Sources de Moncaut, Losse, Landes, France. Photo by author.

PLATE 13. Chapelle de Saint Claude, Senarpont, Picardy, France. Photo by author.

PLATE 14. Fontaine Saint Girons, Suzan, Landes, France. Photo by author.

PLATE 15. Saint Amandus and blind woman at pagan tree shrine, eleventh/twelfth century CE, Valenciennes, France. Médiathèque Simone Veil de Valenciennes, MSS 0502, fol. 27.

PLATE 16. Saint Amandus orders destruction of pagan tree shrine, eleventh/twelfth century CE, Valenciennes, France. Médiathèque Simone Veil de Valenciennes, MSS 0500 (459bis), fol. 66v.

PLATE 17. Yakṣas, Mogao Caves, Dunhuang, Gansu, China, 220–578 CE. Image courtesy of Dunhuang Academy.

PLATE 18. Kṛṣṇa steals the *gopīs*' clothes, Tira-Sujanpur, Himachal Pradesh, early eighteenth century. Image courtesy of Government Museum and Art Gallery, Chandigarh, India.

PLATE 19. Human sacrifice to tree yakkhiṇī, Degaldoruva, Sri Lanka, late eighteenth century. Image courtesy of the Archaeological Survey of Sri Lanka.

PLATE 20. Bherūṃ-jī kā Sāl, Mandor, Rajasthan. Photo by author.

PLATE 21. Birth of the Buddha. Folio from a Prajñaparamitā manuscript, Bihar, India, ca. 1150 CE. Image courtesy of the Regents of the University of Michigan, Department of the History of Art, Visual Resources Collections.

PLATE 22. Tree worship, Pacali Bhairab, Kathmandu. Photo by author.

PLATE 23. Pālanā suspended in *nīm* tree, Puvalī kā Devjī Temple, Ghatiyali, Rajasthan. Photo by author.

PLATE 24. Coconuts in swaddling clothes on Puvalī kā Devjī altar, Ghatiyali, Rajasthan. Image courtesy of Bhoju Ram Gujar.

PLATES 25A AND 25B. Raft *pālanā*, Maharashtra. Images courtesy of Anne Feldhaus.

PLATE 26. Equestrian maiden pursued by mercury, Mughal, eighteenth century. Image courtesy of Ludwig Habighorst.

PLATE 27. Shrine of Hiṅglāj Devī, Lasbela, Pakistan. Photo by Billmirza at English Wikipedia. Reproduction permitted under terms of the GNU Free Documentation License.

PLATE 28. Chandrakup, Lasbela, Pakistan. Courtesy of Getty Images.

PLATE 29. Chandrakup crater, Lasbela, Pakistan. Courtesy of Getty Images.

In a group of modern-day western Indian rituals, the simulacrum that is brought into play is a coconut, with two important differences: rather than a newborn child, it represents an unborn fetus; and rather than being deposited by spirit beings, it is manipulated by the infant's human parents. The logic behind these Indian practices is, however, identical to that underlying the changeling rites: just as a cradle can only be occupied by one infant at a time, so too, a woman's womb can only be occupied by one fetus at a time.[129] In the western European case, the changeling has to be removed before the human child can be restored to the cradle; likewise, in India, the spirit being abusively occupying the womb must be evicted before a viable human embryo can be implanted there. However, whereas in the case documented by

FIGURE 4.20. Tree worship, Bharhut, Madhya Pradesh, 100–80 BCE. Photo by John C. Huntington, courtesy of the John C. and Susan L. Huntington Photographic Archive of Buddhist and Asian Art.

Stephen of Bourbon, the rites performed on the soil covering the remains of the martyred Saint Guinefort rescued human infants from their fairy abductors, in India the performative nature of the rites takes on a different aspect.

In rural Rajasthan, a common reason for newlyweds to visit the shrine of local deities like Bherūṃ-jī is the bride's failure to bear viable children. Childlessness is generally ascribed to the workings of a malevolent household dæmon, often a recently deceased family member. Homologues of the house-dwelling fairies of western Europe, these often turn against their own out of vengeance, for having been denied the proper respect they consider to be their due. Recall here Skanda's admonition to the "Mothers of the World" in the epic narrative mentioned earlier: they are only permitted to devour the children of those who fail to honor them. Several ethnographies attest to just such a scenario as emic explanations for the cults of household tutelary deities. These are the spirits of deceased family members whose worship cult was initiated only after they had displayed their pique, often by possessing a young bride and preventing her from giving birth.[130] Appeased by the new attention they receive—the "carrot approach" once again—they cease and desist.[131]

When, however, a child is born through the intervention of a local deity like Bherūṃ-jī, who in his role as *bhūtanātha* drives away the noxious spirit being blocking conception (the "stick approach"), its birth is considered a blessing from the god, who then receives a defined set of offerings, which are hung from trees in baskets called "cradles" outside his shrine.[132] Rajasthani Muslims engage in similar practices: when childbirth "petitions" (*mannats*)[133] are answered by Thakur Baba, the baby born through the god's intervention is brought to his shrine and placed in a cradle there for the first time, in a rite called *pāl*[*a*]*nā*.[134] Thereafter, the child is said to belong to the god, rather than to its biological parents.[135] Often, the child will also be named after the god who gave it life: this was the case in the epic tale of Jarāsandha; and according to the fifth-century BCE grammarian Pāṇini, children were named after yakṣas for similar reasons.[136] In like manner, at the conclusion of his abduction story, the infant recovered by Pope Sixtus II is named Lawrence after the laurel tree that yielded him up; and one cannot help but see in this episode's depiction on the Undløse church's ceiling the image of a now benevolent faun of the forest returning the swaddled infant to the world of men (see above, fig. 4.4).

In the spring of 1999, I photographed a *nīm* (*Azadirachta indica*) tree hung with basket "cradles" (*pālanās*) in the courtyard of the Puvalī kā Devjī shrine in Ghatiyali (plate 23), which I had been urged to visit by Gold, who, in her classic ethnographic study of that village, noted that

> a common sight at many of Rajasthan's local shrines is clusters of wide straw baskets hanging from tree branches or rooftops.[137] Some appear new; others are weathered by wind, sun, and rain to various stages of disintegration. These baskets, called *pālanā*, or "cradles," are placed there as thank-offerings from pilgrims who have received the boon of a living child's birth. Each basket thus stands for a child born, and a shrine with ample quantities of these baskets on display possesses indisputable testimony of its power to grant fertility.[138]

It will be recalled here that according to his hagiographers, Saint Lawrence was discovered by Sixtus II hanging in a basket (*sporta*) in the branches of his laurel tree. That such hanging baskets were the "cradles" of fairies is also attested in a story recorded by G. F. Abbott at Melenik (northeastern Macedonia) at the turn of the twentieth century. In it, a young prince fathers a child on a sylvan nymph (*yougovitsas*), who hangs its cradle from a tree in her garden.[139] The typical Indian cradle is of the same type: the child lies in a basket cum hammock, which is suspended by a rope from a tripod or a tree branch (fig. 4.21).

In rural Rajasthan, the principal offerings placed in its hanging thanksgiving "cradles" are coconuts swaddled in bolts of red and white cloth. I have already discussed the place and symbolism of cloth in these contexts. What of the coconuts? At these same Rajasthani shrines, coconuts are associated with Bherūṃ-jī in a rite called "pouch-filling" (*jholī bharnā*) through which the process of childbirth is symbolically enacted. Young brides are the principal actors in this ritual, in which they petition the god to grant them viable (male) offspring. In the Indo-Aryan languages, the term employed here for "pouch," *jholī*, also stands as the most common synonym for *pālanā* ("cradle"). Gold's account of the rite, which takes place at the Puvalī kā Devjī shrine of Devnārāyaṇ, the tutelary deity of Ghatiyali village, bears quoting in full:

> The deity (that is, the priest possessed by Devjī's [i.e., Devnārāyaṇ's] agent Bherūṃ-jī) tells his petitioner to bring the "pouch ingredients" on a specified date. . . . When the day arrives, the woman and her accompanying kin present themselves at the shrine, bringing the specified items. . . . They also bring two coconuts and lengths of red and white cloth. One coconut, swaddled in the red cloth, is placed prominently on the shrine's platform (plate 24). The woman desiring a child [has her] customary wrap . . . arranged in a special fashion so that a secure "pouch" [*jholī*] is formed in the front. When her turn comes to stand before the god, the red-clothed coconut is caused to "bow" before the icons just as the infant will be on his first visit if the outcome is successful. Then . . . the priest places the coconut in the pilgrim woman's prepared pouch. Obviously this is a gesture of impregnation, the coconut representing the child-to-be, and the red cloth evoking the blood of birth as well as the

FIGURE 4.21. Typical Rajasthani hanging cradle. Photo by Ann Grodzins Gold.

> vigor of life. Rather than presaging the perilous embryonic state, the coconut seems to stand for the fully developed and safely birthed baby. One evidence for this is the bowing routine; another is that the same coconut, carefully preserved, returns to the shrine in the cradle-basket [*pālanā*] hung as a postpartum thank-offering. . . . Shortly after the birth . . . the cradle-basket is hung and the infant is made to give its first obeisance to the deity who should now be its lifelong protector.[140]

Derived from the verbal root √*jhūl*, "to swing, hang, be suspended," the Hindi *jholī* ("pouch," "small sack") is related to a complex of Indo-Aryan terms, including the Sanskrit *jhaulikā* ("small bag"); *jhoḷī* ("a skirt used as a bag; the lap") in the western Punjabi Lahndā dialect; *jholī* ("nest of eggs") in Sindhi; as well as *jholuṅgo* ("swinging cradle") in Nepali.[141] These philological data confirm the logic of the ritual: through the intervention of the deity, a healthy child (coconut) is safely placed in a woman's womb (pouch/lap/nest/cradle) that had previously been blocked or occupied by spirit beings. After the woman has given birth, the healthy child is presented to the deity beneath the tree in which the coconut (simulacrum of the child), wrapped in red (the blood of childbirth) and white cloth (its swaddling clothes), will later be suspended in its basket-cradle, in a gesture of thanksgiving.

Here, it bears noting that unlike the European practices analyzed by Schmitt, these Indian rituals involve an offering in two phases: first, at the time when the local deity is petitioned, and, following the successful outcome of the rite, to show "thanksgiving."[142] As such, the coconut hung in the basket-cradle is the double of the first swaddled coconut, which had been deposited directly before the image of Devnārāyaṇ at the beginning of the rite. It may be just such a basket that is figured on the left half of the first-century CE Mathura bas-relief discussed earlier in this chapter (fig. 4.10). Here, the gnome-like figures facing the human donor of the basket may be viewed as the local devatās of the tree-shrine, devatās represented in a similar way on first century BCE panels from the Buddhist archeological site of Kanganhalli in eastern Karnataka. One of these is a portrayal of Māyāvatī's presentation of the infant Buddha to a tree devatā, which also features a dwarfish female figure identified by Sonya Rhie Mace as a local "representative of the procreative forces of nature that result in the bearing of children." Another panel shows several squat male figures, "chthonic forces in human form," in the company of a throng of animal-headed devatās, human devotees, assorted wild beasts of the forest, and a tree yakṣa (far lower right) (fig. 4.22).[143]

A variant on the pouch-filling ritual, observed at the western Rajasthani pilgrimage site of Ramdevra, adds a further touch of the miraculous. There, "the candidate for pouch-filling sits by the shore of the lake on the temple grounds. The priest tosses her coconut into the lake. The coconut then, witnesses state, bounces back 'of its own accord' into the woman's pouch—if she is destined to bear a child." As Gold further notes, "in some cases pouch-filling may be accompanied by exorcism. As one informant described an incident witnessed at Ramdevra, it appears that there is no room within the female pilgrim for the auspicious coconut-child and the destructive 'ghost.' One comes in and the other, raucously admitting defeat, departs."[144] These Rajasthani data evoke certain details of western European changeling rites, narratives, and ritual logic in ways that I will summarize at the end of this chapter. However, the two traditions differ radically on this essential point: whereas in Europe the recovery of the abducted infant occurs post-partum, in Rajasthan the child is symbolically restored in the womb itself. A similar

FIGURE 4.22. Wild forest scene with devatās, Kanganhalli, Karnataka. Photo courtesy of Christian Luczanits.

cleavage obtains in the custom of passing the afflicted person through a hole in a tree. At Saint Guinefort's shrine and elsewhere in Europe, it was sickly children who were subject to this practice. However, in the western state of Gujarat, which shares a border with both Rajasthan and Maharashtra, it is childless women who undergo the rite, in order to rid them of the spirit being (*pey*) that is the cause of their failure to conceive.[145]

C

Although the cloth-wrapped coconuts of the pouch-filling rites—coconuts that later reappear in votive hanging basket "cradles"—unambiguously represent the embryo of the child that will be born through the intervention of a *bhūtanātha*, these Rajasthani practices cannot be neatly analogized with the European changeling rituals in which a real or imagined exchange of infants is operative. In interior Maharashtra, however, there exists a rite in which just such an exchange occurs. Here, it is living infants who may be removed from their cradles—and, if all goes well, returned to their parents—by dæmons; however, the exchange takes place not in or beneath trees, but rather in riverine pools. These traditions, documented by Anne Feldhaus, revolve around a grouping of river goddesses among which a heptad of fearsome female spirit deities called the Sātī Āsarā predominates. Their collective name may be read as a vernacular form of the Sanskrit *sapta apsarasa*, the "Seven Water Nymphs"; however, this etymology is unknown to the people who perform this rite.[146] The members of this group are far more ferocious and malign than the ancestral spirits that block the wombs of young Rajasthani brides. More akin to the Mothers, Female Seizers, and their ilk, these occupy a higher rung in the South Asian pandemonium, even if the two distinct types of malevolent beings are sometimes conflated.[147]

Here, the rite is performed in order to prevent or counter the abduction of children by these malevolent female beings that, following patterns found throughout South Asia since at least the time of the NT, prey upon nubile and vulnerable young women. A menstruating young woman wandering alone in proximity to their haunts during the heat of the day is nearly certain to be "caught" by them. Once possessed, she is either unable to bring her pregnancy to term, or incapable of providing sufficient milk to her sickly newborns, who die prematurely.[148] In interior Maharashtra, people who drown in riverine pools are often said to have been pulled down by the Sātī Āsarā into their underwater "temples." In the rare cases in which the drowning victim reappears several days later, the assumption is that the same Sātī Āsarā have returned that person to life.[149]

As in rural Rajasthan, a number of preventative measures may be taken to ensure protection from these Child Abductresses. One of these is a pouch-filling rite, here called *oṭī bharaṇeṃ*, which is identical to the Rajasthani *jholī bharnā*, the sole difference between the two being the venue: rather than beneath a tree, the ceremony takes place on the shore of a river in flood, understood to be the dwelling if not the body of a river goddesses herself, with the coconut and other offerings being cast directly into her waters.[150] One encounters the same polysemy here as with the Rajasthani *jholī*, with *oṭī* denoting "lap," and the expression "let my lap be filled" meaning "let me become pregnant." Such requests are generally made in the context of what in Marathi is called a *navas*—a vow or petition according to which a person binds herself "to make a particular offering or perform a particular ritual if some specific desired goal or object is achieved." The analogue of the Rajasthani *mannat*, the goal or object of the *navas* is the birth or viability and welfare of children.[151]

The riverine goddesses addressed in the *navas* tend to be Āsarās of regional renown, which Feldhaus identifies as "full fledged folk goddesses of rivers" or "exceptional Āsarās."[152] In contrast, women tend not to offer *navas* to the dread Sātī Āsarā, but more commonly attempt to placate them in other ways in order to prevent them from abducting their children outright.[153] A number of physically and psychologically demanding rites are observed at the shrines of both local and "exceptional" (i.e., regional) Āsarās, of which one stands out for its resemblance to the third ritual sequence reported by Stephen of Bourbon for Saint Guinefort's shrine. This rite—which involves babies either born in fulfillment of a *navas*, children belonging to a caste group for which a given Āsarā is the family deity (*kuḷdaivat*), or in some cases the child population of an entire village—brings both cradles (*pālaṇā*s) and baskets (*paraḍī*s) into play.[154] As Feldhaus describes it,

> In this kind of rite, the child is floated on a raft—a *pālaṇā* (cradle) or *par*[*a*]*ḍī* (basket)—in the water near the goddess's shrine. . . . One or more children are placed on the raft, which is already floating on the water, and one or more adults move the raft around in the water (plates 25a–b). . . . At some places where children are floated on a raft, it is said that the raft used to circle around in the water and then come back to shore on its own. . . . The rite of floating babies and children on a raft seems to be a kind of attenuated or mimic sacrifice. The fact that . . . the child's clothes are removed and thrown into the water adds to this impression. . . . The clothes seem to represent the child, who is placed *on* the water when the clothes are thrown *into* it. . . . The babies and children who are floated on the rafts are thereby offered to the goddess. Although their parents do get them back, the parents must nevertheless first give them up, surrendering them to the goddess in the form of the water of her river. A frequent motif in the lore about floating babies and children in the water is that the child's parents must not become frightened. . . . The children who are floated on the raft are thereby being entrusted to the goddess, being put under her protection and care, but also into her power.[155]

In one account of such a ritual gone awry, a woman—who due to fear had lost her raft-borne child—made a second vow, saying: "'If I get another son, I will float him on the raft again.' So in two years' time, the woman got another son, and again he was floated on the raft. But this time, even after he began to be floated, the woman did not get worried that way. After the raft had circled around five times, it came back to the bank. In it were the first child and this child—the woman got [back] both children."[156] One of Feldhaus's informants recounted a dream she had had during pregnancy concerning a son who had died shortly after childbirth. Involving a group of Āsarā she called the "Mothers of Children,"[157] her dream is eerily evocative of European changeling narratives: When she was pregnant with her fourth child, a son, she dreamed about the Āsarā. "'I saw water,' she said. 'Water like this. And in the water there was a nice cradle, and in that cradle a child was lying. I would try to take him, and she [an Āsarā] would take him from the other side. I would go to take him, and she would take him over there. A second one took him over there, and a third one took him over there.'"[158] "Over there" is of course, the world of the dead, of dead babies carried off by spirit-world Mothers, with the cradle representing the protected yet contested space within the domestic sphere and a woman's body where infants are subject to abduction. In a zero-sum game in which "there is no room within the female pilgrim [or cradle] for the auspicious coconut-child and the destructive 'ghost,'" the recovery of the one requires the ouster of the other. As is the case in western Europe, these western Indian rituals of exchange are the means to that end.

6

We have seen that the folktale that was adapted into the martyrdom account of the French greyhound Saint Guinefort was first recorded in an ancient Sanskrit anthology, the *Pañcatantra*, which was successively translated in the thousand years that followed into Pahlavi, Hebrew, Arabic, Latin, and French. However, these were but the written versions of the folktale, which is also attested in numerous oral traditions. Here, it is important to note that there is no intrinsic connection whatsoever between that narrative and the ritual practices at Guinefort's shrine as reported by Stephen of Bourbon in the thirteenth century, and that nowhere else in the world is the folktale type of a "dog defend[ing its] master's child against [an] animal assailant" linked to any sort of ritual complex. Since their inception, tracing networks of influence and exchange among narrative tales has been the primary concern of the disciplines of comparative mythology and folklore studies. Can the same be done for ritual? This is what I suggested in the previous two chapters. However, in chapter 2 the purview of the network was limited to modern-day South Asia, principally Rajasthan and Nepal, with shared textual traditions and the movements of yogis serving as the hypothetical connective tissue between those regions. In chapter 3, the "Silk

Road" was the tangible link that made my claims concerning the connected histories of the evil eye, mirror divination, and demonological devices plausible. In the present case, not only has the range been greatly expanded, but also, in contrast to the dissemination of the canine "Guinefort" folktale, no intermediary witnesses to the three ritual sequences can be found outside of western Europe and western India. Yet, the parallels between the data collected at those two extremities of the Indo-European cultural area are compelling. I review them here. Terms denoting the site of contestation/exchange are given in **bold**; terms denoting the shrine or haunt of the tutelary deity or dæmon ensuring the efficacy of the ritual exchange are underlined; terms denoting transitional ritual objects through which that supernatural being's power or charisma is transferred are given in *italics*.

The European and Indic rites have the same underlying logic. The site of contestation/exchange, the liminal zone of intersection between two worlds, is the **womb** or **cradle**, which is homologized with a **basket** or **pouch**. Only one infant can occupy the site of contestation at a time, which is why the nonhuman infant must be evicted so that the human infant can recover its rightful place. A local deity or dæmon inhabiting a tree or body of water makes the exchange effective, its power being transmitted through transitional ritual objects (*swaddling clothes*, *straw* from the **cradle**, articles of *clothing*) that are placed in contact with the natural elements (spring water, river water, tree, shrub, soil) of his or her shrine. The ritual scenario, tabulated in table 4.1, is comprised of the following elements: (1) An infant is abducted (2) from its **cradle**/mother's **womb**, either directly (changeling, miscarriage) or by inference (death of a sickly child), (3) by a faun, an ancestral spirit, or a malign demon(ess), (4) who replaces it with an alien being: a child of its own type, a simulacrum, or the abductor itself. (5) Sometimes, the abductor lives in the house of the abducted infant. (6) The abducted child is transferred to the abductor's **cradle**, a **basket** hanging in a tree; or the evicted embryo is stillborn. (7) The presence of the alien being at the site of contestation is found out by the infant's mother either empirically (appearance, sickliness) or through subterfuge (boiling water in eggshells), or through the intervention of a religious specialist (exorcist). In nearly all cases, these rites are performed or officiated by women.

Once it has been determined that an abduction/exchange has occurred, (8) swaddling *clothes* or pieces of infant *clothing* are offered to the dæmon of an arboreal/aquatic shrine (9) as a pledge at the time that the dæmon is petitioned. (10) The dæmon's power is transferred through the branches on which the *clothes* have been hung or through the stones or barrier surrounding the aquatic shrine when no trees are present, or through the water itself. (11) The infant's illness is drawn out through the contact of its article of *clothing* with the water/tree.

TABLE 4.1 Synoptic chart of ritual sequences for the recovery of infants abducted by spirit beings

	Saint Lawrence	*Guinefort*	*Other European*	*Rajasthan*	*Maharashtra*	*Other Indic*
1	x	x	x	x	x	x
2	x		x	x	x	x
3	x	x	x	x	x	x
4	x	x	x	x	x	
5			x	x		x
6	x		x	x	x	x
7		x	x	x	x	x
8		x	x	x	x	x
9			x	x	x	x
10		x	x	x	x	x
11		x	x	x		x
12		x	x	x	x	x
13		x				
14	x	x	x			
15				x	x	
16				x		x
17	x			x		x
18		x		x	x	
19		x			x	

(12) The performative aspect of the ritual occurs at the site of the exchange, the shrine of the dæmon presiding over that transfer. (13) The changeling is exposed on the forest floor, on *straw* from the infant's **cradle**. (14) The abducted infant is returned by the fauns or ancestral spirits to the **cradle** *straw* on the forest floor, or to a **basket** in a tree, or to the infant's **cradle** in the home; or (15) the ancestral spirit or malign demon is evicted and a viable embryo implanted in the **womb** through the "**pouch**-filling" rite, with a *coconut* wrapped in red and white "swaddling *clothes*" representing the embryo of a viable infant in the **womb**. (16) After the birth of a viable child, the *coconut* in its swaddling *clothes* is suspended in a **basket** hung in the tree of the arboreal dæmon, as an act of thanksgiving. (17) The recovered/viable infant is presented to/named after the tree dæmon.

(18) The infant/a *coconut* is plunged into the waters adjacent to the tree/aquatic dæmon's shrine, either to confirm that the true infant has been/will be recovered, or as a simulated sacrifice. (19) Floated on/plunged into these dangerous waters (directly, or in a **basket** called a **cradle**), the child either dies (by drowning/exposure) or is returned by malign aquatic dæmons.

What sorts of conclusions can we draw from these structural homologies in rituals whose three sequences are combined in the practices documented by Stephen of Bourbon in thirteenth-century France, but "uncoupled" in modern-day western India? How might they relate to the other mythic, folkloric, and iconographic data reviewed here? At this point, I wish to return to observations I made in my introductory chapter. The similarities between these ritual scenarios and sequences as observed in western India and western Europe are too numerous and complex to be explained on the basis of independent innovation or polygenesis. At the same time, one is hard pressed to find the path by which these rites would have been transmitted across such a wide swathe of land and sea. Unlike the folktale underlying the legend of Saint Guinefort's martyrdom, whose dissemination across Eurasia from India to France has been traced through datable written texts, no such trail of breadcrumbs exists for these ritual sequences. Had they been transmitted via contacts and exchanges between South Asia and western Europe, we would expect to find reports of them in ancient, medieval, or modern-day texts and folkways in Persia, Inner Asia, the Near East, and the Mediterranean world. This is not the case. While Maharashtra's Konkan coast has been dotted with trading ports since at least the time of the circa 60 CE *Periplus of the Erythraean Sea*, none of those ports has ever had direct trading links with ports on the western coastlines of continental Europe or the British Isles, let alone the interior Dombes region of eastern France. Equally implausible are scenarios of mass migration or military invasion.[159]

It is nonetheless intriguing to note, as my colleague Richard Hecht reported to me recently, that the practice of hanging children's clothing in trees, for the purpose of healing or the conception of a viable infant, may also be observed at three sites in modern-day Jerusalem. A new practice in the Israeli context, its actors are Bene Israel Indian Jews, recent immigrants from the last remaining Jewish enclaves of South Asia, in Mumbai and the Konkan region, the coastal strip through which the rivers of inner Maharashtra empty into the sea (fig. 4.23).[160] Given the fact that merchant sailors were obliged to pass months at a stretch on foreign shores while waiting for the monsoons to push their boats across the Arabian Sea, one might surmise that they would have had ample time to become acculturated to the customs of the Malabar Coast, which they would have brought back to Cairo and points north and west. While I cannot infer from this hypothetical ancient history and contemporary connected history that such a rapid and direct transfer of ritual practice could have occurred over a thousand years ago, I also cannot place this scenario outside the realm of possibility.

This notwithstanding, I believe that the most probable explanation for these parallel traditions lies elsewhere. As Stephen's inquisitorial report and modern ethnography make clear, these rites have been perennially performed

FIGURE 4.23. Votive cloth offerings, Jerusalem. Image courtesy of Richard Hecht.

not by cosmopolitan male actors, but rather by members of the rural peasantry, often women. However, as I argued in chapter 2, these "local" dæmonological practices have ancient pedigrees, in some cases going back to archaic vedic traditions. While no vedic prototype exists for this specific ritual sequence or set of rites, we have found certain elements of them reflected in the Buddhist iconographic record dating back to the beginning of the Common Era. This opens the way to the hypothesis of monogenesis. Here, the presence of a homologous sequence of ritual acts, attested at the two extremities of the Indo-European world, may be viewed as survivals of a body of practice observed by speakers of the *PIE language whose western branch, which includes the Celtic, Romance, Germanic, and Slavic languages, split off from the Indo-Iranian languages some five thousand years ago.

Here, one should expect to find the least "contaminated" traditions among those Indo-European societies that were geographically the most isolated from interference by culturally and politically powerful neighbors. This would apply especially to insular Great Britain and Iceland and the South Asian subcontinent, as opposed to Greece, whose mythology was strongly influenced by ancient Near Eastern traditions.[161] Due to the powerful influence of priesthoods whose vocation it was to preserve their ancient lore, certain ancient and medieval Indo-European cultures were particularly conservative. In the case of India's brahmins, the Celtic druids, and Rome's pontifical colleges, the phenomenon of "hieratic entrenchment" was also an important factor in the long-term preservation of ancient traditions. Situated at the periphery of the Indo-European world and in relative isolation from possible interferences from other cultures, religiously conservative elements of the populations of these religiously conservative regions—women and priesthoods—would have preserved these rites, which had been supplanted in all other Eurasian cultural spheres prior to the advent of writing. The fact that they did not appear in written records until a far later time—Stephen of Bourbon's report in the case of the Latin West—may be explained by a change in the *mentalités* of the Western clerics of his time. It was not until the "twelfth-century Renaissance" that European literati began to express curiosity about the wider world. This was a century that saw a broadening of mental horizons, with local folklore, the world of nature, and non-Biblical "wonders" appearing in the writings of clerics like Chrétien of Troyes, Gervase of Tilbury, Alan of Lille and others.[162] In other words, these rites may well have existed, undocumented in the West, for millennia until Catholic inquisitors and open-minded clerics began to report them. This hypothesis, while not entirely satisfactory, is to my mind the least implausible explanation for the existence of these homologous ritual complexes attested in modern-day western India and coastal western Europe alone.

5

Odysseus in Taprobane

1

One of the most popular narratives of ancient and medieval Europe, the Homeric tale of Odysseus's encounter with Circe has been read, recited, translated, and performed for nearly three thousand years.[1] The reason for its popularity is not difficult to gauge: as stories go, it has everything—sorcery, seduction, and the supernatural, all set against a fabulous Mediterranean backdrop. As happens frequently enough in the *Odyssey*,[2] the episode begins with the wily Odysseus and his men cast upon a desert shore. But the island of Aeaea is not entirely deserted, for it is the domain of Circe, a "dread goddess" (*deinē theos*).[3] After lying in harbor for two days with his men, Odysseus sets out on his own and espies smoke rising from Circe's halls.[4] Returning to his ship, he divides his men into two parties, sending a group led by Eurylochus to scout ahead.

> Within the forest glades they found the house of Circe, built of polished stone in a place of wide outlook, and round about it were mountain wolves and lions, whom Circe herself had bewitched; for she gave them evil drugs. Yet these beasts did not rush upon my men, but pranced about them fawningly, wagging their long tails. And as when hounds fawn around their master as he comes from a feast, for he ever brings them bits to soothe their temper, so about them fawned the stoutclawed wolves and lions; but they were seized with fear, as they saw the dread monsters. So they stood in the gateway of the fair-tressed goddess, and within they heard Circe singing with sweet voice, as she went to and fro before a great imperishable web, such as is the handiwork of goddesses, finely-woven and beautiful, and glorious.[5]

Odysseus's men enter her hall and she gives them to eat; but the baneful drug she has placed in their food transforms them into swine, and she pens them up in her sties. Eurylochus, the sole escapee, alerts Odysseus, who then sets out on his own to free his party.

> But when, as I went through the sacred glades, I was about to come to the great house of the sorceress Circe, then Hermes, of the golden wand, met me as I went toward the house, in the likeness of a young man.[6] [He said to me] "Whither now again, hapless man, dost thou go alone through the hills, knowing naught of the country? Lo, thy comrades yonder in the house of Circe are penned like swine in close-barred sties. And art thou come to release them? Nay, I tell thee, thou shalt not thyself return, but shalt remain there with the others. But come, I will free thee from harm, and save thee. Here, take this potent herb, and go to the house of Circe, and it shall ward off from thy head the evil day. And I will tell thee all the baneful wiles of Circe. She will mix thee a potion, and cast drugs into the food; but even so she shall not be able to bewitch thee, for the potent herb that I shall give thee will not suffer it. And I will tell thee all. When Circe shall smite thee with her long wand, then do thou draw thy sharp sword from beside thy thigh, and rush upon Circe, as though thou wouldst slay her. And she will be seized with fear, and will bid thee lie with her. Then do not thou thereafter refuse the couch of the goddess, that she may set free thy comrades, and give entertainment to thee."[7]

Everything goes according plan, and, as Odysseus relates, when neither poison nor wand nor spell could bewitch him,

> I, drawing my sharp sword from beside my thigh, rushed upon Circe, as though I would slay her. But she, with a loud cry, ran beneath, and clasped my knees, . . . [saying] "Nay, come, put up thy sword in its sheath, and let us two then go up into my bed, that couched together in love we may put trust in each other." . . . and she straightway swore the oath to do me no harm, as I bade her. But when she had sworn, and made an end of the oath, then I went up to the beautiful bed of Circe.[8]

Circe bathes and anoints him, restores his men to their human form, and offers a feast for all. The banquet lasts a full year before Odysseus and his men once more take to the wine-dark sea in search of Ithaca and home.

This Homeric tale of Circe bears comparison with a fifth- to sixth-century work composed in the Pali language and attributed to a certain Mahānāma, an erudite Buddhist monk living on the island of Ceylon,[9] likely the same isle as that known to the Greeks as Taprobane.[10] This is the *Mahāvamsa* (MV),[11] the "Great Chronicle" of the island, whose seventh chapter recounts the arrival on the island of "Laṅkā, in the region called Tambapaṇṇi,"[12] of an Indian prince named Vijaya. Here is that chapter given in full. As the Buddha prepares to enter into *parinirvāṇa*,[13] he calls upon the Hindu god Sakka (Indra) to protect Vijaya, who is about to land there:

When the lord of gods heard the words of the Tathāgata he from respect handed over the guardianship of Laṅkā to the god who is in color like the lotus [Viṣṇu]. And no sooner had the god received the charge from Sakka than he came speedily to Laṅkā and sat down at the foot of a tree in the guise of a wandering ascetic. And all the followers of Vijaya came to him and asked him: "What island is this, sir?" "The island of Laṅkā," he answered. "There are no men here, and here no dangers will arise." And when he had spoken so and sprinkled water on them from his water-vessel, and had wound a thread about their hands he vanished through the air. And there appeared, in the form of a bitch, a *yakkhiṇī* who was an attendant (of Kuvaṇṇā).[14] One (of Vijaya's men) went after her, although he was forbidden by the prince (for he thought), "Only where there is a village are dogs to be found." Her mistress, a *yakkhiṇī* named Kuvaṇṇā, sat there at the foot of a tree spinning, as a woman-hermit (*tāpasī*) might. When the man saw the pond and the woman-hermit sitting there, he bathed there and drank and taking young shoots of lotuses and water in lotus-leaves he came forth again. And she said to him: "Stay! thou art my food!"[15] Then the man stood there as if fast bound. But because of the power of the magic thread she could not devour him, and though he was entreated by the *yakkhiṇī*, the man would not yield up the thread. Then the *yakkhiṇī* seized him, and hurled him who cried aloud into a chasm. And there in like manner she hurled (all) the seven hundred one by one after him. And when they all did not return fear came on Vijaya; armed with the five weapons he set out, and when he beheld the beautiful pond, where he saw no footstep of any man coming forth, but saw that woman-hermit there, he thought: "Surely my men have been seized by this woman." And he said to her, "Lady, hast thou not seen my men?" "What dost thou want with thy people, prince?" she answered, "Drink thou and bathe."

Then was it clear to him: "This is surely a *yakkhiṇī*, she knows my rank," and swiftly, uttering his name, he came at her drawing his bow. He caught the *yakkhiṇī* in the noose about the neck, and seizing her hair with his left hand he lifted his sword in the right and cried: "Slave! give me back my men, or I slay thee!" Then, tormented with fear the *yakkhiṇī* prayed him for her life. "Spare my life, sir, I will give thee a kingdom and do thee a woman's service and other service as thou wilt." And that he might not be betrayed he made the *yakkhiṇī* swear an oath, and so soon as the charge was laid on her, "Bring hither my men with all speed," she brought them to that place. When he said, "These men are hungry," she showed them rice and other (foods) and goods of every kind that had been in the ships of those traders whom she had devoured.

(Vijaya's) men prepared the rice and the condiments, and when they had first set them before the prince they all ate of them.

When the *yakkhiṇī* had taken the first portions (of the meal) that Vijaya handed to her, she was well pleased, and assuming the lovely form of a sixteen-year-old maiden she approached the prince adorned with all the ornaments.

> At the foot of a tree she made a splendid bed, well covered around with a tent, and adorned with a canopy. And seeing this, the king's son, looking forward to the time to come, took her to him as his spouse and lay (with her) blissfully on that bed; and all his men encamped around the tent.
>
> As the night went on he heard the sounds of music and singing, and asked the *yakkhiṇī* who was lying near him: "What means this noise?" And the *yakkhiṇī* thought: "I will bestow a kingdom[16] on my lord and all the *yakkha*s must be slain, for (else) the *yakkha*s will slay me, for it was through me that men have taken up their dwelling (on Ceylon)."
>
> And she said to the prince: "Here there is a *yakkha*-city called Sirīsavatthu.... Even to-day do thou destroy the *yakkha*s, for afterwards it will no longer be possible." ... Since he listened to her and did even (as she said) he slew all the *yakkha*s, and when he had fought victoriously he himself put on the garments of the *yakkha*-king and bestowed the other raiments on one and another of his followers. When he had spent some days at that spot he went to Tambapaṇṇi. There Vijaya founded the city of Tambapaṇṇi and dwelt there, together with the *yakkhiṇī*, surrounded by his ministers. When those who were commanded by Vijaya landed from their ship, they sat down wearied, resting their hands upon the ground and since their hands were reddened by touching the dust of the red earth that region and also the island were (named) Tambapaṇṇi.[17]

These two narratives are uncannily similar. In both, a hero and his men have come to a deserted island setting on their ill-fated ships, the prince-regent Vijaya and his men driven there by his father the king for their "intolerable deeds of violence,"[18] and Odysseus by the god Poseidon in revenge for the blinding of his son, the Cyclops Polyphemus. The men of both parties are hungry and thirsty when they are cast upon foreign shores. Odysseus provides for his men by killing a stag on a day when "the might of the sun oppressed him" (10.160); Vijaya's men attempt to collect lotus roots from Kuvaṇṇā's pond, also taking up lotus leaves in order to fetch water (7.12). In both cases, "dogs" are the first creatures the men meet. The mountain wolves and lions that Circe has bewitched fawn around Odysseus's men like hounds (*kunes*) (10.216); the first *yakkhiṇī* attendant of Kuvaṇṇā that Vijaya's men meet appears in the form of a bitch (*soṇirūpeṇā*) (7.9).

Both island mistresses are engaged in the same activity when the men first come upon them: Circe passes to and fro before a great web or loom (*megan histon*); Kuvaṇṇā sits at the foot of a tree spinning (*kantantī*). In Kuvaṇṇā's case, her activity is appropriate both for a Buddhist woman ascetic and for the South Asian sorceress that she is. By her words alone, Vijaya's man is "as if bound" (*baddho va*), and all that saves him from being devoured by the man-eating *yakkhiṇī* is the power of the counter-spellbinding thread (*paritta-sutta*) that had earlier been fixed about his throat by the god Viṣṇu. These *parittas* ("all around protectors") are defensive countercharms, in distinction to Vijaya's noose (*nārācavalaya*),[19] the offensive weapon with which he subjugates Kuvaṇṇā, "binding the binder" being a common strategy of South Asian countersorcery. Circe's sorcery is of an entirely different order. When she is at her most nefarious, Homer calls her a *polupharmakos* (10.276), a term that, commonly translated as "sorceress," literally denotes a person "skilled in drugs or charms."[20] Potions or poisons (*pharmaka*) abound in these verses of the *Odyssey*: it is with a *pharmakon* that Circe bewitches the wolves and lions of her island, transforms Odysseus's men into swine, and attempts to do the same to him. A ploy in which she might well have succeeded, had Odysseus not been protected by a counter-*pharmakon*, the potent *moly* root given him by Hermes, the Greek homologue to, if not the inspiration behind, the MV's Viṣṇu.

Circe imprisons Odysseus's men in pigsties; Kuvaṇṇā casts Vijaya's men into a chasm. Both Odysseus and Vijaya set out alone to save their shipmates; both are recognized for who they are, Vijaya immediately (as a prince) and Odysseus after he has shown himself to be immune to Circe's poison. Both heroes overpower the respective goddesses with drawn swords; and when the women plead for their lives, offering them their sexual favors (as well as a kingdom in the case of Kuvaṇṇā), the respective heroes only spare them when they swear an oath (*horkos*; *sapatha*) to be true to their word. Both Circe and Kuvaṇṇā then become seductresses, taking their respective hero-captors to bed; and, at the latters' commands, feasting their men.

2

These striking parallels have been noted by a number of authors, most notably the MV's first English-language translator, George Turnour, who, in the 1837 forward to his partial translation of the work, made the following observation:

> The fabulous tone of the narrative in which the account of Wijayo's landing in Lanká is conveyed in the seventh chapter, bears, even in its details, so close a resemblance to the landing of Ulysses at the island of Circé, that it would have been difficult to defend Mahanámo from the imputation of plagiarism, had he lived in a country in which the works of Homer could, by possibility, be accessible to him. The seizure and imprisonment of Ulysses' men, and his own rencontre with Circé, are almost identical with the fate of Wijayo and his men, on their landing in Lanká, within the dominions of Kuwéni.[21]

Following which, Turnour quotes in full thirty-eight verses from the Circe story.[22] Turnour's reticence to allow that Mahānāma might have adapted his tale from Homer may be explained by his broader positivist agenda. It was his contention that, unlike the unreliable sources upon which the Hindus of India based their history, the Buddhist MV was a "scientific," that is, an empiricist, historical record of Ceylon.[23] In the nearly two centuries that have followed Turnour's opening broadside, a quiet debate regarding the origins and transmission of the MV narrative has admitted three possibilities: either (1) Mahānāma borrowed the episode of Kuvaṇṇā and Vijaya from Homer; or (2) Homer's episode of Circe and Odysseus was inspired by an eastern source; or (3) both Homer and Mahānāma drew upon a common Indo-European protomyth in crafting their narratives. Contra Turnour, scholars have for well over a century favored the first option.[24] On the one hand, a handful of authors from late antiquity intimated that Homer's works were known to the "Indians";[25] on the other, the *Odyssey* predates the MV by at least 1,300 years. Furthermore, as Albrecht Weber noted in an 1873 study, our MV episode contains a Greek loan word, albeit one not found in the *Odyssey* itself: *suruṅgā*—the word employed for the chasm into which Vijaya's men are thrown by Kuvaṇṇā—is a Pali corruption of *surigx*, an ancient Greek term that meant, among other things, "underground passage."[26]

This should not surprise us, since by Mahānāma's time, the island of Ceylon had for several hundred years been trading with the Mediterranean world in far more than words and stories. Opened following the Greek "discovery" of the Etesian winds in approximately 120 BCE, Indian Ocean trade began to fall under Roman domination in the early decades of the first century CE, a domination that would endure for a few hundred years. The period saw imperial trading cartels launching ships by the thousands across the Arabian Sea, establishing fortified settlements at South Asian ports and exchanging ambassadors with South Asian courts.[27] Already by the middle of the first century CE, Western familiarity with the ports of trade on the west coast of India was extensive, as evidenced in the Greek-language *Periplus of the Erythraean Sea*.[28] Roman coin hoards and numerous trade goods from the first centuries of the Common Era have been unearthed all along Ceylon's western coast, including at Mantai,[29] which was the principal port for Mahānāma's Anuradhapura, the political, economic, and religious capital of the island from the second century BCE to the eleventh century CE. At its height, between the mid-fourth and late-fifth century CE, when Ceylon had eclipsed the subcontinent as the pivot of trade between South Asia and the Mediterranean world, Anuradhapura's trade network extended to China and Rome.[30] Here it should be noted that Roman trade with South Asia was something of an epiphenomenon, eclipsed in importance by India's and Ceylon's long-standing maritime trading networks with East and Southeast Asia, networks that were also main conduits for the spread of Theravāda, Mahāyāna, and tantric Buddhism.[31]

There have been two principal arguments in support of the second option. The first of these takes its lead from the ancient Near Eastern mythology and iconography of Ishtar, which also features the transformation of men into beasts, as well as that goddess's representation as a mistress of wild animals (*potnia therōn*). Here it is urged that Homer, who lived on the Aegean coast of Anatolia in Asia Minor, would have patterned his Circe after the goddess Ishtar of the third-millennium BCE Gilgamesh epic.[32] The second, invoking the wide range of Asian folktales featuring similar transformations of unwitting men at the hands of their sorceress "hostesses," suggests that these traditions would already have been in circulation across Asia prior to Homer's time.[33] The most concerted argument in support of the third hypothesis was advanced by Denys Page in a 1973 study.[34] Page, like Turnour, dismissed as "improbable" any Homeric influence on "such a history of Buddhist Ceylon."[35] Then, working from an analysis of folktale patterns, Page suggested that the sequence of incidents in the Circe episode "deviated from a stricter model,"[36] which he found "more or less intact in the MV account," before identifying the "ultimate source" of both "in the remotest past, before the separation of the Indo-European peoples into their Indian and European branches."[37] A decade later, Page's arguments and conclusions were vigorously rejected by Alex Scobie and Andrew Dyck,[38] and there the issue has remained for over thirty years.

While direct borrowing is a near certainty, given that Mahānāma's account is a virtual palimpsest of Homer's far older version, I believe that both tales also issued from a common stock of narratives fully as ancient as the archaic language that was the source of Homer's Greek and Mahānāma's Pali. Then, in the wake of the Alexandrian Conquest, the opening of overland and maritime trade routes between the Mediterranean world and Inner, South, and East Asia set the stage for a sort of "second act" in the transmission of words, stories, and material culture. In other words, Mahānāma was motivated to "translate" the Circe episode into a South Asian vernacular not only because it was a ripping good story, but also because he found it strangely familiar when he first came upon it.

What was it, then, about the encounter between Odysseus and Circe that spoke to him, a monk from a distant time and place (even if he was unaware of how distant)? What I wish to suggest here is that the certain elements of the Odysseus story were already familiar to Mahānāma, not because he was acquainted with ancient Greek epic, but rather because, at some deeper level, his and Homer's cultures were already inscribed within the same hermeneutical horizon.[39] Their respective languages belonged to the same Indo-European family, which presupposed a common origin, the *PIE language.

Triangulating philological, archeological, and most recently population-scale genomic-sequencing data,[40] scholars have located the original homeland of the speakers of this language in either Anatolia or the Pontic steppes. Then, toward the beginning of the Bronze Age, these *PIE speakers began a series of migrations, eventually pushing north and west into Iceland and south and east into India and the island of "Taprobane." The legacy of these migrations was the spread of the Indo-European languages, ancient and modern, ranging from the Germanic and Celtic subfamilies of northwestern Europe to the Indic subfamily of the northern half of the Indian subcontinent and the island of Ceylon.

3

When he first heard or read it, Mahānāma would have readily recognized Homer's female antagonist as a member of a class of problematic female beings indigenous to his island. In the case of Kuvaṇṇā, he identified her both as a *yakkhiṇī* and as a *devatā*, a tutelary deity of the place—what the Greeks would have called a *daimōn* and the Romans a *genius loci*—entitled to receive tribute offerings (*bali*).[41] She was entitled to these because the piece of land she inhabited, a lotus pond surrounded by trees, belonged to her. It was her domain. Like her fellow devatās, she had been there from time immemorial, and so when Vijaya's men trespassed its precincts, she rightfully expected them to offer her tribute. It is for this reason that she was given the first portions of the meal that Vijaya's men prepared after she had freed them.[42] Although these victuals were cooked, tribute offerings were most often comprised of raw foods, including flesh. As she reported to Vijaya, Kuvaṇṇā had previously eaten men, making Viṣṇu's earlier statement to Vijaya's crew—that because there were no men on the island they had no reason to fear—a case of bad intel. It was only after she had been treated with the honor due to a devatā that she showed herself to be "well pleased."[43] Then, taking on the appearance of a lovely sixteen-year-old maiden, "adorned with all the ornaments" of marriage, she shared her bed with Vijaya, who had taken "her to him as his spouse," and aided him in winning the kingdom she had promised.[44]

Homer first introduces Circe as a "dread goddess possessed of human speech,"[45] but shortly thereafter he calls her a fair-tressed goddess.[46] Just as Mahānāma does for Kuvaṇṇā in the MV, Homer casts Circe as an ambiguous figure, when he has Odysseus's man Polites refer to her as "some goddess or some woman."[47] When Circe removes the spell from Odysseus's men, Homer employs the epithet "queenly" (*potnia*),[48] also calling her a "beautiful goddess" (*dia theaōn*);[49] and when after a year Odysseus and his men are about to depart her isle, a "nymph" (*numphē*),[50] a term he had also used for Calypso in an earlier episode. In Homer's world, nymphs were mistresses of forest groves, mountains and spring-fed pools. As such, Homer's description of Circe's four handmaidens bears noting: "Children are they of the springs and groves, and of the sacred rivers that flow forth to the sea."[51]

As for Kuvaṇṇā's attendants (*paricarikā*s), these are shape-changing *yakkhiṇī*s, who, while they are not so described in this passage from the MV, are local goddesses inhabiting the same sorts of sylvan settings as Homer's nymphs. We see this in a detail not found in Homer, but present in Mahānāma's account: the entire episode is set beneath a tree on the shore of a lotus pond.[52] Ancient Romans would have referred to this as her *lucus*, and Latin usages of this term for a deity's sacred grove attest to a topography identical to that described in the MV. In his authoritative writings on the subject, John Scheid observes that in ancient Italy, the *lucus* was either a clearing in the midst of a dense forest or a spring-fed pool hemmed in by stands of ash and poplar.[53] Trees, often filled with shrieking waterbirds, border nearly every mythological lotus pond in South Asia, several of which we will visit in this chapter.

The lotus ponds of Indic myth are often haunted by yakkhas, male counterparts to the *yakkhiṇī* Kuvaṇṇā. An account of one such pool is embedded in a Jātaka, one of a collection of the stories of the Buddha's prior births that would certainly have been known to Mahānāma. The "Devadhamma Jātaka" (DJ)[54] is the story of an encounter between three princes, the sons of two different queens, and a yakkha. In his 1895 translation, Robert Chalmers chose to read *devadhamma* as "what is truly godlike." This is, however, called into question by the fact that the term *deva* was, in the early Buddhist literature, simply a synonym for a dæmon such as a yakkha or devatā.[55] As such, *devadhamma* would simply denote "yakkha law," "yakkha wisdom," or "yakkha doctrine," these lesser deities' inferior homologue of the Buddha's supreme Dhamma. Here, the senior queen's sons are named Mahiṃsāsa and Canda ("Moon"), respectively, with the elder of the two being none other than the *bodhisatta*, the future Buddha himself. Upon the death of this queen, the king remarries and his new bride bears him a son named Suriya ("Sun"). Learning that his young queen is plotting against his two eldest sons, the king sends them into hiding in the forest. However, as the two are departing, the youngest, Suriya, runs to join them. The three of them then

> entered the snowy mountain (Himalaya). . . . Having sat down at the foot of a tree, the bodhisatta [i.e. the eldest brother] said to Prince Sun, "My little Sun! Go down to that pool and drink and bathe, and then bring some water back to us in a lotus-leaf." Now that pool had been received by a certain

> "water guardian" (*daka-rakkasa*) from Vessavana [the Buddhist "King of the Yakkhas"], and Vessavana said to him: "I authorize thee to eat those who go down into this pool, except those who know yakkha law. Thou art not authorized [to eat] those who do not go down." Thereafter, the water guardian questioned those who went down into the pool [about] yakkha law, [and] he ate the ones who didn't know [the answers].[56]

Entering the pool, Prince Sun is confronted by the water guardian, who, when the boy fails to answer his question correctly, drags him down into the depths and imprisons him there in his underwater lair. Following Sun there, Prince Moon suffers the same fate. Intuiting what has befallen the two, the bodhisatta now takes up his sword and bow, and waits at the edge of the pool. Putting on the guise of a woodsman (because his pond *is* in the midst of a forest), the water guardian attempts to inveigle the bodhisatta into entering its waters.

> "Hail, good fellow! Thou art road weary, so get thee down into this pool, drink [of its water], eat [its] lotus fibers, and deck thyself with [its] lotus flowers to thy heart's content!" Seeing him, and realizing that "this must be a yakkha," the bodhisatta said, "my brothers have been seized by thee." "Yes, by me." "Why?" "Because I am authorized [to eat] all who go down into this pool . . . except for those who know yakkha law. I am authorized [to eat] the rest."[57]

With this, the bodhisatta promises to answer the yakkha's questions, but protests that he is tired from his journey.

> Then the yakkha bathed the bodhisatta, gave him food to eat and water to drink, decked him with flowers, anointed him with fragrant essences, and laid out a couch for him in the midst of a decorated pavilion.[58]

When the bodhisatta answers his questions correctly, the yakkha offers to return one of his brothers to him. The bodhisatta asks for Prince Sun, his young half-brother, upon which the water guardian, marveling at his magnanimity, remits both of the princes to him. The bodhisatta then converts the yakkha to the true law of the Buddhist faith,[59] and the story is at its end. As will be made clear in the pages that follow, the "yakkha law" referenced in this Jātaka included the right of a *genius loci* to pose riddles to trespassers, which they were required to answer at the peril of their lives.

The *Jātaka*s were compiled over a nearly thousand-year period, probably reaching their canonical form in the sixth century CE, the beginning of the period in which Mahānāma's island was becoming a "Pali-Theravāda cosmopolis."[60] As such, I would suggest that the Buddhist monk Mahānāma folded this yakkha tale into Homer's account, which he would have also viewed as a typical yakkha yarn. The symmetry is quite compelling, with the details of the yakkha's show of hospitality also bearing remarkable similarities to that shown by Circe to Odysseus on faraway Aeaea. It is also striking that virtually all of the elements of Mahānāma's tale not found the *Odyssey* are present in the DJ: the "water guardian" is also a yakkha, a local water guardian deputized in this case by Vessavana, the King of the Yakkhas, to guard his pool. Like Kuvaṇṇā, who wishes to eat Vijaya's men, the yakkha of this tale is authorized to devour (*khādati*) all who fail to answer his riddle; also like the yakkhiṇī, he imprisons them in the pool's watery depths (Kuvaṇṇā's "chasm"). In both narratives, the victims enter the pool to bathe, drink, and collect water in a lotus leaf; in both, the heroes arm themselves with a bow and sword; in both, the yakkha antagonists disguise themselves; in both, the heroes see through their disguise at the moment they are invited by them to drink and bathe; and in both, the heroes are offered a lovely caparisoned couch after they have been reconciled with their antagonists. Mahānāma also appears to have inserted a detail from another Jātaka into his story. The "Valāhassa Jātaka," which recounts the plight of five hundred merchants cast upon the shore of Tambapaṇṇi, identifies Sirīsavatthu as a city of yakkhiṇīs. Using their feminine wiles, these lure the unsuspecting merchants into their clutches, eating half of them before the bodhisatta saves the day in the form of a winged horse.[61]

Mahānāma nonetheless chose to omit a pivotal element of the DJ's plot. This was the yakkha's interrogation of the three brothers on the topic of *devadhamma*, yakkha law. This same motif drives the narrative of two tales from a Hindu source, the MBh.[62] One of these—found in the thirteenth and youngest of the great epic's eighteen books (MBh 13)—involves the venerable Seven Sages (*saptarṣi*), who are starving in the wilderness in a time of famine.[63] When they resort to cooking the flesh of a young prince to survive, they provoke the ire of his father the king, Vṛṣādarbhi, who then performs a rite of sorcery. As a result, there arises out of his sacrificial fire a Kṛtyā, a female humanoid simulacrum of the sort discussed in chapter 3, which the king names Yātudhānī, a name attesting to both her demonic nature and the fact that she was created through sorcery.[64]

As is always the case with creatures of her ilk, her first words to her maker are "What am I to do?" The king's answer is a curious one. After she has found the Seven Sages, she is to have them recall their names, "and once you know their names, destroy them all!"[65] After a series of developments, the Seven Sages, together with a figure named "Dog's Buddy" (Śunasakha), stumble upon a beautiful lotus pond of pellucid water, overhung with trees, filled with waterfowl, and guarded by Yātudhānī, whom they see standing on its shore.[66]

Challenged by her, the sages explain that they are hungry and wish to collect a store of lotus shoots. When, as the king had instructed her, she insists that they first tell her their names,[67] they not only comply but also provide her with elaborate and arcane etymologies for them. After each, she admits that she cannot comprehend their etymological explanations, following which she gives them leave to enter the lake and harvest its lotus shoots.[68] When it is the turn of Śunasakha, he submits that he cannot provide her with the etymology of his name, and so saying he strikes her with a magical weapon, reducing her to ashes.[69] Finally, in a deus ex machina scenario frequently encountered in the epic, Śunasakha reveals himself to be none other than Indra, the champion of the gods, who had come there not only to save the sages from Yātudhānī, but also "in order to test" them (*parīkṣārtham*).[70]

While the setting remains the same here, it is hunger rather than thirst that drives the protagonists of this tale to attempt to remove edible lotus parts from the pool. Although the antagonist guardian of the pool is here called a Kṛtyā rather than a *yakṣiṇī* (the Sanskrit equivalent of the Pali yakkhiṇī), she has been deputized by King Vṛṣādarbhi (in much the same way as the DJ's water guardian had been by the King of the Yakkhas) to interrogate those who would enter its waters, and eventually to kill them. Just as Vijaya did to Kuvaṇṇā in the MV ("uttering his name"), the Seven Sages identify themselves by name to Yātudhānī, adding "riddling" etymologies to their responses. Unlike the yakkha antagonists of the Buddhist accounts, however, the option of eating her victims is never raised here.

Another epic narrative of the same sort, in which both hunger and thirst drive its protagonists to seek out the clear waters of a lotus pond, is found in a historically prior and narratively earlier book of the MBh, the "Book of the Forest" (MBh 3). Comprising the book's final chapters, this adventure begins with the epic's young heroes, the five Pāṇḍava brothers, stumbling through the forest in pursuit of a deer. Tired and thirsty and searching for water,[71] they espy a "lake covered with lotus beds," surrounded by trees and filled with the cries of whooping cranes.[72] Then, suddenly, the Pāṇḍavas find themselves in the narrative world of the DJ's three brothers and MBh 13's Seven Sages. As each of the brothers goes down to the pool, he is challenged by a disembodied voice that warns him: "Don't be rash, son! This is my ancient domain. Answer my questions, and only after that mayest thou drink and fetch [my water]."[73] None of the younger Pāṇḍavas heeds the voice, and, "exceedingly thirsty," they drink of its cool water and immediately collapse to the ground. Finally Yudhiṣṭhira, the eldest and most circumspect of the five, approaches the pool, and seeing his brothers lying on its shore wades into its waters. The voice now addresses him: "I am 'Crane' (*baka*), an eater of duckweed and fishes. By me have thy brothers been delivered into the clutches of the spirits of the departed (*pretavaśam*).[74] Thou, O prince, shalt be the fifth if thou failest to expound upon the questions asked of thee."[75]

Then, at Yudhiṣṭhira's prodding, the still invisible speaker reveals his true identity: "I am a yakṣa, if it pleaseth thee! I am not a water bird!"[76] And then, as he draws closer, Yudhiṣṭhira sees the yakṣa in its true form. "He beheld . . . standing on the shore a yakṣa with misshapen eyes and a massive body, towering like a palmyra palm, looking like a flaming sun, unassailable as a mountain."[77] Now threatened by the yakṣa as his brothers had been before him, Yudhiṣṭhira wisely agrees to answer his questions. These are, in fact, the stuff of "yakṣa law" (*deva-dhamma*)—one is tempted to say "yakṣa scholasticism" (*deva-abhidhamma*)—a set of nineteen four-part riddles on arcane matters of sacred lore, patterned on an ancient vedic model.[78] When Yudhiṣṭhira succeeds in answering all, the yakṣa offers him a boon: he may choose which one of his four brothers shall be allowed to live. As in the DJ narrative, the yakṣa is brought up short by the profound goodness of the hero's choice of the brother to be spared. Here, like the bodhisatta of the Buddhist tale, Yudhiṣṭhira requests that Nakula, the lesser of his two young stepbrothers, be allowed to live; and like the yakkha, the epic yakṣa's reaction is supererogatory: all four brothers are allowed to rise up again. Then, in another epic deus ex machina scenario, the yakṣa reveals himself to be none other than Dharma, Yudhiṣṭhira's own divine father, who had also disguised himself as the deer in whose pursuit the Pāṇḍavas had originally come to the fatal pool.[79] Here, Dharma's name also reminds us of the *deva-dhamma* of the Jātaka tale related above: in this story as well, it is the workings of "yakkha (or, in this case, yakṣa) wisdom" or "law" that are narrativized.

While the absence of any threat of anthropophagy distinguishes these epic antagonists from their Buddhist counterparts, the challenges or riddles posed by the water guardian, Kṛtyā, and yakṣa stand in contrast to the behavior of the yakkhiṇī Kuvaṇṇā. Can the same be said of both the water guardian's and the yakṣa's acts of supererogation? Perhaps not, if one characterizes Kuvaṇṇā's offering of a kingdom (*rajjam*) to Vijaya, for which she would later pay with her own life,[80] as supererogatory. Alf Hiltebeitel, who was the first scholar to note the parallels between the MV and the MBh account just reviewed,[81] emphasized this theme of granting sovereignty: I will return to his analysis shortly.

The yakṣa encountered by the Pāṇḍavas is a shape-shifter, even if in the end we learn that his yakṣa form was but one among a great god's many disguises.[82] First appearing as a deer and then identifying himself as a water bird, when he reveals his "true" yakṣa form he manifests as a massive, towering figure with "misshapen eyes." Here, it is worth noting that in the early sculptural record of India, no supernatural beings are represented with images as massive as those of the ancient yakṣas and their female counterparts.[83] And, as Robert DeCaroli has noted, "images of yakṣas and yakṣīs constitute the earliest examples of figural, freestanding sculpture in India and help to explain why the term *devatā* (roughly translated as 'minor god') has the second meaning of 'image' or 'idol.'"[84] One of the most imposing extant images of this type is a circa third-century BCE sculpture of the Buddhist tutelary deity Maṇibhadra, which is better known by the name of the site at which the image was found, about a dozen miles north of the city of Mathura in north central India.[85] In his 1882–83 archeological report, Alexander Cunningham described the then newly found image of the "Parkham Yakṣa" (fig. 5.1) in the following terms:

> Parkham is remarkable for the possession of the oldest statue that has yet been found in the Mathura district . . . a colossal standing figure of a man cut in the round, 7 feet in height from head to foot and 2 feet broad across the shoulders. . . . The figure is clothed from head to foot in a loose flowing garment, which is secured by two broad bands, one round the waist and the other round the loins. The whole body is much too bulky; and seen from the side the two bands look exactly as if they were intended to support its pot-belly. The statue is made of grey sandstone, and still retains many traces of having been highly polished. The figure is called Devata, or "the God," and has been in its present position for an unknown length of time. All the other remains at Parkham are of red sandstone and are comparatively modern. . . . I suspect that the statue was that of a yaksha, or attendant demi-god.[86] . . . As the characters [of the inscription on the base] are those of the Asoka [*sic*] period, the statue must belong to the 3rd century B.C.[87]

When Cunningham viewed it, the image was receiving libations of clarified butter and red lead; and a "Jakhaiyā" (yakṣa) festival, held at Parkham in mid-January and noted by Cunningham in his report, continues to be observed there today. As Whitney Sanford indicated in a recent ethnography of that festival, the village of Parkham "is situated upon a lake,"[88] which local residents expressly identify as that of the MBh 3 tale just reviewed. Sanford also observes that the name of the village was "derived from Parikṣam."[89] The Sanskrit term *parīkṣā* means "examination, test, trial by ordeal of various kinds," which is precisely the type of treatment that the heroes of the DJ, MBh 13, and MBh 3 suffer at the hands of the guardians of their respective bodies of water. As such, the Pāṇḍavas' yakṣa, when he reveals his "true form" as a massive figure standing on the shore of the deadly pool, is the narrative replica of a seven-foot-tall stone devatā hailing from roughly the same place and time as the epic

FIGURE 5.1. Parkham Yakṣa, Parkham, Madhya Pradesh, third/second century BCE. Mathura Museum. Image courtesy of Biswarup Ganguly. Reproduction permitted under terms of the GNU Free Documentation License.

narrative itself. Furthermore, when at the conclusion of the epic account the yakṣa reveals himself to be the god Dharma, he tells Yudhiṣṭhira that he has come there because he "wished to test him."[90]

The Buddhist canon enshrines two other narrative encounters between the Buddha and riddling yakkhas, recorded in consecutive chapters of the *Suttanipāta* (SN, "Falling Down Manual"), one of the most ancient collections of the Pali canon.[91] In the first of these, two yakkhas interrogate the Buddha on topics similar to those submitted to Yudhiṣṭhira in the MBh. When they are satisfied with his responses, they become his followers.[92] In the second, a yakkha named Āḷavaka evicts the Buddha from his dwelling (*bhavana*) three times. When, after attempting to do so for a fourth time, he is resisted by the Buddha, the yakkha threatens him: "I will ask thee a question. . . . If thou dost not answer me I'll drive thee mad or cause thy heart to burst, or grab onto thy feet to fling thee across the Ganges!" Āḷavaka poses three metaphysical questions, which the Buddha answers to his satisfaction, following which that yakkha too becomes his disciple.[93] While these narratives lack much of the detail of other stories, they nonetheless draw from the same pool of ancient mythemes, behind which we may also detect an ancient ritual sequence or protocol. We will return to the riddles of these riddling water guardians later in this chapter, but before we do so, we must first dwell on another recurring motif found in these seven South Asian narratives.

4

When the god Dharma disguises himself as a yakṣa to test the Pāṇḍavas, he refers to his lotus pond as his "ancient domain." When the yakkhiṇī Kuvaṇṇā has been satisfied by the tribute offering to which she is entitled as the tutelary deity of her lotus pond, she transforms herself into a lovely maiden, offers herself to Vijaya, and resolves to grant him a kingdom. All but one of the other South Asian narratives we have reviewed to this point hinge on humans attempting to fetch lotuses from a pond owned or guarded by the *genius loci* of that sylvan haunt; and in all of these, there is a direct relationship between lotuses and property rights, that is, a local deity's dominion over a *lucus*, his or her inviolate plot of land (or, in this case, body of water).

Now, the kingdom that Kuvaṇṇā offers Vijaya, both in return for sparing her life and in return for his tribute offering, represents a domain of a higher order, a supreme or sovereign domain. As Nancy Falk has argued, the wilderness shrines of these figures would have served as sacred seats of ancient South Asian kingship.[94] However, these domains were always site-specific, limited to a single human conurbation, forest grove, tree, or pond: the MMVS's precious "catalog of yakṣas," discussed in chapter 3, provides ample evidence for this phenomenon.[95] So too does yakṣa iconography. As Ananda Coomaraswamy's classic study makes clear, the yakṣa was identified with his or her *lucus*. When the *lucus* was a tree,[96] the yakṣa's body was frequently an element of the tree's morphology; when the *lucus* was a lotus pond, the yakṣa could be portrayed with a stream of water or a lotus rhizome emerging from its jaws.[97]

While these South Asian devatās were local tutelary deities comparable to those of other Indo-European traditions, more than one of those same traditions also knew of a supreme goddess, identified as "Sovereignty," whose broader territorial claims and fortunes were directly linked to the persons of ancient kings pretending to universal kingship rather than to lordship over specific, circumscribed domains. In the first of his groundbreaking studies of the MBh, Alf Hiltebeitel suggested that Kuvaṇṇā was an embodiment of Indo-European Sovereignty, a goddess identified in India with the mythic Śrī and the epic heroines Draupadī and Mādhavī.[98] I believe Hiltebeitel was mistaken on this point for a number of reasons, which I will develop here both as a caution against forcing mythic data into preformated categories, and by way of delineating the specificity of the mythology of local Indo-European dæmons of sylvan water sources. To begin, Hiltebeitel was apparently unaware of Mahānāma's adaptation of the Circe episode, which induced him to make unwarranted connections between the MV's tale of Kuvaṇṇā and the epic mythology of Śrī, on the one hand, and Dharma's testing of the Pāṇḍavas, on the other.[99] Also, because he was not cognizant of the three Buddhist yakkha tales reviewed above and the MBh's tale of Yātudhānī and the Seven Sages, he overlooked the centrality of the interrogation theme to South Asian narratives involving these local deities. On the basis of his incomplete data, he then went on to identify not only Kuvaṇṇā, but also the epic "yakṣa" Dharma—"male this time"—as alloforms of the Indic Sovereignty goddess Śrī.[100] Here, he was also following the lead of Dumézil, whose comparative enterprise generally focused on the socioreligious ideology of tripartition and myths of sovereignty. In addition to the Indo-European folktales discussed in chapter 1, the mythology surrounding guardian deities of freshwater pools appears never to have sparked his interest. The same may be said for his epigones, and so it is that the scope of the field of comparative Indo-European mythology has largely remained limited to the Dumézilian themes of over a half-century ago.

Hiltebeitel based his analysis of the Hindu epic material on a set of secondary elements from the mythology of the Indo-European goddess Sovereignty. This he did not only on the basis of specifically Indic mythemes, but also of mythemes shared with that other primary locus of said mythology: pre-Christian Ireland. As is so often the case in Indo-European mythology, the strongest parallels to the Indic material are to be found at the opposite pole of the ancient Indo-European diaspora, in the geographically and culturally insular traditions of Ireland and Iceland. Those parallels, first analyzed by Dumézil in 1971,[101] comprise the following primary motifs with respect to the goddess Sovereignty's mythology. Sovereignty is (1) embodied in a forest-dwelling female figure who may take the form of a deer, or be closely associated with the deer hunted by a worthy hero who eventually wins her affections and becomes the founder of a line of kings.[102] (2) Through sexual intercourse with this polyandrous goddess, a series of worthy male figures win Sovereignty and thereby enter into a line of kings who embody the three "royal virtues" related to the three functions of Indo-European social ideology.[103] (3) This goddess is also embodied in a draught of sovereignty, an intoxicating beverage whose name is an onomastic match with her own, and which she sometimes shares with the worthy heroes who have won her.[104]

None of these three mythemes is present in the MV tale of Vijaya and Kuvaṇṇā. The yakkhiṇī's offer of a kingdom comes *before* she lies with her hero; in the Indo-European material analyzed by Dumézil, the hero wins Sovereignty *because* he has lain with the goddess. Elsewhere, Hiltebeitel's argument—that Kuvaṇṇā's yakkhiṇī companion who appears as a she-dog is to be equated with the deer of the other Indo-European material—is improbable, particularly when one recalls the parallel placement in the *Odyssey* of the lions and wolves that, enchanted by Circe, fawned around Odysseus's men like hounds.[105] Finally, no connection is made between Kuvaṇṇā and an alcoholic draught of Sovereignty. Three *secondary* mythemes from the Indic or Irish mythology of Sovereignty do appear in MBh accounts, as well, perhaps, as in the MV: the lotus pool setting, the immobilization of the goddess's victims, and shape-shifting.[106] This last mytheme takes the form, in Irish narratives, of what has been termed the "Loathly Bride" motif, which Hiltebeitel sees reflected in the form in which Kuvaṇṇā first appeared to Vijaya and his men.

I will return to this last motif shortly, after reviewing the first two. In spite of her distinction from them, the goddess Śrī and South Asia's local deities of still waters did share certain attributes, of which the most important was the lotus. Śrī's earliest sculptural representation, a first-century BCE medallion from the Buddhist site of Bharhut in central India, shows her seated upon a lotus as a pair of elephants shower her with water (fig. 5.2).[107] As "a lotus in bodily form, dwelling on the surface of the lotus, [and] present in the lotus," Śrī was also embodied in the lotus thrones (*padmāsana*s) that were the seats of power of ancient Indian kings.[108] This was of a piece with South Asian royal ideology, according to which a king was only empowered to rule by virtue of the goddess Śrī's affection for him. Boasts concerning the abduction of Śrī from rival kings were a staple of Indian panegyrics throughout the medieval period; related to these were accounts of the fickleness of Śrī, who was notorious for abandoning kings who had lost their mojo.[109] That the lotus should have been the emblem of a flighty goddess may be explained by its plant behavior. From one season to the next, an entire lotus bed may transplant itself from one pond to another, leaving the former pond empty, to the benefit of the latter. The MBh makes an elliptical statement to this effect, when it says of Kuntī, the polyandrous mother of four possible heirs to the Kuru throne,

FIGURE 5.2. Śrī, Bharhut, first century BCE. Photo by John C. Huntington, courtesy of the John C. and Susan L. Huntington Photographic Archive of Buddhist and Asian Art.

that she is "like [the lotus] that has come from one pond to another."[110] In a sense, the lotus was the symbolic currency of dominion, whether over a forest pool or an entire kingdom. However, only in the latter case did the lotus emblematize royal sovereignty.

Śrī's most extensive mythology is found in the MBh, an epic whose central plot is driven by a dispute over legitimacy in matters of sovereignty. Among the epic's dozens of identifications of Śrī with the lotus,[111] none are more fully developed than those involving Draupadī, the common bride of the five Pāṇḍava princes. Identified as a "portion of Śrī" when she is born,[112] she has lotus petal eyes, and her newborn body exudes the fragrance of the blue lotus.[113] Why Draupadī has been destined to become the polyandrous wife of all five brothers is the subject of an elaborate narrative that features the royal warrior god Indra, Śrī, and lotuses. This myth, which Hiltebeitel highlights in his analysis,[114] features an encounter between Indra and a female figure that he at first fails to recognize as Sovereignty. Here, the high gods of Hinduism, assembled at a sacrifice near the headwaters of the Ganges River, marvel at the sight of a golden lotus floating in its current. Indra strikes out upstream, and coming to the river's primeval source he beholds a weeping maiden bathing in its waters.[115] Wherever one of her teardrops falls onto the water, it becomes a golden lotus.[116] With this, we are brought back to the now familiar mythic tableau of lotuses in pristine waters. Here, however, by way of highlighting the prestige of royal sovereignty, these lotuses are golden and their pool situated at the headwaters of the Ganges, the mother of all rivers. It should be noted, however, that these waters are not placid—the golden lotuses are caught in their rapid flow—and as I will show in the next chapter, the Indo-European mythology of living waters is of an entirely different order than that of the quiet pools under investigation here.

When Indra asks the maiden who she is and why she is weeping, she does not answer directly, but simply says that her stock of fortune has dwindled (*mandabhāgyā*).[117] She then bids Indra to follow her, and the pair comes upon Śiva and his consort Pārvatī playing dice on a nearby mountaintop. The more powerful of the two gods in this epic context, Śiva sets about manipulating Indra in a number of ways, first by paralyzing him with a simple glance.[118] Then, in what appears to be a redundant move, he bids Śrī to bring the god to him; and no sooner does she touch him than does Indra lose complete control of his limbs and fall to the ground.[119] As Hiltebeitel argues, Indra's serial losses of motor skills replicate those of figures from two of the narratives reviewed above: Vijaya's men, who are paralyzed, made to stand "as if fast bound," by Kuvaṇṇā's words; and the four younger Pāṇḍavas who fall to the ground when they fail to answer the "yakṣa" Dharma's riddles.[120]

Hiltebeitel's third basis for comparison is the goddess Sovereignty's shape-shifting powers, which takes the form of the "Loathly Bride" motif attested in several western European narratives. Following Dumézil, Hiltebeitel focuses his analysis on two widely referenced tales, nearly identical in all their features, that hinge on an encounter between a set of princely brothers and a hideous hag (*cailleach*) who reveals herself to be "The Sovereignty" (*In flaithius*) of Ireland.[121] There is general agreement that these two accounts are narrativizations of a Celtic *banfheis rigi*, a "wedding feast of kingship," of which cognate rituals are attested in the epigraphy, iconography, and textual record of other medieval European cultures.[122]

The first of these is embedded in the *Echtra mac nEchach Muigmedóin* ("Adventurous Journey of the Sons of Echu Muigmedóin"), an eleventh-century work concerning a legendary fifth-century ruler named Níall Noigíallach.[123]

Deep in a forest at the end of a hunt, King Eochaid's four sons and their younger stepbrother Níall build a fire to cook and eat their game. Now "athirst and in great drouth," they set out, one by one, in quest of water. Each comes upon a wellspring (*topar*) that has "an old woman guarding it." The loathsome hag is "black as coal . . . with [a] sickle of green teeth . . . in her head," "a nose crooked and hollow," "a middle fibrous, spotted with pustules, diseased, and shins distorted and awry."[124] No man may draw water from her spring unless he first kiss her, and because neither Fergus, Olioll, nor Brian can bring himself to do so, each comes away with none.[125] The fourth son, Fiachra, brings himself to "give a few kisses for it," in return for which she allows that he would one day "visit Tara": as the narrator explains, two of his descendants would later come to rule Ireland. Finally, Níall comes to the well, and when the hag bids that he kiss her he replies "Besides giving thee a kiss, I will lie with thee!"[126] Then

> he throws himself down upon her and gives her a kiss. But then, when he looked at her, there was not in the world a damsel whose gait and appearance was more loveable than hers! . . . "Who art thou?" says the boy. "I am the Sovranty,"[127] she answered and then she said: "O king of Tara, I am the Sovranty."[128] . . . "Go now to thy brothers," she says, "and take water with thee, and the kingship and the domination will for ever abide with thee and thy children. . . . As thou hast seen me loathsome, beastly, horrible at first and beautiful at last, so is the Sovranty: for seldom is it gained without battles and conflicts."[129]

The Sovranty's final advice to Níall recalls the DJ and MBh 3 accounts in which the young half-brothers Prince Sun and Nakula came to be prioritized over their elders. By bartering the water he has won from her, Níall will, as she urges, obtain the gift of primogeniture over his brothers and become the founder of a long line of kings.[130]

The second Irish narrative, embedded in two medieval works of toponymic literature, the "Dindshenchas ["Place Name Lore"] of Carn Máil" and the *Cóir Anmann* ("Fitness of Names"), has for its protagonists a set of brothers, all named Lugaid.[131] The narrative tension of these two nearly identical versions of the tale is driven by a druid's prophecy, made to Dáire Doimthech, that a son by the name of Lugaid would catch a "fawn with a golden lustre upon it," and so win The Sovereignty of Ireland. Dáire fathers five (or seven) sons and names all of them Lugaid. Sometime later, the Lugaids pursue a golden fawn into a "magical mist," bringing it down beside a stream. After dressing the animal and preparing to eat it, they withdraw to a nearby house, into which there enters a hag whose description in the "Dindshenchas of Carn Máil" is fully as lurid as that contained in "The Adventure of Eochaid's Sons." An "obese lustful horror," she

> was hideous, unsightly. Taller was she than a mast upright, bigger than a sleeping-hut her ear, blacker than any visage her form, a weight on every heart was the hag. Broader her row of teeth—what portends it?—than a board set with draughtsmen; her nose stood out far before her, it was longer than a ploughshare. Bigger than a basket full of sheaves was each fist of the misnatured woman: bigger than rough-hewn stone in rampart each of her black bony knees. A paunchy belly she bore, I trow, without rib to the armpits: a scabby black crown with a crop of wens, like a furzy hillside, upon her.[132]

Like Kuvaṇṇā and the water guardian of the DJ, this hag is also a man-eater, and so she delivers an ultimatum: one of the Lugaids shall "sleep with me to-night, or I will devour you all." When Lugaid Laigde, the youngest, agrees to share her bed, "she changed to another wondrous shape: she took on a radiant form, beyond praise; rosy she grew, round-bosomed. . . . Then the young man asked her, 'Fair maiden, whence comest thou? name thy race, tell it now, speak to me, hide it not from me!' 'I will tell thee, gentle youth; with me sleep the High Kings: I, the tall slender maiden, am The Sovereignty of Alba and Erin.' "[133] The *Cóir Anmann* version adds the following detail, which recalls the feasts put on by Circe and Kuvaṇṇā for Odysseus's and Vijaya's men. Here, The Sovereignty provides for Lugaid and his four brothers "the freshest of food and the oldest of ale, and self-moving drinking horns pouring out to them."[134] This is a detail, overlooked by Hiltebeitel, which he might have marshaled in support of his identification of Kuvaṇṇā as an instantiation of the Indo-European Sovereignty goddess. If so, it stands quite alone, given the fact that, apart from the anthropophagous tendencies of both Kuvaṇṇā and one of the two Irish hags, only one other of the Irish motifs appears in the MV tale: like Vijaya and his men, the female figure confronted by Níall and his brothers is the guardian deity of a source of water. As for the multiplicity of "interchangeable" brothers, as well as the elevation of the youngest of a set of (step)brothers in these accounts, this is a theme found in all of the South Asian accounts *except* that of the MV.

Hiltebeitel's final putative common mytheme, the shape-shifting power of the goddess Sovereignty, fares no better. In his words, "just as the Irish Flaith turns from hag to beauty, Kuvaṇṇā the Yakkhiṇī is *transformed* from a *tapasī*—an identity which no doubt connotes ragged clothes, unkempt appearance, emaciated physique—to the loveliest of young maidens."[135] To begin, the MV makes no such statement; rather, it first describes Kuvaṇṇā as "sitting at the foot of a tree spinning, *in the way that a woman-hermit might*."[136] Furthermore, shape-shifting is a power ascribed to a wide variety of supernatural female figures from Indo-European mythology, and it is in no way specific to supernatural embodiments of Sovereignty.

However, let us, for the sake of argument, allow that Mahānāma had "transformed" Kuvaṇṇā from an emaciated hermit into a ravishing sixteen-year-old maiden. Is this sufficient ground for us to follow Hiltebeitel in identifying this as an Indic instantiation of the Loathly Bride motif? I think not, and this for two reasons. The first, and most obvious, is the clear difference between an unkempt, emaciated woman and a monstrous behemoth. The second, and this is my principal reason for this extended critique of Hiltebeitel's treatment of the MV narrative, brings us back to the distinction between a *genius loci*'s property rights—that is, his or her dominion over a *lucus*, a circumscribed plot of land or water—and a supreme goddess's power to bestow universal sovereignty upon a worthy princely hero. An English work that also features a Loathly Bride will aid us in sharpening that distinction.

5

Unlike South Asia, where it is virtually absent, the "Loathly Bride" was a ubiquitous motif of medieval western European literature, appearing in Irish, Welsh, Scandinavian, French, English, and German works from the twelfth century onward. While the relationship between these various literary traditions and their relationship to oral tradition are not settled matters,[137] there is general agreement that the Irish tales of Níall and Lugaid, the first to combine the Loathly Bride motif with that of Sovereignty, were the direct or indirect sources of three English works whose manuscript witnesses date from the late fourteenth to the mid-fifteenth centuries.[138] These are John Gower's "Tale of Florent" (1390–93), Geoffrey Chaucer's "Tale of the Wife of Bath" (1405–10), and the anonymous "Wedding of Sir Gawain and Dame Ragnelle" (WGDR, ca. 1450).[139]

Here I will focus on the last, most detailed—and by far the most humorous—of the English narratives, the WGDR,[140] because, rather than conflating the two, its author distinguishes the figures of a local guardian of a specific *lucus* from a female "Sovereignty" figure. The tale opens with a deer hunt in Yngleswod (Inglewood), an enchanted forest rich in Arthurian lore situated on the borderlands between northwestern England and Scotland.[141] King Arthur, who has strayed from his party, brings down a hart deep in the wilds. As he sets about to dress it, a strange man, "armed well and sure, a knight full strong and of great might," challenges him: "Well met, King Arthur! Thou hast done me wrong many a year. . . . Thou hast indeed given my lands with great wrong unto Sir Gawain."

And as the knight threatens Arthur's life (a threat that will be repeated thirty-eight times in the story),[142] Arthur asks him his name. The man's answer, Gromer Somer Joure, has been interpreted by most to mean a "man" or "groom" (*gromer*) of the festivities of Midsummer (*Somer Joure*), which continued to feature, in sixteenth-century London, carnival-type figures of fully armed "great and ugly gyants."[143] Somer Joure's name also brings us back, perhaps, to a recurrent theme of our Indic accounts; that is, to the time of year in which oppressive heat drives their protagonists to seek the waters of a devatā's pool.

Somer Joure's grievance with Arthur concerns title to the very land on which Arthur finds himself—an issue of dominion in the same circumscribed territorial sense as that found in the South Asian accounts. Somer Joure's noble estate has been usurped by Arthur. Out of revenge, the "strange groom" (*quaynt grome*) will only give Arthur leave to depart with his life, and by extension his sovereignty, on one condition: that the king return in a year's time with the correct answer to the following question: "To show me at thy coming what women love best," adding that "if thou bringest not an answer without fail, thine head thou shalt lose for thy travail."[144] A crestfallen Arthur returns to his castle in Carlyle, sharing his sorrows with Gawain and confiding in him his task to discover "what women desire most." They part ways, each seeking to find the response to Somer Joure's riddle. Eleven months pass, until the day when Arthur, riding "into Yngleswod," crosses the path of a strange and hideous Lady.

> She was as uncouth a creature as ever a man saw, beyond measure. King Arthur marveled transfixed. Her face was red, her nose snotted as well, her mouth wide, her teeth yellow over all, with bleary eyes greater than a ball. Her mouth was not oversmall. Her teeth hung over her lips, her cheeks as broad as a woman's hips. A lute she bore upon her back, her neck long and equally broad, her hanging breasts large enough to be a horse's load, and like a barrel she was made. To recount the foulness of that Lady there is no tongue may tell, surely—of ugliness enough she had. She sat on a palfrey that was richly draped, adorned with gold and many a precious stone. There was an incongruous sight: so foul a creature without measure to ride so handsomely, I assure you it was neither proper nor right.[145]

Addressing him directly, she immediately informs Arthur of her cognizance of Somer Joure's ultimatum, adding that she will only save him—by answering the riddle—if he gives her Sir Gawain's hand in marriage.[146] And as they take leave of each other, she tells him her name—Dame Ragnelle—and utters a cryptic phrase that has long defied interpretation: "There is a bird men call an owl, and yet a Lady I am."[147] Here I would suggest that we see in Ragnelle's avian aspect an echo of the MBh "yakṣa" Dharma who first appears to the Pāṇḍavas as a crane, and of the screeching waterbirds that form a part of several South Asian tableaus of sylvan pools. The gallant Gawain accepts to marry the loathly lady sight unseen, and when Arthur reports this to her, Dame Ragnelle provides him with the answer he has been seeking: "But there is one thing [that] is all our fancy, and that now shall ye know. We desire of men above all manner of things to have the *sovereynté*, no lie, of all, both high and low. For where we have *sovereynté*, all is ours."[148] When on the appointed day Arthur rejoins the menacing Somer Joure and provides him with the correct answer to his riddle, adding "thus they [women] did teach me to rule thee, Gromer Sire," the knight flies into a rage, not against Arthur but against "she that told thee now. I pray to God, I may see her burn on a fire; *for that was my sister, Dame Ragnelle*."[149] Now all that remains is for Sir Gawain to marry Ragnelle, whom Arthur brings to his court, scandalizing Queen Guenevere and her ladies in waiting. The wedding feast becomes another occasion for our author to expand upon Ragnelle's monstrosity. In a hilarious scene, we see her sitting at the place of honor, her "boar's tusks" tearing through capons, curlews, and roasted meats while devouring six times as much as the other guests, and not stopping until all the tables have been cleared and washed. Now it is Ragnelle and Gawain's wedding night, and the hideous hag entreats Gawain:

> "Yet for Arthur's sake kiss me at least; I pray you do this at my request. Let us see how you can fare." Sir Gawain said, "I will do more than for to kiss, and before God!" [And when] he turned toward her, he saw [in] her the fairest creature that ever he had seen, without compare. She said, "What is your will?" . . . And he embraced her in his arms and did kiss her, and made great joy, surely. "Sire," she said, "thus shall ye have me. Choose of the one (so God me save, [or] my beauty will not hold): Whether ye will have me fair on nights and as foul on days to all men's sights, or else to have me fair on days, and on nights [as] the foulest wife."[150]

Gawain weighs the alternatives, and then bids that Ragnelle choose herself:

> "But do as it pleases you, my Lady gay. The choice I put in your hand. Just as you would [have it], I put it in your hand. Release me as you please for I am bound; I put the choice in you. Both [my] body and goods, my heart and every part, is all your own for to buy and sell—that I vow to God!" "Many thanks, courteous knight," said the Lady; "Of all earthly knights blessed may you be, for now I am honored properly. Thou shall have me fair both day and night, and for as long as I live as fair and bright."[151]

With this, Ragnelle explains how she had originally come to be transformed into a monstrous creature. An evil stepmother had put a spell on her that would not be broken unless "the best [knight] of England had truly wedded me, and also he should give me the *sovereynté* of all his body and goods, surely. . . . And thou, Sir Knight, courteous Gawain, hast surely given me the *sovereynté*."[152] The now lovely lady would later bear a son by him, named Gyngolyn, before tragically dying five short years after Gawain had wed her.[153]

Clearly, the stepmother's spell has been broken by the *sovereynté* that Gawain has granted her; and although it is the lifting of that spell rather than an active decision on her part, Dame Ragnelle's beauty by both day and night may be read as an act of supererogation comparable to the sparing of heroes' lives by the various local guardians of South Asian sylvan pools. Here, however, the objection has often been raised that whereas Indic and Irish mythology unambiguously cast Śrī and Flaith as female deifications of royal Sovereignty, the *sovereynté* sought and won by Ragnelle—a woman's domestic primacy in marital relations—was of an entirely different and perhaps incommensurable order. It nonetheless remains the case that while the sovereignty that Ragnelle retained was but a pale image of that of her Irish forebears, her transformation occurred under the same conditions as in the tales of Níall and Lugaid: at the moment that her young hero gave himself up to her sexually.

In a 1993 article aptly titled "The Riddle of Sovereignty," Manuel Aguirre proposed a solution to these issues. Noting the riddle motif as a distinguishing feature of the English versions of the Loathly Bride narratives,[154] he argued that those same versions also retained the specific sense of Sovereignty enshrined in the Irish traditions.

> At the beginning of *Ragnelle*, Sir Gromer Somer Joure complains that his lands have been given away to Gawain by Arthur and that Gawain holds them unlawfully. When Gawain agrees to marry Ragnelle he obtains the answer to Sir Gromer's riddle, who then withdraws his claim, while calling Ragnelle his own sister. In other words, Arthur's bequest to Gawain was not valid; on the other hand, Gromer's lands are effectively taken away from him by his sister Ragnelle, and lawfully assigned by her to Gawain as a result of his marriage pledge. In a significantly obscured way, she is indeed Sovereignty, the power that dispenses territorial rule.[155]

Aguirre goes on to hypothesize that Ragnelle's actual relationship to Gromer Somer Joure was not a sisterly one, but rather that she had originally been his spouse, a "Mother Earth" figure and the Sovereignty to which he had been wed as the lord of his domain. Here I must take issue with his analysis. Even if Ragnelle's transformation had occurred under the same circumstances as did that of The Sovereignty of Irish traditions, with that transformation triggered by a hero's recognition of her *sovereynté*, it remains that she was not "The Sovereignty" embodied. The "groom" Somer Joure was never the lord of a sovereign domain or a pretendant to the throne of Britain; and Ragnelle's resolution of his dispute with Arthur over land ownership (via her wedding to Gawain) was in no way an issue of royal sovereignty.[156] Rather, the dark groom was the Celtic homologue of the South Asian water guardian: a powerful figure fiercely protecting a *lucus*, his ancient circumscribed domain, and threatening death to any who would or could not answer his riddle.

In the final analysis, Dame Ragnelle's ambiguous role is analogous to that of the South Asian lotus and the Celtic deer: like her, both can symbolize dominion over a *lucus* and universal Sovereignty. In the light of these data, I would suggest that with the exception of the Irish Flaith and the Indic Śrī, none of the female figures in these tales, to say nothing of the riddling male *genii locorum* of Indic myth, are mythic embodiments of Sovereignty. Kuvaṇṇā's behavior is that of a male or female *genius loci*, and her beauty of the same fatal sort as that exhibited by South Asian yakkhiṇīs for thousands of years.[157] If the offer she makes to Vijaya of a kingdom is effectively an offer of sovereignty, this would be a piece of literary improvisation on the part of Mahānāma, the transformation of a female guardian of a lotus pond into a kingdom-granting goddess with shades of Homer's Circe.

6

A question left unanswered in the preceding analysis concerns Dame Ragnelle's "redundancy" with respect to her brother Gromer Somer Joure, since she appears to have been a co-sharer in his sylvan domain on the Scottish borderlands. Was this simply a case of literary invention by the WGDR's anonymous author, an ingenious fusion of two strands of Indo-European mythology concerning two types (male and female) of local tutelary deities? Or did this doubling constitute an independent Indo-European mytheme? Here, we should recall that in the DJ narrative, it was Vessavana, the Buddhist "King of the Yakkhas," who deputized the water guardian to challenge and eventually eat persons unschooled in "yakkha law." So too, Yātudhāni was a creature of Vṛṣādarbhi, the king pulling the strings in his attempt to exterminate the Seven Sages at another lotus pond. Even Kuvaṇṇā appears to have been a surrogate for the male yakkhas of Sirīsavatthu, who she fears will slay her for allowing men to trespass onto their island.[158] A recent article by Emily West throws new light on this question,[159] as she suggests that another epic episode, this one from the MBh's first book (MBh 1), be read as an Indic cognate of the Homeric accounts of Odysseus's encounters with the nymphs Circe and Calypso. This she does on the basis of sixteen "building blocks" shared by both traditions.[160] While I find certain elements of her demonstration unconvincing, her hypothesis, that an epic *rākṣasī* named Hiḍimbā was an Indic reflex of Homer's nymphs, is highly compelling.

West's findings have several other implications with respect to the myths I have analyzed in this chapter. First, they support my contention that Mahānāma was able to directly adapt the Homeric tale of Odysseus and Circe because as heir to archaic Indo-European mythic traditions, he was already familiar with its plot. He consciously plagiarized Homer's Greek account while also injecting indigenous material from the DJ's yakkha narrative. In other words, he crafted his story from two strands of an Indo-European mythology of local tutelary deities. At the same time, he would likely have been unaware of similar tales from the coeval Hindu epic, including the Hiḍimbā episode, because he was not a Hindu from the subcontinent, but rather a Buddhist from the island of Ceylon.[161] As such, he would have unwittingly incorporated into his narrative several of the Indo-European mythemes that, while present in the Hiḍimbā myth, are not found in either the *Odyssey* or the DJ.

In developing her argument West does not marshal any of the sources I have discussed above—neither the MV nor any of the other Indic myths, either Hindu or Buddhist.[162] For this reason, she emphasizes certain parallels between the two narratives that I find to be insignificant while passing over others that I will underscore in what follows. Nonetheless, I fully subscribe to her conclusion: that the striking parallels between Homer's Circe and the MBh's Hiḍimbā can only be explained through monogenesis:

> I therefore propose that the identical cores of the three episodes [of Circe, Calypso, and Hiḍimbā] are an Indo-European survival from the Graeco-Aryan roots of the epics. . . . If this argument is correct, and the tale of Circe, or other Homeric episodes previously perceived to be adoptions from folklore are shown to exist in the Indic tradition as well, then the folktale-source hypothesis must be altered to accommodate the Indo-European evidence. . . . There is no reason to dispute the claim that the Homeric epics and folktales must have counter-influenced one another at times when they circulated within the same society. But episodes sharing parallels with the *Mahābhārata* on the order of those discussed here would have shared origins dating to before 2300 BCE.[163]

The striking similarities between the MBh story of Hiḍimbā, Homer's Circe narrative, and the English WGDR will permit us to add another crucial piece to the reconstruction of what we may now identify as a complex Indo-European protomyth of the encounter between a hero and a *genius loci*. This episode opens with the five Pāṇḍavas and their mother Kuntī wandering through the wilderness in the month of March.[164] Exhausted and thirsty, they are lifted up onto the massive arms of the second brother, Bhīma, who carries them across one wilderness tract after another, until he comes upon a great shady banyan tree:[165]

> Tossing them all down, the bull of the Bhāratas said [to Yudhiṣṭhira]: "I'm going to try to find some water in this place. Rest, my lord! These sweetly whooping cranes are waterfowl, and so I suppose there's a big water hole over yonder." Given leave to depart by his eldest brother, [who said] "Go," he went to the place where the water birds were whooping. Then, after drinking the water and bathing there, the bull among the Bhāratas fetched the water [back to the others] with his upper garment.[166]

Finding everyone asleep upon his return, Bhīma decides to stand guard through the night. "While they were sleeping, a cruel, mighty and powerful man-eating guardian named Hiḍimba was perched in a nearby *sāl* tree."[167] The epic's Hiḍimba is a "guardian" (*rākṣasa*) of the forest, the Sanskrit cognate of the *(daka)rakkasa*, the "(water) guardian" of the Pali-language Buddhist DJ. Generally portrayed as colossal nocturnal man-eaters, the "guardians" are a group of indigenous, congenitally malign South Asian dæmons whose demonic nature was already established prior to their absorption into Hindu, Buddhist, or Jain pantheons.

The guardian Hiḍimba is not alone in his *sāl* tree, because he now turns to his sister—whose name Hiḍimbā makes her his double—and commands that she "kill all these humans and bring them to me! There is no danger to you from them who are asleep *in our domain*."[168] She follows his orders, but upon seeing the mighty Bhīma standing guard, she is immediately smitten with him.[169] "A shape-shifter (*kāmarūpiṇī*), she put on her finest human form and quietly approached the strong-armed Bhīma like a timid creeper."[170] With her first words to him, she both betrays her brother and plies her troth with the strapping young hero. Her brother will kill them all, she says, but if Bhīma would but share his love with her, she will spirit him away and save him. The noble Bhīma immediately objects that he could never abandon his mother and brothers to satisfy his lust, to which she replies in desperation that she will do anything to please him.[171] But as Bhīma affirms, no one, whether human or superhuman, can match him in combat, "so bring on that man-eating brother of yours!"[172]

As if on cue, Hiḍimba, who is as "massive as a column of clouds,"[173] comes storming out of the forest to feast on the Pāṇḍavas. Seeing his sister in human form together with Bhīma, he immediately perceives her betrayal and, hurling insults, attempts to kill her. Bhīma then becomes her champion, engaging Hiḍimba in a fierce hand-to-hand combat, and as the day dawns the young hero strangles, slaughters, and breaks the body of Hiḍimba over his knee.[174] The five brothers and their mother then resume their wanderings, with Hiḍimbā in tow. She convinces Kuntī that her love for Bhīma is real, and with his mother's blessing the young hero marries the *rākṣasī*. And from that time forward, she makes love to her man after "putting on the finest body" and "wearing the finest outer aspect."[175] Soon after, a son is born to them named Ghaṭotkaca,[176] who would later play a crucial role in the great epic battle.

7

The Hiḍimbā narrative calls forth several conclusions concerning the Indic, Greek, and Celtic materials reviewed in this chapter. First, we can now be certain that female Sovereignty was not an original mytheme in this Indo-European protomyth. To begin, the lotus pond is an Indic variation on the (watered) forest setting of all other versions of the myth. The forest grove or pool is nothing more or less than the *genius loci*'s circumscribed domain, which empowers him to demand tribute from any who would trespass upon it, or simply to kill any interloper. When, however, he deputizes another figure, nearly always female, to act as his surrogate, she generally betrays him when she offers her bed and body to the hero of the tale.[177] However, she does so at her own peril: Somer Joure would see his sister Ragnelle "burn on a fire," and Hiḍimba attempts to slay his sister. Kuvaṇṇā, later abandoned by her hero, Vijaya, is killed for her treachery by a violent yakkha.[178] Taken together, these Indic, Greek, and Celtic myths may be viewed as variations on the following complex Indo-European protomyth:

(1) A male hero (2) wanders in the wilds (3) in a time of great heat/afflicted by thirst (4), accompanied by a group of men (5) who are his "brothers." (6) One or several of those men (7) approach a *genius loci*'s domain, (8) a forest pond or grove with a watering place. (9) When they attempt, in sequence, to violate that domain, (10) they are challenged by the *genius loci*, (11) a shape-shifter (12) who threatens them with death.

(13) When the *genius loci* is a male figure, (14) he is a giant. (15) He tests the brothers with riddles,[179] (16) which they fail to answer, (17) for which reason he strikes them down. (18) However, the hero is able to answer the riddle, (19) in return for which the *genius loci* offers to revive one of this slain brothers. (20) Nonplussed by the hero's choice, the *genius loci* revives all the brothers.

(21) When the figure encountered by the hero and brothers is female, (22) she is cast as the sister or surrogate of the male *genius loci*. (23) She first

appears in a horrific, nonhuman form to threaten the hero's men (24) with death. (25) She tests the hero's character, (26) and overcome by his cunning, force, beauty, or goodness, (27) she betrays her brother or the male figure for whom she is a surrogate. (28) Taking on an attractive and benevolent human aspect, (29) she promises to do no harm, and (30) gives herself up to the hero, (31) frees his men, (32) and bathes and feasts them. (33) She later bears a son by the hero.[180]

When these mythemes are presented in tabular form, their distribution follows certain patterns (see table 5.1). What we have here, then, are a set of variations on *two* mythemes, the one concerning encounters with male sentinels of watered sylvan *luci* with their ritual entailments, and the other concerning the winning of female Sovereignty, mythemes that were woven together in a variety of ways according to storytellers' and mythographers' cultural situations and literary craft—what Dumézil has termed "secondary causalities."[181] Regardless of their literary genre, he argued, these modes of expression could never be "arbitrary dramatic or lyrical inventions divorced from the social or political order, or from ritual, law or custom; on the contrary, their role was to endorse all of these, to express through images the broad concepts that ordered and sustained them all."[182]

This may explain why the riddling or testing theme was absent from the Homeric account of Odysseus and Circe (and, by extension, Mahānāma's adaptation of it). In the ancient Mediterranean world, the word "oracle" denoted both function (predicting the future, revealing unknown past or concurrent events), place (the sanctuary at which the oracle held forth), and the dæmon, the mantic supernatural being capable of revealing things unknown. These latter communicated through human intermediaries who were often female: the pythoness at Delphi, the prophetess at Didyma, and the many Sibyllae. Persons wishing to gain knowledge of hidden or future events would voluntarily present themselves at these oracles' established shrines to seek answers to their questions.[183] In this light, perhaps the non-Greek tales surveyed in this chapter ought to be read as narratives of another type of "first contact" between humans and dæmons which, grounded in archaic rituals wherein the tables were turned, required that humans respond to often riddling-type questions before being granted access to their sanctuaries.

A comparison with observations made by Jonathan Z. Smith regarding a shift in attitudes toward demons in late antiquity is apposite here. As Smith notes, with the end of the classical order and the replacement of its "locative" worldview with a "utopian" one, demons were no longer to be found on the periphery of "horizontal" cosmologies. With the disappearance of the sacred center, man now found himself "out of place . . . estranged from his true home

TABLE 5.1 Synoptic chart of mythemes in variations on the "Odysseus and Circe" myth

		Indic		*Celtic*	
	Homeric Greek (and Mahānāma)	*Pali (DJ, SN)*	*Sanskrit (Y, Dh, H)*	*English (DR)*	*Irish (N, L)*
1	x	x	x	x	x
2	x	x	x	x	x
3	x	x	x		x
4	x	DJ	x		x
5		DJ	x		x
6	x	DJ	x	x	x
7	x	DJ	x	x	x
8	M	DJ	x	x	x
9	M	DJ	Y, Dh		x
10	M	x	x	x	x
11	M		Dh, H	x	x
12	M		Dh, H	x	x
13		x	Dh, H	x	
14			Dh, H	x	
15		DJ	Y, Dh	x	
16		DJ	Dh	x	
17		DJ	Dh		
18		x	Dh	x	
19		DJ	Dh		
20		DJ	Dh		
21	x		Y, H	x	x
22	M		Y, H	x	
23			Y, H	x	x
24	M		Y		
25	M				L
26	x		H	x	x
27	M		H	x	
28	x		H	x	x
29	x				
30	x		H	x	x
31	x		H		
32	x				L
33	M		H	x	

Note: x: appears in all versions of myths in a given language/tradition; M: appears only in the MV version of the Circe myth; DJ: Devadhamma Jātaka; SN: *Sutta Nipāta*; Y: Yātudhānī; Dh: Dharma; H: Hiḍimbā; N: Niall; L: Lugaid; DR: Dame Ragnelle

'on high.'" As for the demons, these were now "in place," dwelling in their spheres, their "houses," situated between heaven and earth. As Smith observes, "It is the demons in their role as 'Watchers' . . . who will either recognize him as an enemy or alien and seek to expel or destroy him or . . . become his ally. The man proves his right to stand 'on high' by his *gnōsis*, especially by demonstrating his knowledge of the demon's name, place and taxon."[184] In the light of the mythology reviewed in this chapter, we may see that Smith's "locative-to-utopian" scenario is specific to a particular historical context, and cannot be extrapolated to all "utopian" situations and worldviews. In fact, while all of the elements of Smith's analysis are present in the narratives I have reviewed, the valences of virtually every one of them has been turned around in some way. So, while the dæmons of sylvan water sources were often cast as "Watchers" (my "Guardians") "in place" in their *luci*, they were not in place in some vertically ordered cosmos, because they belonged to a locative cosmic order on the horizontal plane of the earth. As we have seen, these dæmons were in many cases themselves tributary to a superior power—the supreme yakkha Vessavana, King Vṛṣādarbhi, etc.—occupying the center of their locative "mandalas." As for the humans who trespassed their domains, these were natives to a locative cosmic order who now found themselves exiled from their true homes on a horizontal plane. Yet, they were often put to the test and required to demonstrate some order of higher knowledge in ways similar to those of humans seeking to prove their right to "stand 'on high'" in a centerless "utopian" universe. Since there can be no question that the protomyth that generated the narratives I have reviewed in this chapter predates late antiquity by at least two millennia, it follows that Smith's "utopian" scenario ought to be viewed less as a paradigm shift than as a ninety-degree axial pivot from the orientation of a prior locus of the encounter between the human and the nonhuman: not a temple of the gods, but rather a *lucus* of ancient Greco-Roman dæmons or their South Asian homologues.[185]

Unlike the Sovereignty mytheme, which has been widely studied by Indo-Europeanists, Celticists, and Indologists, that of the *genius loci* in his or her specific *lucus* has not. This will also be a central focus of the next chapter: the translocal mythology of a set of "local" dæmons, embodied here by two great sentinels standing guard at the confines of the Indo-European world: the Parkham Yakṣa and Sir Gromer Somer Joure.

6

Perilous Fountains

1

Another lotus pool, rectangular this time, and fashioned by human hands. We know so because this pool was depicted not in a word description but rather with an artist's brush. Sometime in the early seventh century, its brushstrokes touched the wall of a Buddhist cave shrine at Dandan-Uiliq, a Silk Road oasis in the kingdom of Khotan on the southwestern edge of the Tarim Basin. Some 1,300 years later, in 1900 or 1901, Sir Aurel Stein photographed that mural in the cella of "Buddhist Shrine D II" (fig. 6.1).[1] Yet another tableau of a lotus pool and its *agonistes*, the work contains its own gloss, which Lokesh Chandra brilliantly interpreted in an obscure 2003 article. That gloss is found in the title of the book held in the hand of the Buddhist monk at the upper left: this is the *Suvarṇaprabhāsottamasūtra*, a work that in this context symbolized the promise of Chinese protection for the Khotanese realm.[2] In addition to the Buddhist monk Ānanda, the mural comprises images of (1) a radiantly beautiful female figure standing in a water-filled lotus tank: this is Hāritī, the most widely worshiped yakṣī in all of Asia; (2) a naked child clinging to her thigh (see figs. 4.16 and 4.17): as was noted earlier, this pan-Asian protectress of newborns has been perennially represented together with multiple infant figures;[3] (3) the Buddha; and (4) a riderless horse. At the southeastern end of the mural is (5) a massive sculpture of the "King of the Yakṣas" Vaiśravaṇa—the same figure as the Vessavana of the Pāli-language DJ tale from the last chapter—standing on (6) the recumbent figure of a "red demon."

As Stein himself noted, the pictorial style of old Khotan was derived directly from Indic models found in Gandhara and its surrounding regions.[4] However, as Chandra convincingly argues, those models were reprised in this western Chinese setting to specific political ends, with the demon representing

FIGURE 6.1. Hāritī, Dandan-Uiliq, Xinjiang, China, seventh century CE. Image courtesy of the Hungarian Academy of Sciences.

the Tibetans, whose armies were a constant cause of Khotanese anxiety and strife throughout the period.[5] This squares with a number of royal annals, which relate how it was that when Khotan was threatened by the armies of the "red-faces," the Buddha marshalled Vaiśravana, Hāritī, and their armies to protect the kingdom and its people (represented by the child at Hāritī's hip).[6] Hāritī's Chinese features and hairstyle make it clear that her protection of the kingdom has been ensured via the Chinese military hand.[7] In his conclusion, Chandra compares Hāritī to Athena, the "national goddess" and divine protectress of the Greek city-state that bears her name to this day.[8]

Chandra's impressive analysis of this mural and sculpture's specific seventh- to eighth-century politico-religious message is, for our purposes, secondary. By this I mean that its primary meaning—that is, what would have made it immediately recognizable to all who viewed it in its setting—was the deeper story that we have seen told across the ancient and medieval Indo-European world. For what are the elements of this tableau? A female figure in a lotus pond, and a colossal male figure treading on his recumbent victim. Standing in her lotus pond, Hāritī is doubled—in the same way as Dame Ragnelle was by Sir Gromer Somer Joure and Hiḍimbā by Hiḍimba—by Vaiśravaṇa, the colossal yakṣa guardian of the kingdom of Khotan. The recumbent demon is to be analogized with trespassers who usurp the local water guardian's domain at their own peril—the princely brothers of the DJ and MBh narratives, as well as Vijaya's men in the MV. To be sure, there are additional figures in this tableau not found in the South Asian and western European sources reviewed in the last chapter,[9] but of course each of those narratives also featured its own "supporting cast" of characters.

As for the saddled but riderless horse, Chandra notes that it "symbolizes the Twenty-eight Yakṣa Generals who are mentioned together with Hāritī and her sons" in the *Suvarṇaprabhāsottamasūtra*. But here as well, one may look behind the specific Buddhist identity of this horse to ponder its simple presence in an ensemble that also comprises an alluring female figure, a dominant male figure, a victim, and a pool of water. Here, as in all of the traditions reviewed in the last chapter, the pool is a placid one: lotuses will not grow in troubled waters. In the balance of this chapter, however, we will see those waters come alive and interact in a specific set of ways with a maiden, a male figure—and a horse.

2

The most masterfully crafted of Chrétien de Troyes's three Arthurian romances, *Yvain*[10] features a series of attacks directed against its eponymous hero at a miraculous yet "perilous" spring-fed pool. Composed in the final quarter of the twelfth century,[11] Chrétien's work likely drew, directly or indirectly, upon motifs found in five literary works that predate *Yvain* by less than a century: the Welsh *Mabinogi*;[12] the Irish *Serglige Con Culainn* ("Con Culainn's Sick Bed")[13] and *Immram Maele Dúin* ("Voyage of Maele Dúin");[14] the British poet Wace's Old Norman *Roman de Rou*; and the anonymous *Vita sancti Kentegerni imperfecta*, a work composed in Scotland.[15] The events surrounding the Perilous Fountain, which occupy the first third of Chrétien's romance—and which essentially frame the entire narrative[16]—include a number of elements not found in these five works. While many of these episodes or motifs have been shown to have been products of Chrétien's literary imagination, we should also allow that others came to him through additional, less traceable folklore and storytelling traditions, both written and oral,[17] including Celtic lore that would have been derived, at least in part, from more ancient Indo-European sources.[18] The adaptation into courtly literature of this folklore and its enchanted world of fairies and monsters was, in Chrétien's time, a recent phenomenon grounded in the emergence of a new social class. As profits from royal and noble landholdings expanded with the clearing of the forests, liege warriors fighting in the service of these princes were increasingly rewarded both with small grants of land, and marriage to women of noble descent. But for the members of this rising class, these alone were insufficient. Here, as Jean-Claude Schmitt explains, "for those members of the lay gentry who had succeeded in founding a noble line by acquiring a wife and castle from a more powerful noble, what was now essential was recognition—by his peers, his superiors and the Church—of the legitimacy of his lineage, his name, and his estate. Here, the *milites* looked to the ambient folk culture—its mythic accounts, local legends, and the burgeoning world of fairies—as a source for their legitimacy. And in order that their claims should endure, they allied themselves with clerics capable of committing these oral traditions to writing."[19] The most gifted of all the storyteller clerics, Chrétien's stock hero was a simple knight who through his feats of chivalry sought to win the hand of his lady. Several centuries later, Cervantes would playfully subvert this scenario in his classic tale of Don Quixote, "the knight of mournful countenance."

In Chrétien's tale, the Perilous Fountain is overhung with the "the most beautiful pine tree that has ever grown on earth,"[20] from which there hangs a golden pail. No placid lotus pool this, for even as they are "colder than marble," its waters are ever "boiling like hot water."[21] More than this, when water is poured from the pail onto an emerald-colored slab lying on the fountain's bank, the heavens open and a tempestuous storm ensues, followed by a symphony of rapturous song from a flock of birds that covers every leaf and branch of the tree.[22] Soon after their chorus ends, however, another sound fills the air: the tumultuous arrival of the fountain's defender, a lone equestrian knight raising the thunder of ten riders.[23] Chrétien, who locates his spring-fed pool in the Forest of Brocéliande, in Brittany, draws nearly every element of his description from Wace's prior account of the place:

> The fountain of Barenton
> Springs up beside a stone.
> In time of great heat, hunters
> were in the habit of going to Barenton
> and of taking the water in their horns
> and wetting the top of the stone;
> this way they used to have rain.
> Thus it used to rain in former times
> in the forest and its surroundings,
> but I do not know why.
> One is accustomed to seeing fairies there,
> if the Bretons are telling us the truth,
> and many other marvels.
> There are nests of goshawks there
> and a great number of large stags . . .[24]

The practice of wetting the stones around the fountain of Barenton in times of drought persisted into the nineteenth century, and a number of medieval western European sources attest to other springs or wells with similar rainmaking properties.[25] However, the storms that Chrétien's Perilous Fountain unleashes are of a violence that far surpasses meteorological norms.[26] Why this should be so is alluded to elliptically in an early part of *Yvain*, where a character familiar with the spring remarks "if you wish to draw near to a fountain that is close by, you will not return easily, *unless you offer it its due in return*."[27] The implication here is that the spring itself is possessed of some right (*son droit*) that trespassers must respect,[28] analogous to the tribute (*bali*) demanded by the yakkhas and yakkhiṇīs of the quiet sylvan pools of South Asia.[29] Here, the Perilous Fountain's "right" is complicated by that of its present landowner,[30] a noble lady named Laudine, who has been identified by a number of scholars as a "water fairy," a common fixture in the *lai* literature of the period.[31] Her noble estate of Landuc, which comprises little more than the land surrounding the fountain and her nearby castle and dependences, requires a male champion to defend it. Whenever that champion, currently her husband, is slain in its defense, she and her hold on the land become vulnerable and undone, as it were, until such time as she is married to a new champion—even when that person is the slayer of her former spouse.[32] This is precisely what happens after Yvain has slain her husband, a towering red knight named Esclados li Ros:[33] Laudine must marry him. Her once-substantial landholding has already been greatly compromised; unless a valiant champion be found quickly, it will be reduced to naught.[34]

Throughout the opening episodes of the Perilous Fountain narrative, Laudine and Esclados li Ros are cast as rivals to the protagonist Yvain. However, unlike any of the accounts reviewed in the last chapter, the danger to the hero comes not only from the guardian of the pool, but more importantly from the fountain itself, which, possessed of rights of its own, unleashes its devastating fury upon the surrounding landscape of Laudine's tiny estate. Esclados says as much as he gallops up to challenge her fountain's first intruder, Yvain's cousin Calogrenant: "Vassal, gravely have you offended me, without proper challenge. You ought first to have challenged me if you had the slightest wits about you, or at least sought to know what was proper before you brought war against me. But, if it be in my power, sir vassal, the evil caused by your great harm will fall back on you. *My witness is my wood, which has been felled all around me*."[35] The defender of the fountain does not so much defend the fountain from outside aggressors as he defends the surrounding landscape from aggression *by the fountain itself* whenever an intruder disturbs its calm. The Perilous Fountain's full fury is most eloquently described near the conclusion of Chrétien's romance, when Yvain pours water from the golden pail onto the fateful slab for a fourth and final time. Tellingly, Chrétien declares that Yvain has done so after resolving to "[do] battle [at] her [Laudine's] spring" (*a sa fontainne guerroier*).[36] Since Yvain is by this time the authorized defender of the fountain, his adversary can be none other than the fountain itself. As Chrétien relates,

> Don't think I'm lying to you: the storm was so violent that no one could tell the tenth part of it, for it seemed the whole forest was about to plunge into the abyss! The lady fears that her castle will come down altogether. The walls shake, the tower trembles, and it would take but little for it to collapse. The boldest among them would rather have been captured in Persia by the Turks than to find themselves within those walls. So fearful were they that they cursed their ancestors: "Cursed be the man who first made this country his home, cursed be those who built this fortress! In all the world they could not find a more hateful place, for a single man can attack and torment and devastate it."[37]

The forest setting and the presence of singing birds at the fountain are reminiscent of the MBh accounts of still waters, but here there are no riddles to answer. Instead, the hero is pressed into armed combat by the defender of the place, or, more properly speaking, its lady's defender against the Perilous Fountain itself. Furthermore, nearly all of these combats take place between Pentecost and mid-August, the "time of great heat" mentioned by Wace above, and evoked in the *Odyssey* and nearly all of the South Asian yakkha narratives of the last chapter as well, perhaps, as in the name of Gromer Somer Joure.[38] Two *Yvain* motifs not found in those myths may be read as authorial invention on Chrétien's part, or, once again, mythemes that he appropriated from a deeper level of Celtic or Indo-European lore. The first of these is the violence of Perilous Fountain itself, whose cold boiling waters erupt in a destructive fury that threatens the surrounding landscape, in apparent defense of its "right." This narrative theme, with its limited cast of characters, will be the focus of this chapter.

3

The second novel element introduced by Chrétien in his account of the Perilous Fountain involves the presence of horses: when they battle, the fountain's trespasser and defender are both mounted on horseback. This detail, so obvious at first blush—an Arthurian knight without a horse was not a knight at all—proves to be significant when viewed in the context of broader European traditions. Consider, for example, the following account recorded in 1884 by T. E. Morris on the subject of the origin of a small lake in Carmarthenshire, Wales, and a rider named Owen (the Welsh cognate of Yvain):

> There was once a man of the name of Owen living on the Mynydd Mawr, and he had a well ("ffynnon"). Over this well he kept a large flag[stone] . . . which he was always careful to replace over its mouth after he had satisfied himself or his beast with its water. It happened, however, that one day he went on

> horseback to the well to water his horse, and forgot to put the flag back in its place. He rode off leisurely in the direction of his home; but, after he had gone some distance, he casually looked back, and, to his great astonishment, saw that the well had burst out and was overflowing the whole place. He suddenly bethought him that he should ride back and encompass the overflow of the water as fast as he could; and it was the horse's track in galloping round the water that put a stop to its further overflowing. It is fully believed that, had he not galloped round the flood in the way he did, the well would have been sure to inundate the whole district and drown all. Hence the lake was called the Lake of Owen's Flag ("Llyn Llech Owen").[39]

Morris goes on to evoke a number of possible medieval antecedents to this piece of nineteenth-century lore. These include a ninth-century "speech poem of a lost tale" contained in the circa 1250 CE *Black Book of Carmarthen*,[40] a manuscript from the same region of Wales as the story of Llyn Llech Owen. Out of pride or arrogance (*traha*), a maiden named Mererid releases the waters of a fountain (*finaun*),[41] inundating "Gwyddno's Field," a land sometimes identified with the kingdom of a debauched royal named Seithenhin.[42] This, the "Welsh Atlantis," is said now to lie beneath the waters of Cardigan Bay.

In one stanza of the poem, Mererid cries out "from the back of a bay horse (*gwineu*)."[43] Horses also figure prominently in a number of medieval Irish sources concerning the fatal eruption of water. The most complete account of this type is found in the *Aided Echach maic Maireda* ("The Death of Eochaid McMaireda"), a work preserved in the twelfth-century *Lebor na hUidre* ("Book of the Dun Cow").[44] Here, Mairid, the king of Munster, has two sons, Echu and Rí. Echu elopes with his stepmother, Éibliu, and the couple leaves the country together with Rí and his men. A thousand in number, they travel with their flocks and herds. Following the advice of druids, the brothers and their men part ways, at which point their fates follow parallel paths. Rí sets out westward, eventually coming to the playing ground of a figure named Midir. Midir kills all of Rí's horses, lending him a single horse in their stead. Loaded with all his men's gear, this horse lies down in the middle of a plain, where it lets its urine flow. The flow becomes a well, which engulfs and drowns everyone. This is the origin of the lake known as Loch Rí. Setting out in a different direction, Echu suffers a similar fate. A tall man named Óengus orders him off of his land, and Echu and his men refuse. Óengus kills all of his horses in the night, providing him a single great packhorse in their stead with the order that "they should not unharness the horse or allow it to stop, lest it should let its urine flow and be the cause of their deaths." After that, they set out "on a Sunday" until they reach the place called "Grey Thicket" (the plain of Líathmuine, in Ulster). There, after they fail to heed Óengus's instructions, the horse urinates, its waters forming a deep well. Echu builds a house over the well with a lid on it, leaving a single woman to guard it. One day the woman neglects to cover the well, and the water rises up and spreads out to form Loch nEchach, drowning Echu and all his children, with the exception of a daughter and two sons.[45] As Ranke de Vries has argued, certain of Echu's actions were questionable on both legal and religious grounds. On the one hand, his refusal to depart with his horses from Óengus's land was nothing less than an abusive attempt to expropriate it; on the other, his Sunday departure was a violation of the Irish "Law of Sunday."[46] We will return to this motif, of this type of punishment for similar "sacrileges," several times in this chapter.

Several ancient Greek sources also draw a link between horses and springs. Poseidon, the god of the waters, but most particularly of the earth's subterranean waters, often bears the epithet Hippios, "Equine." As Bernard Sergent has noted, it is he who, in this role, opened up the earth to allow those waters to first well up to the surface.[47] So it was that the landscape of ancient Greece was dotted with springs known as the "Horse's Fount" (*hippokrēnē*), which were said to have been created at places where Poseidon had once driven his trident into the earth. One of these, located in Boeotia, was the site where Pegasus, Greek mythology's first domesticated horse, originally sprang from the ground: his name is derived from the Greek *pēgē*, "spring." At one of these Horse's Founts, the two elements were inverted: according to Pausanias in his circa 175 CE *Hellados Periēgēsis* ("Description of Greece"), "the earth sent up the water [there] when the horse Pegasus struck the ground with his hoof."[48]

This is not the sole account that Pausanias narrates of water erupting from the earth's surface. In his description of the region of Arcadia, he speaks of Poseidon's sanctuary at Mantineia. After evoking the sanctuary's construction by Agamēdes and Trophōnios and their placement of a woolen thread across its entrance, Pausanias relates that a certain Aipytos, the son of Hippothous, entered the sanctuary by cutting through that thread. For this sacrilegious act, he was blinded by a wave that dashed into his eyes and killed him.[49] The sanctuary at Mantineia, which had a hippodrome located nearby, was dedicated to Poseidon Hippios.[50] This feature of the sanctuary is presented dynamically in Morris's Welsh story, when the "horse's track in galloping round the water . . . put a stop to its further overflowing." With the exception of the Lake of Owen's Flag and Pausanias's account of Pegasus's hoof, these living waters always prove fatal: once they rush up out of the ground, through the presence or impulse of a woman or a horse, they cannot be stopped. They maim, they kill, and they drown everyone and everything in their path. Indeed, when one considers the destructive fury of the Perilous Fountain, which makes walls tremble and towers sway to the point of crumbling,[51] as well as the sixteen inundated towns of Gwyddno's Field,[52] one is reminded of another of Poseidon's epithets: he is *ennosigaios*, the "Earth-Shaker."[53] Boiling waters, earthquakes, deadly waves, radically altered landscapes: at bottom, all of these phenomena are indicators of geothermal activity. There exists a very rich, specifically Indo-European, mythology of geothermal phenomena whose range extends well beyond the borders of western Europe and the Mediterranean, even overflowing the linguistic boundaries of the Indo-European world.

4

In my 1996 study of the Siddha traditions of South Asia, I noted the description of a novel technique for extracting mercury from the "wells" (*kūpa*s) in which it was naturally found.[54] This description appears in seven Sanskrit-language alchemical works from the Indian subcontinent. In chronological order, these are the circa-thirteenth-century *Rasendracūḍāmaṇi* ("Crest-Jewel of the Champion of Essential Elements") of Somadeva and *Rasaprakāśasudhākara* ("Moonglow of the Essential Elements") of Yaśodhara Bhaṭṭa; the thirteenth- to fourteenth-century *Rasaratnasamuccaya* ("Assemblage of Jewels and Essential Elements") of Vāgbhaṭṭa,[55] the fourteenth-century *Ānandakanda* ("Root of Bliss") of Mahābhairava;[56] the fifteenth-to seventeenth-century *Śivakalpadruma* ("Śiva's Wish-fulfilling Tree") of Śivanātha; the 1682–83 CE *Rasakautuka* ("Wonder of the Essential Elements") of Mallārinābha;[57] and the 1709 CE *Śivatattvaratnākara* ("Jewel-Mine of the Essence of Śiva") of Keḷadi Basava.[58] Both Śivanātha's and Mallārinābha's narratives are virtual copies of Vāgbhaṭṭa's account; Keḷadi Basava transcribes the *Ānandakanda*'s description verbatim.

Somadeva, who likely hailed from Gujarat,[59] sets the scene. After describing the various wells in which mercury is naturally found, he writes: "[A maiden] who has had her first menstrual bath has approached [a well of mercury] mounted on a horse, and he who wishes to take her hand in marriage (*jighṛkṣuḥ*)[60] pursues her everywhere for a full *yojana*.[61] Then he returns to the well, but King Mercury (or the Prince Royal, *sūtarāṭ*) settles (*saṃtiṣṭhate*) into a hollow [previously] dug across his path. Then he is collected there by the natives of that place." The two verses that follow refer to the country in which said mercury is found: "Now, that mercury was borne by the Ganges [River], the wind, and [its own] mass;[62] and since it fell in a truly distant land (*dūradeśe*), that country is known as 'Setting the Limit' (*pārada*). In fact, the mercury (*sūta*) that is in the clay (i.e. mercury ore) is extracted through the sublimation method. Setting the limit to diseases (*gadapārada*), [mercury] is to be known as 'setting the limit' (*pārada*)."[63] The

Gujarati author Yaśodhara Bhaṭṭa, whose *Rasaprakāśasudhākara* was either coeval with or slightly later than Somadeva's work,[64] offers a rather laconic description, sans reference to the maiden's menstrual bath.

> West of the Himalaya there is a beautiful peak named "Lord of the Hills." In close proximity to that [peak], the Champion of Minerals (*rasendra*) dwells in bodily form (*sākṣāt*) inside a perfectly rounded well.[65] A beautiful, well-adorned young maiden mounted upon the finest of horses [once] came there. Looking down into the well, she [then] very speedily turned back. Most excellent Mercury (*sūtavara*) rushed [after her and] fell to the earth in the four directions.[66] Nowadays there is a perfectly circular field, which, stirred up by Mercury [at that time], is evenly spread out for twelve *yojana*s in every direction around the well. Sublimated in a sublimation apparatus, the clay (i.e., mercury ore) of that field is truly [a] disease killing [agent]. The mercury that is produced [through sublimation] is manifestly beautiful. It is itself called "setting the limit" (*pārada*).[67]

One to two centuries later, Vāgbhaṭṭa's account is slightly more prolix:

> A well-adorned maiden who has bathed on the occasion of her first menstrual period is mounted upon a horse [and] looking [all around]. Beholding her, Mercury (*rasa*), who is lodged in a well, wishes to take her hand in marriage (*jighṛkṣuḥ*). He suddenly rushes forth, but seeing him, she swiftly takes flight. Mercury (*sūta*) follows her for the distance of one full *yojana*. Then He Who Was Born From Śiva quickly returns to the well [but] he ends up settled (*sthita*) in hollows that have been created along his path. [That is how] they catch the mercury (*pārada*). That mercury, because of its mass, fell from the mouth of Agni in Darada country. It was absorbed into the ground. The people of this and other countries cast that clay (i.e. mercury ore) into a sublimation apparatus and extract the mercury.[68]

About a century later, the *Ānandakanda*, a work likely compiled in the southwestern part of the subcontinent,[69] adds several details:

> An attractive, fine-featured [maiden], well-bathed after her first menstruation, wearing fresh clothing and fine ornaments and anointed with fragrant garlands, is mounted upon the finest of horses. She has shunned sexual intercourse. After reverencing Gaṇanātha and Bhairava, and contemplating the ancient guru Bhairava Who Is the Champion of Minerals (*rasendrabhairava*), she should, O my darling, quickly gaze upon Mercury (*pārada*), who is dwelling in a well. The equestrian maiden should then make off over the distance of one *yojana*, without once looking back. But now the maiden should lead that [Mercury] home [as her bridegroom] (*āharet*). Out of a desire to take her hand in marriage (*saṅjighṛkṣayā*), he rises up from the heart of the well and chases after her. When he has covered a *yojana*, he will suddenly [attempt to]

> re-enter the well; but a native from the Land of Mercury, shall, after purifying himself, take hold of that Champion of Minerals who has settled into hollows [previously] dug on all sides [of the well]. That mercury (*sūta*), because of its mass, fell from the mouth of Agni in the country called Darada. [There] it was absorbed into the ground. Cast into the earthen apparatus called "Sublimation" by alchemists conversant in the Tantras,[70] the collected mercury (*pārada*) is extracted. O Goddess! It is said to be flawless. O Goddess! Perfected Beings (Siddhas) and Wizards (Vidyādharas) everywhere have always inscribed [his name as] the "Champion among Those Setting the Limit" (*pāradendra*) and considered him a provider of supernatural powers.[71]

The mytho-logic behind this extraction technique is clear. The Hindu alchemical tradition identifies mercury (Hg) as the phallic god Śiva's semen in mineral form. Sulfur (S), which is mercury's principal chemical reagent, is the mineral form taken by the uterine or menstrual blood of Śiva's divine consort. The origin myths for Hg and S, found in a number of alchemical works, depict them as the only slightly altered sexual emissions of the primal dyad of Hindu Tantra.[72] This conceptual interplay between sexual fluids and minerals is sufficient for understanding the attraction that a menarcheal maiden would have on mineral semen. Its eruption out of a subterranean well would appear to be orgasmic in everything but name—but to what end? The hollows dug in its path constitute a novel form of contraception.

As for the detail that the maiden is mounted on a horse, this would appear to a piece of South Asian exotica. Traditional South Asian women did not ride horseback. However, women from faraway lands, west of the Himalayas, situated at the limit of the world, apparently could. Such may be seen in a half-dozen extant Mughal miniatures, wherein the landscapes across which Mercury is pursuing the maiden on horseback feature groups of figures in exotic foreign dress (plate 26).[73] The matrimonial language of these accounts also brings equestrianism into the picture, since in traditional Indian weddings the groom rides to the house of the bride to fetch her back to his family compound. Here as well, the reversal of roles would once again be of a piece with the exotic venue of these unconsummated alchemical marriages.

These instructions for the extraction of mercury from its wells enshrine all of the principal Sanskrit terms for mercury: *rasa* ("mineral, essential element"), *rasendra* ("champion of minerals"), *sūta* ("he who was born"), and *pārada* ("setting the limit"). In my translations, however, I have alternated between using the masculine ("he") and neuter ("it") pronouns for (M)ercury. In the first part of each narrative, in which Mercury actively pursues the equestrian maiden, indicating agency, mobility, and volition (*jighṛkṣu*, "wishing to take her hand in marriage [or to catch her]"), I call Mercury "he" or "him."

The language of the *Rasendracūḍāmaṇi*, which refers to him as King Mercury or the Prince Royal (*sūtarāṭ*), as well as that of the *Rasaprakāśasudhākara*, which speaks of the Champion of Minerals as dwelling "in bodily form," even "in person" (*sākṣāt*) at the bottom of his well, is particularly illustrative. In the *Rasaratnasamuccaya*, Mercury is referred to as "He Who Was Born From Śiva," a reference to the fact that these same alchemical sources identify mercury with Śiva's semen, which was "engendered" (*sūta*) after an interminable bout of sexual intercourse with the great Goddess. Mercury is a son of god of sorts, and as such, one should perhaps read the term *sūta* in these accounts as "the Son" (*suta*).

But are these sources imagining him simply as animated "divine semen" or as something more anthropomorphic? In the second part of each narrative, which describes how the metal is extracted from its ore, I call mercury "it," because what is being described is the treatment of a nonsentient, albeit volatile, fluid mineral.[74] Here, I am suggesting that (M)ercury's two modes of being parallel those of the Perilous Fountain, a source of nonsentient, albeit volatile waters that was, at the same time, accorded the status of a legal subject (*son droit*).[75] Also in the light of the Celtic material—as well, perhaps, of the riderless horse in the Hāritī mural from Dandan-Uiliq[76]—our menarcheal maiden's horse may in the end be something more than an exotic oddity. But the mythological *bricolage* does not end here.

It is significant that the younger *Rasaratnasamuccaya* and *Ānandakanda* narratives transform the "distant land" (*dūradeśa*) of Somadeva's account into "Darada Country" (*darada-deśa*) or the "Country called Darada" (*daradāhvaya deśa*). Identified with the modern-day Dardistan—a region to the west of the Himalayas[77]—this land and its people were known as Darada(s) in the South Asian record from about 500 BCE down through the medieval period.[78] As for Somadeva himself, he identifies this distant land by another name, Pārada, which he etymologizes as "Setting the Limit." Like Darada, Pārada was a name both for a mineral and for a faraway land and its people: medieval traditions placed the Pāradas or Pārada country on the Makran coast of southern Baluchistan in modern-day Pakistan.[79] Also located in this region is the ancient shrine of the "Red Goddess" Hiṅglāj Devī, whose name is traditionally derived from the Sanskrit *hiṅgula* ("red cinnabar"). In the vicinity of her shrine is a site called Candrakūp ("Moon Well"), to which I will return at the end of this chapter.[80]

Like *hiṅgula*, *darada* is a Sanskrit term for cinnabar, mercuric sulfide (HgS), the red-colored ore—the "clay" of our narratives—from which mercury is commonly extracted. While Dardistan is not particularly rich in cinnabar, the country of Badakhshan, slightly to the north in modern-day northeastern

Afghanistan, was renowned from antiquity as the source of a brilliant red mineral. A fifth-century BCE Persian document names it *sinkabruš*, the word from which the Greek *kinnábari* and the English "cinnabar" are derived.[81] Now, Darada Country is identified in a number of South Asian alchemical works as the site of a "northern well" of mercury. One of a set of five directionally distributed wells of mercury, this northern mercury is notable for its *red color* and high level of purity.[82] Situated at the extreme northwestern limit of the Indian subcontinent, this may be the sole site at which "indigenous" South Asian mercury is to be found.[83] It is nonetheless possible that our sources identified cinnabar with this country because mercury ore (whose other names include *cīna-piṣṭa* ["Chinese powder"] and *carmāragandhikā* ["that which makes hides stink"]) was carried into the subcontinent from mines in East and Inner Asia via trade routes running through Dardistan.[84] But these trade networks were also conduits of information, which in some cases traveled more extensively than the trade goods themselves. Such was the possible case with the information embedded in these Sanskrit-language mercury extraction accounts.

Slightly later than the Mahābhairava who compiled the *Ānandakanda*, but also hailing from South India, was another alchemical author who also located a mercurial well in a distant country and described the mercury in that well as a living, sentient being. This was the fifteenth- to seventeenth-century Sittar (Siddha) alchemist Irāmatevar, a Tamil Hindu who converted to Islam (and changed his name to Yakoob or Yakoppu) in order to further his alchemical quest.[85] The most salient portion of Yakoppu's account involves his journey to a fabled well of mercury located some five hundred *kosa*s[86] from "Mecca." As he relates,

> I went to Mecca to find the mercury well about which the Arabs spoke with much authority. I swallowed some *kulikai* and set off to the mountainous region when I came across some Nabis, the alchemy masters. I stopped there for a while, served them and then asked for the exact location of the well. They let me know the place and I with one more tablet of mercury went to the location with a gourd pitcher. On seeing the well I slowly lowered the vessel. But I was assaulted by the mercury.[87] I had to fly high and with mercury I went back to Mecca, pretending to be innocent. I treated the mercury with blue vitriol and other chemicals and stabilized the mercury. I thus prepared many kinds of pills. I kept one under my tongue, one in my palm and one in my hip. Thus with a wrapping of mercury, I flew over several mountains, several countries, and met many alchemists. I exchanged my knowledge and learned many new techniques from them.[88]

On the basis of the vocabulary and other data found in Yakoppu's accounts of his travels, I believe his well was located far closer to the Indian subcontinent than it was to "Mecca"; and I would opine that his mercurial well was none other than the Candrakūp situated in the proximity of Hiṅglāj Devī.[89]

Regardless of its location, the mercury found in this well, like that of the extraction accounts, appears to be sentient, mobile, and possessed of free will. However, rather than pursuing a human female, even a prospective bride, out of attraction to her, he here assaults a human male on the basis of a motivation perhaps redolent of that of Yvain's Perilous Fountain. Yakoppu's testimony has yet another wrinkle to it, since in another of his works, the *Tantakam 110*,[90] he identifies Valai as the patron goddess of Tamil alchemists. However, as Kanchana Natarajan has noted in her study of this alchemist's works and legend, the Tamil term *valai* denotes both a prepubescent maiden and mercury.[91] This is of course at variance with the Sanskritic alchemical canon, which identifies mercury as the semen of the phallic god Śiva; and Yakoppu makes a point of using the male Sanskrit term *sūta* for the mercury that "assaulted" him.[92] These "reversals," as structuralists of yore would have called them, recall the alternating genders of the dæmon guardians of still waters of the previous chapter, as well as of the equestrian figures that approach the "perilous fountains" of various geothermal phenomena.

What are we to make of the seeming humanization, if not divinization, of a being—called King Mercury or Prince Royal, or He Who Was Born From Śiva—who springs out of the well in which he dwells "in person" in order to pursue marriageable maidens and assault foreign alchemists? Its possible human qualities aside, the mercury of South Asian alchemy was, in its purest form, assumed to be possessed of the power of flight.[93] This power is referred to throughout the alchemical canon, and it also appears in the yogi lore of medieval and early modern India. We find the technical term for such mercury in Yakoppu's account: the Tamil *kulikai* is a cognate of the Sanskrit *guṭikā* ("globule," "pellet," "pill"). In its most highly refined state, alchemical mercury becomes a solid pellet, possessed of the autonomous power of flight. When held in the mouth of an alchemist—a practice called *guṭika-bandha*—it allows him to fly.[94] An amusing seventeenth-century tale relates how a yogi possessed of just such a pellet once flew into the Emperor Akbar's harem and promptly fell asleep. While he was sleeping, the mercurial pellet fell from his mouth. Akbar, learning of the situation, nonetheless showed himself to be more interested in the pellet than in any liberties the yogi might have taken with his women.[95]

5

In an 1895 article Fernand de Mély discussed the possibility of exchanges in matters alchemical between medieval China and Greece. De Mély's primary data source was a mercury extraction technique reported in nearly identical terms in a circa 800–1000 CE Syriac work attributed to Zosimos of Panopolis, on the one hand,[96] and on the other, in an entry in the *Ho han sans ts'ai t'ou hui*, a seventeenth-century Chinese encyclopedia.[97] These accounts are nearly identical in all their details to the Sanskrit alchemical narratives discussed above. De Mély's Chinese source turns out to be a relatively late adaptation of a description found in several earlier works, including the *Bencao Gangmu* of Li Shizhen, a sixteenth-century Ming anthology.[98] However, the earliest extant Chinese version, which appears in Zhu Derun's 1347 CE *Cun fuzhai wenji* ("Collected Works on Preserving, Restoring, and Purifying"), dates from about the same period as our Sanskrit-language sources. As Zhu explains, he had learned of this mercury extraction technique in 1345 from two former Yuan imperial guards, to whom it had been described by members of an embassy from Fo-lin sometime between 1314 and 1320. Zhu's narrative reads as follows:

> Their country lies in the region where the sun goes down. The land is extremely vast and has seventy-two tribal elders. There is in this country a sea of quicksilver, spanning about forty to fifty *li* in circumference.[99] The way in which the inhabitants extract [the quicksilver is the following]: First they dig several tens of well shafts at a distance of ten *li* from the shore, and after that they dispatch strong men [to that place] on horses that are so light-footed that they can keep up with a flying falcon. The men and the horses are all covered in gold leaf and ride abreast in tight formation skirting along the meanders of the sea's shoreline. When the sun glints off the gold, [it emits] a dazzling brilliance; then the quicksilver boils up like a tidal wave and comes forth, as if it were intending to cling fast [to the gold leaf] with the strength of a viscous glue. Thereupon, the men immediately turn their horses around and ride off with the greatest of speed, and the quicksilver pursues them. Were they to move only slightly more slowly, then the quicksilver would strike and drown them. By the time the men and horses have raced back, the quicksilver's strength has receded and its vigor diminished. As they retreat further back to the well shafts, the quicksilver trickles and accumulates therein. Then the inhabitants immediately fetch it out. They boil it down with aromatic herbs, such that it all turns into fine silver [lit. "flower silver"].[100]

Although the virginal maiden on horseback has been replaced here by a band of male riders, most of the details of the Sanskrit-language South Asian narratives are present in this Chinese account. The process takes place in a distant land far to the west, and mercury, after pursuing its quarry over a specific distance, is captured and immobilized by means of well shafts dug across its return path. It too is processed through sublimation ("boiling"), and the "flower silver" into which it is transformed is evocative of refined quicksilver. This being a sea rather than a well of mercury, it boils up "like a tidal wave," but as in the South Asian accounts, it is possessed of volition, "intending" as it does to cling fast to the gold leaf. Here, however, the attraction is chemical rather than sexual: when mercury amalgamates with gold, it truly appears to cling to it prior to consuming it entirely. At this point, mercury's viscosity is comparable to that of a thick glue-like or binding agent.[101]

Walter Fuchs, who in 1958 published the earliest transcription and (German) translation of this account, suggested that the envoys in question were from Moorish Granada,[102] and that the mercury source to which they were referring was none other than the Almadén mine, famous then as now for the abundance and quality of its mercury ore.[103] However, Fuchs also noted that in Zhu's time Asia's mercury supply came from "China, Persia, Transoxiana and the Near East." Zhu's mention of the toponym Fo-lin is a likely variant on Fu-lin, a common Chinese word for Byzantium or Roman Syria;[104] and as De Mély noted in his 1895 study, Bir es Zeibaq ("Well of Mercury"), the site named in his seventeenth-century Chinese source, was a contemporary "Syrian" toponym, situated in modern-day Israel where no native mercury is found.[105]

A thousand miles to the northeast of this Israeli site, reports of naphtha (*naffāṭat*) springs, "volcanoes," wells of fire, and off-shore eruptions near the petroleum-rich Caspian coastline at Baku (in modern-day Azerbaijan) began to appear in Arabic, Persian, and European sources from the tenth century onward.[106] One of these, the 1226 CE *Mu'jam al-buldān* ("Dictionary of Countries"), the work of Yāḳūt al-Rūmī, an Arab geographer of Greek origin, described a large naphtha spring (an above-ground seepage of oil) in the Baku region. Close by was a "spring from which flows white naphtha like oil of mercury (*duhnu al-zibaq*), ceasing neither by day nor by night."[107] Describing Baku's "naphtha springs," the Persian historian Ḥamd-allāh Mustawfī (d. 1349) relates that "over a tract of land they have dug dry wells to get down to the Naphtha source, and the water which rises in these wells carries the naphtha on its surface."[108] Might this site and its extraction techniques have been the basis for the report Zhu received indirectly from "Fo-lin" emissaries? I will return to this region, situated in close vicinity to the homeland of the original speakers of *PIE,[109] at the end of this chapter.

Zhu's account also places his sea of mercury "in the region where the sun goes down." This recalls Somadeva's "distant land" (*dūradeśa*) named "Setting the Limit" (*pārada*) that was situated to the west of the Himalayas. Here, we should also recall that Iramatevar-Yakoppu locates the "mercury well about which the Arabs spoke with much authority" in the direction of "Mecca."[110]

By his time, Mecca, Antioch, and the former Byzantium had been absorbed into the Ottoman Empire. But as De Mély noted, the Chinese account just reviewed appears to have been derived from a narrative embedded in a circa 800–1000 CE Syriac version of the *Treatise* of Zosimos of Panopolis, a work translated into French by Rubens Duval in 1893. This version is presumably a translation of an earlier Greek-language work, but because that work is no longer extant, one cannot know whether it included the following narrative.[111] I am grateful to Matteo Martelli of the University of Bologna for his translation of this passage, which, based on his own concise edition of the *Treatise*, is superior to that of Marcellin Berthelot, whose edition Duval had relied upon for his 1893 translation:

> In the furthest region of the West,[112] where tin [*zws*, lit. "Zeus"] is located, there is a spring of water[113] that gushes out and pulls him [i.e. Zeus] up[114] like water. When the inhabitants of this region see that he is ready to overflow out of the spring, they have a virgin girl of outstanding beauty stand naked in front of him; she [stands] in a depression, in front of a deep hole in the field, so that he lusts after the beauty of the young girl; for he rushes upon her in a leap with the desire to take possession of her. But she is accustomed to running quickly, and there are young people standing next to her bearing axes in their hands. As soon as they see him draw near to the virgin girl, they beat and cut him; and he goes his way into that deep hole, and he congeals by himself and hardens. They cut this *zws* into pieces [lit. into nodules or lumps] and make use of it. That is why they give the name of "river water" to the mercury that comes from tin (*onko*). They use this name because it runs like the water that flows away in the fields and it is similar in shape to a rebel and bright dragon.[115]

In his 1893 summary of this passage, Berthelot explained that "they offer a virgin girl to the deity of this spring, in order to lure him outside."[116] This of course brings us back to the nature of the fluid being contained in its spring, well, or sea: was it a living dæmon or a flowing metal? It is for this reason that Martelli employs the personal pronoun "he" for the tin of the first part of this account. In fact, the Syriac term for "tin" is *zws*, which is also the transcription of the Greek "Zeus." This is quite common in Syriac alchemical works, where the name of the Greek god (or better still, the planet) is usually used to refer to "tin."[117] However, at the end of the passage, when Zosimos discusses the extraction of mercury from said tin, he uses a different term, *onko*, which unambiguously refers to the metal alone.[118] We have already seen the same alternation in the South Asian versions of this extraction account: when Mercury is pursuing the maiden, he is a living being, whereas when its sublimation is being described, mercury is treated as a volatile metal.

As was the case in the later South Asian and Chinese accounts, Zosimos attributes volition, emotion, and mobility to the fluid dæmon: he "lusts after" the young girl and "rushes upon her in a leap with the desire to take possession of her." This version also provides us with a possible explanation for the verbal constructions based on the root √*sthā* ("stand," "settle") in the four Sanskrit-language accounts: drawing on a tradition that was likely their common source, theirs were descriptions of how mercury, once trapped in hollows in the ground, "congeals by itself and hardens." Now, it is true that the fluid dæmon or metal of Zosimos's narrative is *zws*, "tin," which only yields up "mercury" (*zīwag*) after it has been processed by the natives of the place. This detail notwithstanding, this extraction account clearly flows from the same mythological tradition of living waters as that attested in the nineteenth-century Welsh account of how a gushing well came to be tamed by a rider circling it on horseback. Finally, we cannot overlook the fact that, while Zosimos's maiden isn't riding horseback as she does in the Sanskrit accounts, she is naked, standing in front of the hollow that will trap the fluid metal that rushes upon her. Here we are far from Zhu's or Yakoppu's accounts of male mercury assaulting male humans. As in the South Asian extraction narratives, the attraction here is patently sexual, a male dæmon streaming out of the ground in pursuit of a lithe maiden. Here as well, the fluid metal's capture involves catchment basins and, in this case, chopping.

6

I now summarize the extraction narrative embedded in these four sources, which I will indicate hereafter as **SAN** (Sanskrit), **T** (Tamil), **C** (Chinese), and **SYR** (Syriac):

> In a distant western land, a (naked [**SYR**]) maiden (on horseback [**SAN**]; or else a mounted band of men clad in gold leaf [**C**] or a lone male alchemist [**T**]) attracts the attention of a living, sentient fluid mineral being by passing (or standing [**SYR**] or flying [**T**]) in proximity to the well [**SAN, T**], spring [**SYR**], or sea [**C**] in which he resides. Possessed of a desire or intention to marry, catch [**SAN**], possess [**SYR**], cling to (the golden armor of [**C**]), or assault [**T**] the approaching human(s), that living being (who is identified with a dæmon [**SAN, SYR**]) rushes after her [**SAN, SYR**] (or him [**T**], or them [**C**]). He pursues his quarry, but when, after a specific distance he turns around and attempts to return to his abode [**SAN, C**], he is trapped in a naturally occurring depression [**SYR**], or hollow [**SAN**] or set of well shafts [**C**] that have been dug to that end by the people of that land. Now reduced to the state of an inert mineral or metal, he is no longer referred to as a living sentient being or dæmon [**SAN, C, SYR**]. The natives of the land then process that mineral in order to stabilize and optimize it [**SAN, C, SYR, T**].

While the manuscript sources for the **SYR** account can be firmly dated to an earlier time than those of the **SAN**, **C**, or **T** accounts, it is unlikely that any of these borrowed from it directly (although it is likely that **T** was directly inspired by **SAN**). I say this because of a number of inexplicable differences among them. Why, for example, is the virgin maiden naked in **SYR** and clothed in **SAN**, and replaced by "strong men" in **C**? Why is the fluid entity's attraction amorous in **SAN** and **SYR**, but strictly chemical in **C**? Why do **SAN** and **C** speak of the fluid being's attempt to return to its source after pursuing its quarry for a specific distance, when **SYR** says nothing of the sort? Finally, why do **SAN** and **C** feature horses, when none are present in **SYR**?

For all this, their similarities far outweigh their differences. Clearly we are in the presence of connected (hi)stories, of the transmission of a tradition across linguistic and cultural boundaries, in all probability via the same medieval trade routes as those over which mercury and other minerals were transported in the medieval period. While there is insufficient data to localize the archetype narrative, whether oral or written, from which these four versions drew their inspiration, one cannot help but note that nearly every retelling places its action in a "western" locale. Zhu says as much in the introduction to **C**: the technique had been reported to him by two former envoys to Byzantium or Roman Syria. Both **SYR** and **C** situate their well or sea on the western edge of the world, while Yaśodhara Bhaṭṭa's is found to the west of the Himalayas, and Irāmatevar's to the west, in the general direction of "Mecca." And, as we have seen, medieval reports of geothermal activity near Baku, where there is a "spring from which flows white naphtha like oil of mercury," also point to a western—i.e., Middle Eastern—location.

Like the western European myths, literary works, and folk narratives with which we began this chapter, these mercury extraction accounts may be viewed as variants on a far more archaic Indo-European protomyth of "fire in water," inspired by human encounters and interactions with geothermal phenomena in an ancient time. The complex Indo-European protomyth of fire in water was first discussed by Georges Dumézil in 1963, and greatly expanded by him in 1973.[119] In the decades that have followed, a number of other scholars—including Jaan Puhvel,[120] Ellison Banks Findly,[121] Heinrich Wagner,[122] Dominique Briquel,[123] Claude Sterckx,[124] Bernard Sergent,[125] and Jean Kellens[126]—have further elaborated upon this Indo-European dossier.[127] While much of what follows in this section is a summary of the work of these scholars, I have made several additions of my own, some of which reprise the Old French, Irish, and Welsh material discussed earlier in this chapter. Here, I review the most important extant witnesses to the protomyth, which appear in (1) a set of vedic hymns of praise to the god Apám Napāt; (2) the

Indo-Iranian mythology of the god Apąm Napāt; (3) Roman accounts of the overflowing of the waters of the Alban Lake; (4) the Irish mythology of Nechtan's well; (5) a Greek account of a *nymphaion* at Apollonia in Greek Illyria; (6) a Greek account, already summarized,[128] of an Arcadian sanctuary dedicated to Poseidon; (7) a Greek account of the well of Asbama in Cappadocia; and (8) a Latin-language praise of thermal spas dedicated to the Gaulish Apollo in eastern France.

A

The earliest extant versions of the fire in water myth, found in the Vedas—and thereby likely composed somewhere to the northwest of the Indus River valley toward the beginning of the second millennium BCE—are the least coherent. Liturgical hymns of praise, these contain no plot, although certain of their expressions clearly anticipate several of the motifs found in the Old French, Irish, and Welsh material, as well as in the alchemical myths analyzed above. Two rigvedic hymns[129] praise a divine figure named Apā́m Napāt (the "Descendant of the Waters"), who is associated with horses[130] and possessed of igneous properties.[131] These hymns associate him with women in three ways. First, he is "kindled by youthful women," who surrender themselves to him when he approaches them eagerly.[132] Second, "three goddesses" wish to provide him with food;[133] and finally, he is described as "stretching himself out in the waters as if toward just 'made' (*kṛ́tā*, i.e., deflowered) women."[134] Giving off light without fuel, Apā́m Napāt is also described as being clad in a "garment of ghee."[135] This is an especially evocative image: when poured into fire, clarified butter becomes an incandescent stream of pure flame, and so what the vedic poets are describing here is a flammable and potentially explosive liquid burning in the midst of a body of water. A vedic ritual, called the *pravargya*, which simulates this natural phenomenon, climaxes with the pouring of ghee into a pot of boiling milk. In the words of one scholar, the reaction is "volcanic." Of course, these vedic liturgies are metaphorical, referencing two levels of reality, the one natural and the other ritual.[136]

Apā́m Napāt is also said to beget all beings, some of which go directly to the vessel of the sea (*ūrvá*) "that the rivers fill."[137] In his commentary on this verse, the venerable fourteenth-century commentator Sāyaṇa glosses *ūrvá* as the "mare fire in the ocean,"[138] an image that collapses four essential elements from the broader mythology of living waters: *ūrvá* is a female "equine" eruption of fire in water. Sāyaṇa's interpretation is the end product of a long history of postvedic mythologization, which I summarize here. In ṚV 8.102.4, a certain Aur[a]va is paired with the vedic sage Bhṛgu, as they conjointly call upon "the gleaming one, upon Agni (Fire), whose garment is the sea."[139] The MBh and several Purāṇas etymologize Aurva's name, not on the basis of *ūrvá* ("sea"), but rather of *ūru* ("thigh"), relating how he was born directly from his mother's thigh. Regardless of his origins, his later mythology underscores his igneous nature, describing him either as a raging fire burning at the bottom of the ocean, or as the human or superhuman agent who creates and manipulates that fire.

In both scenarios, that fire is related to horses, inasmuch as the epic and later sources identify the "Aurva fire" (*aurvāgni*) with the "mare-fire" (*bāḍava*), which is so called because it burns in the mouth of a submarine mare (*baḍavāmukha*).[140] The MBh's version of the myth is significant in this regard. In the epic's first book, Aurva is introduced as an effulgent brahmin child and scion of the vedic sage Bhṛgu whose brilliance, once he has been born from his mother's thigh, blinds the eyes of the craven warrior barons (*kṣatriyas*) responsible for the earlier massacre of his brahmanic lineage. When he subsequently threatens to incinerate the entire universe, the shades of his ancestors urge him to divert his fiery rage into the ocean. There it becomes a great horse's head (*mahaddhayaśiras*) that belches fire from its mouth and drinks up the ocean's waters down to the mythical present.[141] It was in the medieval Purāṇas that that "great horse's head" at the bottom of the sea came to be identified as a submarine mare (*baḍavā*). Still later, after geometric models of planetary motion based on the idea of the circularity of their orbits were introduced into India, the mare at the bottom of the sea became identified as the "mare's mouth" at the south celestial pole.[142]

According to one puranic source, that mare was originally a river, whose mouth (in both senses of the term) was associated with fire.[143] Several puranic myths expand on this theme. At large in the world and devouring all the gods, the mare-fire is only pacified after it has been led by the river goddess Sarasvatī to "dwell in the waters." In one case, Sarasvatī carries the fire in a golden vessel; in another, she bands together with four other river goddesses to transport it to the ocean.[144] This Indic mythology of the submarine mare recalls the Greek records of the various "Horse's Founts" that first rose up out of the ground through the intervention of a divine equine figure, either Poseidon or Pegasus;[145] it may also be analogized with the Old French, Welsh, and Irish narratives of explosive, overflowing springs and fountains. Also like the Welsh tale of the Lake of Owen's Flag, these epic and puranic myths of the mare-fire suggest that these burning equine waters could somehow be controlled or diverted.

Another myth from the MBh appears to be a greatly fractured reworking of the same themes. This is the tale of the sons of a king named Sagara.

The king has two wives, one of whom gives birth to a single, and singularly evil, son named Asamañjas, who is eventually banished from the kingdom for his violent behavior. In the words of the epic's compilers, he was wont to seize weakling townspeople *by their hooves* and throw them screaming into a river.[146] But it is the misadventures of the sixty thousand sons of Sagara's second queen that bring together a number of fire in water mythemes, albeit in a most curious way. Sagara is in the midst of performing a vedic horse sacrifice when the sacrificial stallion, straying to the shore of a "waterless ocean" (*nistoyaṃ samudram*), suddenly disappears. (The ocean is waterless at this time because it has been drunk dry by the sage Agastya; it will soon be refilled at the behest of Sagara, which is why the Sanskrit word for "ocean" is *sāgara*). Not finding the horse anywhere on the earth's surface, Sagara's hapless sons come to a chasm and begin digging down through its floor and into the dry ocean bed. Finally, when they break through to the underworld, they find the missing horse grazing in the vicinity of a sage named Kapila, whose asceticism has set him aglow "like a fire with its flames."[147] The sixty thousand manage to enrage the sage, who forthwith reduces them all to ashes with his burning gaze. Old King Sagara now turns to his grandson Aṃśumat, the son of the exiled Asamañjas, to set things right. Aṃśumat petitions Kapila for two boons: that the sacrificial horse be returned to his grandfather the king, and that water be brought to cover the ashes of his sixty thousand calcinated uncles. As he explains, that purifying water is needed in order that they attain heaven.[148] The horse is duly restored. As for the water supply, Kapila instructs Aṃśumat to bring the Ganges River down from heaven to earth. Aṃśumat prays to the heavenly Gaṅgā, and he, together with the goddess, "rapidly filled up the ocean, the abode of Varuṇa" with her waters.[149]

Behind this narrative's two anomalies—townspeople with hooves, an ocean without water—are a number of mythemes found in the broader mythology of living waters. Here, the fire kindled by Kapila's asceticism—a reflex of Aurva's effulgence—is burning on a dry ocean's floor. The sacrificial horse that falls through to the ocean's bed via a chasm in the earth may be likened to the Pegasus of the Greek "Horse's Founts." However, rather than causing Poseidon's subterranean water to surge to the surface of the earth through a blow from its hoof, here the horse indirectly causes the subterranean realm of Varuṇa, a god of the waters and Poseidon's epic cognate, to fill with water that flows down from above. The MBh's very late thirteenth book takes up the Aurva myth a second time, here linking his fire to Hindu eschatology and the end of a cosmic cycle: "That greatly effulgent one, named Aurva, will have the splendor of the blazing sun. In his rage, he will kindle a fire for the destruction of the three worlds, a fire that will reduce the earth with its mountains and forests to ashes. Then, after some time that great hermit will extinguish that same fire, throwing it into the mouth of the mare in the ocean."[150]

B

This eschatological theme, which becomes a leitmotiv of later Hindu submarine mare mythology, is also linked to the vedic Apā́m Napāt's Iranian cognate—a deity named Apąm Napāt—who is glorified in a myth from the circa 600 BCE nineteenth book of the *Zamyād Yašt* (ZY, "*Yašt* of the Munificent Earth").[151] Unlike the ṚV's liturgical hymns to Apā́m Napāt, the ZY myth actually features a narrative plot, which contains nearly every mytheme found in the narratives reviewed to this point.[152] Here, the avestan cognate of the Indic ocean or sea is the Vourukaṣ̌a, a great mythic sea "having wide (*vouru*) shores (*kaṣ̌a*),"[153] located either far to the north or in heaven.[154] As in the puranic mythology of the Aurva- or mare-fire, the activity of the *x^varənah*, the luminous essence of divine and human sovereignty in Iranian mythology, is also projected onto the cosmic end time, in this case in the context of a prophecy:

> We worship the . . . x^varənah, which will (have) come over to . . . the Victorious Savior . . . when he will make existence brilliant . . . so that the dead will rise again. . . . Imperishable will be the world of truth. . . . Deceit will be done away, (sent) back to the place whence it has come.[155]

The avestan myth of fire in water is relatively straightforward. The x^varənah, the luminous glory or majesty that haloes the head of Iran's divinely sanctioned Kayanid or Kavyan kings, has absconded from the royal person of the sacrilege Yima. That fallen majesty, now become an object of contention between the cosmic forces of Good and Evil, withdraws to the waters of the Vourukaṣ̌a Sea, where it is recovered by Apąm Napāt: "Then Apąm Napāt of swift horses reached for it, and in doing so, Apąm Napāt of swift horses urgently wishes (*iziieiti*), 'I want to gain hold of this Glory (*hangrəfšāne x^varənō*) . . . (lying) at the bottom of the abyssal sea, at the bottom of the deep lakes.'"[156] This he does, following which Ahura Mazdā enjoins all mortals to strive after the same x^varənah, which is a source of abundance, fortitude, and martial valor.[157] Here it is also worth noting that the term *hangrəfšāne* ("I want to gain hold") in this statement is a present subjunctive form of the Old Iranian root √*grab*,[158] and thus a match for *jighṛkṣu*, the desiderative form of the Sanskrit root √*grah*, which I translated in the **SAN** mercury extraction accounts as "wishing to take (a woman's) hand in marriage" or "wishing to catch (her)."

The ZY next introduces "the Turanian scoundrel [named] Fraŋrasiian" who sacrilegiously attempts to lay hold of the x^varənah for himself. Three times Fraŋrasiian attempts to carry off the x^varənah, and three times he fails, with three new outlets to the Vourukaša being created through his attempts.[159] The last of these, Lake Haētumant,[160] which continues to harbor the x^varənah down to the mythic present, flows back into the Vourukaša, making that sea both the source and catch basin of all earthly watercourses.[161] As a number of scholars have noted, Dumézil's analysis abusively conflated the fire in water of these myths with its divine guardian or custodian.[162] The distinction between the two is most clearly presented in the Iranian material, in which, in contrast to the unworthy Fraŋrasiian, the x^varənah allows itself to be taken by Apąm Napāt. Given that no such explicit distinction is found in the vedic hymns, the proper name Apā́m Napāt denoting both the phenomenon of "fire in water" and the god that protects it, Findly's remarks are illuminating:

> The name Apām Napāt, then, becomes significant in two ways. He is, on the one hand, the "child of the waters," who abides in the midst of the fertile and mothering river waves and, as their fiery custodian, guards those waves from illegitimate intruders. But he is also the "child of the waters," who abides in the sanctified wave which is mixed with Soma and, as a fiery essence, is completely compatible with the intoxicating properties of the ritual drink. Thus, we might summarize the dual nature of the Vedic Apām Napāt as follows: when we view the waters as "natural," Apām Napāt is primarily a custodian; when we view the waters as "ritual," Apām Napāt is primarily an essence.[163]

Earlier, we saw the MBh making an identical distinction when it differentiated between the figure named Aurva and the fire he created and later diverted into the sea.[164] So too, we find a similar sort of cleavage in the nature of (M)ercury as both dæmon and fluid metal. These passages also recall Chrétien of Troyes casting of the relationship between the Perilous Fountain and its defender whose role it was to guard (against) the explosive forces it unleashed when its waters were poured onto the emerald-colored slab lying on its shore.

C

The Latin-language version of the fire in water myth, which Dumézil explored in particular detail, is embedded in the prodigy of the Lacus Albanus as recounted by six different Roman authors.[165] In spite of the Roman historicization of the myth, it is at bottom an account of a sacrilege perpetrated by Roman officials with respect to Jupiter Latiaris and what Dionysius of Halicarnassus termed "the local deities and dæmons of the Alban Lake."[166] A water-filled volcanic crater, the lake suddenly overflows its banks, its floodwaters threatening to engulf Rome itself. Both the Delphic oracle and an Etruscan diviner are called upon to interpret the will of the gods, with the two concurring that Rome will fall to its enemies if the outflow is allowed to reach the sea. Following their counsel, the Romans succeed in saving the eternal city through a lightning feat of hydraulic engineering, thanks to which the floodwaters are harmlessly channeled into the countryside through a network of canals and trenches.[167] In fact, the region had already been honeycombed with an ingenious drainage system of subterranean and above-ground conduits, the work of the ancient Etruscans.[168]

While the Roman Neptūnus was not directly implicated in the overflow of the Alban Lake, Dumézil offers a wealth of supporting data to argue for that god's identity as the Roman instantiation of the Indo-European dæmon of fire in water. The first of these was his name, which Dumézil relates to the Indo-European **nep(ō)t*, the *PIE term for "descendant" that also generated the vedic and avestan names for their cognate deities.[169] In addition, if only by virtue of his close identification with the Greek Poseidon, Neptūnus was also a water deity closely associated with horses.[170] Furthermore, as Dumézil has noted, certain features of his cult indicate that, more than merely a god of subterranean waters, Neptūnus was "an active and violent energy indwelling in the waters," an energy found in the name of Salācia, one of his female consorts. While her name is derived from the Latin *saliō*, to "bound" or "surge," it is also related, as Dumézil indicates, to the adjective *salax*, whose primary sense is "salacious."[171] These etymological associations recall the behaviors of the (male) dæmons of the **SAN** and **SYR** mercury extraction accounts, as well, perhaps as the vedic Apā́m Napāt's possible erotic relationship with the water goddesses that surround him. While this detail (together with Apā́m Napāt's equine connections) is evocative of mercury's attraction to the equestrian menarcheal maiden of the **SAN** mercury extraction accounts, as well, perhaps of Zws's attraction to a naked virgin in the **SYR** account, they are far from identical. On the one hand, a "just deflowered woman" is quite the opposite of a virgin,[172] and on the other, it is the Son of the Waters and not an equestrian maiden who is the master of horses in the vedic account. Furthermore, whereas in the vedic account he is the descendant of a group of goddesses, mercury is in the alchemical account the son of his father Śiva. However, as Dumézil has demonstrated time and again, inversions such as these often serve to strengthen the argument for a common origin.

But was there fire in Neptūnus's water? Because the Roman accounts appear to be lacking in any reference to the presence of either fire or an igneous fluid in the water of the Alban Lake, Dumézil adduced a solar connection through the Neptunalia, Neptūnus's annual festival. The Neptunalia fell on July 23, the date in the Roman calendar that ushered in the Dog Days of summer, a period in which the sun's heat was redoubled by the heliacal rising of the "Dog Star" Sirius.[173] As such, the Neptunalia would have fallen during the period in which the provoked eruptions of Yvain's Perilous Fountain occurred, between Pentecost and mid-August.[174] Commenting on the Roman material, Puhvel noted that there was embedded in Livy's version of the prodigy a "formulaic petrifact . . . an ancient versified formula in the indigenous Saturnian meter" that Dumézil had overlooked. That formula was scripted by the historian into the Delphic oracle's pronouncement:

> Roman, beware of keeping the Alban water confined in the lake,
> beware of letting it flow by its own stream into the sea.
> You should send it out through the fields to water them;
> you shall scatter it in channels and put it out.[175]

The oracle's juxtaposition of the terms *aquam* and *exstingues* brings us back to the igneous properties of the fluids in the mythology of fire in water: like the Aurva-fire of the Indian tradition, the waters of the lake must be "put out," extinguished. In Puhvel's words, the oracle's language is "a phraseological survival from the ritual of the Roman protomyth . . . originally indicating what to do when there was eruptive fiery water pouring forth and running amuck [*sic*] from Neptūnus's mythical lake."[176]

D

As Dumézil first argued in 1963, nearly all of the same elements reappear in a narrative found in the circa 1150 CE manuscript known as the "Rennes Dindshenchas" concerning the name and origin of Ireland's greatest river, the Boyne.[177] Here, Nechtan is the name of the infernal dæmon of a fairy mound (*síd*) that encloses a secret well (*tobair*) containing the waters of life and poetic inspiration,[178] but "from which gush[es] forth every kind of mysterious evil."[179] However, Nechtan's mound is said to be lodged in the house of another figure, named "Elcmaire of the Horses."[180] Apart from Nechtan and his three "cupbearers," anyone who approaches his well suffers bursting of the eyes, due to a deadly source of heat or light in its depths. Either out of hubris (*dimus*) or in order to innocent herself for having cuckolded her husband and master of the house, a woman named Boand approaches the well "to make a trial of its power."[181] She circles it counterclockwise three times, upon which three waves rise from the well and break over her, severing a thigh, a hand, and an eye. The greatly maimed Boand flees with Nechtan's burning fluids in hot pursuit, thereby creating a river in her wake, until she drowns in its estuary by the sea, some seventy miles away.[182] This river (the Boyne), which bears her name, is said to be the source of many of the world's great rivers, flowing all the way to "Adam's paradise" before returning to Nechtan's mound.[183] In this detail, the Irish material aligns with that found in the ZY: like the well beneath Nechtan's mound, the Vourukaṣ̌a Sea is the source of all the world's rivers, from which they flow and to which they return.[184] It also recalls the puranic intervention of five Indian river goddesses to carry the raging "mare fire" to the ocean, as well as the taming of the waters of the well of Mynydd Mawr in Morris's late nineteenth-century Welsh folktale. Finally, it parallels the **SAN**, **SYR**, and **C** alchemical accounts wherein Mercury, whenever he attempts to return to his original well or sea, is trapped in trenches, depressions, or well shafts lying across his path. While the waters of the Alban Lake were not made to return to their source, the act of channeling was also present, through a feat of hydraulic engineering. Here, the floodwaters were diverted from Rome and the sea through a system of canals and trenches that emptied into farmers' fields, an echo of which is found at the conclusion of the **SYR** mercury extraction account, when it identifies the fluid mercury with "river water . . . because it runs like the water that flows away in the fields."[185]

The same theme reappears, quite remarkably, in a Cornish folk tradition concerning the chapel and sepulcher of a certain "Saint Nectan" located in a deep glen known as Saint Nectan's Kieve. According to an account recorded in the nineteenth century, after Saint Nectan died, "two strange ladies from a foreign land came and took possession of his oratory." Placing the saint's remains as well as his worldly possessions in an oaken chest, "they turned the waters of the fall aside, and dug a grave in the river bed, below the Kieve, in which they placed this precious chest. The waters were then returned to their natural course."[186]

E

Three Greek-language accounts, all dating from between 150 and 250 CE, describe male deities present at and identified with sites of geothermal eruptions. In two of these, the god is aggressive, rushing out from his lair to punish perjurers and sacrileges. In the third, described in about 200 BCE by Cassius Dio, the behavior of the divine fire is oracular. The *nymphaion* at Apollonia in Greek Illyria is a fire that, fueled by bituminous deposits, bursts out of fissures in the ground. As he explains, this is considered an abode of nymphs because of its verdant setting and the effects of rainwater upon it.

FIGURE 6.2. Nymphs at fiery pool, coin of Apollonia, Illyria, ca. 100 BCE. Image courtesy of the Bibliothèque Nationale de France.

> What I have marveled at above all is that a great fire issues from the earth near the Aoōs River and neither spreads much over the surrounding land nor sets on fire even the place where it dwells nor dries it out, but has grass and trees flourishing close by. In pouring rain, it increases and rises high. For this reason it is called a *nymphaion*, and provides an oracle in this way: you take incense and after making whatever prayer you wish, cast it into the fire to carry the prayer. And if your wish is to be fulfilled, the fire accepts it readily, and even if it falls outside, runs out, snatches the incense and burns it up, But if the wish is not to be fulfilled, the fire does not go to it, but even if the incense is carried near, it recedes and flees.[187]

Here, we are given a clue as to why both (the god of) fire in water and Mercury are portrayed as not only rushing outward from their well or pool, but also returning to it—either fleeing, as in the case of the ZY's account of the flight of the x^{v}arənah, or reversing its direction, as in the case of Mercury. Furthermore, ancient coins from Apollonia (fig. 6.2) depict three nymphs dancing around a fire that represents the (god of the) fiery eruption itself. That deity, figuring on the obverse of these coins, is Apollo, Celtic Gaul's most exalted divinity, whose major shrines were situated at hot springs. I will return to this Gallo-Roman Apollo shortly.[188] On this ancient coinage, the nymphs are shown as three in number. Is their triplicity significant here? If so, then they are comparable to the three goddesses attending on the vedic Apā́m Napāt, as well, perhaps to other groups of three.[189]

F

Earlier in this chapter, I summarized Pausanias's account of events that transpired at Poseidon's sanctuary at Mantineia, an account that Heinrich Wagner compared in a 1981 article to the Irish myth of Nechtan's well.[190] Here is Pausanias's text in full. After describing the sanctuary's construction by Agamēdes and Trophōnios, Pausanias writes:[191] "They set up no barrier at the entrance to prevent men from going inside; but they stretched across it a thread of wool. Perhaps they thought that even this would strike fear into the religious people of that time, and perhaps there was also some power in the thread. It is notorious that even Aipytos, the son of Hippothous entered the sanctuary neither by jumping over the thread nor by slipping under it, but by cutting it through. For this sin he was blinded by a wave (*kuma*) that dashed into his eyes, and forthwith his life left him."[192] Pausanias concludes by evoking an old legend according to which the seawater that rises at Mantineia does so "through divine will."[193] Like the Roman Neptūnus, the Greek Poseidon gushes out from his sanctuary in response to a violation of its sacred precincts; like the Irish Nechtan, he takes the form of a wave that blinds and kills the trespasser. More than this, as Sergent has argued, Poseidon is, like Nechtan, a god of ordeals. When Boand circles Nechtan's well three times, she is voluntarily undertaking an ordeal—in which she fails—to prove herself innocent of the taint of adultery. In the Irish tale of *Aided Echach maic Maireda* as well, the deaths of the brothers Echu and Rí are attributed to their violations of ancient Irish law. Many of Poseidon's victims, including several heroes of Greek mythology, suffer a similar fate.[194] This also appears to be the motive behind Mercury's pursuit of Yakoppu in the **T** version of the mercury extraction account: he assaults the fledgling alchemist when he attempts, abusively, to lower a gourd pitcher into his well. However, there appears to be no trace of fire in Poseidon's blinding and fatal waters.[195]

G

Another Greek witness to this sort of ordeal is Philostratus's *Life of Apollonius of Tyana*. Dated to 225 CE, this pseudo-biography of an illustrious wonder-worker of the ancient world is some fifty years younger than Pausanias's account. As Philostratus relates with respect to Apollonius's home town in central Cappadocia,

> Now there is near Tyana a well sacred to Zeus, the god of oaths, so they say, and they call it the well of Asbama. Here a spring rises cold, but bubbles up like a boiling cauldron. The water is favourable and sweet to those who keep their oaths, but to perjurers it brings hot-footed justice; for it attacks their eyes and hands and feet, and they fall the prey of dropsy and wasting disease; and they are not even able to go away, but are held on the spot and bemoan themselves at the edge of the spring, acknowledging their perjuries.[196]

H

A final witness to this archaic body of myth is embedded in a 310 CE document from trans-Alpine Gaul. Here, an anonymous orator welcomes the future emperor Constantine to a sacred shrine in the Vosges region of eastern France. A functionary in the service of Rome, his Latin is elegant, but as his speech makes clear, he takes great pride in his Gaulish homeland and its Gallic deities.[197] Foremost among these is the Gallo-Roman Apollo, the most exalted god of Celtic Gaul and the master of two renowned hot springs in the region. The description of their boiling waters recalls certain elements of the fire in water protomyth, as well as the role of living waters in ordeals. The first of these, the renowned thermal spa of Apollo Grannus at the site of the modern-day village of Grand in the Vosges region, was the object of a vision beheld by the young general Constantine.[198] As Jean-Jacques Hatt has argued, the details of Constantine's vision of 310 were likely inspired by a representation of the god that he had viewed at the Grand thermal spa itself. In a sculpted image recovered at Grand, Apollo is mounted on a horse,[199] and it is to this god that our anonymous panegyrist refers when he says to Constantine, "You have deservedly honored these august temples . . . in particular that of our Apollo *whose burning waters punish perjurers*."[200] Then, evoking the thermal spa located at his native Autun (Burgundy), a sister city to Rome,[201] he describes "the sacred *lucus* of Apollo, its sacred temple and its hot springs' steaming pools . . . and the shrine of your protector god and his burning waters that rise up from ground containing no trace of heat . . . [waters whose] purity in taste and odor is the same as [waters from] cold springs."[202] Over eight centuries later, Chrétien of Troyes would use similar language to describe the Perilous Fountain: it is a spring "that boils and yet is colder than marble."[203] As for the power of dæmons like the Gallo-Roman Apollo to punish evildoers, this is also attested by a number of so-called "curse tablets" recovered from thermal spas in Britain and other western parts of the Roman Empire.[204]

7

A synoptic reading of these eight sources, together with the material found in the myths and accounts examined in the earlier sections of this chapter, yields an Indo-European protomyth comprised of the following mythemes: (1) A subterranean dæmon (2) whose name **nep(ō)t* means "Descendant of the Waters" (3) is embodied as a fluid numinous being immersed in a body of living water. (4) He is frequently associated with horses. He is (5) roused to action by a provocative, often sacrilegious, act committed by a man (or men) or a woman (6) who approach(es) or trespass(es) his abode. (7) After erupting from his basin, well or depths, the (8) dæmon in his caustic, fiery, superheated or volatile form (9a) pursues the individual(s), blinding, maiming, drowning and in some cases killing them—and sometimes flooding or laying waste to an entire region in the process—(9b) or else he flees. (10) The advancing (or fleeing) igneous fluid (dæmon) may be controlled or diverted through channels or trenches, which in some cases redirect him/it back to his/its source.[205] No single version of either the Indo-European protomyth or its alchemical, literary, or folkloric adaptations contains every one of the mythemes listed above: each contains an assortment of mythemes, with inversions or reversals occurring from one version to the next. While there can be little doubt that all of the narratives reviewed above are variations on the same myth, it is also clear that certain versions are more archaic and therefore closer in time to the oral narrations of the Indo-European protomyth. Of the eight fire in water accounts, the earliest are likely those in which the subterranean dæmon's name is a variation on the proto-Indo-European **nep(ō)t*, that is, the vedic, avestan, and Roman versions.[206] While the Irish, Greek, and Gallo-Roman narratives are further removed from the original, all are interrelated through monogenesis. Here, a primordial myth, shared among the original speakers of the proto-Indo-European language living in their Anatolian homeland some time prior to the fourth millennium BCE, would have been carried eastward and westward as those people migrated outward across Europe and much of Asia. In this case, transformations of the myth would not only have been the result of adstratal transmission across cultural and language barriers, but also the effects upon the superstratal protomyth of thousands of years of retelling, as well as of interactions between the carriers of this mythology with the various non-Indo-European speakers with whom they cohabited, intermarried, or entered into a hegemonic relationship. As for the medieval and modern French, Irish, and Welsh tales of living waters with which we began this chapter, theirs is probably a mixed legacy, a combination of superstratal tradition and adstratal exchange: a similar "layering" of mythologies was noted in the opening pages of the last chapter.

Here, a number of general observations are in order with respect to the chronology of these respective mythic traditions. As Dumézil demonstrated across the three volumes of his *Mythe et épopée*, many of the traditions recorded in the Indo-European epics are far more ancient that those enshrined in the myths found in such "chronologically prior" sources as the Vedas. Like fossil creatures embedded in amber, a corpus of archaic narratives and mythemes had persisted for hundreds, even thousands of years—and long before the emergence of the great "pagan" religions of Europe and Asia or the advent of writing—through bardic recitation, often in specific ritual contexts. As such, the dates assigned to each of the versions reviewed in this chapter only refer to the periods in which they first appeared, but these have been reckoned in two different ways for the traditions in question. In the case of the Latin, Irish, Welsh, Greek, postvedic Sanskrit, and Old French material, dating carried out on the basis of manuscripts or inscriptions is relatively precise. For the vedic and avestan versions of the mythology of Apā́m/Apąm Napāt, which bring undatable but clearly archaic oral traditions into play,[207] it is the hypothetical origin of this or that oral tradition that has been proposed. This, however, begs the questions of (1) the periodization of the oral traditions undergirding the Latin, Irish, Greek, and postvedic Sanskrit versions of this, or for that matter, any *PIE myth; and (2) the process of textualization specific to each literary tradition.[208] So while it is true that the *medium* of the ancient Indo-Iranian languages became fixed in their vedic and avestan forms earlier than did the four other Indo-European language traditions treated here, the *message* of the fire in water mytheme could not but have been communicated through the archaic *PIE language. Had this not been the case, the superstratal Indo-European protomyth would never have come into writing in the Rome, Gaul, and Greece of late antiquity, or medieval Ireland. This being said, I will adhere to the reigning "double standard" for dating the Indo-European material, identifying the Indo-Iranian **nep*(*ō*)*t* versions as the most archaic and the medieval Irish manuscript-based fire in water accounts as the most recent.

8

As five of the eight versions of the Indo-European protomyth make plain, the subterranean dæmon identified with fire in water is also described as a "master of horses" or is closely associated with them. The "descendant of the waters" of the vedic and avestan versions, as well as Elcmaire in the Irish version are all identified as masters of horses. Elsewhere, two solemn vedic rites also bring a horse into play in connection with subterranean fire and infernal waters. In the first sequence of the *agnicayana* rite, a horse is made to step onto the soil of the loam pit from which the clay used to fire the bricks of the fire altar will later be taken. As Theodore Proferes observes, "the mantra that accompanies this act makes plain that it is not mere soil that is being collected, but the fire itself, hidden within the ground. . . . The fire itself selects the material from which the pot that will carry it will be made, and which itself is really fire."[209] Likewise, in the *agnyādheya* rite, a horse is made to step into the offertory fire pit, such that the coals lying there become embedded in its hoofprint. With respect to this horse, here named "Fire-foot" (*agnipada*), the Atharvan *Gopatha Brāhmaṇa* prescribes the use of pacification (*śānti*) waters to appease it after it has been "led . . . up from the surging caustic [and] violent pool."[210] In the eleventh-century *Kriyākālaguṇottara*, a scriptural manual of tantric medicine, it is a donkey rather than a horse that is related to geothermal eruptions. In describing the origin of so-called "flame donkeys" (*jvālāgardhabhas*), insect-like "demon donkeys" whose bites cause skin inflammation, this source states that once, when Śiva pressed against Mount Kailash with his toe, a subterranean flame (*jvālāmukha*) arose, which was worshiped long ago in the form of a donkey.[211]

As was noted earlier, the Greek Poseidon's epithet of Hippios denotes one of his many equine connections, and the mythic horse Pegasus both generates springs and is generated from a spring.[212] Pausanias's account of Mantineia, where Aipytos was identified as the son of Hippothous ("Impetuous Stallion"), adds an additional layer of complexity. As a number of Greek authors including Pausanias himself noted, Hippothous was none other than Poseidon's own son, born after that god had ravished a princess named Alopē. Alopē had the infant carried off and exposed on a mountain, where two shepherds later discovered it being suckled by a mare. Alopē was found out and cast into prison, where she died, following which her body was transformed by Poseidon into a spring that bears her name.[213] To summarize: an equine god's fatal waters rose up to slay an equine trespasser (Aipytos, his own grandson!) at his inviolable shrine. Here we are also reminded of the scenario found in *Yvain*, and, to a lesser degree, the Welsh folklore of the Lake of Owen's Flag, and to the puranic mythology of the sixty thousand sons of Sagara. The same may be said for the legend of the flooding of Gwyddno's Field, in which Mererid, the probable instigator of the flood, cries out "from the back of the bay horse." While Pausanias's "Horse Founts" are generated by Poseidon's trident or Pegasus's hoof, the most unusual horse-related founts are those described in the "Death of Eochaid McMaireda," in which gushers spewing directly from horses' urethras cause the fatal flooding of Irish plains.[214] In all of these narratives, a horse, whether mounted or not, is an external agent, even *the* external agent, responsible for provoking an explosive and sometimes deadly counter-reaction. The same may be said for the **SAN** and **C** mercury extraction accounts. Even if Mercury's motives for gushing to the surface are different in the two versions, he is provoked in both by the passage of one or several equestrians in close proximity to his well or spring.

How, then, are we to explain the horse's perennial presence—either as protagonist, antagonist, or as their agent—in the mythology of living waters? Would Pausanias's mention of the racetrack at Poseidon's shrine in Mantineia and the Welsh account of the equestrian Owen's circling of the flooding waters of the Lake of Owen's Flag be mythic survivals of an archaic ritual practice? A passage from the ZY includes a reference to horse racing in what appears to be a reprising of the same work's Apąm Napāt narrative. Here, the "Turanian scoundrel Fraŋrasiian" once again figures as the archenemy of the gods, with Haosrauaah, the "Well Famed," replacing Apąm Napāt as the champion who defeats him:[215] "So that Kauui Haosrauaah came closer to that robber on that long racecourse through the forest of nine glades. When the agile-minded villain fought him in the chariot race, Kauui Haosrauaah, the lord, was victorious in all respects over the Turanian villain Fraŋrasiian."[216] In this passage, Haosrauaah is the name of a Kauui, a legendary Kayanid dynast who shares his name with that of Lake Haosrauaah, the first of the three outflows of the Vourukaṣ̌a Sea in the Apąm Napāt narrative.[217] According to Humbach and Ichaporia, this is because the dynast and the lake are one and the same figure—a water dæmon identified with his waters.[218] If then, it was a lake, an outflow of water from the sea, that defeated a usurper in a chariot race, then this is a retelling of the rescuing of the x^{v}arənah, the avestan fire in water, by Apąm Napāt "of swift horses," from Fraŋrasiian—this time in a chariot race on a closed racetrack.[219] In yet another parallel passage, the x^{v}arənah cries out to a figure named Vitāpa, who may also be identified with Apąm Napāt, to save it from being captured by Fraŋrasiian.[220] If this is correct, then the son of the waters who is the guardian of the fiery x^{v}arənah is also a horseman whose closed racetrack lies somewhere near his watery abode.[221]

Already in his 1963 article, Dumézil underscored the parallels between the pitfalls of the Iranian Fraŋrasiian and the Irish Boand;[222] and it was on the western shores of Scotland, Ireland, Brittany, and Norway that folk traditions surviving down into recent times also brought together a number of the equine references found in these sources. Many of these involved the ritual racing, processing, or bathing of horses at turning points of the year (Christmas Day, St. Stephen's

Day, Michaelmas, etc.).[223] In the first case, horses were raced on a circuit between human settlements and a lake, a well, the sea, or some other specific body of water.[224] In Norway, this took the form of the "second day's horse race":

> Early in the morning of the second Christmas Day [December 26], people drove out to water the horses in so-called *fro-brunnar*, special springs or special places at rivers or lakes. These were springs which never froze, or openings in the ice which kept open throughout the winter. The water in these springs was thought to be especially powerful and health giving. When the horses got to drink this water on the morning of the second Christmas Day, they were supposed to thrive and become especially healthy. People competed to come first to the springs, for then the water was thought to be the best.[225]

In the Highlands, the connection between horses and waters has run deeper still, for it is here that the depths of Scotland's rivers and lochs are identified as the abodes of the so-called "water-horse" (*each uisge*). Folk traditions cast these as shape-shifters that take on various human forms to seduce women, abduct children, and kill—or, if captured, be put to the plow. As Aude Le Borgne describes it, "their common characteristic, which allows us to recognize all these stories as being 'waterhorse stories,' is found at the end of the narratives: the waterhorse, in the shape of a horse, plunges back into its loch, alone or carrying off its victim(s) on its back."[226]

Yet another set of data sources, which in no way clarifies the waters of this complex of motifs, are the myths of individual demons or a class of demons named Netun(s), Neptun(s), or Noiton(s) in Old French sources, and Nuton(s) in several Celto-Roman vernaculars, with all of these names being derived from the Latin Neptūnus.[227] As Claude Sterckx has demonstrated in a remarkable article on the subject, the rich philological and mythological data on the celticized Neptūnus made him out to be exclusively a dæmon of freshwater springs and living waters, often reduced to the status of a rustic gnome.[228] A certain Netun makes a cameo appearance in Chrétien's *Yvain*: in one of his adventures, the knight defeats "two sons of the Devil" that had been born from "a woman and a Netun."[229] Netuns are linked to horses in another Old French work from Chrétien's time, the circa 1150 CE *Roman de Thèbes*, which speaks of a black Arabian horse "from across the sea, born from a mare and a neitun." In another passage from the same work, the aquatic connection is more strongly suggested in the description of a "very swift horse": "By the sea it was born, on a lofty shore, born of a noitun and a mare. His father was a marine noitun, his mother a wild mare."[230]

Perhaps the emerging picture we have of horse domestication in the Eurasian steppe will provide new clues to this enigma. What is known is that existing herds were restocked through the capture of wild mares; and one might hypothesize that the ecosystems surrounding hot springs and warm-water lakes were the places at which these mares congregated and were most readily captured.[231] Or, perhaps, these horses were simply metaphorical. Commenting on the vedic myth, Parpola simply states that Apā́m Napāt was "conceived as a horse-shaped sun-fire in the waters."[232] As Dumézil has suggested, the tendency of gushing, racing waters to "bound" and "surge" may explain the presence of the horse in so many of these myths. Ancient and modern Greek, French, English, Irish, and Welsh expressions liken foam-capped waves to horses; and the Greek Pegasus, who burst forth from the earth at a spring (*pḗgē*), may have been a literalization of this metaphor.[233] We must not lose sight of the fact that these were, among other things, accounts of fire in water, of troubled pools of fluid fire, whose rapid expansion and darting movements may have been compared poetically to those of racing equines.

9

At this point, I must bring my analysis down to earth—or, perhaps more accurately, up to the surface of the earth. If we accept Dumézil's theory of monogenesis for the Indo-European mythological corpus, then we must also allow that our protomyth took shape or was consciously crafted in a specific geographical location near the "homeland" of the *PIE speakers where a specific geothermal phenomenon would have constituted what Mircea Eliade long ago referred to as a "hierophany," a manifestation, if not an eruption, of "the sacred" into profane existence. That remarkable presence, of a "fire" burning in the midst of a body of "water," spurred some segment of the population of that place and time to innovate a body of ritual practice, together with a corresponding liturgy and mythology that referenced the unpredictable geothermal eruptions occurring in the region. The numinous dæmon embodied in the very matter of those eruptions would have served as an oracle, and would have been the object of some sort of ritual ordeal. Then, as those proto-Indo-European speakers fanned out into the Asian and European continents over the centuries and millennia, they carried that local tradition with them, such that, whenever they came upon a site at which subterranean fluids, often heated, surged to the earth's surface in some remarkable way, they and their heirs would have recognized it as the same divine presence, a local instantiation of the original "Descendant of the Waters." There, they would have attached their portable myth with its attendant ritual to the geothermal dæmon of the newly consecrated *lucus*. Such a cult would have required priestly specialists, and the presence of priests of one sort or another are mentioned or implied in Irish, vedic, Roman, and Greek accounts.

A clue to the real-world source of this mytheme may be found in the fifth- to sixth-century lexicographer Hesychius of Alexandria's entry for the obscure Greek term *napas*: "an oil-producing well in the mountains of Persia." Hesychius further links *napas* to the word *naphtha*, a term the Greeks borrowed from an ancient Semitic language: Aramaic, Akkadian, or Syriac. This term, *naftu*[*m*], which is found on Babylonian cuneiform texts dating from the eighteenth century BCE, denoted a type of oil or heavy bitumen pitch that was set on fire and used as military ordnance.[234] Working from Hesychius's etymology, Puhvel suggested that "perhaps oil seepage and oil flares on the Caspian shores were not unknown to the Indo-European proto-habitat,"[235] with the Indo-European theonym **nep*(*ō*)*t* being the source of mundane petrochemical terminology.[236]

While geothermal activity is a geological datum in this region of the "Indo-European homeland," the same cannot be said for many of the other sites reviewed in this chapter, a fact that would appear to undermine my claim of a moment ago concerning the link between these mythic variants and crustal geology. With the exception of the vedic Apā́m Napāt liturgies, every version of the Indo-European protomyth is linked to a specific aquatic *lucus* and to the local dæmon (or dæmons) of the site: Mantineia in Greece,[237] the well of Asbama in Turkey, the Alban Lake in Italy, the source of the River Boyne in Ireland,[238] the thermal spas at Grand and Autun in France, as well, perhaps, as the Aral Sea on the border of Kazakhstan and Uzbekistan or the Helmand River in Afghanistan. With the exception of the sites in France, Greece, and Turkey, none of these is known for geothermal activity or violent eruptions of subterranean waters. Trinity Well in County Kildare, the source of Ireland's greatest river, the Boyne, is a placid spring most notable for its immediate proximity to three of Ireland's primary Neolithic burial tumuli.[239] And, in fact, while the flooding of rivers is common in Mediterranean lands, it is unknown in Ireland, additional proof, if such were needed, that neither the "Dindshenchas" account of the flooding of Nechtan's well nor "The Death of Eochaid McMaireda" narrative of the flooding "Grey Thicket" waters originated in Britain and Ireland.[240] The same may be said for the Alban Lake, whose hydrology and geology would have made such an overflow impossible.[241] In other words, while the fire in water protomyth is possibly a reference to geothermal eruptions in the "Indo-European homeland" in a far distant past, the geothermal or hydraulic activity at the sites to which it was later linked was of a less spectacular if not nonexistent order.

What, then, of the alchemical versions of the fire in water myth? Are these too simply pale memories of ancient oil flares in the Caspian region?

Here, I wish to return to South Asia, and specifically to Hiṅglāj, long regarded as the westernmost extension of the Hindu ecumene, as well as the cult site of a local "Red Goddess" whose name may be construed as "She Who Was Born from Red Cinnabar" (*hiṅgula-jā*), the prime mercurial ore (plate 27).[242] A river by the same name (today called the Hingol) flows by her shrine, which draws Hindu pilgrims—and recently, since the opening of a modern highway through the region, Pakistani tourists—to what was formerly an extremely remote and inaccessible spot. This opening of the Makran Coast has, over the past few years, generated a wealth of Internet postings of photographs of Hiṅglāj and other nearby sites of interest. These generally confirm word descriptions made by Persian and British travelers going back to the first decades of the nineteenth century. It is generally accepted that the name by which Hiṅglāj is known locally—Bībī Nānī—is a variation on the ancient Near Eastern Nanā or Innana, who is also referenced in the apocryphal Old Testament "Second Book of Maccabees" as Nanea.[243] Images of the sun and moon, carved into the living rock near the shrine, may be the same as those reported in the Greek traveler Ctesias of Cnidus's *Indika*,[244] which was written in about 400 BCE, shortly after his exile to the Persian court of Artaxerxes II, where he served as that emperor's personal physician. As such, Hiṅglāj's shrine may originally have belonged to Nanā. The great bulk of Ctesias's data on "India" came from his Persian hosts, and Hiṅglāj's geographical location made it an ancient pivot between those two great civilizations.

Travelers' descriptions of this zone of the Makran Coast also mention Candrakūp, the "Moon Well" referred to in section 4 of this chapter. None of these has described the site in richer detail than a slightly fictionalized 1978 Hindi-language travelogue written by Devadatt Shastri on the basis of a pilgrimage he had taken there in 1940.[245] Shastri, whose journey was undertaken in the old-fashioned way (a camel caravan lasting forty-five days from Karachi to Candrakūp, Hiṅglāj, and back),[246] paints a vivid picture of the place. It is a terrifying three-hundred-foot peak, constantly belching superheated mud, into whose boiling sludge (*kīcaḍ*) pilgrims toss chunks of country bread (*roṭ*), coconuts, and chillum pipes packed with marijuana. Pilgrims make these offerings to pacify the temperamental Bhagavān Candrakūp ("Almighty Lord Moon Well")—or more familiarly, "Candrakūp Bābā" ("Father Moon Well")—to absolve them of their sins or foretell their destiny.[247] Elsewhere, Shastri cryptically notes that "although it was called a fire pit, no fire burned there,"[248] and less cryptically calls it a "well of death" in which "there was not the slightest whiff of the divine . . . rather, it appeared to be a hulking demon (*mahādānav*)."[249]

In fact, Candrakūp is not a well: rather, it the world's tallest mud volcano (plates 28 and 29).[250] The word *kūp*[*a*] here does not mean "well," but rather "crater," and as such Candrakūp may be viewed as an alloform of the water-filled crater of the Italian Alban Lake. In this respect, Candrakūp stands as a modern-day survival of an ancient hierophany: a superheated fluid that, dwelling in a well, crater, or pool, is venerated as a fearsome dæmon who makes his presence—and his mood—known when he boils up to the surface.[251] At Candrakūp, the bubbles of mud in the crater are themselves worshiped as an embodiment of the Nāth Yogi Gorakhnāth, here called Bhabaknāth, a name derived from the Hindi *bhabaknā*, "burst into flames."[252] Candrakūp may also be the actual site of the **SAN** accounts of Mercury, whose "perfectly rounded well" was situated in the western "Land of Setting the Limit" (*pārada-deśa*), located by ancient and medieval geographers on the same Makran Coast. Submarine mud volcanoes, which occasionally erupt out of the abyssal plain located off this coast, may also have been the inspiration behind the mythology of the *bāḍava*, the submarine mare-fire.[253]

Fabrizio Brighenti recently noted that atop a hill close to the cave shrine of Hiṅglāj herself there is a "pool of water from whose bottom bubbles of gas, perhaps having the same source as the gas vent of the mud volcanos of Makran, rise to the surface of the water carrying mud in suspension."[254] In 1914, the British folklorist William Crooke referred to this as a "well," and quoting a pilgrim who had recently visited the site, noted that when the water rose up with a bubbling noise Hindu pilgrims would throw into it offerings of cloves, betel nuts, cardamoms, and coconuts. When the water's rise slowed or ceased, "pilgrims in the most abject manner call[ed] on Mātā [Hiṅglāj] to give them a sight of herself, exhorting each other to reveal their sins and inwardly repent." In the light of which Crooke suggested that this was "an example of those oracular wells from which omens are taken in many parts of the world,"[255] in other words, a place of ordeals of the sort documented in Ireland, Greece, Turkey, and France. There is a Greek work that locates a testing well or "Well of Truth" in "India" itself: this is Philostratus's aforementioned *Life of Apollonius of Tyana*. While neither Apollonius nor Philostratus ever traveled to India, much of the content of the *Life* was adapted from travelers' accounts of the time. As Philostratus tells it,

> Apollonius says that he went up the hill roughly from the south following the Indian. The first thing that he saw was a well four fathoms deep, from which a deep blue light rose to the surface. . . . He later learned that the soil at the bottom of the well was realgar, and that the Indians considered the water magical, and so neither drew nor drank from it; the whole region of India round about considered it a pledge of oaths. Near this, he says, there was a fiery crater, which gave off a lead-colored flame, but no smoke came from it or even an odor, and this crater never overflowed, but rose in such a way as never to spill

> out of its hollow. There the Indians purify themselves from accidental crimes, and for that reason the Wise Men call the well "the Well of Proof" and the fire "the Fire of Forgiveness."[256]

The realgar referred to here is arsenic sulfide, also known as "ruby sulfur" for its brilliant red hue, shared by the "Red Goddess" Hiṅglāj.[257] Traces of these mineral and mercurial ores naturally occur at sites of geothermal activity. As the *Shorter Oxford Economic Atlas* notes, "almost all the world's mercury is obtained from the red sulphide mineral cinnabar, HgS, but a little of the metal occurs naturally as small globules associated with cinnabar in certain rocks in the neighborhood of old volcanic regions where the minerals were deposited from hot aqueous solutions during volcanic activity. Many hot springs in such regions are still depositing some cinnabar."[258] Even in places like South Asia, where no mines of mercury were to be found, trace quantities of the "Champion of Minerals" could have been extracted from the soil around geysers, hot springs, mud volcanoes, and sites where underground superheated fluids, "fire in water," boiled up to the surface.

In the light of these data, the medieval mercury extraction accounts whose mythology and attendant ritual practices drew upon a far more ancient Indo-European protomyth also had some basis in ancient scientific knowledge. The Indo-European myth of fire in water may well be the narrativization of an ancient human experience of the supernatural, the numinous, the sacred, as glimpsed in the fiery fluids spawned by geothermal activity. Unlike the other sites linked to it, Pakistan's Candrakūp is a place where the conditions that inspired that millenarian myth—as well as the ritual activity targeting the dæmon of that myth—persist down to the present day.

10

Scriptural and iconographic data indicate that Hiṅglāj first dawned on Hindu mental horizons in about the tenth century CE. Her cult, which now overspreads the entire subcontinent, was subsequently carried eastward through the migrations and periodic movements from the Baluchistan-Sindh region of communities who worshiped her as their lineage goddess (*kuladevī*). These included the Charans and the Nāth Yogis, two groups closely linked to royal lineages in western India.[259] But there is also solid evidence that Hindus—merchants, pilgrims, and yogis—also journeyed far beyond the boundaries of the subcontinent to venerate *jvālāmukhī*s in such distant places as Iraq and Azerbaijan, as well as, perhaps, Uzbekistan. Unlike the singular "mare-fire" (*bāḍava*) discussed earlier in this chapter,[260] *jvālāmukhī* is a generic Indic

FIGURE 6.3. Ateshgah Fire Temple, Baku, Azerbaijan.

term, applicable to any place from which there issues a subterranean fire or inflammable gas: at one point, Shastri refers to Candrakūp as such.[261] Traditional custodians of Hiṅglāj's shrine as well as a bubbling pool of water adjacent to the cave shrine of the goddess Jvālāmukhī—a renowned gas vent in the Kangra Valley of Himachal Pradesh[262]—the Nāth Yogis also venerate Hiṅglāj in the form of a portable *jvālāmukhī*, a flaming wick of cotton suspended in a jar of pure water.[263]

Azerbaijan's Black Sea coastline boasts the world's highest concentration of mud volcanoes, while its Caspian coastline has long been renowned for its geothermal eruptions of "naphtha," particularly in the region of Baku.[264] Situated astride a caravan route linking it to India, Baku had already long been home to a sizable South Asian merchant community when, in the early eighteenth century, a Hindu "fire temple" was erected on the outskirts of the town at Surkhany, the site of an "everlasting fire . . . of a very extraordinary nature"[265] (fig. 6.3). Now a World Heritage Site, eighteenth- and nineteenth-century votive plaques on the temple's walls in Devanagari and Gurmukhi scripts attest to its patronage by Hindu and Sikh pilgrims.[266] While the gods invoked in these inscriptions include Rāma, Kṛṣṇa, Hanumān, Agni, and the goddess Jvālā-jī herself, the nineteenth-century presence of a trident projecting from its cupola indicated the Śaiva identity of the temple's custodians, who were yogis.[267] The earliest report of these, made by the British traveler Jonas Hanway who visited the temple in 1743, speaks of

> forty or fifty of these poor devotees, who come on a pilgrimage from their own country . . . Their business is to make expiation not for their own sins only, but for those of others,[268] and they continue the longer time, in proportion to the number of persons for whom they have engaged to pray. They mark their foreheads with saffron, and have a great veneration for a red cow. They wear very little clothing, and those who are of the most distinguished piety, put one of their arms upon their head, or some other part of the body, in a fixed position, and keep it unalterably in that attitude.[269]

As we saw in chapter 2, it was Bhairava-worshipping Nāth Yogis that were responsible for spreading the *mail*-based protective rites currently observed in both southern Rajasthan and the Kathmandu Valley. According to Nāth legend, yogis also journeyed beyond the borders of the Indian subcontinent, with the illustrious Ratannāth's travels taking him as far afield as Nepal, Afghanistan, and Mecca.[270] The Baku temple priest that C. E. Stewart met in 1866 "had for some time been a priest at the Jowalla Mukhi Temple, near Kangra . . . [and] had heard there from other priests of this greater Jawála Ji, as he called it, and had come on a pilgrimage to visit it, and remained for many years."[271] Another "Hindu Fakir" whom Stewart met near the Persia-Afghan border spoke of his intention to visit "another Hindu fire temple which he had heard of in Bokhara territory." And, in fact, the fourteenth-century geographer Mustawfī noted the existence of white naphtha springs in that region of modern-day Uzbekistan, just as Hanway would do for Baku's Absheron peninsula in the eighteenth century, noting that some of the naphtha collected there was "carried into India as a great rarity."[272]

These data confirm the persistence, down into the twentieth century, of oral traditions concerning networks of sites of geothermal activity, traditions that were maintained by itinerant Indian ascetics. More tantalizing still is the likelihood that with their westward journeys from Kangra to the "greater Jawála Ji," these Indian wanderers were closing the circle of an archaic Indo-European tradition of fire in water, returning unbeknownst to themselves to the geothermal "hierophany" that had been its western Asian source in a far distant past.

7

Imagining a Connected History of Religions

l'histoire est entièrement vraie, puisque je l'ai imaginée d'un bout à l'autre . . .
BORIS VIAN, *L'écume des jours*

In this historical study of dæmonological contacts and exchanges, I have continually circled back to three interrelated themes: narratives, rituals, and artistic representations involving human encounters with dæmons in their natural habitats; the human combat against malign demons as documented through narrative and ritual; and the demonization of "nondemonic" dæmons by partisans of official religion. As we have seen, the boundaries between these three areas of inquiry are fluid. Human actors have carried their inner demons with them as they have traveled across Eurasian landscapes, even as they have recognized and venerated the dæmons of old landscapes in new places. In spite of condemning them as demons, representatives of various official religions have had private recourse to dæmons, foreign and domestic, for comfort in the face of their personal needs and crises. All of which is to be expected, given the fact that the most distinguishing feature of dæmons has been their ambiguity.

It may be argued that these are universal themes, as ancient and widely attested as human culture itself. If, however, we were to follow this line of inquiry, we would be drawn back inexorably into the outmoded approaches of the dinosaurs of comparative religion. As I hope to have made it abundantly clear in these pages, my goal here has not been to generate a set of universal typologies concerning dæmons, demons, and dæmonology, and it is for this reason that I have limited the geographical range of these studies to the Eurasian expanse. My endeavor has rather been to write their connected histories, which, until the European "Age of Exploration," were connected by the movements of human actors within the Eurasian ecumene alone. This being said, I believe that the universality of dæmonological traditions such as those I have treated here ought to lead us to nuance the ways we "imagine religion."

Here, I cannot do better than to quote the Lord and Savior of the Christian world, who famously admonished his disciples to "heal the sick, cleanse the lepers, raise the dead, [and] cast out demons."[1] If these are the foundations of official Christianity, then demonology lies at the heart of this "great religion." If such is the case with the world's other "great religions"—and I would argue it is—then religion has as much to do with immediate concerns as it does with ultimate concern, with dæmonology as much as theology.

Here, it is useful to recall a distinction that the cultural anthropologist David Mandelbaum made in the 1960s between "transcendental" and "pragmatic" religion.[2] The former is the prerogative of universalist "official religion" and its proponents: persons with the social status and leisure to devote themselves to such proactive, transcendent concerns as world maintenance, the worship of supreme deities, scriptural norms, and economies of salvation. The latter is instantiated in local dæmonological traditions, which respond to people's immediate needs and fears in their quotidian struggle against disease, hardship, misfortune, madness, and untimely death. One ought not to assume, however, that the cleavage between the pragmatic and the transcendental tracks with socioeconomic or political class hierarchies. With this, I wish to refer back to the remarks I made at the end of chapter 2 concerning official and vernacular religion. Everyone, including the ordained representatives of official religion, always already inhabits the world of the vernacular as his or her default mode of being. All have their inner demons, their existential anxieties, which are on full display whenever they let down the masks of their official personas.[3] This we have seen most spectacularly in the person of Kirdēr, the Sasanian high priest responsible for the execution of the prophet Mani as well as for the persecution of countless Jews, Buddhists, Hindus, Christians, and Manicheans.[4] Remarkably, it was the same Kirdēr who (by his own account, engraved in stone!) resorted to the altogether un-Zoroastrian dæmonological practice of mirror divination in order to have a vision of his post-mortem fate. Back in Christian Europe, the person who attempted to initiate the young John of Salisbury into the same divinatory technique was himself a Catholic cleric who saw fit to siphon off the holy chrism to what were clearly unorthodox ends.[5] So too, Plutarch, a priest at the oracle of Delphi and an exemplary upper-class intellectual of Roman antiquity, was sufficiently fascinated—figuratively if not literally—by popular evil-eye traditions as to devote a dialogue to explaining their scientific foundations.[6]

The primacy of vernacular over official discourse is a matter of fact, reflected in virtually every one of the dæmonological traditions examined in the preceding chapters, in which one hears the hegemonic voices of official religion being all but drowned out by those of more humble actors, by those of Everyman (or Everywoman). So, for example, in the matter of changelings, Martin Luther's opinion that the little devils should simply be drowned was an official position, anticipated in the legend of Saint Stephen, according to which that adult saint had his demonic simulacrum consigned to the flames.[7] However, as the great volume of European changeling lore makes plain, it has been simple women and not clerical ideologues who have negotiated the safe return of their infants from the fairy mothers who spirit them away on the basis of shared maternal instincts. The same may be seen in iconography, in which one also observes both forms of "discourse." Here, a comparison of the artistic representations of the changeling episodes in the lives of Saint Stephen and Saint Lawrence will serve to illustrate my point. Whereas Martino di Bartolomeo's lurid polyptych panels hew closely to Stephen's official *Vita*, in which it is none other than a bat-winged Satan himself who carries off the infant (plate 11), Danish church frescoes, painted by artists from local workshops, portray Saint Lawrence's abduction and recovery in a vernacular mode. In these, it is skinny ludic imps that carry off the infant, with a chubby "tree spirit" remitting him to the hands of Pope Sixtus II (figs. 4.2–4.4). The same country church walls and ceilings are replete with examples of other vernacular—if not heretical—themes, featuring visual riddles, rebuses, fables, and sexual and scatological imagery that had no correlate in official Church doctrine.[8]

Turning to India, we have seen the lines between the official and the vernacular blurred time and again by religion as practiced on the ground, with the *mail*-related ritual strategies of rural Rajasthan and urban Kathmandu breaking down the static binaries of oral and written, and "great" and "little" tradition, as well as the boundaries between the categories of religion, science, and superstition. As has been the case throughout South Asia from time immemorial, the priestly officiants of these vernacular rites have generally hailed from the lower echelons of society, with adherents of the official Hindu, Buddhist, and Jain faiths nowhere to be found—except as their perennial clients![9] Throughout rural western India, it has more often been heterodox yogis rather than orthodox brahmins who have filled the sacerdotal needs of the populace, yogis whose own religious aspirations have generally been at variance with those sanctioned in orthodox scripture.

As we saw in chapter 6, one such "Hindu Fakir," encountered near the Persia-Afghan border, had practical knowledge of "Hindu fire temples" at both Baku and Bukhara, sites situated over a thousand miles as the crow (or yoginī) flies from his Indian homeland.[10] His practical knowledge of these sites had nothing to do with deep structures of human thought; nor are we authorized to assume that his motivation to walk those fantastic distances had anything to do with some enchanted experience of the "sacred." What we can say is that this anonymous yogi was sharing in a pan-Eurasian system of dæmonological knowledge that, in the case of these geothermal hierophanies, may well have had its origins in the early Bronze Age. In this context, we would do better to view myths of ancient *luci* not as expressions of ideology, but rather as useful information, even instructions for use that were carried and transmitted by human actors across Eurasian climes.

At the same time, certain South Asian narrative and iconographic data discussed and described in chapters 4 and 5 may be entered as evidence in support of Lincoln's social engineering model of (official) religion. So, for example, several South Asian narratives of encounters with massive spirit guardians may be read as so many instances of hegemonic discourse on the part of translocal Hinduism and Buddhism over and against rustic local custom. The great yakṣa that briefly takes the lives of four of the Pāṇḍava brothers appears to be enforcing local statutes—the requirement that trespassers on his domain submit to his testing riddles—until he reveals himself to be none other than universal Hindu Law itself, the god Dharma "in person." The early Buddhist accounts are more explicit still: readily converted to the one "true law" (*saddharma*) of Buddhism by the bodhisattva brother of Princes Sun and Moon, the water-guardian returns his victims to life, abandoning anthropophagy and the "yakkha law" (*devadhamma*) of which he had been the erstwhile enforcer.

This submission to higher authority is also very much in evidence in the architectural programs of South Asian stūpa complexes, where the various local spirit deities of South and Inner Asia are figured on the pillars of these monuments' surrounding walls, called *vedikas*. Since the word *vedika* denoted the railing surrounding a yakṣa's local *caitya*, the message of these stūpa complexes was clear: the yakṣas with their rustic traditions were now tributary to the universal dispensation of the Buddhist Dharma cum Buddha relics residing in the stūpa whose great dome their images surrounded.[11] The same message appears in these stūpas' iconographic programs, as, for example, in depictions of Māyāvatī's presentation of the newborn Buddha to a tree devatā. Rather than accepting the offerings of the precious bolts of cloth that are his due, the yakṣa instead bursts out of his *caitya-vṛkṣa* to bow before the newborn universal savior (fig. 4.14). Elsewhere, it will be recalled that when Prince Vijaya had slain the yakkhas of Sirīsavatthu, he "himself put on the garments of the *yakkha*-king and bestowed the other raiments on one and another of his followers."[12] This specific body of tradition may therefore be read as an ancient South Asian instantiation of the general rule of the demonization/appropriation of dæmons that I proposed in the opening pages of this book. In the light of which, one might well assert that the meaning of these narrative, architectural, and iconographic "texts" revolved around the subordination of local practice to translocal ideology, in this case of Hinduism and Buddhism triumphant.

Also following Lincoln, we may view certain of these works as expressions of subaltern resistance to official authority,[13] beginning with the first-century CE Amaravati image, just mentioned, of Māyāvatī's presentation of the newborn Buddha to a sylvan devatā. "Official" museum captions of this and cognate images identify the tree-spirit as "Śākyavardhana Yakṣa," the tutelary deity of the Buddha's clan. However, as Mace has recently argued, that identification is based on a textual source from northern India, which relates that it was the Śākya *men* who presented the infant to their clan deity "in the city at a built structure," whereas "the southern Indian presentation scenes [at Amaravati, Kanganhalli, etc.] all concern *women* and take place in nature, revealing a different world than that which has been recorded in the Sanskrit sources, the world of women and their rites pertaining to fertility and maternity."[14] Here, we are once again reminded of the cleavage between the religious life of women and the official religion of churchmen.

Another echo of vernacular/female resistance to official/male hegemony may be seen in the tale of Dame Ragnelle's "sovereignty," whose author was, as has been noted, likely a "practitioner of lower-class storytelling styles," with "folktale justice" prevailing at his tale's conclusion.[15] The same may be said of the origin myth of the western Indian excrement goddess Meladī Mātā, who coerces a pair of divine representatives of official Hinduism to worship her after "drinking her water."[16] These sorts of narratives may be taken as representative of a more general rule, as articulated by A. K. Ramanujan, who noted that in India the same tale could serve as either a myth or a folktale depending on the context. For whereas the gods of "official" puranic mythology have bodies without bodily functions, in folk traditions they are supernatural beings whose bodies suffer from hunger and thirst, sometimes satirically presented, and who are possessed of the human emotions of discomfiture and shamed susceptibility to blackmail.[17] In medieval Europe, it was often Catholic clerics themselves—figures like Chrétien de Troyes—who served as culture brokers, transmitting and transforming vernacular traditions into "high" literary form, initiating what Jacques Le Goff has termed a twelfth- to thirteenth-century "great wave of folklore" that washed into the early twentieth century. As Karen Sullivan has shown, this officialization of vernacular traditions was the work of twelfth- and thirteenth-century clerics who introduced "marvels" (*mirabilia*) as a mediating category between Church-sanctioned "miracles" and demonic "magic."[18]

In these respects, the relationships between oral and written account, folktale and literary work, secular literature and sacred text, mythic and historical narrative, and popular systems of knowledge and scientific ethnography have been as multi-sided as those obtaining between official and vernacular religion. The written has never supplanted the oral, nor has the highbrow ever definitively replaced the lowbrow: rather, these have continued to cross-pollinate one another in countless ways.[19] As Subrahmanyam reminds us, whether official or vernacular, European or (South) Asian, cultures are open-ended systems "formed in the crucible of processes of acculturation, whether defined by circuits that had their limits within the Indian subcontinent, or extending outside of it."[20] In a time of identity politics and religious nationalism, this perspective is preferable to that of the comparative historian who would view these as so many self-contained systems.

In a recent article on Rembrandt's art, Russell Shorto described an Amsterdam art collector's special appreciation for a series of portraits, painted by the master, of his own seventeenth-century ancestors. With the realization that the eyes looking out at him from the portraits were genetically his own eyes, "he began looking at paintings in a new way. They went from being flat representations of dead people to aesthetic expressions serving as portals into history."[21] By juxtaposing two or more phenomena from the past, analogical comparison lifts both out of their historical context, flattening them as it were in the mind of the scholar making the comparison. By providing "the means by which *we* 're-vision' phenomena as *our* data in order to solve *our* theoretical problems,"[22] both are shunted off into the modern-day scholar's present and ultimately shorn of their historical specificity, depth, and connectedness. In my opinion, generating insights into the abstract nature of "religion" is a far less rewarding and relevant pursuit than recovering the lifeworlds of our human brethren, both ancient and contemporary. Their experiences of time, space, and their lived environments are not the same as our own. This is not exoticization on my part: these are things we know from the expressions they have left us of their experiences,[23] expressions serving as so many portals into our connected histories. So, for example, when the mother of a sickly child left it exposed on the forest floor of thirteenth-century France, her angst was of an order unknowable to a modern-day (male) scholar, armchair or otherwise. For during those few minutes when that child was out of her sight and earshot, a wolf could very well have carried it off forever—a possibility that Stephen of Bourbon entertained, even as he identified the eventual wolf with the Devil himself.[24] Even as their histories are connected, however tenuously, to our own, it is their stark otherness that makes dæmons and the people whose lives they haunt so compelling.

If my reconstructions are correct, many of these ancient and medieval dæmonological traditions have persisted down to the present day through rituals such as those observed by barren women in western India and carried to Israel over recent decades by expatriate South Asian Jews. However, the fact remains that many of my reconstructions are hypothetical. For while the connected histories approach would have it that Lincoln's islands of weak comparison are but the exposed summits of mountains having their roots in ancient, but now submerged, land bridges of human contacts and exchanges, its connections can never be verified or proven as nonfalsifiable in the same way as the truths of the positive sciences. Even when such is a desideratum,[25] the productions of the humanities can never rise to the same level of objectivity as the latter to become full-fledged *sciences humaines* or Religions*wissenschaften*.

Historians craft their narratives out of traces left on paper, in stone and other materials, or through living folkways, with the connected histories you have read in these pages being largely absent of identifiable historical actors. Like the statuette of Śītalā unearthed at Urgench, the dæmonological materials I have recovered—myths, rituals, images, technologies, and systems of knowledge—are but mute traces of contacts and exchanges occurring between nameless, faceless human individuals. Which begs the following question: can hypothetical reconstructions of connected histories, generated on the basis of traces alone, be valid? To which I would answer: yes, when traces are all we have. Here it bears noting that cutting edge research in particle physics also relies on traces to confirm its theoretical constructs and recover the past. Using the massive technological resources of particle accelerators and quantum computing, physicists have for the past decades been testing and "proving" their mathematical models concerning the origin of the universe, the ink on this page, and the light by which you are reading these words. The quantifiable data that have permitted them to go back in time to the beginning of time (and of space and energy and matter), the data upon which their historical arguments are founded, consist of nothing other than traces, in this case, traces left by the collisions of subatomic particles—bosons, leptons, muons, quarks, and the like. Most recently, they have read in those traces the "signature" of the grail of particle physics, the elusive Higgs boson, named for the Scotsman Peter Higgs and the Indian Narendra Bose—modern-day giants in the mold of the Parkham Yakṣa and Gromer Somer Joure. Their search for the origins of the universe is not grounded in some sort of "nostalgia for paradise":[26] rather, they simply wish to know *wie es eigentlich gewesen*. So too does the empirical historian of Eurasian dæmonology, who, following the traces of contacts and exchanges along the "Silk Road," would seek to recover their connected histories. The portals to those lifeworlds will open to us if we will but allow ourselves to freely deploy the most powerful tools we have at our disposal: our imaginations.

Acknowledgments

A cooperative effort between my inner demons and my better angels, this book owes much to a host of institutions, colleagues, and former strangers, mainly from the academic world, who responded generously to my queries concerning their fields of expertise. They are Rajesh Aggarwal, Tejas Aralere, Ranjani Atur, Audrius Beinorius, Lisa Bitel, Irmine Blanc, Catherine Clémentin-Ojha, Aline Debert, Rob DeCaroli, Beatrice Delaurenti, Debra Diamond, Jacco Dieleman, Mathew James Driscoll, Isabelle Duvivier, Daniel Ehnbom, Anne Feldhaus, Ann Grodzins Gold, Caterina Guenzi, Bhoju Ram Gujar, Richard Hecht, Stephanie Jamison, Bert Jaski, Sarah Iles Johnston, Rob Kritzer, Y. Tzvi Langermann, Roland Lardinois, Catherine Laugée, Sébastien Laurier, Patrick Lavaud, Lug Lebel, Todd Lewis, Po-ming Lin, Francis Longuemaux, Jean-Pierre Louvet, Sonya Rhie Mace, Victor Mair, Matteo Martelli, Ludovic Moignet, Pratapaditya Pal, Stefano Pellò, Dinesh Prasad Saklani, Whitney Sanford, William Sax, Sam van Schaik, John Scheid, Jean-Claude Schmitt, Martin Schwartz, Shai Secunda, Sudharshan Seneviratne, Bernard Sergent, Sylvain Sionneau, Fred Smith, Dominic Steavu-Balint, Kirsten Trampedach, Ulrike Unschuld, Somadeva Vasudeva, Michelle Wang, Colin Webster, Shalva Weil, and Dominik Wujastyk. The collaboration of these specialists has aided me in countless ways, providing invaluable context to my text. Without the assistance they have accorded me, this book would no doubt contain more errors than it does; and any errors that have remained in this book are entirely my own responsibility.

I am grateful to the following institutions for the support they provided for this project: the American Council of Learned Societies, the Fondazione Giorgio Cini, the University of California–based "Middle Ages in the Wider World" project, and the Department of Religious Studies and Academic Senate of the University of California, Santa Barbara. I also owe a deep debt of thanks to the curators of several library, archival, and museum collections, as well as to a number of private individuals, for providing me with the high-resolution images of the artwork and manuscript folios that constitute this book's iconography: they are acknowledged individually in image captions and in endnotes. Among the many web-based platforms to which I had recourse while researching for this book, I wish to acknowledge four remarkable websites: the Internet Archive (archive.org), the Göttingen Register of Electronic Texts in Indian Languages (gretil.sub.uni-goettingen.de), the Encyclopædia Iranica (iranicaonline.org), and the Digital Dictionaries of South Asia Program (dsal .uchicago.edu).

Portions of chapters included here have appeared in prior publications. Chapter 2 is a revised version of an article that appeared in French under the title "Amulettes et lambeaux divins: «superstition», vraie «religion» et «science» pure à la lumière de la démonologie indienne," in Ines G. Županov and Caterina Guenzi, eds., *Divins remèdes. Médecine et religion en Asie du Sud* (Puruṣārtha 27) (Paris: Éditions de l'EHESS, 2008), pp. 135–62. Chapter 4 is an extensive revision of "*Netra Tantra*, at the Crossroads of the Demonological Cosmopolis," *Journal of Hindu Studies* 5, no. 2 (July 2012): 145–71. Chapter 6 is an expanded version of "Variations on the Indo-European 'Fire in Water' Mytheme in Three Alchemical Accounts," *Journal of the American Oriental Society* 137, no. 4 (2017): 679–98.

Notes

Chapter One

1. Mus 1934: 1–44.

2. A classic analysis of the gray area between sorcery and countersorcery is Favret-Saada's 1977 participatory ethnography of sorcery in the Bocage region of northwestern France.

3. White 2012. I have revised much of the analysis and several of the conclusions drawn in that study in chapter 3 of the present work.

4. Pollock 2006: 12.

5. Reprinted in Smith 1978a: 172–89. See esp. pp. 187–89.

6. Recently, Ferrari (2015) has argued that Śītalā has always been a goddess of healing rather than a disease demoness. In South Asia, dæmons frequently both cause disease and release their devotees from the same.

7. Auboyer and Mallmann 1950: 209.

8. Kalleres 2015: 31, 262, note 22.

9. Filliozat 1937.

10. Anderson 1932; White 1991: 52–56; Subrahmanyam 1997: 755–57; Ogden 2012; Stoneman, Erikson, and Netton 2012; Zuwiyya 2012.

11. Almond 1987; Uhlig 2018.

12. See below, chapter 4, notes 32–34.

13. White 1991.

14. MBh 2.28.44, 47. For discussion, see Wittkower 1942: 164; White 1991: 52–67.

15. By "medieval," I am referring to the period between the decline of the Gupta Empire and the rise of the Mughal Empire in India (although it must be allowed that the Delhi Sultanate, whose territories were as extensive as those of the Mauryan and Mughal Empires, ruled India for nearly all of the thirteenth and fourteenth centuries). The period between the Gupta and Mughal empires corresponds quite precisely to that comprised between the fall of the Roman Empire and the rise of the imperial nation-states of Europe. By "early modern," I am referring to the period between approximately 1500 and 1800 in both India and the West. A recent thoughtful study of this periodization for South Asia is Ali 2012: 7–12. See also below, notes 77–86.

16. This is the title of Mines's fine 2005 ethnography of a Tamil village.

17. White 2003: 3; White 2006: 107.

18. For a lucid and fine-grained history of the advent of bhakti in early modern north India, see Burchett 2019.

19. According to Gisèle Krauskopff's (1989: 187) felicitous expression, "the gods are represented as 'landscaped' categories (*catégories 'paysagées'*) because they are the landscape." Cf. Berti 1999: 66–69, on "territorial deities" in South Asia.

20. The earliest extended account of the Hindu *tīrtha*s, found in MBh 3.80–89, gives greater prominence to devatās and other demigods as the local gods of those sacred sites, as well as to ancestral deities (*pitṛ*s) who are to be honored at them, than they do to the emerging high gods of classical Hindu theism.

21. For specific examples see White 2000: 19; and White 2003: 40–41. See also below, chapter 2, notes 83–86.

22. *Oxford English Dictionary*, s.v. "pagan" and "peasant." A notable exception is Gervase of Tilbury, a Catholic administrator and jurist whose early thirteenth-century *Otia Imperialia* draws freely on his first-hand knowledge of (mainly) southeastern French folk traditions: Banks and Binns 2010: lx and passim.

23. Schmitt 1988: 441.

24. The universality of these "local" traditions was an important focus of the graduate seminar I taught at the University of California, Santa Barbara between 2003 and 2018. Titled "Worship without Devotion: A History of South Asian Polytheism," its extensive reading list was heavily weighted toward historical ethnographies of specific regions and locales of South Asia. Online at https://www.academia.edu/37164788/RS_206J_Seminar_in_Indic_Religious_Studies_Worship_Without_Devotion_History_of_South_Asian_Polytheism.

25. *Dæmon* is the Latinate form of the ancient Greek *daimōn*.

26. *Phædo* 107d, in Emlyn-Jones and Preddy 2017: 486–87. Plato's *daimōn* is more or less equivalent to Socrates' *daimonion*, an adjective modifying the oracular "voice" that guided him from his youth: *Apology* 31c, in ibid., 158–59. For a general discussion, see Burkert 1985: 179–81.

27. Boyer 1994: 49–51.

28. But see Smith's (1978b: 432) typology, for ancient Greece, of the *theos* as an individualized anthropomorphic object of a cult versus the *daimōn* as a member of an undifferentiated group of non-anthropomorphic beings not receiving worship.

29. A lucid survey of the taxonomy of dæmons in the ancient world is Marx-Wolf 2016: 38–70. On Origen's interpretation, see ibid., 65–66. Cf. Flint 1999: 281–92 for the demons of classical antiquity, pp. 292–96 for the demons of Jewish antiquity, and pp. 327–29 for pagan demons in Christian angelology.

30. Karetzky 2012: 1–45, who also indicates the presence of winged deities in ancient Iranian bas-reliefs (ibid., fig. 1), and who traces the transmission of this western motif into the Buddhist art of India in the last centuries before the Common Era. On the transmission of the bat-wing motif into Europe, see Baltrušaitis 1993: 155–75. Cf. White 2020: 76–79.

31. This engraving is from Picart 1728: following p. 222.

32. Callieri 2001: 12. However, as Callieri notes (ibid., p. 12, note 4), not all scholars agree. See, for example, Witzel 2001: 1. *Daēva* and *dēw* are Iranian cognates of the Indo-Aryan *devatā*.

33. The *yakku* of modern-day Sri Lanka carry forward this legacy: Scott 1994: 4 and passim.

34. Henning 1947: 47–51. The catalog of *yakṣa*s that this source draws upon is contained in the *Mahāmāyūrīvidyārājñī-sūtra* (MMVS), a work that will be discussed in chapter 3, section 1.

35. For example, in his *On Abstinence*, the third-century Neoplatonist philosopher Porphyry describes how, by gorging themselves on the blood and smoke of animal sacrifices, good

dæmons became heavy and moist and fell to the lower regions of the sublunary sphere: Marx-Wolf 2016: 66.

36. Excellent overviews of the pagan substratum and the strategies of demonization/diabolization in late antiquity are Flint 1999 and Kalleres 2015. See also Smith's (1978b: 435) "complex model" of the demonic in the ancient world.

37. The ṚV mentions the *rakṣas* (called *rākṣasas* in later literature) over fifty times, and the *piśācas* once: Macdonnell 1897: 163–64. See below, chapter 2, note 58; and chapter 3, notes 1 and 25 for further discussion.

38. A pivotal figure in this transition would have been the "sādhaka-magician," who, as Hélène Brunner (1985: 435) opined, would have been the direct descendant of "popular magicians versed in the science of spells (*mantravāda*), botanicals, metals, etc." His practices, which will be discussed at length in chapter 3, comprised both "black magic" (sorcery, manipulation of demonic beings) and "white magic" (protection of the king and society at large from the same): ibid., 432–33, 436–38. See below, chapter 3, note 231. Cf. White 2011: 575.

39. Philological variations on the Sanskrit terms *grāma-devatā* (village deity, *genius loci*) and *kula-devatā* (ancestral, lineage deity) are attested in virtually all modern South Asian languages. See Nagano and Ikari 1993.

40. Vaudeville 1999: 17–196; Sanford 2005: 89–110.

41. Mitterwallner 1984: 12–31. Cf. Banerjea 1941: 126–28 for the early numismatic record. As indicated above (text to note 1), Southeast Asia had analogous lithic representations of territorial deities.

42. Cort 1987: 235–55; DeCaroli 2004: 182–83. On Hāritī, see below, chapter 4, note 102; and chapter 6, section 1.

43. Bitel 2018: 81.

44. While it bears the title *Religious Studies: A Global View*, Alles 2008 is rather a survey of individual world religions and of the sociology of academic knowledge concerning world religions. It retains the Area Studies approach to religious traditions that has been dominant for several decades.

45. Originally published in French in 1949 under the title *Traité d'histoire des religions*.

46. Chakrabarty 2000: 29, 40–41, 93–94, 106.

47. Eaton (2000: 58, 60–63), who notes (p. 63) that one of the group's founders, Ramachandra Guha, went on to lament (1995: 2056–58) that Subaltern Studies had become "bhadralok studies," that is, the study of elites.

48. Chakrabarty 2000: 16, 113. In a 2006 article, I offer an extended critique of Chakrabarty's theoretical positions by adducing evidence for "linear" historical thinking on the part of subalterns, and by suggesting that in making his arguments, Chakrabarty conflated "thinking historically" with "historicist theorizing": White 2006: 5–14.

49. Spivak 1993: 86–91. This chapter originally appeared in a 1988 collective volume: see bibliography. Spivak claims for herself the "permission to narrate" (for) the subaltern on the basis of "birth and education" (ibid., 76, 79). She bases her arguments on a superficial, archive-based analysis of *satī*/suttee (ibid., 93–103). The most serious and sensitive treatment of the subject, based on both archival and field research, remains Weinberger-Thomas 1999.

50. Chakrabarty 2000: 40.

51. Jamison 2016: 238.

52. This effect has recently been quantified. A recent report from the Modern Language Association indicates that colleges shuttered more than 650 language programs between 2013 and 2016: Johnson 2019.

53. Chakrabarty 2000: 77, 108, 239.

54. According to such law books as the *Manu Smṛti* (2.22–23), the territory of *āryāvarta* was enclosed by the eastern and western seas (i.e., the Arabian Sea and the Bay of Bengal) and the Himalaya and Vindhya mountain ranges. The same source (2.24) also speaks of a broader geographical range, "where the black antelope naturally roams," as distinguishing "the country fit for sacrifices" from the "land of the barbarians" beyond. For discussion, see Witzel 2001: 1–93; Subrahmanyam 1997: 742–45.

55. White 2014: 84–85.

56. Reprinted in Eliade 1969: 54–71.

57. Published in Smith 1978a: 104–28.

58. First broached in Smith 1971: 67–90.

59. Smith 1982: 21–22, 25–26; Smith 1990: 53, 143; Smith 2004: 25–30.

60. Smith 1971: 67–90; Smith 1990: 47–49, 112–13. At the same time, Smith underscored "*the recognition and role of historical development and change*" with regard to comparison, evoking the "*historical processes of reinterpretation*" that comprise tradition (Smith 1990: 106–7; italics in original). Smith (1982: 29) also acknowledged, without pursuing the idea further, that history should have a place in the comparative approach: "We have yet to develop the responsible alternative [to earlier failed attempts]: the integration of a complex notion of pattern and system with an equally complex notion of history."

61. For discussion, see Espagne 1994: 112–21; Subrahmanyam 1997: 735–62; Subrahmanyam 2005: 102–3; and Stanziani 2018: 89–114, 119–20.

62. Smith 1978a: 88–103, 172–89.

63. Smith 1982: 90–101.

64. Smith 1990: 52.

65. Lincoln 1985: 268–69; Lincoln 1991: 123; Lincoln 2012: xiii; Lincoln 2014: 22; Lincoln 2018: 26. Lincoln's purview is also narrowed by his nearly exclusive reliance on mythological and ritual texts from the archive.

66. "Theses on Comparison," in Lincoln 2012: 121–23, and Lincoln 2018: 25–27; "Theses on Method" in Lincoln 2012: 1–3; "protocols for dealing with texts" in Lincoln 2012: 9; "definition of religion" in Lincoln 2012: 75–76.

67. Lincoln 2012: 123; Lincoln 2018: 12, 13, 40, 70, 109, 113, 128, 147, 153, 183.

68. Smith 1990: 53.

69. Lincoln 1985: 268–69; Lincoln 1986: 164–65; Lincoln 1991: xvi; Lincoln 1994: passim; Lincoln 2012: 1–3, 6–7; Lincoln 2018: 23–24. This position is anticipated and contextualized in White 1987: 13–14. On myths of resistance, see Lincoln 2014: 23–24. For a critique of this type of analysis, see Subrahmanyam 2005: 134.

70. Lincoln 1999: 216.

71. Bloch (1928: 18) laid the theoretical foundations for this focus, which rejected Weber's style of comparative history for a connected approach: "To undertake parallel studies of neighboring and contemporary societies, perennially influenced by one another and subject during their development, precisely due to their proximity and their contemporaneousness, to the same great historical forces, and going back, at least in part, to a common origin. This is the equivalent, in history per se, of historical linguistics (of Indo-European linguistics, for example)." For discussion, see Stanziani 2018: 119–21. The research institute founded by Le Goff in 1978, and which was directed by Schmitt until 2014, was named Groupe d'Anthropologie Historique de l'Occident Médiéval (GAHOM). Its name was recently changed to Anthropologie historique du long Moyen Âge (AHLOMA).

72. White 1991: 130–39.

73. Burkert 1992: 7–8.

74. Subrahmanyam 1997: 735–62.

75. Subrahmanyam 1997: 761–62.

76. Burkert 1979: 27–28.

77. Subrahmanyam 1997: 737.

78. Vagnon 2017: 193.

79. Subrahmanyam 2005: 103.

80. Subrahmanyam 2005: 12. Subrahmanyam's articulation of this relationship was anticipated by Espagne 1994: 115–16.

81. Subrahmanyam 2005: 50.

82. Inglebert 2009: 128–29, 136.

83. "Modern World-system" is the term coined in 1974 by Immanuel Wallerstein for the modern period.

84. Mukherjee 2017: 350; Beaujard 2017: 389.

85. See above, notes 10–14.

86. Beaujard 2017: 389–411; see especially figs. 2–5. As Mukherjee (2017: 357) describes it, "the medieval Indian Ocean became a networked sea with regional entrepots as new powers emerged: the Khmers at Angkor (944), the Songs in China (960), the Fatimids in Egypt (969), the Cholas in peninsular India (985), the Ly in North Vietnam (1009), and the Burmese in Bagan (1044)."

87. Inglebert 2009: 137–39.

88. Gills and Frank 1992: 621–87, especially 632–47, which treats of the period between 3000 BCE and 100/50 BCE. An extensive bibliography of these two scholars and a presentation of their model may be found online at "Andre Gunder Frank: The Five Thousand Year World System in Theory and Practice": http://rrojasdatabank.info/agfrank/theory_praxis.html (accessed April 30, 2019).

89. Puhvel 1987: 4; Dumézil 1981: 35; Dumézil 1986b: 78–80, who speaks of a "common heritage."

90. Bouckaert et al. 2012: 957–60; see esp. p. 959, fig. 2. Bouckaert's analysis is based on linguistic evidence, and as such counters Marija Gimbutas's long-prevailing archaeology-based theory of a homeland in the Pontic steppes. Gimbutas's theory continues to be embraced by many Indo-Europeanists, and also finds support on the basis of DNA evidence: Haak 2015: 207–20. However, see Haak's "Extended Data Figure 4," which maps out Indo-European expansion according to the two contending theories, and his discussion in ibid., 211. Parpola (2015: 35–68) gives an exceptionally fine-grained account of the Indo-European homeland as a nexus of agriculture, pastoralism, and metallurgy, as well as the use of the horse-drawn war chariot.

91. Lampooned by Lincoln 1999: 76–100.

92. This is the year in which, according to Dumézil himself, he found a solid foundation for his comparative research (Ewald 1986: 17), bringing comparative mythology back from its erasure from "the catalogue of serious fields of study": Dumézil 1986a: 11.

93. Lincoln 1991: 231–43, 259–68; Dubuisson 1993: 21–123; Lincoln 1999: 121–37. Other critics include Arnaldo Momigliano, Cristiano Grottanelli, and Carlo Ginzburg: see Lincoln 1999: 270, note 14.

94. Derrida 1972: 254.

95. Guyénot 2011: 27, 35, 94; Boyer 2014: 73–74.

96. Pirart 2007 is one of the most convincing critiques of Dumézil on this point, arguing that through selective omissions and philological sleight of hand, Dumézil imposed his trifunctional

schema upon nontrifunctional Iranian pantheons of gods and demons. Lincoln (1991: 244–58) makes a similar argument concerning Dumézil's selective use of data, marshaled for ideological ends.

97. Boyer 2014: 74.

98. Gould 1989: 52.

99. Scheid 1993: 19. Related to the Latin *lux*, it is a cognate of the vedic √*ruc*, which generates the term *loka*, "world." The early Heidegger would be pleased.

100. Scheid 2008: 633.

101. Graça da Silva and Tehrani 2016: 1–11. Only one of these folklore types is discussed in this book. See below, chapter 4, note 32.

102. Here, I am using this term in the generic (and relatively rare) sense of "amulet," and not according to the specific Jewish usage: *Oxford English Dictionary*, s.v. "phylactery[3]."

103. For chapter 5, White 2003: 64; for chapter 6, White 1996: 206.

Chapter Two

1. Ghatiyali (Ajmer District) is the village that has anchored Ann Grodzins Gold's ethnography for the past four decades. It was she who alerted me to the existence of this temple, and I am grateful to her and to Bhoju Ram Gujar, who was my host and guide during my stay there.

2. *Tel-sindūr* is the more common name for the mixture of oil and vermilion powder that forms the colored paste applied to both iconic and aniconic images across north India.

3. Less well known than fall Nine Nights festival, which is better known as Daśaharā or Durgā Pūjā. In Rajasthan, the term *navarātri* is used, rather than *navarātra*, which is more commonly employed in other parts of India.

4. Bouillier 2017: 50, note 10.

5. At their paired shrines in Mandore, the old Rathor capital located five miles to the north of Jodhpur, one finds massive iconic images of the two gods alongside their original aniconic forms in a shrine adjacent to the so-called "Hall of Heroes" there: two conical foil-covered stones with eyes painted upon them.

6. In the Bhanswara District of Rajasthan, Bherūṃ-jī's Bhopā priests offer *māḷīpanā* to the deity on the sixth night of the dark lunar fortnights of the months of Bhādrapada (August–September) and Māgh (January–February): Sehgal 1974: 73.

7. On the Gosains, see below, note 22.

8. Personal communication from Komal Kothari, Jodhpur, Rajasthan, April 2, 1999. Also known as Bayasāb Mātā or Bayānsā, her name is applied to a collectivity of seven sister goddesses. She also has several regional shrines, including one at Nimgarh, in the Beawar District of southern Rajasthan, which she shares with Bherūṃ-jī: Mayaram 1999: 106–7, 110 and note 6.

9. The Bhopās are the Rajasthani homologues of the Ojhas of the Gangetic plain, the Bhuvos of Gujarat, and the Baigas of Madhya Pradesh. Healers, sorcerers, exorcists, and the traditional priests of village shrines, their practices are generally more "shamanic" than brahmanic. Traditionally, Bhopās are members of the Bhil tribe. This particular Bhopā was from the Chīpā *jāti*, whose traditional occupation was to print patterns onto textiles using wood blocks: personal communication from Bhoju Ram Gujar, Ghatiyali, Rajasthan, November 29, 2006.

10. The colors red, yellow, and black are noxious to evil spirits: Crooke 1928: 444. At the Kāl Bhairo Nāth temple in Benares, worshipers receive black woven threads to this end.

11. The bodily secretions of holy persons are considered to have protective properties: Crooke 1928: 446.

12. Personal communication from Komal Kothari, Jodhpur, April 2, 1999. Mayaram (1999: 114) also mentions *mail* in the context of Rajasthani exorcisms.

13. In 1999, the *pūjārī* of this temple was Manorji, a member of the Gāchī (milkman) *jāti*. His position was not hereditary, and not reserved for any particular *jāti*.

14. One encounters the same forms in modern Indic languages. *Mal* or *mail* means "filth" or "bodily secretion" in Hindi, while the Telugu term for ritual pollution, *maila*, draws on the same Sanskrit root and the same semantic field of meanings: Knipe 1989: 130. See below, notes 74–75.

15. Sakaria and Sakaria 1982, s.v. "māḷīyo" and "māḷīpanā."

16. Melaḍī Mātā also figures on a poster of *kuldevīs* that I purchased in Jodhpur in the mid-1990s. Her winnowing fan and ass vehicle are also features of the iconography of the smallpox goddess Śītalā. The region's seven other *kuldevīs* are Mahīṣāsura Mārdinī (Durgā), Momāī Mātā, Kālī, Bahucarājī, Khodīyār Mātā, Santoṣī Mātā, and Gel Mātā.

17. Pocock 1973: 64.

18. Marriott 1976: 128.

19. As do many of the goddesses of Nepal, Bhairab accepts sacrifices of five animals: water buffalo, goat, sheep, duck, and chicken.

20. This was the situation in 1999. In the fall of 2006, however, the original image was found to be scrubbed clean, with only the temple priests authorized to collect and redistribute the *tel-sindūr* and other detritus from beneath the feet of the image: email message from Peter Moran, November 22, 2006.

21. This term is related to *jaḍī būṭī*, "medicinal herb," because of its healing properties: personal communication from Sthaneswar Timalsina, Kathmandu, June 18, 1999.

22. Pinch 1996: 43–45.

23. Lorenzen 1972: 46.

24. Russell and Lal 1993: vol. 3, p. 153.

25. Sontheimer 1989: 95, 203.

26. Sontheimer 1989: 27, 97.

27. Sontheimer 1989: 198.

28. According to Bouillier (2017: 37), Bhairava is, after Gorakhnāth (of late identified with Śiva) and the Goddess, the most important deity in Nāth Yogi ritual, and the most ubiquitous deity in their temples. See also ibid., 38–39, 192–201, and passim.

29. Bouillier 1989: 193–202, esp. p. 197; Bouillier 1991: 1–21; Bouillier 2017: 165; White 1996: 310–11, 343–46; White 2009: 227–29.

30. Unbescheid 1980: 181–82.

31. Joshi 1977: 245. The Hindi-language term *ṭoṭkā* used here denotes both a "charm, spell, or amulet" and a "black earthen pot placed in a field to avert the evil eye": McGregor 1995: s.v. "ṭoṭkā."

32. Campbell 1976: 29.

33. On the date and provenance of this work, see Sanderson 2004: 243.

34. In his analysis of the ayurvedic demonological canon, Smith (2006: 481) notes that the term *bhūta* is generally applied to male agents of possession, with *graha* applied to females. However, Smith also observes (537) that in the ayurvedic literature, the term *graha* is used in a way analogous to the tantric use of the term *bhūtanātha* or *bhūteśvara*: these are beings who achieved supernatural powers through austerities and other practices, who control possessing

entities but who do not themselves possess. As will be discussed in chapter 3, this gender-based division of labor appears not to apply in the tantric literature.

35. NT 19.59a, 61a–62a, 68ab, 71ab, in Shastri 1939: 147–48, 150, 152.

36. NT 19.207a–211a, in Shastri 1939: 208–9.

37. *Jayākhya Saṃhitā* 29.172b–173a, 178b–180a, in Rastelli 2003: 146–47.

38. Mitra 1939: 174–75.

39. KSS 7.3.109–10, 128, 137, 153–56 in Sastri 1970: 170–71.

40. Sontheimer 1989: 27–29, 36.

41. NT 19.15b–22b, in Shastri 1939: 64–67; SS 6.37.11–22, in Vaidya 1975: 669–70. See below, chapter 3, note 66.

42. MBh 3.207.2–3.219.43. For an extended discussion of this myth in the MBh, see White 2003: 36–63. See also below, chapter 4, notes 96 and 101.

43. MBh 3.218.45, 49. Her ancient and modern cult are discussed in White 2003: 40–43. On the rites related to her modern cult in Bengal, see Sircar (2018: 45–46), who notes that "stones (or other items) can be tied with [these same colored threads] in small pieces of cloth to . . . tree branches."

44. The fifth-century image of the god unearthed at the Raj Ghat archeological site in Benares, and his ninth-century image from Hadigaon, Kathmandu, show identical necklaces. On the latter, see Slusser 1982: vol. 1, p. 259, note 188, and vol. 2, pl. 419. These are comparable to the protective charm necklaces placed on six-month-old children described in an early twentieth-century gazetteer from Mandi District in Himachal Pradesh: Emerson 1920: 94. In fourteenth- to fifteenth-century Italian art, the infant Jesus is sometimes shown with a coral amulet affixed about his throat, to ward off the evil eye: Simpson 2002: 122.

45. In the relatively rare cases in which endogenous causes are diagnosed, the emphasis is placed on imbalances in the wind humor (*vāta*): Smith 2006: 544. In modern-day Sri Lanka, *yakṣa dōṣa*s are humoral imbalances caused by malign *yakku*s: Scott 1994: 35.

46. Buddhist sources, such as the circa sixth-century CE version of the MMVS contained in the Bower Manuscript, present similar data, including lists of demonic agents of childhood disease: see below, chapter 3, section 1.

47. Wujastyk (1998: 39–41) dates this work to the period between the third century BCE and the fifth century CE. The redaction of the SS is more or less coeval with that of the CS: Wujastyk 1998: 104–5.

48. CS 6.9.89–94, in Acharya 1992: 474, translated in Smith 2006: 538–39.

49. Gail 1991–1992: 44–45. A seventh-century brass sculpture from Kashmir has been identified as "Śiva as Bhūteśvara," mainly on the basis of the goat that he holds in his left hand, which also figures on the OHþO coin: Pal 2003: 58.

50. Vaudeville 1999: 29–30.

51. CS 4.8.62, in Acharya 1992: 352.

52. SS 6.31.7–8, in Vaidya 1975: 665. An indication of the continuity of these traditions is attested in the names of the trees from whose wood the beads of these protective amulets are fashioned: *varaṇa* is listed as an amulet wood in the AV (10.3.1–25) as well as in its ancillary literature: KS 19.22; ŚK 2.19.8; and Atharvan *Pariśiṣṭa* 32.18. *Varaṇa* and other amulet woods mentioned in the AV are also prescribed in the *Yogaratnākara*, an eighteenth-century ayurvedic work: Shastri 1973: 451.

53. Whereas *pratisara* is a common Sanskrit term for an amulet or phylactery, the use of a feminine ending (*pratisarā*) is unusual. In both Hindu and Buddhist Tantra, Pratisarā is the

name of a protective goddess who, like the phylactery, repels malign beings, spells, and magical weapons. See below, note 60; and chapter 3, notes 215–18.

54. *Aṣṭāṅgasaṃgraha* 6.4.15a, 17ab–18a, 21a, in Athavale 1980: 648.

55. *Aṣṭāṅgasaṃgraha* 6.4.35, in Athavale 1980: 648.

56. *Aṣṭāṅgasaṃgraha* 6.4.41–42, 55, in Athavale 1980: 649–50. A wet nurse also appears in Skanda's epic birth myth: MBh 3.215.21. See below, chapter 4, note 101.

57. *Cikitsāsaṃgraha* 20.44–45, translated in Smith 2006: 542; *Ayurveda Saukhyam* 1.30, translated in Dash and Kashyap 1980: 59; *Yogaratnākara* in Shastri 1973: 451.

58. AV 1.16.1–4; 1.29.1–4; 2.4.1–6; 2.9.1–5; 3.5.1–9; 3.9.2–6; 4.10.1–7; 6.81.1–3; 6.127.1–3; 8.5.1–22; 10.3.1–25; 10.6.1–35; 19.34.1–10; 19.46.1–7; etc.

59. While the primary meaning of the term comes to be "jewel" or "gem" in later Sanskrit, its earliest meaning of "necklace" is related to the ancient Greek (*mánnos*) and Latin (*monile*), both terms for "necklace," as well as to the English "mane": Monier-Williams 1984: 774, s.v. "maṇi."

60. Gonda 1937: 311–15.

61. For a general discussion, see Geslani 2018: 20–71. On the dating of the AV canon, see ibid., 12–13, 24–26. The latest collection, that of the Atharvan *Pariśiṣṭa*s, "date(s) from the early centuries of the second millennium CE": ibid., 80–81. These contain several rites of protection that call for the tying of *pratisara*s: Atharvan *Pariśiṣṭa*s 4.4.9, 6.1.11, in Bolling and Negelein 1976: 42, 47. Modak (1993: 474, notes 18 and 19) lists over fifteen references from this collection, in which some type of amulet is used against various malign human and nonhuman beings.

62. Modak 1993: 73. Cf. Geslani 2018: 25.

63. KS 7.15–21, in Bolling 1928: 469; Bloomfield 1972: 23; Caland 1900: 11–12.

64. KS 25.1–35.19, in Bloomfield 1972: 67–96. See also Modak 1993: 72.

65. Zysk 1985: 25. According to Zysk (ibid., 27), *rapas* is possibly dracunculiasis or guinea-worm disease.

66. KS 28.17–20: English translation and discussion in Zysk 1985: 27. See also Zysk's discussion of the use of a barley amulet for the same purpose in AV 6.91.1. Zysk surmises (ibid., 129) that the barley in question was wrapped into a poultice, which was applied to the affected region of the body (in this case the foot).

67. Bolling 1904: 84; Bolling 1928: 472. This text takes its name from the fact that it contains the ritual for the *adbhūtamahāśānti*, or "great ceremony for averting the evil effects of omens and portents": Bolling 1904: 79. An edition (and English translation) of the ŚK is found in Bolling 1904; an edition of a previously unknown introductory chapter is in Bolling 1913.

68. ŚK 2.22.2, in Bolling 1904: 107. The *amṛtā-mahāśānti* has been recently treated in depth in Geslani 2018: 54–70, 237–41. For his discussion of the language of this specific ritual (based in part on Bolling 1904: 121–22), see ibid., 58–59, 63, 267–68. The mantras that comprise AV 5.10.1–8 are said to be for "defense from all quarters." Note that these mantras are taken from the AV chapter that immediately follows AV 5.9 (entitled "for protection"), whose mantras form the liturgy of the KS (28.17–20) ritual described just above (note 66). The mantras of AV 5.10 are employed in a KS (51.14–16) rite for the protection of a house or field: Whitney 1905: vol. 2, p. 236; Caland 1900: 177; Modak 1993: 133.

69. ŚK 2.22.3–5 in Bolling 1904: 107. The liturgy for this rite is comprised of mantras from AV 3.26 and 3.27, hymns of homage to the gods of the quarters.

70. This hymn (AV 11.4.13) notably identifies barley and rice as the in-breath and out-breath.

71. ŚK 2.24.6, 2.25.1, in Bolling 1904: 109 (English translation p. 122).

72. *Sāmavidhāna Brāhmaṇa* 2.2.1 in Bolling 1928: 472. See below, chapter 4, notes 140 and 155.

73. See Malamoud 1989 for his penetrating studies on the notion of "remains" in brahmanism (ibid., 13–33), and on the raw and the cooked in vedic and modern-day India (ibid., 68–70).

74. The *malam* that comprises the fetter is in fact threefold: Sanderson 1986: 191.

75. Brunner, Oberhammer, and Padoux 2000: 181, s.v. "āṇavamala."

76. See also NT 19.130 and above, notes 37 and 48.

77. On this Jain deity, see Cort 1997: 115–33.

78. Daya 1990: 74.

79. Behind all of these modernist categories one may glimpse the evolutionist theories of Sir James Frazer, according to which the human mind passes through the stages of "magical" and "religious" thought before reaching its *telos* of "scientific" thought. However, Frazer (2002: 48–49) noted the common ground shared by magic and science, over and against religion. "The magician does not doubt that the same causes will always produce the same effects. . . . He supplicates no higher power: he sues the favour of no fickle and wayward being: he abases himself before no awful deity. Yet his power . . . is by no means arbitrary and unlimited. He can wield it only so long as he strictly conforms . . . to what may be called the laws of nature as conceived by him." I am grateful to Keith Cantú for bringing this passage to my attention.

80. Fuller 1992: 27–28.

81. Smith 2006: 55.

82. Bentley 2006: 17. In place of pre-modern, James Ketelaar (2006: 62–79) has proposed the term "non-modern" to denote societies that not only predate "modernity" but also contemporary traditional societies that have remained relatively untouched by modernity, i.e., subalterns, tribals, peasants, minorities, etc.

83. Primiano 1995: 46.

84. Chakrabarti 2001: 61–62. Another excellent study of local-translocal negotiations of this type in medieval India is Cohen 1998.

85. Chakrabarti 2001: 24.

86. Guyénot 2011: 51–52; Sullivan 2018: 7–8, 39–40, 52. For a pertinent example of the circularity, i.e., the mutual borrowings between elite and popular culture, see Schmitt 2001: 190. His case involves an exemplum penned by the thirteenth-century Dominican inquisitor Stephen of Bourbon, who documented the rituals surrounding the unauthorized cult of Saint Guinefort: see below, chapter 4, section 2.

Chapter Three

1. *Saddharmapuṇḍarīka Sūtra* 401.4–402.1, quoted in Dietz 1997: 86–87. Cf. SPS 398.1–2, 474.8–10.

2. Lévi 1915: 118, 121. The ancient core of the MMVS was the *Ātānāṭiya Sutta*, a Pali-language Hinayana work: Sørensen 2006: 91. The mid-third-century Endere Inscription refers to the Kushan emperor Huviṣka as a champion of Mahāyāna: Lam 2013: 441.

3. Toponyms referenced here were spread across much of KGB, including Gandhara, Bactria, Kashmir, eastern Iran, the valleys of the Indus, Swat, and Oxus rivers, as well as Chinese Turkestan: Lévi 1915: 71–79, 100–102, 104–15. In his summary, Lévi notes (ibid., 116–17) that "the northwest"—largely comprised within the KGB region—was of special interest to the author of the yakṣa list. On urban yakṣa cults, see DeCaroli 2004: 14, 23, and below, chapter 4, note 82. Deshpande (1959: 68–69) locates a number of the yakṣa sites mentioned in the MMVS along ancient Maharashtran trade routes.

4. Ed. and tr. Hoernle 1893–1912. On the language and date of the Bower Manuscript, see Meulenbeld 2000: 4–6; Wujastyk 2003: 149.

5. The earliest manuscript witnesses for the *Mahāpratisarā-mahāvidyārājñī*, another early Buddhist demonological work incorporated, like the MMVS, into the Pañcarakṣā (named for five protector mantra-goddesses) canon, are also from Eastern Turkestan and Gilgit: Hidas 2012: 7, 37–41. See also below, note 216.

6. On the links between the trading oases of the Tarim Basin and the Bactrian and Kushan Empires, see Schwartzberg 1992: 175; La Vaissière 2002: 97; Inglebert 2009: 136; Christopoulos 2012: maps I.1, I.4, and I.5, following p. 79.

7. This notwithstanding, the principal conduit for east-west trade throughout this period was maritime: on this, see Acri 2016a: 1–25, and below, chapter 5, notes 27–31. It was often the case, however, that goods carried overland would be loaded onto ships at South Asian port cities (Barygaza, etc.), and thence freighted onward to Rome, China, and other destinations: Fitzpatrick 2011: 44.

8. Salles 2017: 58; Mukherjee 2017: 352, 354; Schwartzberg 1992: 18 (plate III.B.4ab), 20 (plate III.C.1), 173–74. A trade route dating from Achaemenid times linked the eastern Mediterranean to the Bactrian region: Inglebert 2009: 128.

9. La Vaissière 2002: 42; Grenet 2015: 221, note 62; Cunliffe 2015: 288 (map 7.20).

10. Cohen 2013: 225–28; Pollock 2006: 265; Lecuyot 2007: 159–60; Verardi 1994: 51, note 73. While the date of the city's founding is uncertain, it is known to have been abandoned by the Greeks in 145 BCE: Lecuyot 2007: 156.

11. Lohuizen-de Leeuw 1975: 28; Fitzpatrick 2011: 44.

12. Lévi 1934: 15–19.

13. Grenet 2006: 88–91; Grenet 2015: 206–37. A brilliant analysis of the political calculations behind Kushan coinage is Michon 2015: 112–51.

14. Verardi 1994: 66–79 (figs. 12–28).

15. See below, notes 123–24.

16. Scott 1993: 92–93, 100–104.

17. La Vaissière 2002: 97; Schwartzberg 1996: 21 (plate III.C.2), 175–76.

18. Shenkar (2017: 195, 200) makes the distinction between the "Sogdian variant of Zoroastrianism" practiced by commoners and the Indic religions cultivated by the aristocracy.

19. Grenet 2006: 89–96; Grenet 2016: 220–21; Durkin-Meisterernst 2016: 155–56, 159.

20. Grenet 1996; La Vaissière 2002: 18, 62, 74–75, 82–85, 89–90, 96–97, 152–53, and map 3 following p. 66. Sogdians were already trading with China in the second century BCE, and with India in the third century CE.

21. Durkin-Meisterernst 2016: 155–65; Cunliffe 2015: 314 (map 8.12); Stanziani 2018: 173. The eighth-century tantric Buddhist translator Amoghavajra, initiated by Vajrabodhi, was a Sogdian who appears to have combined his role as a merchant with that of an apostle of Buddhism: Grenet 1996: 67, 69; Parkin and Barnes 2002: 104. Translations were also carried out by Parthian, Indian, and Yuezhi merchant-monks: Mukherjee 2017: 342.

22. Grenet 1996: 65; La Vaissière 2002: 85–88.

23. Lévi 1915: 24–28; DesJardins 2002: 20–28. The earliest of these three complete Chinese translations (Taisho 984), a pivotal work compiled in about 516 CE by Sengjiapoluo (= Saṅgabhadra), a monk from Funan in southern China whose knowledge of Sanskrit was poor, corresponds in part to the Sanskrit version of the MMVS transmitted in the Bower Manuscript: Sørensen 2006: 90; DesJardins 2002: 23. This may explain some of the bizarre spellings of names of demons contained therein.

24. Summarized in Lévi 1915: 21–22.

25. Takubo 1972: 1, 3, 11–12, 27, 37, 42, 48, 50, 57.

26. In his translation of the Bower Manuscript version of this passage, Hoernle (vol. 2 [1897], p. 227) tentatively reads *ostāraka* as "a misspelling for *dus-tāraka*," which "might be the evil eye." I find this interpretation to be implausible.

27. Here, I have emended *karmaṇāḥ* to *karṣaṇāḥ*.

28. *Kiraṇa*, *cicca*, and *preṣaka* are all defined in the same way in Edgerton (1953: 183, 229, 394), citing the MMVS for each entry, as "a kind of malevolent supernatural being."

29. *Duśchāyā*[*ḥ*] is anomalous in a number of ways. On the one hand, the -ā ending could signal a simple feminine singular, or a masculine or feminine plural, dropping the final *visarga* before the sonant h- in the word that follows (*hatā*). Furthermore, it is the sole member of the list of six terms in which it is embedded that does not have a past passive participial form.

30. Takubo 1972: 38. Similar passages are found in ibid., 3, 28, 42, 57. These passages are also reprised in the *Mahāpratisarā-Mahāvidyārājñī* and *Suvarṇaprabhāsottamasūtra* (Hidas 2012: 153).

31. Commenting on the language of the portion of the Bower Manuscript containing these passages, Meulenbeld (2000: 4) notes that "the author . . . was not conversant with scholarly Sanskrit: these treatises are written in a mixed type of language." He refers to this nonstandard Sanskrit as resulting from "the influence of Prakrit."

32. Throughout this chapter, I will capitalize Chāyā when the term unambiguously refers to a demon, and I will use the lowercase italicized form (*chāyā*) when it is used in a more generic sense.

33. Monier-Williams 1984: 406, s.v. "chāya." In the ṚV and later sources, Chāyā is the name of a simulacrum created by the Sun god's wife to stand in for herself (O'Flaherty 1980: 175–78). She is said to be the mother of Śani (Saturn): see below, notes 120–21.

34. Takubo 1972: 11–12. The same treatment is given to all the demon and demigod types listed here.

35. Turner 1931: 195, s.v. "chāyā."

36. Tulpule and Feldhaus 1999: 247, s.v. "chāyā." Email message from William Sax, February 26, 2018.

37. Weinberger-Thomas 1999: 20; Mayaram 1999: 112. There are several synonyms for voluntary or induced possession and its effects. These include *chāyā ānā*, *bhāv ānā*, *ghumna*, *bārtan ānā*, and *battarai ānā*: personal communication from Komal Kothari, Jodhpur, Rajasthan, March 23, 1999.

38. Varma 1981: 342, s.v. "chāyā."

39. Dasa 1965–75: 5079, s.v. "sāyā."

40. Shakespear 1834: 1035, s.v. "sāya."

41. Fallon 1879: 74, s.v. "sāya."

42. Platts 1884: 258, s.v. "sāya."

43. Raverty 1867: 574, s.v. "sāya'h."

44. Gharib 1995: 367, s.v. "sy'k(h)"; MacKenzie 1971: 74, s.v. "sāyag."

45. DesJardins 2002: 24, 354–56. In addition to the three Chinese translators, Śākyaprabhā's ninth- to tenth-century Tibetan translation also appears to work from the same Sanskrit archetype manuscript: Overbye 2016: 262. The circa 800 CE Tibetan translation of the *Garbhāvakrānti* ("Descent of the Embryo"), another Sanskrit-language Buddhist work with strong demonological content, also contains references to *chāy*(*ā*)-*graha*s, references that are absent from all earlier (Chinese) translations: email message from Rob Kritzer, January 29, 2018. An exhaustive study of this text is Kritzer 2014a, who notes that Chos grub, who inserted the *chāy*(*ā*)-*graha*s into his

Tibetan translation, probably lived in Dunhuang, in the Tarim Basin. The list of demons found in his translation closely follows the demon lists of the MMVS. Cf. Kritzer 2014b: 190, 192.

46. On the topic of the *chāy(ā)*s, the Bower Manuscript's excerpt of the MMVS (book 6, fol. 1, line 3 to fol. 2, line 1) is virtually identical to Takubo 1972: 3. In both, there is a long list of names of the same demons and demigods, compounded with the ending *-grahato*, and followed by kṛtyākarmaṇak(āḥ)khordavetāḍakiraṇaciccaka-preṣakadurbhuktaduścharditaduśchāyā.

47. Sax 2009: 83–90. Throughout his study, Sax transliterates these Garhwali terms as *chhaya*, *chhal*, and *chhidra*.

48. Sax 2009: 83–84.

49. Sax 2009: 85. Numerous other examples may be cited from modern ethnographies, such as Nabokov's (2000: 74) discussion of the possession of young women by *peys* in Tamilnadu. Tantric manuscripts held in private collections in Garhwal, and dating back to the eleventh to twelfth centuries, consistently describe *chaḷ*s as demonic afflictions arising from fear: email message from Garhwal University historian Dinesh Prasad Saklani, October 12, 2010. See also below, note 67.

50. Sax 2009: 86.

51. Sax 2009: 84. On the cognate Sātī Āsarā of Maharashtra, see below, note 58; and chapter 4, notes 152–54. Among the Tharu populations of the Terai region of southern Nepal, several hundred miles to the southeast of Uttarakhand, *masān* denotes the malevolent spirit of a person who died a violent death or who has died in a desolate place; or the spirit of some "outsider" group: Krauskopff 1989: 118. As such, these would be the Tharu cognates of the Chaḷs of Uttarakhand.

52. See below, note 67.

53. Sax 2009: 70, 86–87.

54. Confusingly, Sax (2009: 88) uses Masan here in the plural, but it is clear that he is referring to the Chaḷs.

55. Sax 2009: 88–89.

56. Sax 2009: 89.

57. Sax 2009: 54, 89–90.

58. Traill 1828: 220–21. As Turner (1966: 23) indicates, the Garhwali *āchri* ("heavenly damsel") is a cognate of the Sanskrit *apsaras*. So too are the Sātī Āsarā ("Seven Apsarasas"), the dread river demonesses of Maharashtra: see above, note 51.

59. Crooke 1968: vol. 1, p. 260. Cf. Oberoi 1994: 175, on the sāyās of the Punjab.

60. According to Hidas (2012: 241), another Sanskrit term relating to the evil eye is *duḥprekṣita*, which I translated in the passage above as "those who are beheld with evil intent." See above, note 30.

61. See above, notes 5 and 22. The two valleys were linked by a spur of the Silk Road: Whitfield 2004: 6–7.

62. Brunner 1974: 127; Sanderson 2004: 293.

63. Included in these works were ritual instructions for the mastery of Vetālas (Sanderson 2006: 149), a theme to which I will return in section 5 of this chapter.

64. An edition and translation of selected chapters of the *Kriyākālaguṇottara* is found in Slouber 2017: 133–279.

65. NT 19.2–6.

66. NT 19.15–21.

67. NT 19.25–30a. Later, the NT (19.175) speaks of *hiṃsaka*s that, "fond of tribute offerings (*balikāma*), gathering together in a windy space [or the place of wind in the body: *vātasthānam*],

arise as 'wind-born' [demons]." The same is said of phlegm-born and bile-born beings (19.176). See also above, note 49.

68. RA 18.186–87.

69. KSS 7.1.79–89 (in Sastri 1970: 161). This tale is illustrated in a Persian manuscript likely commissioned by Akbar: Franke 2010: 333, 347 (fig. 57).

70. *Kāśyapa Saṃhitā* 8.6.6, in Sharma 1998: 188. Cf. Tewari 1996: 174–75. This work has been dated to the seventh century by Meulenbeld (2000: 41).

71. MBh 3.207.2–3.219.43.

72. The earliest myth involving "Long-Tongue" is found in *Jaiminīya Brāhmaṇa* 1.161–63, translated and discussed in O'Flaherty 1985: 100–103.

73. *Kāśyapa Saṃhitā* 8.6.7, in Sharma 1998: 189. Cf. Tewari 1996: 175.

74. NT 19.34–44. Several of the pathologies (*nidānas*) listed here reproduce those found in *Aṣṭāṅgasaṃgraha* 6.3.4. One of these is "delusional fear" (*mohabhaya*), which Kṣemarāja glosses (*ad* NT 19.36a, in Shastri 1939: 138) as "fear caused by the *chāyās* and so forth."

75. I have emended *snātvā*, which makes no sense, to *asnātvā*.

76. NT 19.45a–47d, 49a–51b. The *sādhaka* is the principal ritual actor in these demonological and countersorcery rites. The term appears some sixty times in the NT. On his central role in protecting the king and society at large, see Brunner 1975: 432–38. See also above, chapter 1, note 38.

77. Meulenbeld 2000: 25. Only two manuscript witnesses of the *Kāśyapa Saṃhitā* are extant. While one is of unknown provenance, the other is from Nepal, which may indicate that this work also originated from somewhere in the Himalayas or beyond.

78. *Kāśyapa Saṃhitā* 8.6.8 in Sharma 1998: 189–90. Cf. Tewari 1996: 177–78. The same information is related in similar language in *Kāśyapa Saṃhitā* 8.6.63–66.

79. Osella and Osella 1999: 188.

80. *Harivaṃśa* 38.77b–78a.

81. CS 6.9.21 (in Acharya 1992: 470); *Aṣṭāṅgasaṃgraha* 6.3.4.4ab.

82. Brunner, Oberhammer, and Padoux 2004: 257, s.v. "chidra 2."

83. *Tantrāloka* 30.96b–97a, in Gnoli 1999: 592.

84. *Prabandhacintāmaṇi* 4.42, in Sastri 1932: 155: tacchidreṇa tānpraviśya lūtāvyādhirbādhāmaghāt. The full text reads: "Owing to the curse of the very virtuous mother of Lakṣarāja the king of Kaccha, it [the disease] was handed down to all the descendants of Mūlarāja and in consequence of this transmission, it came to pass that [when Hemacandra briefly replaced Mūlarāja's descendant Kumārapāla, thereby becoming Mūlarāja's successor], the disease of leprosy penetrated into the sage by that opening (*tacchidreṇa*)" (Tawney 1899: 150).

85. chidramaraṇye rodanādi.

86. NT 19.42c: "[Women who are] wailing, shrieking, [and] who have their hair unbound." I am grateful to Somadeva Vasudeva for suggesting this connection to me in an email message dated October 24, 2010.

87. Another use of the term comes from neighboring Himachal Pradesh, where *chidra* signifies the ritual slicing of a lamb's foot as a means to "breaking open" a political and meteorological crisis ascribed to the displeasure of the local territorial deities: Berti 1999: 68, 83, 87–88.

88. *Aṣṭāṅgahṛdayasūtra* 6.4.6. On this, see Braverman 2003: 64.

89. ṚV 10.146.4: vásann araṇyām sāyám ákrukṣad íti manyate.

90. Sommer 2007: 55. Cf. White 2020: 79–80.

91. See below, note 267.

92. Brunner, Oberhammer, and Padoux 2004: 257, s.v. "chidra 1."

93. Email message from William Sax, February 28, 2018.

94. In his introduction to NT 1–5 (in Shastri 1939: 127), he writes: chāyācchidradṛṣṭipātādi.

95. NT 19.45–46.

96. NT 19.17b; Kṣemarāja's opening invocation and introductory verse to the NT's nineteenth chapter (in Shastri 1939: 127); his commentary on NT 19.3a (in Shastri 1939: 128) and 19.36a (in Shastri 1939: 138); and his introductions to NT 19.5–7 (in Shastri 1939: 128) and 19.53 (in Shastri 1939: 144). This last reference is particularly evocative: "and what of the person who is possessed of [or by] a malign Chāyā (kiṃca duṣṭachāyāvatām)?" The other six mentions of *chāyā* in this chapter are too ambiguous to determine whether a shadow or a demon (or both) is denoted.

97. NT 19.5b. See above, note 65.

98. Brunner, Oberhammer, and Padoux 2004: 256, s.v. "chalam."

99. TSBh 16.164, quoted in Kṣemaraja ad NT 19.71, in Shastri 1939: 153.

100. Turner 1966: 274, s.v. "chala"; and 276, s.v. "chāyā."

101. Kṣemarāja *ad* NT 19.182, in Shastri 1939: 199.

102. NT 19.52–54. These are therapeutic measures: for apotropaic measures against these forms of aggression, see NT 19.207–211, discussed above, chapter 2, note 36.

103. The identities of these leaders, detailed in the NT 19's following section, have already been discussed. See above, chapter 2, note 35.

104. E.g., on earthen mounds at the edge of a settlement: Kṣemarāja *ad* NT 19.80–81, in Shastri 1939: 157. Here, I have emended Shastri's lacunary reading to read "grāmāntaṃ dhiṣṇyo sthāpitaḥ."

105. NT 19.74a–75a. This was also the case with the *chaḷ pūjā* described by Sax: see above, note 57.

106. Kṣemarāja *ad* NT 19.71: see above, note 98. Several tantric sources classify the Yoginīs in an analogous way, with some "arisen in the body" and others belonging to various landscapes: fields, mounds, etc.

107. NT 19.55–81, with the commentary of Kṣemarāja (in Shastri 1939: 144–58). See above, chapter 2, notes 48 and 56.

108. Sanderson 1986: 181–85.

109. White 2010: 200–215.

110. Forrest 2011: 18.

111. The Avesta also documents a demoness of the evil eye named Aγaši: Sakurzada and Omidsalar 1998: 44.

112. *Greater Bundahišn* 186.12. See Daryaee 2009: 94; and Kanga 1987: 873. I am grateful to Stefano Pellò for his assistance with this passage.

113. "For a demon of such violence is the demon of menstruation that, [where] the other demons do not strike things with the evil eye, this one strikes [them] with the evil eye": *Šāyest nē šāyest* 3.29, translated and discussed in Secunda 2014: 96.

114. Secunda 2014: 97–98.

115. Secunda 2014: 92, quoting *Dēnkard* 3.26. In a long catalog of demons, *Dēnkard* 3.20.41 (tr. Skjærvø 2011: 78) also mentions an evil eye demon "with salty eyes, who strikes people with the eyes." Paragraph numbering of these passages varies from one source to another.

116. The *Zand* comprised a broad Sasanian project to translate (into Middle Persian) and elucidate the original Avesta. The Pahlavi-language *Vidēvdād* is a portion of that broader project: Secunda 2014: 93, note 33. As such, it, like the *Šāyest nē šāyest*, predates the fall of the Sasanian Empire (ibid., 96). See below, note 255.

117. White 2003: 60–63.

118. Guenzi 2013: 272, quoting *Bṛhatparāśarahorāśāstra* 9.13. Cf. ibid., p. 348, note 8. On the date of this work see Pingree 1981: 86–88.

119. Guenzi 2013: 310. Guenzi is using Hindi-language terminology here. We have already seen the term *lagnā* in Sax's ethnography; the same verb is employed for involuntary possession by a spirit being in Rajasthan: personal communication from Komal Kothari, Jodhpur, March 23, 1999. A Sanskrit equivalent is the verb *sajj*, found in the *Kāśyapa Saṃhitā*, which I translated above as "latch onto." See above, notes 49 and 78.

120. Knipe 1995: 219, 223–25. He is said to be the son of the sun god and a goddess named Chāyā: Marchetto and Hoefer 2016: 53. See also above, note 33.

121. Guenzi 2013: 328, quoting Shrivastava 2001: 7. Shrivastava's title may be translated as "Save Yourself from Saturn's Rage."

122. Frontisi-Ducroix 1995: 26.

123. White 2003: 60.

124. The dates of both of these authors and their works have been thrown into question by Bill M. Mak. In the light of his findings (Mak 2013: 17–18), both texts are to be dated from sometime between 22 CE and the seventh century CE. The malevolence of Saturn (Kēwān) is also featured in Pahlavi sources dating from the sixth century, where he is cast as the "heavenly body of death" and "lord of darkness" who afflicts creatures with death, evil, and poverty. As with India, Persian astronomy was influenced by Greek traditions, which themselves drew upon ancient Mesopotamian sources: Raffaelli 2010: 78, 80, 83.

125. Heliodorus, *Aethiopica* 2.24.6, in Athenian Society 1897: 115–16. Cf. Yatromanolakis 1988: 198.

126. Heliodorus, *Aethiopica* 2.25.3, in Yatromanolakis 1988: 199.

127. Heliodorus, *Aethiopica* 2.25.2, in Athenian Society 1897: 117–18. On the important distinction between *prosōpeion* as actor's mask and *prosōpon* as the face, see Frontisi-Ducroix 1995: 14–17.

128. When its object takes the accusative, the Greek *prosballō* denotes the act of casting or striking, on the part of both a celestial body and the (evil) eye (Liddell and Scott 1996: 1504, s.v. "prosballō I.3"; Elliott 2016: 51). As such, it is the semantic cognate of the Sanskrit causative root √*pāt* ("cause to fall, cast") that generates (*dṛṣṭi*)-*pāta*, the "casting of the evil eye."

129. Cataloged in Elworthy 1895; Seligman 1922; Maloney 1976; and Dundes 1992. The phenomenon of the evil eye is not universal, however. Geographical distribution patterns (Maloney 1976: xii–xiii) and historical data (Roberts 1976: 229–34) indicate that only 36 percent of world cultures have possessed a belief in the evil eye, and that most of these are of either Semitic or Indo-European origin. The phenomenon is first attested in the ancient Near East (ca. 2500 BCE).

130. A useful general survey is Gross 1999.

131. Plato, *Timaeus* 45b–d, in Bury 1929: 100–103.

132. Aristotle, *On Sense and Sensible Objects* 437b.11–438b.17, in Hett 1957: 220–27.

133. On Alhazan, see Elias 2012: 192–97.

134. Gautama, *Nyāya Sūtra* 3.1.34. For a general discussion, see White 2009a: 123–26. Cf. Śrīdhārāchārya, *Nyāyakandalī* ("Bean-Sprout of Logic") 166 (in Jetly and Parikh 1991: 436–37), which defines perception as a fourfold contact between the self, the mind, a sense organ and an object.

135. Dharmaraja, *Vedānta Paribhāṣā* ("Explanatory Rules of Vedānta"), in Madhavananda 1942: 15. Dharmaraja was a seventeenth-century commentator.

136. For an extended discussion, see White 2009a: 151–66.

137. Gross 1999: 62–63.

138. Rakoczy 1996: 291–309.

139. Liddell and Scott 1996: 310, s.v. "baskainō"; Ernout and Meillet 1959: 218, s.v. "fascinus." Most helpful is Elliott 2016: 67, note 77, who summarizes the terms of the *bask-* family as they appear in Heliodorus's *Aethiopica*.

140. Dickie 1991: 18, 20–24; Elliott 2016: 65.

141. Alexander of Aphrodisias, *Problemata physica* 2.53, in Ideler 1841: 67–68; Elliott 2016: 113–14. In his 1600 CE *Disquisitiones Magicae* (in Maxwell-Stuart 2000: 256), the Jesuit inquisitor Martín del Rio reproduces Alexander's explanation quite precisely, adding, intriguingly, that "the skin of the night-wandering hyena, when worn upon the forehead or preserved in secret, repels frightening magic glances."

142. NT 19.34. See above, note 74.

143. Secunda 2014: 90.

144. Aristotle, *On Dreams* 460a.1–12, quoted in Secunda 2014: 94.

145. Secunda 2014: 94.

146. Plutarch, "Quaestiones Conviviales" (QC) (*Moralia*, Table Talk) 5.7.680c–683b: ed. and tr. Clement and Hoffleit 1969: 416–33.

147. Casanova 2012: 151–57.

148. Elliott 2016: 63.

149. Plutarch, QC 5.7.680f–681a: ed. and tr. Clement and Hoffleit 1969: 420–21.

150. Plutarch, QC 5.7.681e–681f: ed. and tr. Clement and Hoffleit 1969: 424–25. See above, text to note 135, on an Indic formulation concerning the proximity of the mind or soul (*antaḥkaraṇa*, the cognate of the Greek *psyche*) to the eye. A cognate tradition linking envy to the evil eye is attested in Sasanian Iran, which likely drew on prior Semitic traditions: Callieri 2001: 31.

151. Plutarch, QC 5.7.682f–683a: ed. Clement and Hoffleit 1969: 432–33. The translation of this passage is my own, with the helpful assistance of my graduate students Ranjani Atur and Tejas Aralere.

152. Liddell and Scott 1996: 483, s.v. "eidōlon"; Clement and Hoffleit 1969: 433; Elliott 2016: 56; Dickie 1991: 25.

153. Simon 2004: 336.

154. SS 6.60.19, quoted in Smith 2006: 431–32 and 463, note 75; RA 18.186. See above, note 69.

155. Baldes (1975: 103–5) follows Theophrastus in arguing for the absurdity, "confusion and chaos" of Democritus's doctrine of visual impressions.

156. Webster 2014: 142.

157. As Gordon (1999: 221) notes, Plutarch's discussion of the evil eye may have been more influenced by "the Empedoclean-Leucippan theory of emanations" than by Democritus's intromission theory. In his account of intromission, Epicurus employs the plural *eidōla* to denote the subtle sheaths of atoms emitted from the surface of objects, which cause us to see them when they penetrate our eyes: Simon 2004: 336. Cf. Elliott 2016: 57.

158. Plutarch, QC 5.7.683b: ed. and tr. Clement and Hoffleit 1969: 432–33.

159. Webster 2014: 142.

160. Homer, *Iliad* 5.451; *Odyssey* 4.796, cited in Salem 1996: 216.

161. Salem 1996: 216.

162. Plutarch, "On the Obsolescence of Oracles" (*Moralia* 17.419a), in Babbitt 1936: 400–401. Democritus's statement is reported in similar terms by another ancient author, the circa 160–210

CE Sextus Empiricus (Gordon 1999: 221): "Democritus says some *eidōla* approach men, some of them beneficent, some maleficent; that is why he desired to 'encounter propitious images.'"

163. As Salem (1996: 216) notes, this reading of Democritus was held as canonical for at least a millennium, as attested in the writings of the early fourteenth-century Byzantine writer John Katrares, who indicates that Democritus equated the *eidōla* with *daimonas* "and declared that the air was full of them." The "astrological intellectuals" of fifteenth- and sixteenth-century Europe's understanding of the *eidōla* was virtually identical to that of the ancients: Quinlan-McGrath 2012: 50–80.

164. On the demon of envy, see Chariton, *Callirhoe* 3.2.17 and 6.3.11, in Goold 1995: 146, 290. Cf. Elliott 2016: 138–39. Elliott further links the Greek evil eye demon as tormentor of infants to the ancient Near Eastern Gulla and Lamashtu.

165. Basil of Caesarea, *Homilia* 11 ("De Invidia"), in Migne 1857–64: vol. 31, col. 380, lines 37–42, referenced in Cairns 2011: 46, note 38.

166. NT 19.46–47. See above, notes 97–98.

167. Baumbach 2015: 38–44; Weststeijn 2010: 150–56.

168. ṚV 7.104.2; AV 4.9.6, 19.35.3.

169. Forrest 2011: 83–85. In the Avesta, the evil eye is represented by the demon *ayaši* (< *aya* "evil" and *aši* "eye" [of demons]): Sakurzada and Omidsalar 1998: 44.

170. The measures taken by Calasiris at the end of *Aethiopica* to conjure the evil eye are comparable to both modern Greek practice (Yatromanolakis 1988: 202) and the prescriptions of NT 19.52–54: all combine bathing, unguents, incense, medicinal herbs, and spells. However, the same combinations of "snake oil" are employed in dozens of other forms of magical healing, from traditions across the world.

171. Scott 1994: 38–66.

172. Favret-Saada 1985: 220, note 12.

173. Sax 2009: 89.

174. Guenzi 2013: 335–36.

175. Takubo 1972: 3, 57. See above, notes 1 and 25.

176. The *Kriyākālaguṇottara*, a work combining tantric medicine with demonology, refers to the use of the same reflective surfaces as means to determining a patient's vitality. If the tantric healer does not see his patient's "own reflection" (*ātma-chāyā*) on their surfaces, he is advised to abandon his treatment: *Kriyākālaguṇottara* 7.2 in Slouber 2017: 229.

177. P. Lond. Demot. 10070 and P. Lugd. Bat. J 383: Betz 1992: xxiii, lv–lvii.

178. On the language and history of these manuscripts, and the Egyptian provenance of much of the content of both the Demotic and Greek magical papyri, see Johnson 1992: lv–lviii. Johnson is the translator of all of the Demotic papyri edited in Betz 1992.

179. Graf 1997: 6.

180. Pollard 2013: 18.

181. All are contained in "Demotic Magical Papyri" xiv, translated (by Johnson) in Betz 1992: 195–99, 219–20, 222, 223–24, 224–25, 225–26, 232, 235, 237, 239, 240.

182. "Demotic Magical Papyri" xiv, lines 412–425, in Betz 1992: 219–20. I am grateful to Jacco Dielemann for providing me with the Demotic term for "god" in this passage.

183. Some accounts of the practice stipulate that the child be a "youth who has not yet gone with a woman": "Demotic Magical Papyri" xiv, line 769, in Betz 1992: 235. In her seminal article on this practice, Johnston (1999: 101) states that "the practitioner blindfolds the child and then calls a god or spirit into him." None of the Demotic accounts of mirror divination allude to

induced possession of this sort. A Greek magical papyrus containing a greatly abbreviated description of lamp divination is the sole reference I have found in this canon to a magician calling upon a "spirit . . . [to] enter into the boy's soul": PMG vii, lines 560–63, in Betz 1992: 134. None of the other examples adduced by Johnston (1999: 101, note 9) involve mirror divination.

184. Delatte 1932: 14.

185. *Policraticus* 1.12.22–24 (408c) in Webb 1965: 52; and Boudet 2006: 104. About fifty years after John's account, Gervase of Tilbury refers to the practice as "experiments of the sword, the mirror, the finger-nail, or the circle," for which "only a virgin's eyes are effective": *Otia Imperialia* 1.17 in Banks and Binns 2002: 96–97.

186. *Policraticus* 2.28.12–32 (474ab) in Webb 1965: 164; and Boudet 2006: 101.

187. Trachtenberg 2004: 219–22; Schäfer 1990: 89. The Talmudic period dates from 70 to 640 CE; the bulk of the documents recovered from the Cairo Geniza date from the tenth to thirteenth centuries.

188. Delatte 1927; Delatte 1932; Strickmann 1996: 216, 220–21, 227; Strickmann 2002: 206–7, 212–17, 237, 278–79; Smith 2006: 421–32. A case study of Western catoptromancy, based on a fifteenth-century German "necromancer's manual," is found in Kieckhefer 1998: 96–125.

189. On Kirdēr's powerful place in the Sasanian imperial hierarchy, see Daryaee 2009: 75–77.

190. Schwartz 2007: 365–66. Schwartz abundantly cites an earlier study by Grenet (2002). Later studies incorporating Schwartz's reinterpretation are Grenet 2011 and Agostini 2014.

191. Schwartz 2007: 372. Schwartz (ibid., 373–75) adduces a small number of divinatory precedents in the Zoroastrian Gathas, but these wholly lack the level of detail found in Kirdēr's vision. A number of Greek and Latin sources, including Varro (116–27 BCE) and Strabo (d. 23 CE)—both of whose lives and works predate the earliest Greek and Egyptian magical papyri by over a century—identify lecanomancy as a Persian invention: Johnston 2001: 104, note 19. There is no prior documentation from Persia to support their claims, and in any case, simple mirror divination—which is attested in Babylonian documents going back to the second millennium BCE (Johnston 2001: 98; 101, note 11)—is not the subject of the present discussion; rather, it is a specific configuration of actors and practices that I am highlighting here.

192. His analysis hinges on his phonological interpretation of the expression *'dwyn mhly* as *āyēn mahr*: Schwartz 2007: 369–72. Cf. Agostini 2014: 62–63.

193. According to Shaul Shaked, the same divinatory complex is found in Jewish, Muslim, and Ethiopic texts: Schwartz 2007: 386, note 25. Schwartz also references an 1830s account of a Maghrebi magician employing a boy medium whose visions occurred reflected in a pool of ink: Schwartz 2007: 368. See Mokhtarian 2015 for a detailed, nuanced account of Jewish rabbis and magicians in the Sasanian Empire.

194. Boudet 2006: 105.

195. Buddhaghosa *ad* DN 1.26 in Rhys Davids and Carpenter 1890: 97: "asking questions after bringing a god down into a mirror; asking questions after causing a god to descend into the body of a maiden."

196. *Niśītha Cūrṇi*, quoted in Smith 2006: 423. As Smith indicates (ibid.), an early twentieth-century Prakrit-Hindi dictionary containing the entry *pasiṇa* (Sheth 1928: 580) cites two pre-Common Era Jain works as its source; however, like Smith, I was unable to locate the term in those sources, and so I follow Smith in concluding that the entry was referring to later medieval commentaries.

197. Smith 2006: 424. The (male) deity is named Po-ssu-na in Chinese sources; the practice is termed *pra pha-pa*, "bringing down the *pra*" in Tibetan: Strickmann 2002: 214–15. According

to Smith (2006: 426), this is a translation of the Sanskrit *pratisenā* ("prognostic image"). The original source of this terminology has not been found.

198. Davis 2001: 97–98.

199. *Niḥśvāsaguhya* 3.24–27, in Vasudeva 2014: 380–81.

200. TSBh 9.375–79, in Vasudeva 2014: 381–85.

201. *Jayadrathayāmalatantra* 2.5.27–30, cited in Goodall and Rastelli 2013: 543, s.v. "prasenā, prasīnā, prasannā, pratisenā."

202. CST 43.13, in Gray 2007: 345; Gray 2012: 209.

203. Strickmann 2002: 206–7, 211–12; Giebel 2016: 281–88. Vajrabodhi's work is Taisho 1202.21.23–24; Amoghavajra's is Taisho 1277.329b–331a.

204. RA 2.92, 98–103, in Ray and Kaviratna 1910: 27–28. My translation of the first chapter of the RA appeared in White 1995.

205. Strickmann 2002: 206. Vajrabodhi is said to have converted to Buddhism the "Persian merchants" of thirty-five ships departing from Ceylon to Sumatra in the year 717. With the exception of the ship on which Vajrabodhi himself was traveling, the entire fleet was shipwrecked: Grenet 1996: 71.

206. Strickmann 2002: 206–7. Davis (2001: 124) cites two other eighth- to ninth-century Chinese works of esoteric Buddhism (Taisho 895 and Taisho 1202) treating of *aweishe*, in which children were made to gaze into a mirror "empowered by the divinity" and answer questions based on what they saw. Similar data is found in the eighth- to tenth-century Taoist *Yijian zhi* (Davis 2001: 94, 97–98). Later Tibetan-language works in which this terminology is found, or in which mirror divination with child clairvoyants is described, include the Tibetan translation of the *Subahuparipṛcchā*, and the *Kālacakra Tantra* and its commentaries: Orofino 1994: 612–28. Cf. Hemacandra, *Yogaśāstra* 5.173–76, quoted in Smith 2006: 431.

207. Smith (2006: 442) states, without documentation, that *prasenā* disappeared from the subcontinent "by the sixteenth century." On early modern Tibetan practice, see Orofino 1994: 616–17; and Strickmann 2002: 215–17. Smith (2006: 450) notes the modern-day mirror divination practice of an elderly Tibetan woman in the south Indian refugee colony of Bylakuppe.

208. Here, I take issue with the overarching analysis of Smith, whose richly documented history of *svasthāveśa* I have drawn upon widely in this section. All of the chronological inconsistencies that Smith himself acknowledges (Smith 2006: 432, 433, 434, 455) are resolved if one separates mirror divination from oracular possession.

209. Strickmann 1996: 174. See above, note 195.

210. Sanderson (2004: 290, note 149) defines *yantra* as "a Mantra-inscribed diagram written in various colours and with various inks on cloth, birchbark, the hides of various animals and the like, wrapped up and then employed in various ways (by being worn as an amulet, by being burned in a cremation ground, and so on) for purposes such as warding off ills, harming an enemy, of forcing a person to submit to the user's will."

211. Kṣemarāja *ad* NT 18.1a–4a, in Shastri 1939: 73. One of Kṣemarāja's sources may have been Bhaṭṭotpala's tenth-century commentary on *Bṛhatsaṃhitā* 68.37 (in Tripathi 1968: 794), which defines a Kṛtyā as a woman who is, through sorcery spells, made to rise up out of a fire for the slaughter of one's enemies.

212. NT 18.3d–4d. I have emended *duṣṭāni* to *duṣṭān*.

213. *Ṛgvidhāna* 4.6.4, quoted in Bahulkar 2004: 20. According to an epic source (MBh 5.17.5–7), Aṅgiras was the original author of the Atharvanic spells.

214. Sādhana 220, cited in Sen 1965: 72.

215. Hidas 2012: 7–8, 21–35.

216. Mevissen 1991: 358–69; Mevissen 1999: 99–129; Hidas 2012: 26–31.

217. Gonda 1937: 315–19. On the *paritta*, the "all around protector," see below, chapter 5, note 19. On the *pratisara*, see above, chapter 2, note 60.

218. AV 8.5.1–6.

219. AV 10.1.1–3, in Bahulkar 2004: 15–16.

220. A "Hot Vetālī" (Uṣṇavetālī) appears in a list of Female Seizers in certain noncritical readings of the *Harivaṃśa* (appendix 1, no. 24, line 108, in Vaidya 1971: 195). On the distinction between a "hot" and a "cold" Vetāla, see Dezső 2010: 399.

221. *Bṛhatsaṃhitā* 68.37 (in Tripathi 1968: 794). Cf. Dezső 2010: 399. Further discussion of *vaitālīya* practice is found in *Bṛhatsaṃhitā* 103.59 (in Tripathi 1968: 1104).

222. Buddhaghosa *ad* DN 1.13 in Rhys Davids and Carpenter 1886: 84.

223. By the late sixth to early seventh centuries, elaborate instructions for controlling a Vetāḍa/Vetāla were extant in the Buddhist *Mañjuśrīmūlakalpa* (chapter 55, quoted in Goodall et al. 2015: 80–81).

224. NT 19.132.

225. NT 18.87–90. Śrī is identified as the consort of the supreme god/mantra Mṛtyujit/Mṛtyuñjaya in NT 18.62–69.

226. Compare NT 19.5d–6a (chalaṃ [tathā] prakurvanti sadā) and NT 18.89bc (kuhakānī ca yāni ca kariṣyanti). In his commentary on *Bṛhatsaṃhitā* 2.15, Utpala equates *kuhaka-* with *indrajāla*, "magic, illusionism": Smith 2006: 424.

227. See above, note 98.

228. NT 19.48.

229. NT 18.4cd, 90ab.

230. Kṣemarāja *ad* NT 18.89–90, in Shastri 1939: 111.

231. Kṣemarāja *ad* NT 16.34, in Shastri 1939: 17. On *sādhaka* initiations, see Brunner 1985: 416–30, who quotes NT 5.4–6 (ibid., pp. 429–30 and note 65).

232. Kṣemarāja *ad* NT 19.132, in Shastri 1939: 176. See above, note 220. Dezső (2010: 393–98) translates and comments on a number of sixth- to eighth-century Hindu tantric works that describe rituals for animating and controlling Vetālas, which are unambiguously cast as zombies, i.e., corpses reanimated for the purpose of attaining wealth, supernatural powers, sexual gratification, and the destruction of enemies. He also provides an extensive overview of Vetālas in early medieval Indic literary works: Dezső 2010: 398–412.

233. *Haracaritacintāmaṇi* 2.125a, in Sivadatt and Parab 1983: 23.

234. *Rājataraṃgiṇī* 4.94, 5.239–40, in Pandey 1985: 82, 143; Stein 1979: vol. 1, pp. 128, 218.

235. Sanderson 2004: 290–92.

236. *Nagaropamasūtra* 2.11.25, quoted in Dietz 1997: 85.

237. Dutt 1984: vol. 1, p. 100, line 9.

238. Dutt 1984: vol. 1, p. 13, lines 10–11.

239. *Mahāpratisarā-Mahāvidyārājñī* 13.8, 36.7, 44.3, in Hidas 2012: 111, 153, 171.

240. Schopen 1977: 141.

241. Waldschmidt 1965–2008: no. 4, p. 272, quoted in Dietz 1997: 88.

242. This work was translated into Chinese four times between the late fifth and late eighth century, with its final Chinese translation, undertaken by a Kashmiri monk named Prajñā, completed in 798 CE: Osto 2009: 166–67.

243. *Gaṇḍavyūhasūtra* 214.6–7 (chap. 30, v. 14), quoted in Dietz 1997: 89. A literary text, the tenth-century *Bṛhatkathākośa* (102.9, quoted in Dezső 2010: 407) also identifies the term *vetāla*

with a spell. However, a Tibetan Buddhist work titled the [*'Phags pa*] *Ro langs bdun pa zhes bya 'gyurs* (= *[*Ārya*] *Saptavetālakanāmadhāraṇī*) gives instructions for the use of a *dhāraṇī* by means of which Vetālas, here identified with (Mahā)bhūtas, "become stiff," i.e., are paralyzed: Walter 2004: 15.

244. The earliest Chinese translation of this work dates from the early fifth century; the Tibetan translation is from the eighth century.

245. Walter 2004: 13–46.

246. For a compendium of *ro laṅs* tales involving "risen corpses," see Berglie 1982: 37–44. Another tradition, found in the TSBh and *Mṛgendratantra*, rather identifies Vetālas as Śaiva practitioners who have been reborn in demonic bodies as karmic punishment for illicit sexual activities: Vasudeva 2012: 292–93.

247. Nobel 1958: 230–33, note 3.

248. Schopen 1977: 141.

249. Dietz 1997: 85–86.

250. Dietz 1997: 92.

251. Burrow (1935: 781) notes that "no example is given of the akṣara *-rd-* in the account of the alphabet (*Khar. Inscr.*, p. 315). It would naturally be quite uncommon, and possibly is intended here and has been confused in the transliteration with *-rn-*."

252. Boyer et al. 1997: 19–21; Burrow 1940: 13–14.

253. Forrest 2011: 66–67.

254. *Yasna* 3.9, 12, 16, cited in Schwartz 1970: 389.

255. On the basis of philology, mythology, and geographical and other references contained in them, both the Old Avesta and the Vedas are datable to circa 1500–1000 BCE. The Avesta as we know it was not compiled until the Sasanian period, and its earliest (lacunary) manuscripts date from the thirteenth and fourteenth centuries: Skjærvø 1995: 161. See above, note 116.

256. Witzel 2006: 172.

257. Christensen 1941: 14–15, 55–59.

258. Grether 2010: 102, 134.

259. Forrest 2011: 66–67; Pocock 1973: 64. See above, chapter 2, note 17.

260. In the fifth century CE, the Sasanian Empire extended westward into eastern Armenia; and after the fall of the Kushans in the third century, eastward to Kashgar at the western entrance to the Tarim Basin, directly north of Kashmir: Daryaee 2009: 140; Schwartzberg 1992: 176.

261. Russell 1987: 443; Turner 1966: 201.

262. This term is derived from the verb "kerėti" (inf.): to cast a spell, bewitch, charm, conjure, enchant, fascinate, hex, and as such also has a very close relation to the vedic root √*kṛ* and the term *kṛtyā*: Email message from Audrius Beinorius, dated May 14, 2013. In Lithuanian, *kaūkas* means "fairy demon, ghost, dwarflike ghost": Pokorny 2007: 1562, s.v. "kəu-2."

263. Schwartz 1970: 390.

264. A series of similes from this source include *vetālayantrapratimā* (2.133) and *māyāvetālayantra* (2.152): Walter 2004: 39, note 13.

265. Burnouf 1876: 443; Weinberger-Thomas 1999: 20.

266. NT 18.90.

267. Schwartz 1970: 391.

268. For these terms, see Puhvel 1987: 127.

269. Pollock 2006.

270. Smith 1978b: 187.

271. Burkert 1992: 42. Cf. Kalleres 2015: 31, 37, describing the itinerant religious specialists who traversed Hellenistic Antioch. One of the earliest Chinese mentions of Daquin ("Rome") concerns a group of "Roman" magicians brought to Luoyang in 120 CE, the gift of a Burmese king: Inglebert 2009: 132.

272. Strickmann 1996: 174.

273. Subrahmanyam 2005: 12.

Chapter Four

1. Gad 1971: 172.

2. Documented in Jørgensen and Johannsen 1981: 357–97, esp. 367–68 and fig. 11.

3. Documented in Jørgensen and Johannsen 1983: 809–46, esp. pp. 825–26 and fig. 17. Nothing is known of the individual artists responsible for Denmark's *kalkmalerier*, although art historians have managed to identify the influence of various workshops (*værksteder*) on particular styles in particular periods. Although these two churches are situated fewer than five miles apart and their gothic-style frescos date from the same century, their *kalkmalerier* reflect the stylistic marks of two different workshops: Haastrup and Egevang 1985: xvi. Denmark's churches and frescos are richly detailed on the Denmark's National Museum's website: http://natmus.dk/salg-og-ydelser/museumsfaglige-ydelser/kirker-og-kirkegaarde/kalkmalerier-i-danske-kirker/

4. Baudoin de Gaiffier 1967: 176, note 5, mentions an altarpiece from Coire in Switzerland, which shows the third and final scene of Lawrence's birth legend.

5. This detail is no longer visible, due to a fire in the church and a subsequent restoration of its frescoes in 1972. It appears, however, on a photograph taken in 1909 by E. Rothe of Denmark's National Museum. It is this photograph that appears on fig. 17 of Jørgensen and Johannsen 1983, cited above: email message from Karin Trampedach, Denmark Nationalmuseet, June 16, 2016.

6. *Gesta Romanorum*, chap. 201, app. 5, in Oesterley 1872: 612–14. The Codex Pommersfeld 2793, which is the earliest manuscript of the *Gesta* to contain this episode, is dated to 1394: Baudoin de Gaiffier 1967: 175, note 3.

7. Oesterley 1872: 612–13.

8. Baudouin de Gaiffier 1967: 172. A third saint and martyr, Bartholomew, is also the subject of a set of medieval changeling accounts: ibid., 176–81.

9. Schmitt 1979: 116.

10. The manuscript, preserved in the Biblioteca Marciana, Venice (Latin MSS VI.51, 14th–15th c., fols. 327–328v), is translated and transcribed in Baudouin de Gaiffier 1967: 174 and 181–84.

11. In one version of the late twelfth-century chanson de geste titled *Le chevalier au Cygne*, a holy hermit discovers seven infants abandoned in a forest. When he calls upon the Christ for succor, a doe appears to suckle them: Guyénot 2011: 273.

12. Harf-Lancner 1984: 221–41. For additional examples, see Guyénot 2011: 100 (a white boar), 148 (a white doe), 167, and 173; and Sullivan 2018: 235–38 (a white stag).

13. Drescher et al. 1916: 357–58; Drescher et al. 1919: 9.

14. For other early modern sources, see Doulet 2002: 287.

15. Schmitt 1988: 439.

16. *City of God* 15.23, in Dyson 1998: 681. A more elaborate scenario, involving the hoarding of human semen, obtained from a *succuba* by a demon to be "poured out" during his intercourse with a human woman, is proposed by the Spanish Jesuit Martín del Rio, whose 1600 CE

Disquisitiones Magicae was the most erudite work on demonology, witchcraft, and magic of the early modern period: Maxwell-Stuart 2000: 90.

17. On the ancient Roman distinction between *silva*, *nemus*, and *lucus*, see Scheid 1993: 19.

18. Martianus Capella, *De Nuptiis Philologiae et Mercurii* 2.167, tr. in Stahl and Johnson 1977: 54–55. A classic, albeit idiosyncratic discussion of the oracular powers and longevity of the (nonetheless mortal) *daimōns* is Plutarch's "On the Disappearance of Oracles" in *Moralia*. For the history of interpretations of this theme, see Bourgeaud 1983: 254–83.

19. Guyénot 2011: 140–43; Hennard Dutheil de la Rochère and Dasen 2011: 16. Cf. *Oxford English Dictionary*, s.v. "fairy."

20. Schmitt 1979: 109–10.

21. McCulloch 1910: 358. For Scandinavia, where terms like "evil spirits" (*onda andarna*), "the underworldly ones" (*de underjordiske*), and "mountain folk" (*bjergefolk*) are used for the "fairies," see Burjam 1917: 24 and Møller 1940: 239.

22. Harf-Lancner 2003: 45; Gaignebet 1986: vol. 1, p. 164. Ulrich von Zatzikhoven's late twelfth-century *Lanzelet* opens with a water fairy carrying off Lancelot after his mother had briefly left the child unattended next to a spring. He passes fifteen years in her "golden palace" before being returned to the world of men: Guyénot 2011: 205–6.

23. "Wife of Bath's Tale," vv. 857–61, 864–68, 872–74, 878–81, in Mann 2005: 241–42. Limitours are mendicant friars.

24. As in the case of the legend of Saint Stephen, Church doctrine maintained that the changeling was a demon or the Devil himself, who had changed his form to appear in the guise of a sickly infant: Schmitt 1979: 112.

25. Grimm 1999: vol. 2, pp. 468–69. This is stated explicitly in a tale recounted in Doulet 2002: 30.

26. See below, note 115.

27. Schmitt 1979.

28. An analogous practice, dating from the Middle Ages but still observed in modern-day Greece, involves passing a child (or the child's garments) three times through an opening above the icon screen in the church of Saint Pakhys ("Saint Chubby") on the island of Naxos. By virtue of the practice, feeble and sickly children are restored to robust health: Stewart 1991: 32–33.

29. Stephen of Bourbon, *Tractatus de diversis materiis prædicabilibus* (par. 370), in Lecoy de la Marche 1877: 326–27. English translation by Martin Thom in Schmitt 1983: 5–6. A modern-day account of the return of an abducted child by its fairy captor is in Pradère 1872: 58–59.

30. Schmitt 1979: 14, 17.

31. Schmitt 1979: 15, 17.

32. This is motif 178A in the index: Uther 2004: 122.

33. Viṣṇuśarman, *Pañcatantra* 5.17–21.

34. Saintyves (1930: 412–27) and Schmitt (1979: 63–74) provide rich compendia of the literature. Schmitt (1979: 74–96) offers a formal analysis, which he concludes by noting themes unique to the Guinefort legend (ibid., 97–99).

35. Schmitt 1979: 66.

36. Schmitt 1979: 105–6.

37. "Saint Guinefort, Pour la vie ou pour la mort": Schmitt 1979: 152, 154, 160, 163, 164.

38. Doulet 2002: 196–97; Stewart 1991: 156.

39. For other examples of exposure, as well as the logic behind plunging infants into water, see Doulet 2002: 287, 298–99.

40. Schmitt 1979: 117, 118.

41. Doulet 2002: 92.

42. Doulet 2002: 197, 278; Ottonelli 1994: 136. Ottonelli's study is based on ethnographic research conducted in the Italian Alps in the 1980s.

43. Schmitt 1988: 441.

44. Schmitt 1979: 15, 32, 112.

45. Schmitt 1979: 105; Sébillot 1906: 413–14.

46. Marliave 2018: 13.

47. Gaidoz 1892: 1–54, esp. 10 (for sheep), 12–19, 21, 36. Cf. Saint-Mars 1817: 429.

48. Vayssière 1879: 216–17. According to Schmitt (1979: 192), the last documented case of a woman visiting Guinefort's sylvan shrine for the purpose of healing a sick child dates back to 1940. All traces of the shrine and the sainted greyhound's cult had disappeared by 1962. However, in the wake of the publication of Schmitt's monograph those practices have been renewed at the site: personal communication from Jean-Claude Schmitt, October 7, 2016.

49. Schmitt 1979: 108, citing Saintyves 1918: 299–300.

50. For France, Saintyves 1918: 296–300, Harlé 1917: 441–42, and Harlé 1919: 369–70; for Wales, Morris 1893: 55–59 and Rhys 1901: 354–60; for Ireland, O'Sullivan 1853: 91–92. Hartland (1893: 451–70) offers a general survey, extending across Europe and into Africa and Asia. See also Gaidoz 1883: 5–16.

51. On the ancient Celtic origins of this pairing, of a tree and a well, see Ross 1967: 36.

52. For Wales, see Rhys 1901: 354–62, and Jones 1954: 10, 18–19, 94–95; for Scotland, see Le Borgne 2002: 29–40; for Ireland, see Carroll 1999: 33–35.

53. For the modern-day Landes region, see Lavaud 1986; Marliave 2018; and Laurier 2016. I am grateful to Sébastien Laurier and Patrick Lavaud for the assistance they provided when I was conducting fieldwork in this region in March 2018.

54. For the kind assistance I received while conducting fieldwork in the French regions of Nord-Pas-de-Calais and Picardy in September 2017, I am grateful to Irmine Blanc, Lug Lebel, Jean-Pierre Louvet, and Isabelle Duvivier. On the Belgian data, see Marchant 2013: 87–91.

55. In French Picardy and Flanders, these are referred to as "arbres à loques." They are called "moniès" in Occitan: Blondel 2011: 119. In the British Isles, the term "clootie tree" is common. "Clootie" is "cloth," and "loques" are "rags."

56. In 1618, Christ's Well at Mentieth, Scotland, was described as "all tapestried about with old rags": Jones 1954: 95. In 1798, stone cairns surrounding the Holy Pool of Strathfillian in Perthshire, Scotland, were reported as "covered with old halters, gloves, shoes, bonnets, night-caps, rags of all sorts, kilts, petticoats, garters, and smocks": Hartland 1893: 462. A similar report, concerning the Fontaine de Moniès near the village of Dourgnes in the region of Castres in southwestern France, is given in Saint-Mars 1817: 430–31.

57. Hartland 1893: 462–66.

58. There nonetheless exist some "all-purpose" healing springs, such as that of Notre Dame des Douleurs ("Our Lady of Afflictions"), situated in the commune of Garosse in the central Landes.

59. Flint 1991: 267; Lescarret 1980: 178; Lefebvre 1888: 97; Blondel 2011: 148. This reprises a theme from the ancient mythology of Poseidon: see below, chapter 6, note 47. An analogous motif is found in early modern Rajasthan in India, where, according to tradition, a spring erupted at the place where a sixteenth-century saint named Agradās thrust his fire tongs into the ground: Burchett 2019: 202.

60. Lavaud 1986: 39. As such, Saint Eutrope is, together with the Virgin Mary (Notre Dame) and Saint Christopher, the saint/virgin most commonly called upon to heal childhood ailments: Marliave 2018: 13.

61. "Remetteuse" is the term employed by Lavaud (1986: 56–65). In the 1980s, he was able to interview one remetteuse as well as the grand-daughter of another. Several "recommandaïres," now deceased, are discussed in Marliave 2018: 17–19, 78, 138, 145, 190, 198 (with photo), and 218. I saw the term "recommandeuse" employed on a panel at the trailhead of the path leading to the fountains of Saint Antoine de la Traverse, Saint Luce, and Saint Cô, near the village of Escources. This is the term employed in Blondel 2011: 72. Cf. Caulier 1990: 89–93.

62. Madame Marié (d. 1988), the recommandaïre of Potenx-les-Forges, quoted in Marliave 2018: 16.

63. Marliave 2018: 17; Lescarret 1980: 180; Lavaud 1986: 59; Boudreau 1976: 19. Like the lotus beds of the MBh (see below, chapter 5, note 110) and the avestan x^{v}*arənah* (see below, chapter 6, section 6B), springs can, when "offended," flee and move to another location overnight: Blondel 2011: 105.

64. A possible exception is the seventh- to eighth-century Saxon poem *The Dream of the Rood*, which describes the hanging of a wooden cross with garments and other objects, "as were some of the simulacra and trees in the non-Christian shrines" of the period: Flint 1991: 259.

65. *Vittae* were linen headbands or fillets worn by priests and sacrificial victims, but also by Roman matrons and unmarried women: MacMullen 1997: 65, 197. Cf. *Oxford Latin Dictionary*, vol. 2, p. 2294, s.v. "vitta." The oldest oracle of the ancient world, the Zeus of Dodona was a simple tree sanctuary, presided over by three female mediums called "doves": Burkert 1985: 114.

66. Brunaux 1993: 57–65; Ross 1967: 14, 34–38.

67. Brunaux 2016: 131–33.

68. Brunaux 2016: 134; Fercoq du Leslay 2017: 100–101. I am grateful to Lug Lebel and Ludovic Moignet for introducing me to this remarkable archeological site in the fall of 2017.

69. Graus 1965: 184–90; Flint 1991: 204–12; Hooke 2013: 231.

70. Theodosian Code 16.12.2 in Pharr 2001: 474: "But if any person . . . should bind a tree with fillets . . . such person, as one guilty of the violation of religion, shall be punished by the forfeiture of that house or landholding in which it is proved that he served a pagan superstition." Cf. the 1026 CE decree of Burchard of Worms (book 10, chap. 10, in Migne 1841–66: vol. 140, cols. 834C–834D), which dictated that trees consecrated to *dæmons*, which the common people cultivated and venerated, were to be cut down, chopped up, uprooted and burned. Several similar edicts and prohibitions are reviewed in Hooke 2013: 231.

71. On the implementation of this strategy in medieval France and northern England respectively, see Schmitt 1988: 442–50; and Flint 1991: 257–59.

72. Bollandus and Henschenius 1658: 853 (chap. 6, p. 24); Krusch and Levison 1910: 447.

73. The Valenciennes image (plate 15) may have been an accurate representation of Gaulish shrines, which Jean-Louis Brunaux (2016: 149) also likens to those found in India.

74. The two dwarflike figures are generally identified as *gaṇas* of Śiva: email message from Sonya Rhie Mace, Cleveland Museum of Art, October 25, 2017.

75. Abbott 1903: 243.

76. A photograph of the shrine of the martyred saint Imam Husayn, locally known as Pīr Bābā in the Pali District of western Rajasthan, shows the dargah's prayer screen thickly hung with bundles of five multicolored hemp threads symbolizing the five Pīrs: Mayaram 1999: 112, 115.

77. Papas 2016: 342–44. *Tugh* is the Turkish word for "pole."

78. Papas 2016: 343–50 and figs. XV–XXIV. In Japan, sacred trees are decorated with fringes formed of straw rope and pendants of straw and paper: Abbott 1903: 243.

79. *Yakṣas* are also identified, rather mysteriously, as *itarajanāḥ*, "other folk": DeCaroli 2004: 1.

80. *Aupapātika Sūtra* 2–10, in Leumann 1966: 22–25. For a general discussion of these forest shrines, see Falk 1973: 3–4.

81. MBh 5.192.20–21, 5.193.31c–32c.

82. The third- to second-century BCE *Mānava Gṛhya Sūtra* (2.14.28) stipulates that offerings are to be made to yakṣas and various malign spirit beings on raised mounds or slabs at the crossroads of villages, towns, and marketplaces. Stories such as the "Sutano Jātaka" narrativize the transfer of yakkhas/devatās from sylvan to urban settings: DeCaroli 2004: 48.

83. See below, chapter 5, section 6, for the tale of Hiḍimba and Hiḍimbā. Forty-three of the Buddhist Jātakas cast the bodhisattva as a tree (*rukkha*) devatā, who invariably dwells in a tree. These include birth stories 18, 38, 74, 105, 109, 113, 121, 139, 187, 205, 209, 217, 246, 247, 253, 255, 272, 278, 283, 294, 295, 298, 307, 311, 361, 400, 465, 475, 520, and 536. However, as Viennot (1954: 104) notes, citing *Samyutta Nikaya* 4.302–4, *rukkha-devatās* always have feminine names.

84. This accords with scripture: the *Mānava Gṛhya Sūtra* (2.14.28) prescribes cooked and uncooked rice, raw and cooked meat, raw and cooked fish, flour cakes, fragrant substances, alcoholic beverages, garlands, and "red, yellow, white, black, blue, green and multicolored pieces of cloth."

85. Granoff 2004: 50, note 60.

86. *Bhāgavata Purāṇa* 10.22.1–28. On Kṛṣṇa's "identity" with the forest yakṣas of the region, see Vaudeville 1999: 26, 68–71. Another site in the same region was Khaṇḍacelaka, a name suggesting votive offerings made of strips of cloth: Entwistle 1990: 19. On the Parkham Yakṣa, see below, chapter 5, notes 85–88.

87. At Amaravati, a stele depicting "several people worshiping at two trees whose bases have been enclosed by rail fences" is inscribed with the words *bahuputra caitya*, "the multiple children shrine": DeCaroli 2004: 28.

88. *Aṭṭhakathā* (commentary on the *Dhammapada*) 1.1.6–13, in Tatia 1973: 4.

89. Long considered, on the basis of textual sources, to be an image of Śākyavardhana, the Buddha's tutelary yakṣa, this image has been re-identified by Sonya Rhie Mace as an unnamed devatā of the forest: Quintanilla 2017: 130–35. In *Aṭṭhakathā* 2.1.6, we read of the devatā (later called a *devarājā*) of a banyan tree who, after providing food and water to a group of ascetics, bursts out of the trunk of that tree to reveal himself: Tatia 1973: 173.

90. In spite of Buddhism's historical importance there, one does not find trees so decorated in China: email message from Victor Mair, June 16, 2017.

91. Coomaraswamy (1931: 9) reviews a number of Jātakas (nos. 50, 347, 398) with this theme. Cf. DeCaroli 2004: 49–50. See also *Matsya Purāṇa* 180.10a, which characterizes yakṣas as flesh-eaters (*kravyādāḥ*), as does Caitanya's sixteenth-century biographer, Vṛndāvana-dāsa: Dimock 1989: 112.

92. "Dummedha Jātaka" (no. 50), in Fausböll 1877: 259.

93. Holt 1996: 76–79.

94. Coomaraswamy (1928: 31–32) notes that an alternate reading of their name is *vṛkṣakās* ("female dryads"), and that they are depicted in early sculpture as standing beneath a tree (usually a mango or *aśoka*), or half visible among the leaves of a tree, with a face, hand, or part of a body emerging from the branches.

95. MBh 3.220.16. See Viennot 1954: 97 and pl. 2b; Coomaraswamy 1956: 267, fig. 152.

96. MBh 3.219.30, 33–34, 36–37. See above, chapter 2, notes 42–43.

97. However, see below, note 107.

98. Couture and Schmid 2001: 173–92.

99. White 2003: 35–66. A male yakṣa is also identified as a devourer of infants in the Buddhist *Therāgātha* (9.518, in Rhys Davids 1913: 245).

100. MBh 3.219.14–17. For discussion, see White 2003: 44–45.

101. MBh 3.219.19–20.

102. Ahuja 2019: 35–37 and figs. 1 and 7abc. The Yusufzai Hāritī is held by the British Museum (1886,0611.1). Cf. White 2003: 63–64.

103. Chandra 2003: 293–302; Cohen 1998: 381–92.

104. MBh 2.17.1, insertion *185, in Sukthankar et al. 1927–66: vol. 2, p. 94. The demonic Youths referred to here are comprised of two males and seven females. These form Skanda's entourage in MBh 3.219.24–30.

105. Gold 1989: 61.

106. Gold 1989: 66.

107. Schömbucher 1999: 177–78.

108. Here and throughout, I use "motif" as defined by Sircar (2018: 51) on the subject of folklore motifs: "a motif is . . . an actor, an object or an incident. . . . A motif summary lets us see what is the same and what is different across the local tales within a tale type and its links with other tale types and the tales within them."

109. Sébillot 1882: 118–19.

110. In some versions of the changeling narrative, the changeling was not a fairy child, but rather a fairy that transformed itself into a child: Doulet 2002: 126.

111. Guyénot 2011: 28–29, 74. Ginzburg (1992: 111–12, 115) makes a similar observation concerning the "good ladies" of the "Celtic" lore of western and southern Europe: "It is through a provisional death that one gains access to the world of these beneficent female figures who lavished prosperity, wealth and knowledge. Their world is the world of the dead."

112. Bitel 2018: 81–82; Guyénot 2011: 17–79, 233–36; Harf-Lancner 2003: 329; Doulet 2002: 320. As Guyénot acknowledges, he draws heavily upon Czarnowski 1919 and Harf-Lancner 1984. Fairies who abducted their chivalric lovers in life, later allowing them to return to the world of the living, have been classified as *mélusiniennes*, while those who take dead heroes as their husbands are *morganiennes*. On this typology, see especially Harf-Lancner 1984: 26–57, and Harf-Lancner 2003: 25–101. As Harf-Lancner (2003: 47–48) notes, it was Dumézil who in his 1929 monograph, *Le problème des Centaurs*, coined the term "mélusinienne," applying it to the vedic nymph Urvaśi.

113. Doulet 2002: 347–78. Cf. Ottonelli 1994: 132–36.

114. An exhaustive compendium is found in Legros 1952, 1964, and 1967.

115. Legros 1952: 174; Doulet 2002: 125–26. Nine-hundred-year-old fairy babies imply fairy mothers of still greater age, a further indication that fairyland was the world of the ancestral dead of pagan western Europe.

116. The impersonality of the ancient Greek *daimōn*s, in association with the concept of fate and their role as attendants at birth, contributed to their later demonization: Smith 1978b: 433.

117. Harf-Lancner 1984: 34–42. The "Wedding of Sir Gawain and Dame Ragnelle" (WGDR) may be a quirky variation on this theme: see below, chapter 5, section 5.

118. Doulet 2002: 20.

119. Harf-Lancner 2003: 29, quoting Tertullian, *De anima* 39.2.

120. Harf-Lancner 2003: 29–30.

121. Harf-Lancner 1984: 27–34. The Norns of Nordic tradition have identical roles, perhaps because this tradition was adapted from Greco-Roman material by the Icelandic poets: Boyer 2014: 155–61.

122. *Mānava Gṛhya Sūtra* 2.14.28.

123. Hackett 1861–62: 257–58 and footnote b. Outside of Rajasthan, a recent monograph by Taneja (2018: 213–14) attests to the hanging of clothing on a yellow oleander tree in Delhi's Bhuli Bhatiyari Park. Reputed to cure skin diseases, the tree is visited by "people from Gurgaon and Faridabad" who bring their own water to bathe beneath and water the tree, leaving their clothes and presumably their skin conditions behind.

124. Coomaraswamy 1928: 34: however, different sources identify the tree as a mango, *plakṣa*, or *aśoka*. The Buddha's *parinirvāṇa* also took place beneath a *sāl* tree: Coomaraswamy 1928: 23.

125. For a discussion of this shrine, see above, chapter 2, note 7.

126. Email message from Bhoju Ram Gujar, July 8, 2016.

127. Schmitt 1979: 117.

128. Doulet 2002: 126–29; Harf-Lancner 2003: 329.

129. Unless, of course, the woman is pregnant with twins, triplets, etc.

130. Gold 1989: 79. An excellent nuanced summary of the nature and hierarchy of these spirit beings is Fuller 1992: 224–36. See above, note 101.

131. Nabokov 2000: 120, 125–50; Dietrich 1998: 45.

132. Personal communication from Komal Kothari, Jodhpur, Rajasthan, April 2, 1999.

133. With reference to practices by Bengali Muslims, Chaudhuri (1935: 570) gives the following definition: "*Manat* means an offering which is promised to a god in order to be cured of some malady, generally chronic or fatal. . . . It is a promise or lure of sacrifice held out to the god to induce him to grant some specific relief." *Man*[*n*]*at* is an alloform of *manaut*[*i*], the term used by Hindu populations in Rajasthan: Weinberger-Thomas 1999: 155.

134. Singh 2012: 390–91.

135. Gold 1989: 154.

136. DeCaroli 2004: 92. See above, note 104.

137. They are also on display in the *ḍhok* tree overhanging the Eight Bherūṃ-jīs (Aṣṭabhairava), inside Ghatiyali's Līlāḍ Temple compound: see above, chapter 2, note 2.

138. Gold 1989: 149.

139. Abbott (1903: 248) uses the term "cot." According to the *Oxford English Dictionary* (s.v. "cot," 4), a cot is "a small bed for a child; properly one suspended so as to swing between uprights."

140. Gold 1989: 150–52.

141. Turner 1966: 299, s.v. "jhōla."

142. Quintanilla 2017: 129–30, 136. See above, note 49.

143. Ibid., pp. 117–19, 131, 133, and figs. 16, 17, 19, and 21.

144. Gold 1989: 152. Ramdevra is a pilgrimage site sacred to the regional deity Rāmdevjī, situated some three hundred miles west northwest of Ghatiyali, in Rajasthan's Jaisalmer District.

145. Boulnois 1989: 131–32.

146. Feldhaus 1995: 82. Another group of malevolent goddesses, whose names are also vernacularizations of the Sanskrit *sapta apsarasa*, are the Āccharī of Uttarakhand: see above, chapter 3, notes 51 and 58.

147. For example, Mines (2005: 190) reports that a "fierce" tree deity responsible for the death of a young man from the dominant Thevar group has been conflated with his victim, both being known as Panaiyatiyan Cāmi, "The God at the Foot of the Palmyra Tree."

148. Feldhaus 1995: 129. Cf. Nabokov 2000: 74–75; Sax 2009: 85. See above, chapter 3, notes 49–50.

149. Feldhaus 1999: 127–28.

150. Feldhaus 1999: 43–45.

151. Feldhaus 1995: 121.

152. Feldhaus 1995: 48–49.

153. Feldhaus 1999: 156.

154. Feldhaus 1995: 122–23. Feldhaus lists sixteen riverine goddess shrines at which these rites have been observed in the past or present. In cases where the rite is not performed in thanksgiving for the fulfillment of a *navas*, even "children" approaching marriageable age may be floated on these cradle baskets.

155. Feldhaus 1995: 123–24. While the abandonment of infants on floating baskets is a relatively common fixture of world mythology (Moses, Karṇa, etc.), such myths lack the specificity of the rite described here.

156. Feldhaus 1995: 124–25.

157. Feldhaus 1995: 135.

158. Feldhaus 1995: 136.

159. Among these, Littleton's and Malcor's 1994 hypothesis that the tales of King Arthur originated among the Alans and Sarmatians of Scythia.

160. Personal communication from Richard Hecht, University of California, Santa Barbara, February 25, 2019; email message from Shalva Weil, Hebrew University, February 28, 2019. Hecht and Weil observed "rag trees" at three sites in Israel: the Sheikh Badr cemetery, situated near the Knesset in Jerusalem; the Meron for Rabbi Shimon Bar Yohai; and the Aharon Abuhatzera or the Baba Sali in Netivot.

161. Puhvel 1987: 21–31. The same applies to language: As Boyer (2012: 25) explains, the (Old) Icelandic language has remained so stable that "a twelve year-old from modern-day Reykjavik can read a thirteenth-century text with ease."

162. Chenu 1969: 1–48; Banks and Binns 2002: lv. Gervase completed his *Otia Imperialia* in the early years of the thirteenth century (ibid., xxxix). See below, chapter 7, note 18.

Chapter Five

1. Paetz 1970; Yarnall 1994; Escola and Rabau 2015; Bettini and Franco 2010: 351–62.

2. The Circe episode is edited and translated in Murray 1966: 354–71.

3. *Odyssey* 10.136.

4. *Odyssey* 10.149–50.

5. *Odyssey* 10.210–23.

6. *Odyssey* 10.275–78.

7. *Odyssey* 10.281–98.

8. *Odyssey* 10.321–23, 333–35, 346–47.

9. Bullis 2012: 3.

10. Onesicritus, a companion of both Alexander the Great and Megasthenes, introduced the name "Taprobanē" for an island situated in the portion of the Indian Ocean known at the time as the Erythrean Sea. According to Kessler (2016: 437), the toponym was likely derived from the word "Tambapani" found on the rock edicts of the emperor Aśoka. However, Marcotte (2016: 40)

notes that Jean Filliozat's suggestion that the name was derived from the Tamil *Tāmpirapaṉṉi* has been widely accepted.

11. MV 6.1–61. Edition Geiger 1908: 62–68; translation in Geiger and Bode 1912: 55–58; edition with commentary: Malalasekera 1977: 254–61.

12. MV 6.47.

13. There is no consensus concerning the date in the calendar year in which the Buddha's *parinirvāṇa* took place. In some parts of the Buddhist world it is celebrated in March, in others in May; however these dates can neither be supported nor refuted on the basis of Buddhist scripture.

14. She is named Kuveṇī in the *Vaṃsatthappakāsinī* commentary: Malasekera 1977: 255.

15. bhakkho 'si mama tiṭṭhā. Here, I diverge from Geiger, who translates *bhakkha* as "prey."

16. Here, I have emended Geiger's translation of *rajjam*. In this verse, he translates the term as "kingship," whereas in MV 7.22, he translates it as "kingdom."

17. MV 7.2–32, 35, 37–42. *Tamba-paṇi* means "copper [-colored] hand" in Pali.

18. MV 6.39–40.

19. According to the work's anonymous commentator, this is "a noose formed by bending the ends of the cord into a circle": Malasekera 1977: 257. This is the same shape as the *pratisara* or *pratyaṅgira* amulet, discussed above, chapter 2, note 53.

20. See, however, Heubeck and Hoekstra's (1989: 64, *ad Odyssey* 10.388–99) comment that Homer makes Circe out to be both a "poisoner" and a "sorceress who uses her wand and incantations to metamorphose her victims."

21. Turnour 1837: xliv.

22. *Odyssey* 10.251–61 and 321–47, in Turnour 1837: xliv–xlv.

23. Discussed in Walter 2000: 154–59.

24. Weber 1873: 24–27; Crooke 1908: 179; Coomaraswamy 1956: 2; and Winternitz 1972: 215.

25. Dio Chrysostom (*Logoi* 53.6), Plutarch (*De fortuna alexandri*, frag. 328d), Aelian (*Varia historia* 12.48), and Philostratus (*Vita Apollonii* 3.12, 16), quoted in Derrett 1992: 49.

26. Weber 1873: 26–27, with reference to MV 7.15.

27. Inglebert 2009; Fitzpatrick 2011: 38–46; Marcotte 2016: 34. Roman Indian Ocean trade peaked in the third century; Roman relations with India ended in 640 CE: Mukherjee 2017: 347; Lambourne 2016: 372.

28. Marcotte 2017b: 6. "Erythrean Sea" is an ancient denomination, the name by which the Indian Ocean had been known to the Greeks for over six centuries prior to the *Periplus*'s composition.

29. Silva 1990: 1–14.

30. Bopearachchi 1999: 20–21; Holt 2004: 795; Tomber 2008: 119, 127, 145–46; Inglebert 2009; Bullis 2012: 114–15; Lambourne 2016: 372.

31. Wink 1990: 45–108; Inglebert 2009; Fitzpatrick 2011: 43–45; Alpers 2014: 26–36; Acri 2016a: 1–25.

32. Yarnall 1994: 29, 50–51; Page 1973: 59–60; Bettini and Franco 2010: 130–37; Scobie 1983: 187–90.

33. Scobie 1983: 229–57. Saint Augustine relates a version of this story in *City of God* (58.18), cited in Baroja 1993: 24.

34. Page 1973: 62–65, 69.

35. Page 1973: 64.

36. For example, that Odysseus's concern for his crew should delay his eating together with Circe, but not his sleeping with her: Page 1973: 56.

37. Page 1973: 64.

38. Scobie 1983: 234–37; Dyck 1981: 196–98.

39. See below, note 163.

40. Allentoft 2015: 167–83; Callaway 2015: 140–41; Haak 2015: 207–20.

41. MV 7.61, in Geiger and Bode 1912: 60 and note 2.

42. MV 7.26.

43. This ambiguity is of a piece with that of the ancient Greek *daimōns*, as discussed in chapter 1. According to Kapferer (1991: 163–64), anthropologists of modern Sri Lanka disagree on the semantic range of the term *devatā*, with some viewing them as minor, intermediate deities; others identifying them with the gods (*deviyo*) themselves; and Kapferer himself characterizing them as "supernatural beings who are transitional between the classes of deity and demon." Scott (1994: 22–23) translates devatā as "tree deity" and notes that it can also be used as an honorific when addressing a *yakku*, the modern-day Sinhala term for a malevolent *yakṣa/yakkha*.

44. MV 7.22, 31.

45. deinē theos audēessa: *Odyssey* 10.136; 11.8.

46. theas kalliplokamoio: *Odyssey* 10.220.

47. ē theos ēe gunē: *Odyssey* 10.255.

48. *Odyssey* 10.394, 549.

49. *Odyssey* 10.400, 487, 503.

50. *Odyssey* 10.543.

51. *Odyssey* 10.350–51. Here, their role was to prepare the botanicals Circe would use to make her potions, since they "card no fleece and spin no woolen threads" (*Odyssey* 10.264–65). Ovid, in his adaptation of this episode, identifies Circe's handmaidens as nereids and nymphs.

52. DeCaroli 2004: 16. The same author (ibid., 12) refers to the occasional use in the South Asian record of the term *naivāsika* as a word for "local genius" or "dwelling deity."

53. Scheid 2008: 628–30.

54. Jātaka 6, in Fausböll 1877: 127–33; Chalmers 1895: 23–26.

55. Lévi 1934: 12–15.

56. Fausböll 1877: 128.

57. Fausböll 1877: 129.

58. Fausböll 1877: 129.

59. "True law" is an apt translation of the Sanskrit *sad-dharma*, the first compound in the title of the SPS, the "Manual of the Lotus of the True Law," referenced in the opening sentence of chapter 3.

60. Law 1933: 273–74; Frasch 2017: 66–76.

61. Jātaka 196, in Fausböll 1879: 127–30. A Mahāyāna version, titled the *Siṃhalasārthabāhu Avadāna*, has been analyzed and translated from the Nepali in Lewis 1995. In this version, the cannibalistic female demons are called *rākṣasīs*, a group whose resemblance to the Greek Sirens has been noted by Penzer (1926: 282): see also below, notes 66 and 161. A Tibetan version places the action at the southern tip of India: Templeman 1983: 41–42. Sirīsavatthu is identified as the yakkhas' city in MV 7.32b. See above, note 17.

62. MBh 3.295.1–3.298.6. See below, notes 71–79.

63. MBh 13.94.2–13.95.86.

64. MBh 13.94.39–41a. On Kṛtyās, see above, chapter 3, section 5.

65. MBh 13.94.41b–43a.

66. MBh 13.95.14–19. The Sanskrit verb "to guard" (√*rakṣ*) is the same root that generates *rākṣasa*, the cognate of the Pali *rakkasa*, the "[water] guardian" of the DJ account. These are a class of malevolent spirit deities, whose nature and behaviors overlap those of the *yakṣas*.

67. MBh 13.95.23.

68. MBh 13.95.20–44.

69. MBh 13.95.47–48.

70. MBh 13.95.78–80. For further discussion of this episode, see White 1991: 94.

71. MBh 3.295.15b; 3.296.6.

72. MBh 3.296.8, 45–46.

73. MBh 3.296.12, 18, 37: mā tāta sāhasaṃ kārṣīr mama pūrvaparigrahaḥ/ praśnānuktvā . . . tataḥ piba harasva ca//. The yakṣa's ultimatum to Arjuna is a paraphrase (3.296.26); it is later repeated verbatim (3.297.12) and in a slightly altered form (3.297.23) to Yudhiṣṭhira.

74. In the epic period, the term *preta* likely meant the "departed" (*pra-ita*) spirit of a recently deceased person. The language of this episode is ambiguous, such that the question of whether the four brothers have actually died, or simply been immobilized into a comatose state, remains open.

75. MBh 3.297.11.

76. MBh 3.297.18a. He is nonetheless described as standing on one foot, as would a crane: MBh 3.298.2a.

77. MBh 3.297.20a–21a. The *Tilakamañjarī*, an early eleventh-century CE Jain prose poem, describes a yakṣa standing by a lake as resembling "a man of terrifying strength, his body straight and beautifully dark like the trunk of a *priyaṅgu* tree that has been thoroughly scraped, his belly slightly fat, watching . . . with unblinking sharp-pupiled eyes looking somewhat angry, and repeatedly tossing a huge Banyan tree held in his right hand . . .": Dezső 2010: 87–88.

78. As Agrawala (1970: 195) notes, some of the questions posed to Yudhiṣṭhira are directly borrowed from the *brahmodya* chapter of *Yajur Veda* 23.

79. MBh 3.297.22–3.298.13. The question of intertextuality is an interesting one here. Another Jātaka, titled the "Kurudhamma," appears to make explicit reference to the Pāṇḍavas, who are of the Kuru lineage in the epic. In it, a figure named Dhanaṃjaya shoots arrows over a pool controlled by a yakkha named Cittarāja in order to bring rain in a time of drought (Jātaka 276, in Fausböll 1877: 372). In the epic account related here, Arjuna, one of whose epithets is Dhanaṃjaya, releases a rain of magically consecrated arrows and other projectiles over "Crane's" pool before entering into the water and succumbing (MBh 3.296.28–31). None of the other Pāṇḍavas do so. A truncated version of this account comprises the twenty-first story of the circa 1595 CE *Kathāratnākara* ("Jewel-Mine of Stories") of the Jain author Hemavijaya (Municandrasuri 1997: 29–31). Here, the riddles posed to Yudhiṣṭhira are of a more cryptic order, conforming to the *malhor* trope specific to the Kuru homeland (*kuru-janpad*): Sharan 1953: 70–74.

80. MV 6.64.

81. Hiltebeitel 1976: 181–91.

82. Hiltebeitel's (1976: 190) explanation for the Pāṇḍavas' yakṣa's "sex change," from a female embodiment of Sovereignty, is unnecessary and unsatisfying.

83. Coomaraswamy 1928: 38.

84. DeCaroli 2004: 20.

85. An 1885 photograph of the Parkham Yakṣa in situ on its mound in the center of the village of Parkham (Sanford 2005: 103) may be viewed online at http://www.bl.uk/onlinegallery/onlineex/apac/photocoll/f/largeimage58912.html (accessed August 10, 2016). Coomaraswamy (1928: 38) refers to this figure as the Yakṣa Kuṇika.

86. Cunningham's statement is based on the textual traditions of "classical" Hinduism and Buddhism, which reduced the yakṣas to this subaltern role, even as the high gods of Mahāyāna and Vajrayāna Buddhism retained many yakṣa attributes. See below, chapter 7, notes 11–12.

87. Cunningham 1885: 40–41.

88. DeCaroli 2004: 62–63; Sanford 2005: 103. Buddhist tradition speaks of the Buddha's conversion of a yakṣa "protector of the lake" at Nandivardhana, one of the sites listed in the MMVS's catalog of yakṣas: Lévi 1915: 79.

89. Sanford 2005: 103. A local *nirukti* has it that Parikṣam's name means "one who can protect himself from demons": email message from A. Whitney Sanford, August 15, 2016.

90. MBh 3.298.10a.

91. Norman 1983: 84–85.

92. *Suttanipāta* 1.9.1–28 (Hemavatasutta), in Andersen and Smith 1965: 27–31.

93. *Suttanipāta* 1.10.1–12 (Āḷavakasutta), in Andersen and Smith 1965: 31–33. A far richer Sinhala version of this tale is recounted in Scott 1994: 6–10.

94. Falk 1973: 3–4.

95. Lévi 1915: 19–138. Lévi (118) assigns the compilation of this work to the first centuries CE, but its extant recensions date from between the fourth and sixth centuries CE: Overbye 2016: 257, 261–62. See above, chapter 3, note 2.

96. For example, in the "Sutano Jātaka," Vessavana grants a yakkha the right to eat anything that comes under the shade of its banyan tree: DeCaroli 2004: 47–48.

97. On the iconography of tree yakṣas/devatās, see above, chapter 4, notes 80–85. On the iconography of aquatic yakṣas/devatās, see Coomaraswamy 1931: 80–81 and plates 34, 35, and 36.

98. Hiltebeitel 1976: 143–91, 203–6.

99. Hiltebeitel (1976: 182) adduces Viṣṇu's protector role, which Mahānāma modeled, as we have seen, after Homer's Hermes.

100. Hiltebeitel 1976: 190.

101. Dumézil 1986b: 316–51.

102. Dumézil 1986b: 324, 336. As Hiltebeitel (1976: 180) notes, the earliest hymn to the Indic sovereignty goddess Śrī relates that she took the form of a deer; she also appears together with a deer on a first-century BCE Kuninda coin.

103. Dumézil 1986b: 324–27, 335–39. Cf. Jaski 2000: 69–71.

104. These are the names of the Indian Mādhavī (Dumézil 1986b: 327–30) and the Irish Medb (Dumézil 1986b: 339–40; Jaski 2000: 68–69; Kelly 1992: 77–84; Rees and Rees 1961: 75). Dumézil also notes (1986b: 339) the near onomastic match between the Irish *flaith*(*ius*) (Sovereignty) and *laith* (beer). As Jaski (2000: 67) notes, several sources from 700 CE onward highlight the theme of a woman dispensing the sovereignty of Ireland "by handing over a drink to her partner or successive partners (in which case she is often a supernatural being) and/or by sleeping with her partner or successive partners (in which case she is often a queen)." See also below, note 134.

105. Hiltebeitel 1976: 185–88. Cf. *Odyssey* 10.216 and MV 7.9.

106. Hiltebeitel 1976: 177, 184, 190.

107. Early on, this configuration of a goddess flanked by asperging elephants came to be identified with Lakṣmī, the Hindu goddess of abundance. It remains central to her modern-day iconography, wherein she is referred to as Gaja-Lakṣmī.

108. MBh 12.210.14, 20. Already in the ancient Brāhmaṇas (*Jaiminīya* 2.25; *Aitareya* 8.12.3), the cushion of the royal throne was identified with the royal quality of *śrī*: Gonda 1969: 188.

109. See, for example MBh 12.217.57–59 and 12.220.44–46. These and other epic references to her fickleness are discussed in Hiltebeitel 1976: 163–65.

110. MBh 5.88.91b.

111. Others concern queens or queen mothers, including Gaṅgā, the divine mother of Bhīṣma, the rightful Kaurava heir (MBh 1.92.26); Jarā, the demoness indirectly responsible for the birth of the Magadhan dynast Jarāsandha (MBh 2.16.51; see also above, chapter 4, note 104); Śakuntalā (MBh 1.65.3), progenetrix of the Bhārata line; and Damayantī (MBh 3.65.9–16), the queen of King Nala.

112. MBh 1.61.95.

113. MBh 1.155.42–43.

114. Hiltebeitel 1976: 166–75. The myth is also discussed in Dumézil 1986a: 111–12.

115. *yoṣā rudatī*: according to Sāyaṇa, *yoṣā* can also signify "mare," in which case this expression could be read as "a mare braying": see below, chapter 6, notes 138–50, 230–31.

116. MBh 1.189.9–11.

117. MBh 1.189.12–13.

118. MBh 1.189.16.

119. MBh 1.189.18. Indra also "trembles like a ficus leaf in the wind" out of his fear of Śiva: MBh 1.189.22.

120. Hiltebeitel 1976: 171, 184, 190.

121. Elsewhere, the *cailleach* represented both the land (and specific landforms) and the continuity of the Gaelic peoples and races, and was a protectress of herds of wild deer: Rees and Rees 1961: 135; Ross 1967: 336; Eichhorn-Mulligan 2006: 1026.

122. Jaski 2000: 58, 68, 71; Bromwich 1960–61: 445.

123. Eichhorn-Mulligan 2006: 1015, 1017. The tale has been preserved in a twelfth-century poem and a fourteenth-century prose work. On the four extant manuscripts of the work, see Jaski 2000: 163. Edition and translation of the prose version in Stokes 1903: 196–203 and O'Grady (1892: vol. 1, pp. 328–30 [Irish text], and vol. 2, pp. 370–73 [English translation]). The salient portions of the story are contained in paragraphs 9–19.

124. *Echtra mac nEchach* 9–11, in Stokes 1903: 196–97. Cf. Eichhorn-Mulligan 2006: 1023–24.

125. *Echtra mac nEchach* 12–13, in Stokes 1903: 198–99.

126. *Echtra mac nEchach* 14, in Stokes 1903: 198–99. O'Grady's (1892: vol. 2, p. 371) translation reads, "I will give it! . . . I will even hug thee!" Cf. Eichhorn-Mulligan 2006: 1026–27.

127. This is Stokes's spelling of his translation of *misi in flaithius*.

128. *rí Temra is mé in flaithes*.

129. *Echtra mac nEchach* 15, in Stokes 1903: 200–201.

130. *Echtra mac nEchach* 16, in Stokes 1903: 200–201. Cf. Eichhorn-Mulligan 2006: 1017. See Jaski 2000: 164–65 for the relationship between this narrative and ancient Irish rules of royal succession.

131. The "Dindshenchas of Carn Máil" is part 29 of the *Metrical Dindshenchas*, in Gwynn 1924: 136–43. The tale of the four Lugaids comprises verses 37–140 of this poem. The same tale comprises verses 67–70 of the *Cóir Anmann*: ed. and tr. in Stokes and Windisch 1891: 318–23. Bitel (2018: 84) dates this corpus to about 900–1200 CE, but notes that these draw on more ancient medieval sources. Jaski (2000: 168–69) suggests a ninth-century *terminus ad quem* for the *Cóir Anmann*.

132. "Dindshenchas of Carn Máil" 18–22, in Gwynn 1924: 138–41. Cf. Eichhorn-Mulligan 2006: 1028.

133. "Dindshenchas of Carn Máil" 26–28, 31–32, in Gwynn 1924: 141–42, who translates *In flaithius* as "the Kingship." The same quote is translated by Bollard (1986: 47) as "I am the *flaithius* and it is the kingship of Ireland that will be taken."

134. *Cóir Anmann* 70, in Stokes and Windisch 1891: 320–21.

135. Hiltebeitel 1976: 185 (my italics).

136. MV 7.11: katantī tāpasī viya.

137. Maynadier (1901: 79) suggests that this is a "pan-Celtic" motif; it also appears in an Icelandic saga: Child 1965: 293. Cf. Folks and Lindahl 2002: 245–46.

138. Maynadier 1901: passim; Bromwich 1960–61: 444–47, 470–72; Child 1965: 292–93; Bollard 1986: 41–48, 56; Bugge 2004: 198, 207–10.

139. The "Tale of Florent" is found in book one (lines 1407–1875) of Gower's *Confessio Amantis*: edition and translation in Peck 2006. The "Tale of the Wife of Bath" is one of Chaucer's *Canterbury Tales*: edition in Mann 2005: 211–54; "Wedding of Sir Gawain and Dame Ragnelle": edition and translation in Hahn 1995.

140. Ragnelle's name, which is first given in WGDR, verse 319, had medieval associations with "an exotic pagan god or devil": Hahn 1995: 76. Like Chaucer, the anonymous author of this work was a "practitioner of lower-class storytelling styles," with "folktale justice" prevailing at the conclusion of both narratives: Lindahl 2002: 144.

141. Hahn 1995: 71–72.

142. Bugge 2004: 204.

143. Hahn 1995: 73, citing Puttenham 1936: 153.

144. WGDR, vv. 91, 97–98.

145. WGDR, vv. 228–51.

146. WGDR, vv. 255–314.

147. WGDR, vv. 316–17. For references to the sinister symbolism of the owl in the ancient and medieval west, see Bugge 2004: 203. *Bruja* (also spelled *bruxa*), the Spanish word for "witch," also denoted a species of owl in early modern Spain: Baroja 1993: 21. The owl had similar associations in ancient India. See White 2020: 76–78.

148. WGDR, vv. 420–25.

149. WGDR, vv. 471–75.

150. WGDR, vv. 635–44, 654–62.

151. WGDR, vv. 677–89.

152. WGDR, vv. 695–701.

153. WGDR, vv. 799, 820.

154. Aguirre 1993: 275.

155. Aguirre 1993: 278–79.

156. All that Arthur says to him (vv. 471–72) is "thus they [women] did teach me to rule thee, Sir Gromer" (Thus they me dyd ken to rule the, Gromer Syre). The conclusion of the WGDR (vv. 811–16), concerning the final relationship between Arthur and Somer Joure, is equally ambiguous: "She prayed the king for his gentleness 'To be good to Sir Gromer, indeed, insofar as he hath offended you.' 'Yes, Lady, that shall I now for your sake, for I know well he may not make amends [for the fact that] he acted uncourteously toward me.' "

157. Tarabout 1999: 322; White 2003: 63–66.

158. See above, note 17.

159. West 2014: 144–74.

160. West 2014: 148.

161. However, Bopearachchi (1999: 20) points to archeological, inscriptional, and textual evidence for trade links between Ceylon, coastal Gujarat, northwestern India, and Arachosia (southern Afghanistan). See chapter 3, note 11; and above, notes 28–31.

162. West (2014: 164) indirectly references the MV narrative by citing Page's (1973: 56) contention that Homer's narrative had "deviated from a stricter model." As was noted above (notes 34–37), Page championed the MV narrative of Kuvaṇṇā and Vijaya as adhering to that model.

163. West 2014: 170–71. Here, she is echoing Bernard Sergent's hypothesis (2002b: 217), which he had articulated twelve years earlier.

164. The episode immediately follows that of the "Fire in the Lacquer House," which, although the epic account is somewhat garbled, appears to have fallen on the dark fourteenth of the month of Phalguna, a night celebrated in the Purāṇas and down to the present day as Śivarātrī (although the epic makes no mention of this): MBh 1.133.30; 1.135.4; 1.136.1.

165. MBh 1.137.19–1.138.9.

166. MBh 1.138.10–13.

167. MBh 1.139.1a–2a. On this tree (Hindi *sāl*; Pali *sāla*; Sanskrit *śāla*), see above, chapter 4, note 124.

168. MBh 1.139.9: hatvaitānmānuṣānsarvānānayasva mamāntikam/ asmadviṣayasuptebhyo naitebhyo bhayamasti te//.

169. MBh 1.139.11–16.

170. MBh 1.139.17a–18a.

171. As West (2014: 163–65) indicates, this passage closely resembles Odysseus's reaction to Circe's offer to share her bed, which, as I have noted above (end of section 1), is echoed in Vijaya's reaction to Kuvaṇṇā.

172. MBh 1.139.19–32.

173. MBh 1.140.2a.

174. MBh 1.140–1.142.30.

175. MBh 1.143.21a (kṛtvā ca paramaṃ rūpaṃ); 1.143.26b (bibhratī paramaṃ rūpaṃ).

176. MBh 1.143.34.

177. The *daka-rakkha* of the DJ is male; Yātudhānī does not truly betray King Vṛṣādarbhi, and being a humanoid simulacrum, is indifferent to whatever male charms the Seven Sages might have possessed.

178. MV 7.64.

179. It bears noting here that while riddles and riddling are a common motif of folk and fairy tales, the complex scenario developed here is nowhere found among the standard catalog of "international tale types": Uther 2004: vol. 3, p. 249.

180. Although, according to later mythology, Circe does bear a son named Telegonos by Odysseus, this motif is absent from this episode of Homer's *Odyssey*.

181. Dumézil 1986b: 113.

182. Dumézil 1986a: 10. Cf. Dumézil 1986b: 361.

183. Burkert 1985: 114–18.

184. Smith 1978b: 438.

185. This shift, from the horizontal to the vertical plane, is one I discussed in White 1991: 89–91.

Chapter Six

1. Chandra 2003: 293–302; Rhie 1988: 38; Stein 1975: 254–55 and accompanying plates. The Digital Silk Road website (http://dsr.nii.ac.jp/rarebook/03/index.html.en) indicates that Stein

was unable to remove the fragile wall to Britain. According to Sam van Schaik (email message, August 7, 2018), one would assume that it remains in situ; however I have been unable to locate a photograph of the wall in its present state.

2. Chandra 2003: 296–98, 301. Several Khotanese-language fragments of this work have been found, attesting to its popularity there: ibid., 296. The Khotanese version is based on a Central Asian recension that was in circulation around the year 700 CE: Kumamoto 2005: 80.

3. Chandra 2003: 293–94.

4. Stein 1975: 255. Cf. Rhie 1988: 29, who speaks of the "international style" of "Buddhist art . . . from Kashmir to Afghanistan to the heart of China and, by extension, beyond to Korea and Japan." Rhie (1988: 38) draws stylistic comparisons between the Khotan Hāritī and Buddhist images from Pendjikent (Tajikstan) and Fondukistan (Afghanistan).

5. Chandra 2003: 296.

6. Chandra 2003: 297–98. Here, I disagree with Chandra (295), who argues that the child symbolizes Hāritī's five hundred sons, who together with her protect their devotees.

7. Chandra 2003: 298. I would add that the rectilinear borders of Hāritī's pool also symbolize the foursquare order of the Middle Kingdom, a bulwark against foreign barbarian invasion. On this theme, see White 1991: 164.

8. Chandra 2003: 301.

9. Chandra also speculates (2003: 299) that in addition to the Buddha, the bodhisattva, and the monk Ānanda, Vaiśravaṇa, the yakṣa guardian of the north, would have also been accompanied by three other great yakṣas of the cardinal directions.

10. The work is also known as *Le chevalier au lion*. The original Old French is found in Pierreville 2016 and Kibler 1985. My translations and verse numbering are adapted from the edition established by Pierreville 2016, which, based on manuscript fr. 794 of the Bibliothèque Nationale and six other manuscripts, is the finest to date.

11. Houdebert and Lambert 2017: 366; Duggan 2001: 15–17.

12. Ford 2008: 80–81.

13. Brown 1903: 34–46, 84–85.

14. Brown 1903: 86–94, 125. Brown suggests that Chrétien would have known of this source via a Latin or Norman-French version of the "Voyage of Saint Brendan."

15. Duggan 2001: 232–38.

16. It forms the subject matter of vv. 173–2292 of the 6,808-verse work, and reappears in vv. 6507–45. See below, note 23.

17. He seems to say as much at the end of his romance (vv. 6804–8): "Thus Chrétien concludes his romance of the *Knight with the Lion*; he hasn't heard any more about it." See also Brown 1903: 9, 25–26; Duggan 2001: 13.

18. Morgan 1909: 331–41; Bradbury 2000: 348–50.

19. Schmitt 1988: 499. Although Chrétien himself was patronized by French royalty.

20. *Yvain*, vv. 411–13.

21. *Yvain*, vv. 378–79, 421.

22. *Yvain*, vv. 458–75. Cf. Blondel 2011: 43.

23. The scenario is repeated three times. In the first Esclados li Ros defeats Yvain's cousin Calogrenant (vv. 476–551); in the second, Yvain defeats Esclados (vv. 809–958); in the third, Yvain defeats Kay (vv. 2220–92). Now the defender of the fountain, Yvain returns there two additional times, alone, once without unleashing the storm (vv. 3484–3521), and once to unleash it a final time (vv. 6507–45) at the end of the romance. See below, note 36.

24. Duggan 2001: 233–34.

25. Villemarqué 1861: 235; Brown 1903: 126–27; Hamilton 1911: 356–57, 362–75.

26. An early precedent is reported in the sixth-century Gregory of Tours's *Liber in Gloria Confessorum* (in Migne 1841–66: vol. 79, col. 831ab; French tr. Schmitt 1988: 446) with regard to a pagan custom observed annually at a lake in the Lozère region of southeastern France. Peasants who gathered there would throw pieces of cloth, cheese, bread, and so forth into the lake. Three days of animal sacrifice and feasting would follow, but on the fourth day as they were leaving, a violent storm would break out, with thunder, lightning, and a life-threatening rain of stones.

27. *Yvain*, vv. 368–71: "[Mes] se tu voloies aler ci pres jusqu'a une fontainne, n'en revandroies pas sanz painne, *se ne li randoies son droit*." Cf. the Middle High German of verse 554 of Hartmann von Aue's *Iwein*: "und tuostû im sîn reht gar" (Edwards 2007: 26).

28. Discussions of the fountain's *droit* are generally unsatisfying. Baumgartner (1988: 38, note 15) notes that, according to one manuscript reading (by Guiot), Chrétien "accentuates the necessity, in order that he may depart, of carrying out the ritual act." Pierreville 2016 (163, note 28) suggests that trespassers must honor the fountain's due by pouring water onto its stone. Other authors translate *droit* as the "custom" of the fountain.

29. The seventh-century Chinese pilgrim Xuanzang tells of a *nāga* that, inhabiting a lake, caused fierce storms to erupt. Eventually, the emperor Kaṇiṣka had a monastery built on the lake's shore that had a calming effect, "and if storms ever began to arise the resident monks would beat a drum in the monastery in order to remind the *nāga* of his vow to behave": DeCaroli 2004: 61.

30. *Yvain*, v. 1851. She is referred to as *la dame* [de Landuc], rather than by her name, throughout most of the work.

31. Bradbury 2002: 347; Baumgartner 1988: 44. As Baumgartner notes (ibid., 32), three late twelfth- to early thirteenth-century French lays (*Graelent*, *Guignamour*, and *Désiré*) feature an encounter with a fairy at a spring. See Guyénot (2011: 148–52) for summaries; and Burgess and Brook (2016: 39–49, 52–60, 63–73) for full English translations.

32. Earlier, Laudine's father, Duke Laududet, had been the defender of the fountain. After his death, his heiress Laudine required a male defender to replace him: Houdebert and Lambert 2017: 167.

33. Esclados is "a whole head taller" than ordinary men (v. 520). He is not named until long after his death (v. 1972).

34. *Yvain*, vv. 2090–2106, 2166–71.

35. *Yvain*, vv. 489–99 (my italics).

36. *Yvain*, v. 6509.

37. *Yvain*, vv. 6525–45. Chrétien's "single man" is anyone who would unleash the fountain's fury by pouring its water on the stone.

38. *Yvain*, vv. 6 and 2576. The night of Saint John, the first night of summer, is frequently evoked, as, for example, in the Old German version of *Yvain* (v. 897, in Edwards 2007: 44).

39. Morris 1893: 64–65. The same story is recounted in Rhys 1901: 379–80.

40. Bromwich 1950: 221, 225.

41. Bromwich 1950: 217, 219. Bromwich (ibid., 228) translates *traha* as "the sin of presumption," and ascribes it not to Mererid but to Seithenhin.

42. Minard 2002: 128–30, 140. Cf. Morris 1893: 67–68.

43. Bromwich 1950: 218, 220, 222.

44. The earliest source, the pre-900 CE *Liber causis*, makes no mention of horses. Two pre-1100 CE *dindshenchas* sources add significant detail concerning the role of horses in the flooding of the two Irish plains; these are combined in the *Aided Echach maic Maireda*. For a summary of these sources, see Vries 2012: 1–17.

45. The edition and translation of the portion of the text summarized here are in Vries 2012: 200–203. The legend is also summarized in Mac Mathúna (2010: 23–24) and in Rhys (1901: 381–82), who provides several additional examples of wells flooding lands after a negligent woman has neglected to cover it with its "flag": however, horses do not figure in these accounts.

46. Vries 2012: 152–56. Rhys (1901: 381–82) refers to the horse of the legend as "a kind of water horse": see below, notes 226–30. Minard (2002: 125–26) quotes from two modern-day folk narratives, one Irish and one Welsh, in which horses are absent.

47. Pausanias, *Description* 2.31.9, in Jones 1918: 420–21. Cf. Sergent 2004: 466, 471, 475. This is a common trope, also found in the lore of the healing springs of modern-day France: Blondel 2011: 65–71. For a western Indian instantiation of this theme, see above, chapter 4, note 59.

48. Pausanias, *Description* 8.10.3–4, in Jones 1933: 392–93. For the full account, see below, note 192.

49. Wagner 1981: 18; Sergent 2004: 477.

50. *Yvain*, vv. 6525–45. See above, note 37.

51. These appear in later "popular" versions of the original ninth-century poem: Bromwich 1950: 228.

52. Sergent 2004: 475.

53. White 1996: 203.

54. *Rasendracūḍāmaṇi* 15.13–15, in Misra 1984: 289–90; *Rasaprakāśasudhākara* 1.13–16, in Joshi 2011: 10. A Rajasthani-language compilation, the *Dhātūtpatti* of Ṭhakkura Pherū (17–19), which also contains a version of the account, may be found in Sarma and Sahai 1995: 162.

55. *Rasaratnasamuccaya* 1.85–88, in Sharma 1962: 14. Meulenbeld (1999: 670–71) dates this work to the sixteenth century. While this is likely the case for the iatrochemical chapters found in the latter part of this work, I find chapters 1–11 to be substantially earlier.

56. *Ānandakanda* 1.53b–62a, in Radhakrishna Sastri 1952: 6. The chronology of five of these works is discussed in White 1996: 158–59, 167–69.

57. *Śivakalpadruma*: Anup Sanskrit Library, Bikaner, mss. 4349, fol. 2v1–4. Since this and virtually every alchemical manuscript in the Anup Sanskrit Library were collected by the Bikaner Maharaja Anup Singh (1669–1698), this work's terminus ante quo is the late seventeenth-century. *Rasakautuka*: Anup Sanskrit Library, Bikaner, mss. 4203, fol. 4r6–9. The date of this work has been established by Wujastyk 2008: 150, note 24.

58. *Śivatattvaratnākara* of Keḷadi Basava 6.33.45–50, in Rama Shastry 1969: vol. 2, p. 169. For the date of this work, see Krishnamachariar 1937: 272.

59. White 1996: 158.

60. *Jighṛkṣuḥ* may also be read as "he who wishes to catch her." See below, note 68.

61. About nine miles: Monier-Williams 1984: 858, s.v. "yojana."

62. This is a reference to the origin myth of mercury, which is found a few verses earlier (*Rasendracūḍāmaṇi* 15.4–12). Mercury is produced from Śiva's semen, which he ejaculates into the mouth of Agni who flies on the wind to the Ganges River. There, the mercury falls from his mouth. The river goddess Gaṅgā pushes the mercury to her shore, from which, due to its mass, it burrows down into a well. See below, note 72.

63. *Rasendracūḍāmaṇi* 15.14–15. For the Sanskrit of this passage, see White 2017: 680.

64. White 1996: 117, 160–61.

65. Here I am translating the name "Indra," the supreme divine warrior of the Vedas, in the more generic sense of "champion." The semantic field of *rasa* is not limited to "mineral"; however, that is the specific sense of the term here.

66. While "most excellent Mercury" is the literal reading of *sūtavara*, it may be that a double entendre is intended here, with the compound also denoting the maiden's "mercurial suitor." Such would align with the use of desiderative forms of the verb √*grah* in the three other Sanskrit-language accounts translated here. See above, note 60 and below, note 158.

67. *Rasaprakāśasudhākara* 1.13–16. For the Sanskrit of this passage, see White 2017: 680.

68. *Rasaratnasamuccaya* 1.85–88. For the Sanskrit of this passage, see White 2017: 681.

69. White 1996: 168.

70. I have emended Sastri's reading of *rasakovidaḥ* to *rasakovidaiḥ*.

71. *Ānandakanda* 1.53b–62a. For the Sanskrit of this passage, see White 2017: 681–82.

72. For mercury: *Rasendracūḍāmaṇi* 15.4–12, in Misra 1984: 287–88; *Rasaratnasamuccaya* 1.60–66, in Sharma 1962: 9–10; *Ānandakanda* 1.8–15, in Radhakrishna Sastri 1952: 2. For sulfur: RA 7.57–66, in Ray and Kaviratna, 1910: 101–2; *Rasaratnasamuccaya* 3.2–12, in Sharma 1962: 38–39; and *Kākacaṇḍīśvarakalpatantra* 44.2–3, in Pandey 2003: 131–32.

73. For a discussion, see Sarma and Sahai 1995: 155–60. While the background figures in plate 26 are either Mughal or Inner Asian, they are portrayed in European garb in the eighteenth-century miniature painting of the same subject held by the Bodleian Library (Arch. O. b. 7 = MS. Douce Or. a. 2, fol. 12).

74. Although the *Ānandakanda* calls mercury *pāradendra* in the final verse of its flowery account.

75. See above, note 28.

76. See above, section 2 of the present chapter.

77. This is where the *Rasaprakāśasudhākara* locates its well. See above, text to note 65. Dardistan is situated between the headwaters of the Kishen Ganga and the Indus Rivers and borders on northern Pakistan, Afghanistan, Kashmir, and Ladakh.

78. Schwartzberg 1992: 109, 168, and maps on pages 13, 14, 15, 16, 27, 31, 32, 137 (map quadrant 2CD); Wink 1990: 232; and Sircar 1990: 34, 35, 68. These are likely the same people as Ptolemy's Daradrai: White 1996: 205.

79. Schwartzberg 1992: 14, 27, 137 (map quadrant 4AB).

80. White 2013: 222–23; Shastri 1978: 29–47, esp. pp. 44–45. See below, section 9.

81. The identity of the mineral nonetheless remains contested: La Vaissière 2002: 23.

82. The five wells are discussed in the *Ānandakanda* (1.15–23), *Śivakalpadruma* (fol. 2r10), *Rasakautuka* (fol. 3r1–5), and the fifteenth-century *Rasasindhu* of Viṣṇudeva (Anup Sanskrit Library, Bikaner, mss. no. 4276, fol. 1r10–2r2). The same sources identify *pārada* as the white-colored mercury of the *eastern* well (even if geographers placed Pārada country at the western edge of the Indian subcontinent, in Baluchistan). On a remarkable "red mercury" hoax, originally propagated by various spy agencies and embraced and woven together with preexisting folk traditions by Islamic State bomb makers in the early 2010s, see Chivers 2015: 36–39, 58.

83. The Chitral River, which runs through the border region between northeastern Pakistan and Afghanistan, has mercury tailings in its waters: Sharma 1962: 199. Elsewhere, Murthy (1979: 83–86) argues, on the basis of textual data, for the presence of mercury ore in the Siddhipur region of the western Indian state of Gujarat.

84. Sharma 1962: 207; White 1996: 66. Important Asian cinnabar deposits are found at Khaidarkan in southern Kirghizstan, a few hundred miles to the northwest of Dardistan, as well as Wuchuan and Wanshan in the Guizhou Province of southwestern China, far to the east of the Indian subcontinent: Pattelli 2014: 243, fig. 1. See also White 1996: 380–81, notes 93–94. However, it cannot be known whether mercury was being extracted at these specific sites in the thirteenth to fifteenth centuries.

85. Natarajan 2004: 256–57 and note 10.

86. An uncertain unit of measurement whose etymology is contested. Most sources equate it to somewhere between two and three miles: Yule and Burnell 1968: 261–62, s.v. "coss."

87. Highly dramatized versions of the same procedure are found in Jinaratna's 1285 CE *Līlāvatīsāra* (6.163–83 and 14.314–27), in Fynes 2005: 394–97 and Fynes 2006: 442–45.

88. *Yakoppu Cunnam* 151–60, translated in Natarajan 2004: 264–65. In a footnote (37) to this passage, the author indicates that the term that Yakoppu uses for mercury when it "assaults" him is the Sanskrit *sūta*, which is so called, according to her, because mercury is "that which is born or generated . . . [and] mercury is generated from the well according to him."

89. White 2013: 222. See below, section 9.

90. It is a commonplace of medieval Tamil works to include the number of verses in the title. The *Tantakam* is 110 verses in length.

91. Natarajan 2004: 260–61.

92. Natarajan 2004: 265, note 37.

93. RA 2.89; 3.9, 17–20; 11.98–107, 162–63, in Ray and Kaviratna 1910: 25, 36–38, 172–73, 182. See also White 1996: 487, note 220.

94. RA 12.336–37, 380, in Ray and Kaviratna 1910: 262, 272. See also White 1996: 487, note 220.

95. Khan 1927: 371.

96. My dating of this work is based on an email message from Matteo Martelli, July 31, 2014. See also Berthelot 1967: v. See below, note 111.

97. De Mély 1895: 332–34.

98. Email message from Ulrike Unschuld, February 19, 2014.

99. The traditional Chinese *li* measured approximately one-third of a mile or half a kilometer.

100. Edition Zhu Derun 1997: vol. 5, fol. 14b–15a. The original Chinese is also found in White 2017: 686. I am grateful to my colleague Dominic Steavu-Balint for his translation of this passage.

101. This dramatic process may be viewed online at https://www.youtube.com/watch?v=gKxCw889qck&feature=youtu.be (accessed July 19, 2015).

102. Letters from the Cairo Geniza document the maritime trans-shipment of Spanish cinnabar to India: Gotein and Friedman 2008: 754. See also ibid., 228, 229, 301, 407, 511.

103. Fuchs 1958–59: 127–28. Fuchs's transcription and translation are found in ibid., 124–26.

104. Needham et al. 2000: 337. De Mély (1895: 333) identifies it with Syria. For the uncertain location of Fu-lin in three late thirteenth-century Chinese sources, see "From the *Sung-shih*, ch. 490"; "Ma Tuan-lin, *Wen-hsien-t'ung-k'ao*, ch. 330"; and "Chao Ju-kua, *Chu-fan-chih*," in Arkenberg 2000. These sources situate Fu-lin in the region of Cilicia, Armenia, and the Black and Mediterranean Seas, and identify Antioch as its capital. These documents appear to reproduce the data found in more ancient Chinese histories, dating from as early as the fifth-sixth centuries CE.

105. De Mély 1895: 334. A 1939 notice held on the Israel Antiquities Authority website (http://iaa-archives.org.il/zoom/zoom.aspx?folder_id=17616&type_id=&id=89618) documents a small ruin at a site called Bir ez-Zeibaq, situated on the "Ramla-Lydda Road," that is, between the modern towns of Ramla and Lod, approximately fifteen miles southeast of Tel Aviv.

106. The earliest report of Baku's "springs of white naphtha" comes from Al-Mas'ūdī in his 943 CE *Murūj al-dhahab wa ma'ādin al-jawāhir* ("Meadows of Gold and Mines and Gems"): Barbier de Meynard and Courteille 1863: 25–26.

107. Lockhart 1939: 10. I am grateful to Y. Tzvi Langermann for this reference.

108. Le Strange 1919: 199.

109. See above, chapter 1, section 5, and chapter 5, note 40.

110. Yakoppu is likely referring here to the Arabic-language work titled *Muṣḥaf aṣ-ṣuwar* ("The Book of Pictures"). See below, note 112.

111. As Berthelot (1967: xxiii) notes, only a short passage from Zosimos of Panopolis's original Greek-language *Treatise* has survived, in the form of a transcription. If the mercury extraction account found in the Syriac were to have existed in the Greek original, it could be dated back to as early as the fourth to sixth centuries CE, Zosimos's traditional dates.

112. A circa 850–1000 CE Arabic translation of, or compilation based upon, this Syriac version calls this distant land *magrib*, i.e., the Magreb, Mediterranean North Africa: Abt and Fuad 2011: 458. This version, which is found on fol. 161v of Istanbul Arkeoloji Müzesi, mss. 1574, generally hews very closely to the Syriac account.

113. The expression "of water" is not completely clear in the manuscript, since the ink is quite faded: email message from Matteo Martelli, September 17, 2015.

114. The verb √*sleq* ("to go up, ascend") seems to be a technical term; in the *aphel* form (*'aseq*) it also means "to distill, sublimate": email message from Matteo Martelli, September 17, 2015.

115. Martelli's edition of this passage from the Syriac *Treatise* of Zosimos (Cambridge University Library MSS 6.29, fols. 58r8–58v3) has been reproduced in White 2017: 688. The same passage was translated into French by Rubens Duval (in Berthelot 1967: 244–45) on the basis of Berthelot's edition.

116. Berthelot 1967: xxxii.

117. Email message from Matteo Martelli, September 17, 2015. See also Duval 1893: 294.

118. In this case we find the Syriac term *'onko* that refers to "tin." This term, whose common meaning is "tin," does not have any connection with Zeus: email message from Matteo Martelli, September 17, 2015.

119. Dumézil 1963: 50–61; Dumézil 1981: 21–89.

120. Puhvel 1973: 379–86 and Puhvel 1987: 277–83.

121. Findly 1979: 164–84.

122. Wagner 1981: 1–28.

123. Briquel 1981: 293–306.

124. Sterckx 1994: 39–79.

125. Sergent 2000: 197–218; Sergent 2002a: 81–97; and Sergent 2004: 475–81.

126. Kellens 2016: 175–81.

127. Several of the contributions to Capdeville 2004 also treat of this mytheme.

128. See above, note 48.

129. ṚV 2.35 and 10.30, in Nooten and Holland 1994: 133–34, 494; translated in Jamison and Brereton 2014: vol. 1, pp. 452–54, and vol. 3, pp. 1422–24. Cf. Dumézil's discussion (1981: 21–24) of the vedic myth. Apā̃m Napāt is invoked a total of thirty times in the ṚV: Findly 1979: 168.

130. ṚV 2.35.1, 6.

131. ṚV 2.35.4, 11.

132. ṚV 2.35.11; 10.30.6ab.

133. ṚV 2.35.5b.

134. ṚV 2.35.5c: kṛ́tā ivópa hi prasarsré apsú. "Deflowered" is the reading of *kṛ́tā* proposed by Oldenberg 1970: vol. 1, p. 217, and, most recently by Jamison and Brereton 2014: vol. 1, p. 453. It should nonetheless be noted that this interpretation has been seriously disputed: for a summary of other readings of the term *kṛ́tā*, see pp. 46–47 of Jamison and Brereton's online commentary to their translation of the ṚV: http://rigvedacommentary.alc.ucla.edu/wp-content/uploads/2015/04/II-5-8-16.pdf.

135. ṚV 10.30.4a; 2.35.11.

136. Smith 2009: 728, note 1. Ghee is also the sacrificial food offered to this deity in both vedic and avestan liturgies: for a discussion, see Kellens 2016: 180–81. See also below, note 163.

137. ṚV 2.35.3.

138. ūrvaṃ samudramadhye vartamānaṃ baḍavānalaṃ: Sāyaṇa *ad* ṚV 2.35.3, in Kashikar and Sontakke 1936: 148. ṚV 3.1 describes the birth of Agni in the waters, which are here identified as (1) his "sisters"; (2) "seven young women"; and (3) "mares" (ṚV 3.1.4).

139. I am grateful to Stephanie Jamison for this reference. In this passage, the word for "sea" is not *ūrvá*, but rather *samudra*, a term that would come to mean "ocean" in later Indic parlance.

140. Monier-Williams 1984: 221, s.v. "ūrva"; MBh 1.60.45; 1.170.8. Aurva's post-epic mythology has been treated in detail in O'Flaherty (1980: 213–37), whose puranic citations I follow here. The birth of Aurva from Ūrva's asceticism is developed explicitly in the *Harivaṃśa* and *Matsya Purāṇa*: O'Flaherty 1980: 227.

141. MBh 1.169.21–1.171.23.

142. Pingree 1981: 12.

143. O'Flaherty 1980: 214, citing *Brahma Purāṇa* 116.22–25.

144. O'Flaherty 1980: 229, 231, 232, citing *Skanda Purāṇa* 7.1.33.1–50; *Padma Purāṇa* 5.18.159–98; and *Brahma Purāṇa* 110.85–210.

145. See above, note 47. Sergent (2004: 471) suggests an improbable parallel between the mythic origin of Pegasus and the MBh (3.115.10) account of a thousand horses that emerged out of a river at a site called "Equine Watering Place" (Aśvatīrtha). This mythic toponym is nonetheless significant in the light of the fact that the Asian horse trade transited through Kushan lands in this period: see above, chapter 3, note 21, and below, note 231.

146. MBh 3.106.10b: khureṣu krośato gṛhya nadyāṃ cikṣepa durbalān [paurān].

147. MBh 3.105.9–25.

148. MBh 3.106.27a; 3.107.18.

149. MBh 3.108.16b: pūrayāmāsa vegena samudram.

150. MBh 13.56.4–6.

151. The deeds of Apąm Napāt are only treated in ZY 51–52. However, these belong to a broader mythic tableau, embedded in ZY 34–69, edited and translated in Hinze 1994: 191–318 and Humbach and Ichaporia 1998: 38–50, 111–43. Hintze (1994: 43) dates this passage to the sixth century BCE. Cf. Dumézil's discussion (1981: 24–27) of the Iranian myth.

152. Kellens (2016: 177–78) identifies a formal parallel between the description of the Iranian deity in ZY 19.52, and that of the vedic deity in RV 2.35: both receive sacrifices, both are referred to as *asura*/*ahura*; both are related to equine fire; and both have waters as their wives (although the rigvedic deity is also their child and lover), etc.

153. ZY 5.5, in Humbach and Ichaporia 1998: 137. Another *Yašt* (8.46, quoted ibid., p. 137) evokes the sea's "beautiful subterranean channels."

154. Tafazzoli 2000: vol. 10, fasc. 2, p. 201. Humbach and Ichaporia (1998: 189, col. 3) identify Vourukaṣ̌a with the Aral Sea.

155. ZY 19.89–90, in Humbach and Ichaporia 1998: 163–64.

156. ZY 19.51, in Humbach and Ichaporia 1998: 130–31. Humbach and Ichaporia note the change of tense in the clause introducing the direct discourse, but offer no explanation for it.

157. ZY 19.53, in Humbach and Ichaporia 1998: 132.

158. Humbach and Ichaporia 1998: 182, s.v. "√grab."

159. ZY 19.56–62, in Humbach and Ichaporia 1998: 135–40. These are the Haosrauaah, Vaŋhazdå̄, and Aβždānauuan Rivers.

160. This is the Helmand River, which forms the border between Afghanistan and Iran: "Helmand River" 2003: 171–72.

161. ZY 19.66, in Humbach and Ichaporia 1998: 141. Cf. Puhvel 1987: 278–79.

162. Puhvel 1973: 383; Oettinger 2009: 189–96; Kellens 2016: 176–77, 180–81.

163. Findly 1979: 183. Kellens (2016: 179–80) has identified a liturgy identical to that of ṚV 10.30, the hymn upon which Findly bases her conclusions, in two Old Iranian texts, the *Ātaš Niyāyišn* ("Liturgy of Fire" = Yasna 62) and the *Āb Zōhr* ("Offering of the Water" = Yasna 63–70). In both cases, as he notes, "natural" waters are transformed into "ritual" fire and water.

164. See above, note 140.

165. Dumézil 1981: 39–85. The six authors are Livy, Plutarch, Dionysius of Halicarnassus, Cicero, Valerius Maximus, and Zonaras. In addition to Dumézil's extensive discussion, see Sterckx (2004: 305, note 11) for bibliographical references to the six authors' quotes.

166. Dumézil 1981: 50–51 (quoting Livy, *History of Rome* 5.16.9–5.17.3); and ibid., 59 (quoting Dionysius of Halicarnassus, *Roman Antiquities* 12.16: tous katexontas ton topon theous kai daimōnas).

167. Dumézil 1981: 49–50, 53–54.

168. Dumézil 1981: 70–72.

169. Dumézil 1981: 41–42.

170. Dumézil 1981: 40; Sergent 2004: 475, 482.

171. Dumézil 1981: 41. A more recent philological analysis, which also incorporates Norse and Greek data, is Oettinger 2009: 189–94. On the etymology of Salācia's name, see Ernout and Meillet 1959: 590, s.v. "saliō."

172. Unless one were to read "just made" here in the sense of menarcheal, which would fit precisely with the biological state of the maidens in the alchemical accounts. However, Jamison and Brereton (2014: 47) are likely correct in pointing out that in the following line, Apā̃m Napāt sucks at the three goddess's breasts, a situation that would require prior deflowering and childbirth.

173. Dumézil 1981: 63–66.

174. See above, note 38. Like the eruptions of Perilous Fountain, the prodigy of the Alban Lake (as well, perhaps, as other of the narratives reviewed here) may have been linked to meteorological or astronomical phenomena such as the heliacal rising of Sirius.

175. Romane, aquam Albanam cave lacu contineri, cave in mare manare suo flumine sinas. Emissam per agros rigabis dissipatamque rivis exstingues: Livy, *History of Rome* 5.16.9–11, quoted and translated in Puhvel 1973: 384.

176. Puhvel 1973: 385.

177. There are two sources for this work. One is the circa 1150 CE manuscript known as the "Rennes Dindshenchas": edition and translation in Stokes 1894: 315–16. A poetic work known as the "Metrical Dindshenchas" contains additional detail on this episode. It has been translated in Gwynn 1913: 27–32 ("Boand I") and ibid., 37–38 ("Boand II"). Cf. Dumézil's (1963: 54–61 and 1981: 27–38) study of the Irish myth.

178. "Rennes Dindshenchas" 19, in Stokes 1894: 315. Cf. Sterckx 2004: 305. As Dumézil notes (1963: 55), Nechtan was the name of an ancient Irish god, one of the Tuatha Dé Danann, who, like them, has now been transformed into a *genius loci* of the *síds*, the Neolithic burial mounds of Ireland and other portals to the otherworld, as well as the otherworld itself. On these, see Bitel 2018. See below, note 239.

179. "Metrical Dindshenchas" 2.11, in Gwynn 1913: 29.

180. "Metrical Dindshenchas" 3.7, in Gwynn 1913: 37; Mac Mathúna 2010: 21. On the distinction between Elcmaire, in whose house the well was located, and Nechtan, the lord of that well, see Sergent 2004: 478–79.

181. "Rennes Dindshenchas" 19, in Stokes 1894: 315; "Metrical Dindshenchas" 2.14 and 3.11, in Gwynn 1913: 31, 37. Minard (2002: 131) compares Boand's *dimus* to Mererid's *traha* in the "Drowning of Gwyddno's Field" account: see above, note 41.

182. "Rennes Dindshenchas" 19, in Stokes 1894: 315–16; "Metrical Dindshenchas" 2.15–18, in Gwynn 1913: 31.

183. "Metrical Dindshenchas" 2.1–9, in Gwynn 1913: 28–29.

184. Dumézil (1963: 57) also adduces a cognate Nordic tradition: a "boiling cauldron" that is the source of all the rivers of the world.

185. See above, text to notes 115 and 167.

186. Hunt 1908: 280. Cf. Delpech 2010: 133–55, especially 141–44.

187. Cassius Dio 41.45, in Larson 2001: 162.

188. Larson 2001: 163, and fig 4.7. On the Gallo-Roman Apollo, see below, section 6H.

189. Nechtan's three cupbearers; the three waves that break over Boand; and the three outlets of the Vourukaṣ̌a.

190. Wagner 1981: 17–22.

191. Online at https://www.google.com/maps/place/Mantineia (accessed October 7, 2015).

192. Pausanias, *Description* 8.10.2–4, in Jones 1933: 392–93. Pausanias repeats this information in an abridged form at 8.5.5.

193. kata tou theou gnōmēn: Pausanias, *Description* 8.10.4, in Jones 1933: 392–93.

194. For the Irish material, see Vries 2012: 152–57; for the Greek material, see Sergent 2000: 212; Sergent 2004: 480–82.

195. Briquel (1988: 51–64) makes an unconvincing case for a relationship between Poseidon and the fire in water motif.

196. *Life of Apollonius* 1.6, in Jones 2005: 42–43. A milder form of this ordeal, undergone in the River Styx, is described in Achilles Tatius's third-century *Leucippe and Clitophon* 8.12–14 (in Gaselee 1969: 434–41). Cf. the first-century CE Pliny the Elder, who in his *Natural History* (31.18.23, in Rackham 1975: 390–91) evokes the waters of the river Alcas in Bithynia (northwestern Turkey), which "flows by Bryazus—this is the name both of a god and of his temple—the current of which perjured persons are said to be unable to endure, as it burns like a flame."

197. Gallettier 1952: 31–34, 43–44.

198. Hatt 1950: 433.

199. Hatt 1950: 432 and pl. 10, fig. 2.

200. Gallettier 1952: 72–73 (*Panegyricus Constantino dictus* [7].21.7). The language of a "curse tablet" from the Gallo-Roman thermal spa of Chamalières in the Puy-de-Dôme region of central France has been linked by Sergent (2000, 2002a) to the Irish myth of Nechtan's well. His daring analysis, however, is based on a translation of the tablet (Lambert 2003: 153) concerning which there is no scholarly consensus: on this see, for example, Meid (1994: 40) and Mees (2007: 18–19).

201. Gallettier 1952: 73, note 1.

202. Gallettier 1952: 72–73 (*Panegyricus Constantino dictus* [7].22.1–2). My translation.

203. See above, note 21.

204. The Latin term for these curse tablets is *defixio*, a derivate of the verb *defigere*, "fasten, bind": Ogden 1999: 5. In the imperial period if not before, subterranean bodies of water became privileged depositories for these tablets (ibid., 23), one of which requests that its target "become liquid as water": Cunliffe 1969: 65–66. Among the primary types of curses found on these tablets, of which hundreds have been excavated and interpreted over the past decades, litigation curses, competition curses, erotic curses, trade curses, and prayers for justice figure prominently: Ogden 1999: 31. Ritual cursing of the same sort was attested at Saint Elian's Well in Wales as late as 1861: Morris 1893: 57, 73–74.

205. My summary is a reworking of that found in Puhvel 1987: 279.

206. This is manifestly the case for the vedic Apā́m Napāt and the avestan Apąm Napāt. As Dumézil (1981: 36–38) argued, it may also apply to the Roman Neptūnus. Ernout and Meillet (1959: 438, s.v. "Neptūnus") support Dumézil's hypothesis concerning Neptūnus, as well, perhaps, as his more problematic contention (1963: 58–60; 1981: 40–43) that the name of the Irish Nechtan can also be etymologically related to **nep*(*ō*)*t*.

207. Parpola 2015: 14–16.

208. See above, chapter 1, section 5.

209. Proferes 2007: 120–21. The mantra, found in the *Taittirīya* (4.1.2.3) and three other vedic *Saṃhitā*s, reads: "Having trodden the earth, O prize-winner, seek the fire by its glow! Having selected (the spot) of ground, tell us from where we are to dig it!"

210. taṃ [aśvaṃ] ghorāt krūrāt salilāt sarasa udāniyus: Geslani 2018: 46, note 103 (I have emended Geslani's translation, which appears ibid., 45). In his discussion (ibid., 44–46), Geslani also quotes related passages from *Āpastamba Śrauta Sūtra* 5.14.14, *Vaitana Śrauta Sūtra* 2.1.10–11, and *Gopatha Brāhmaṇa* 1.2.18.

211. *Kriyākālaguṇottara* 30.5ab, in Slouber 2017: 174, 257. See below, part 10.

212. See above, note 47.

213. Pausanias, *Description* 1.39.3 and 1.5.2, in Jones 1918: 24–25 and 208–9. Graves (1973: 172–73), who summarizes this story, also refers to Hyginus, *Fabulae* 38 and 187, and Aristophanes, *Birds* 533. Apart from his rape of Alopē, Poseidon also fathers a child on a maiden named Hippothoē ("Impetuous Mare"): Graves 1990: 40.

214. Another Irish witness, the *Táin Bó Cúalnge* ("Cattle Raid of Cooley"), relates that when one of the hero Cuchulainn's warhorses entered into it, the waters of the Black Lake "began to boil": Guyonvarc'h 1994: 287. See above, note 46.

215. ZY 19.77, in Humbach and Ichaporia 1998: 150–53.

216. According to Humbach and Ichaporia (1998: 150, 153), it is Fraŋrasiian's brother Kərəsauuazdah whom Haosrauaah defeats in the horse race and then binds before slaying Fraŋrasiian.

217. ZY 19.56, in Humbach and Ichaporia 1998: 135. The avestan Kauui Haosrauaah is known as Kay Khosrow in the Pahlavi sources.

218. Humbach and Ichaporia 1998: 137.

219. This is not the same as the "unappropriated *x*ᵛ*arənah*" of the Apąm Napāt passage. In these chapters, which highlight the ancient Kauuis, it is the "kavyan *x*ᵛ*arənah*" that is at stake: Humbach and Ichaporia 1998: 15–18.

220. ZY 19.82–84. Humbach and Ichaporia (1998: 158–59) suggest Vitāpa's identity with Apąm Napāt. *Tāpaiti* means "is warm" in avestan (Pokorny 2007: 3095), and the noun *tāpa*

means "heat" or "glow" in several Indo-Aryan languages (Turner 1966: 328). *Vi-* is a distributive prefix, making Vitāpa's name ("Widespread Heat") an apt description of the igneous Apąm Napāt as guardian of the luminous submarine x^{v}arənah.

221. Humbach and Ichaporia (1998: 151–52) explicate the track's shape (closed, with nine turns) and location (in or around a wooded forest).

222. Dumézil 1963: 56.

223. In France, Saint Stephen was considered the patron saint of horses; in the Scottish Hebrides, Saint Michael played this role: Le Borgne 2002: 110, note 14.

224. Le Borgne (2002: 96–118) devotes an entire chapter to these rites, surveying reports of such "cavalcades" from over twenty sites, mainly in the Hebrides, spanning the past three hundred years.

225. Le Borgne 2002: 109.

226. Le Borgne 2002: 119.

227. Sterckx 1994: 51–52; Pignatelli and Gerner 2006: 272–73. The name of the Etruscan god Nethuns, whose iconography and functions were assimilated with those of the Greek Poseidon, is also a cognate of the Latin *Neptūnus*: Cristofani 1984: 165.

228. Sterckx 1994: 39–79, especially 39–50, 54, 65. Sterckx (ibid., 54, 57–58) singles out an episode from the 1268 CE Old French *Cristal et Larie* as a reflex of the *PIE "fire in water" myth, and more specifically, the Irish account of Nechtan's well.

229. *Yvain* 5265–67. Here, just as several Catholic clerics before him had done, Chrétien of Troyes reduces the pagan god to a malign demon: Frappier 1969: 51; Sterckx 1994: 52.

230. *Roman de Thèbes* 607–9 (in Constans 1890: vol. 1, p. 273), and 8968–72 (ibid., vol. 2, p. 74).

231. Warmuth 2012: 8202–6. Cf. the MBh (3.115.16) toponym Aśvatīrtha, an "Equine Watering Place" frequented by thousands of wondrous horses. See above, note 145.

232. Parpola 2015: 114.

233. Dumézil 1986a: 186–87. Cf. Sergent 2004: 470–71.

234. *Oxford English Dictionary*, s.v. "naphtha."

235. Puhvel 1989: 279–80. Cf. Dumézil 1963: 59. For (the unlikely) *ta aphoda*, Kurt Latte (1966: 696) conjectures *tēn aphtha*, while Schmidt (1868: 580, s.v. "napas") suggests rather its equivalent, *to naphtha*. It is likely that Puhvel was working from the Schmidt edition, but he gives no references. In either case it should be noted that the "oil" in "oil-producing" is based on a conjecture, though a plausible one.

236. See Lockhart (1939: 1–12) for a compendium of ancient and medieval references, both European and Asian, to Persian naphtha.

237. In his notes on Mantineia, Frazer (1898: 421) describes a cavern from which "a stream strongly impregnated with salt gushes copiously . . . and flows in a large body into the sea."

238. See above, sections C, D, and G.

239. The site, known as Brug na Bóinne, comprises the mounds of Newgrange, Dowth, and Knowth-in-Meath: Sterckx 2004: 303. Irish pre-Christian funerary mounds are called *síd*s. Their underground denizens are called *áes síde*, who are none other than the Túatha Dé, the native spirits of the island: Bitel 2018; Guyénot 2011: 28; Dumézil 1963: 54–56.

240. Ó hUiginn 1992: 40. If Mac Mathúna (2010: 21) is correct in adducing a Gaulish parallel in Borvobo[v]indo[n]a, a name that means "'the Boiling White Cow' (referring probably to the boiling water of hot springs)," then this would constitute further evidence for a geothermal origin far removed from Ireland.

241. Desnier 2004: 302, note 43.

242. Crooke 1914: 715. The earliest record of a pilgrimage to Hiṅglāj dates from 1499 CE; in the same century the site was identified as a *śākta pīṭha* and the site at which the dismembered goddess Satī's *brahmarandhra* fell (Schaflechner 2018: 46, 102). The shrine's general layout and the goddess's representation have changed significantly over the past decades (Schaflechner 2018: 213–29), in ways similar to the Bhairava shrines documented in chapter 2.

243. Second Maccabees 1.13–15. See also Crooke 1914: 715. Brighenti (2016: 43–44) surmises that the Islamicization of Nanā into Bībī Nānī would have taken place in the seventh century CE. Recently, Harry Falk (2015: 265–94) has convincingly demonstrated that in the ancient world, this goddess was identified with the conjunction of the planet Venus with the constellation of Leo. This also explains the leonine mount of the goddess, from the Babylonian Innana to the Indian Durgā.

244. Ctesias's work has survived in the form of an epitome embedded in the ninth-century CE *Bibliotheca* of Photius. For Ctesias's reference to these carvings (in *Bibliotheca* 46a.13–19), see Henry 1947: 136. Cf. Brighenti 2016: 41–43, who notes Nanā's close association with the crescent moon. For discussion and a photograph of these carvings, see Schaflechner 2018: 243–44 (fig. 5.18).

245. Shastri 1978: 6.

246. For a map of this route, see Schaflechner 2018: 102 (fig. 3.1).

247. Shastri 1978: 40, 45; Brighenti 2016: 35.

248. Shastri 1978: 44: use agnikuṇḍ kaheṃ to āg nahīṃ jaltī thī.

249. Shastri 1978: 44: candrakūp meṃ devatvakā leś nahīṃ wah to mahādānav-sā pratīt ho rahā thā.

250. Schaflechner (2018: 196–97) suggests that an alternate spelling of the volcano's name, Candra-gup, may be read as "the moon's mud." He also indicates that the site is comprised of "three mud volcanoes . . . located in closed proximity."

251. As Brighenti (2016: 36) notes, "during the Makran earthquake of 1945 the ignition of large volumes of methane gas that erupted under great pressure near Hinglāj caused a red methane gas cloud to appear in the sky which could be seen from a great distance . . . the flames of the great fireball leapt thousands of feet into the sky and were seen burning for days over two mountains north of Hiṅglāj."

252. Brighenti 2016: 39, note 26. Nāths from the Nāgnāth Akhāḍā in Karachi were the traditional guides for pilgrims journeying to these sites: Shastri 1978: 4, 6; Schaflechner 2018: 129, 133–34, 190, 193, 242.

253. Brighenti 2016: 35. The submarine mare's femininity aligns with the intrinsically feminine nature of sulfurous geothermal phenomena in South Asia. Given the alchemical identification of the goddess's menstrual emission with sulfur, several such sites, scattered across the Indian subcontinent, are identified with tantric goddesses, including Hiṅglāj herself: Brighenti 2016: 37–39. See above, note 72.

254. Brighenti 2016: 35.

255. Crooke 1914: 716.

256. *Life of Apollonius* 3.14, in Jones 2005: 248–51.

257. On references to the presence of red mercury (ore) in this region, see above, note 82.

258. *Shorter Oxford Economic Atlas* 1959: 88. For an image and account of this process at a site in southern Italy, see Kroonenberg 2013: 38–39. See also Pattelli et al. 2014: 244. Interestingly, the mercury-rich area surveyed in this study of central Italy is located slightly to the north of the Alban Lake and its surrounding region of extinct volcanic craters.

259. Briggs 1953: 347; Weinberger-Thomas 1999: 156–57; Brighenti 2016: 33–34. See above, chapter 2, notes 29–30.

260. See above, note 140. However, a *bāḍava-kuṇḍa* ("pool of the mare-fire") exists in the vicinity of the renowned shrine of the goddess Kāmākhyā in Gauhati, Assam: White 1996: 234.

261. Shastri 1978: 44. Monier-Williams 1984: 428, s.v. "jvāla," cited in Brighenti 2016: 37. A gas vent at Muktinath in Nepal is locally known as Jvālā Māī: ibid., 38. See also above, note 211.

262. Called Gorakh Ḍibbi ("Gorakh's Case"), this is a pit of cold boiling water that bursts into flames when a lighted incense stick is thrust into an adjacent waterhole: Erndl 1993: 47–48.

263. This the Nāth Yogis of Ghatiyali, Rajasthan, do in the context of their death rites: Gold 1989: 102–3. One feature of Kangra's Jvālāmukhī is a small water body bubbling with combustible gas, which, ignited by temple priests, is actively worshiped: Brighenti 2016: 38. Brighenti (ibid.) also summarizes the accounts of the British travelers Wilford, Stewart, and Williams Jackson, referred to below.

264. Four hundred of the world's one thousand mud volcanoes are found in Azerbaijan, on the northern shore of the Black Sea: Planke et al. 2003: 258–59; Kroonenberg 2013: 211–14.

265. Hanway 1753: 381; Forster 1808: 256.

266. That Sikhs also venerated Jvālāmukhī at Kangra is confirmed by the fact that none other than Ranjit Singh donated a golden roof to her temple in 1813, to mark his victory over the Afghans: Erndl 1993: 47.

267. Stewart 1991: 312; Williams Jackson 1911: 43, 50.

268. See above, note 256.

269. Hanway 1753: 381. Other British travelers refer to these as "Hindoo mendicants," "Sunyasses," or "Hindu Fakirs": Forster 1808: 257, 291; Stewart 1897: 314.

270. His Muslim sobriquet, Hājji Ratan, indicates that he undertook the Hājj pilgrimage to Mecca where, according to tradition, he conversed with the Prophet himself: Bouillier and Khan 2009: 563–64, 575. Cf. Rose (1990: 407), on the "Muhammadan Yogis" known as Rāwals who made their way to Europe, where they "practice as quack occultists and physicians."

271. Stewart 1897: 312. Wilford 1799: 378 tells of another naphtha spring situated near the city of Kirkuk in Iraq, which Indian pilgrims he met there referred to as "a *Juálá-muc'hi*, or the flaming mouth."

272. Stewart 1897: 314; Le Strange 1919: 198–99, s.v. "naphtha"; Hanway 1753: 383.

Chapter Seven

1. Matthew 10.8. It may be argued that raising the dead was a "transcendent" reference, given the fact that, as the apostle Paul argued in First Corinthians (15.12–13), Jesus's resurrection prefigured the resurrection of the dead at the end of time, which lay at the core of his teachings. However, the reference to resurrection in Jesus's time, as recounted in Matthew 10.8, would have involved such immediate concerns as the raising of Lazarus from the tomb.

2. Mandelbaum 1966: 175–91.

3. Here it is should be noted that the word *persona* is derived from the Latin translation for the ancient Greek *prosōpon*, the mask through which a ritual or dramatic actor's voice sounded: *per-sonare*: Frontisi-Ducroix 1995: 17.

4. Daryaee 2009: 74–77.

5. See above, chapter 3, notes 189–94.

6. See above, chapter 3, notes 146–48. "Fascination" is an abstract form based on the Latin *fascinus* ("evil spell, bewitchment"), itself derived from the Greek *baskanos* ("sorcerer, one who bewitches"): see above, chapter 3, note 139.

7. See above, chapter 4, notes 8–12; and Schmitt 1979: 115, fig. c, and ibid., 117.

8. It bears noting, however, that with the advent of Lutheranism and its anti-Catholic iconoclasm, all of these rich frescoes were plastered over. Since the early twentieth century, Denmark's National Museum has been carrying out their careful restoration. See also above, chapter 4, note 3.

9. See, for example, Pocock 1973: 65–66, 72–73.

10. See above, chapter 6, note 272.

11. DeCaroli (2004: 71–73) links the names of several of these figures, labeled on the gateways and railings of the first-century BCE Bharhut *stūpa*, to those listed in the MMVS's catalog of yakṣas and other Buddhist works from the same period. As he notes (ibid., 75), "each of these would presumably have had its own *caitya*, but here they are relegated to the periphery of the stūpa itself, standing as visual markers of the Buddhists' success in taming and converting spirit-deities."

12. See above, chapter 4, note 89, and chapter 5, note 17.

13. Lincoln 2018: 145, 163.

14. Quintanilla 2017: 129 (my italics). See above, chapter 4, note 89.

15. Lindahl 2002: 144. Cf. Chaucer's satirical treatment of the mendicant friars in his introduction to the "Wife of Bath's Tale." See above, chapter 4, note 23, and chapter 5, note 140.

16. See above, chapter 2, note 17.

17. Summarized in Sircar 2018: 85, note 35.

18. Le Goff 1977: 230; Sullivan 2018: 60–70.

19. Among the many discussions of these topics, see Favret-Saada 1977: 16–19; Schmitt 1979: 233–37; Schmitt 1981: 5–20; Schmitt 1988: 499; Nicolaisen 1995a: 1–6; Lord 1995: 7–29; Minard 2002: 18–33; Doulet 2002: 14; Guyénot 2011: 14–15, 24–26, 50–51; Boyer 2014: 71–74; and Bitel 2018: 80–81.

20. Subrahmanyam 2005: 12.

21. Shorto 2019.

22. Smith 1990: 52.

23. See, for example, Schmitt 2018.

24. Schmitt 1979: 107.

25. This is not the place to rehearse, yet again, the positions of postmodernist criticism, for which the arrogant presumption of objectivity lies at the foundation of the mainly nineteenth-century modernist metanarratives that have bequeathed us the horrors of the twentieth and twenty-first century.

26. Lincoln 1991: 123.

References

Abbott, G. F. 1903. *Macedonian Folklore*. Cambridge: Cambridge University Press.

Abhinavagupta. *Tantrāloka*. See Dwivedi and Rastogi 1987; Gnoli 1999.

Abt, Theodor, and Salwa Fuad, ed. and tr. 2011. *The Book of Pictures Muṣḥaf aṣ-ṣuwar by Zosimos of Panopolis*. Zurich: Living Human Heritage Publications.

Acharya, Jadavji Trikamji, ed. 1992. *Charakasaṃhitā by Agniveśa, revised by Charaka and Dṛidhabala with the Āyurveda-Dīpikā Commentary of Chakrapāṇidatta*. 5th ed. Mumbai: Venkatesvar Steam Press, 1941; reprint Varanasi: Chaukhamba Surbharati Prakashan.

Achilles Tatius. *Leucippe and Clitophon*. See Gaselee 1969.

Acri, Andrea. 2016a. "Introduction: Esoteric Buddhist Networks along the Maritime Silk Routes." In Acri, ed., *Esoteric Buddhism*, pp. 1–25.

———, ed. 2016b. *Esoteric Buddhism in Mediaeval Maritime Asia: Networks of Masters, Texts, Icons*. Singapore: ISEAS-Yusof Ishak Institute.

Ad-Damīrī, Muḥammad ibn Mūsá. *Ḥayāt al-Ḥayawān*. See Jayakar 1908.

Adhami, Siamak. 2010. "Pairikā." In Ehsan Yarshater, ed., *Encyclopædia Iranica*. Online at http://www.iranicaonline.org/articles/pairika. Accessed July 31, 2018.

Agostini, Domenico. 2014. "Eschatological Seers and Otherworldly Travellers in Zoroastrianism." *Journal Asiatique* 302, no. 1: 47–73.

Agrawala, Vasudeva S. 1970. *Ancient Indian Folk Cults*. Varanasi: Prithivi Prakashan.

Aguirre, Manuel. 1993. "The Riddle of Sovereignty." *Modern Language Review* 88, no. 2 (Apr.): 273–82.

Ahuja, Naman P. 2019. "One Mother, Many Tongues." *Marg: A Magazine of the Arts* 70, no. 4: 32–51.

Ali, Daud. 2012. "The Historiography of the Medieval in South Asia." *Journal of the Royal Asiatic Society*, 3rd series, 22, no. 1: 7–12.

Allentoft, Morton E., et al. 2015. "Population Genomics of Bronze Age Eurasia." *Nature* 522 (June 11): 167–83.

Alles, Gregory D., ed. 2008. *Religious Studies: A Global View*. London: Routledge.

Al-Mas'ūdī, Abū al-Ḥasan. *Murūj al-dhahab wa ma'ādin al-jawāhir*. See Barbier de Meynard and Courteille 1863.

Almond, Philip. 1987. "The Buddha of Christendom: A Review of the Legend of Barlaam and Josaphat." *Religious Studies* 23, no. 3: 391–406.

Alpers, Edward A. 2014. *The Indian Ocean in World History*. New York: Oxford University Press.

Ānandakanda. See Radhakrishna Sastri 1952.

Andersen, Dines, and Helmer Smith. 1965. *Sutta-nipāta*. New ed. London: Luzac & Company Ltd.

Anderson, Andrew Runni. 1932. *Alexander's Gate, Gog and Magog, and the Inclosed Nations*. Cambridge, MA: Medieval Academy of America.

Ankarloo, Bengt, and Stuart Clark, eds. 1999. *Witchcraft and Magic in Europe: Ancient Greece and Rome*. The Athlone History of Witchcraft and Magic in Europe, vol. 2. London: Athlone Press.

Ankarloo, Bengt, and Gustav Henningsen, eds. 1993. *Early Modern European Witchcraft: Centres and Peripheries*. Oxford: Clarendon Press.

Aristotle. *On Sense and Sensible Objects*. See Hett 1957.

Arkenberg, J. S. 2000. "East Asian Sourcebook: Chinese Accounts of Rome, Byzantium and the Middle East, c. 91 B.C.E.–1642 C.E." Online at http://depts.washington.edu/silkroad/texts/romchin1.html.

Assayag, Jacky, and Gilles Tarabout, eds. 1999. *La Possession en Asie du Sud: Parole, Corps, Territoire* (Puruṣārtha 21). Paris: Editions de l'EHESS.

Atharva Veda. See Roth and Whitney 1966; Whitney and Lanman 1984.

Atharva Veda Pariśiṣṭas. See Bolling and Negelein 1976.

Athavale, Ananta Damodara, ed. 1980. *Śrīmad Vṛddhavāgbhaṭaviracita Aṣṭāṅgasaṃgraha Induvyākhyāsahitaḥ*. Pune: Srimad Atreya Prakashan.

Athenian Society. 1897. *Heliodorus (The Aethiopica) literally and completely translated from the Greek, with introduction and notes*. Athenian Society's Publications, 5. Athens: Athenian Society.

Atkinson, Edwin T. 2002. *The Himalayan Gazetteer; or, The Himalayan Districts of the North Western Province of India*. 3 vols. Allahabad: North Western Province and Oudh Government Press, 1882–86; reprint: New Delhi: Low Price Publications.

Aṭṭhakathā. See Tatia 1973.

Auboyer, Jeanine, and Marie-Thérèse de Mallmann. 1950. "Śītalā-la-Froide. Déesse indienne de la petite vérole." *Artibus Asiae* 13, no. 3: 207–27.

Augustine of Hippo, Saint. *City of God*. See Dyson 1998.

Aupapātika Sūtra. See Leumann 1966.

Babbitt, Frank Cole. 1936. *Plutarch: Moralia*. Vol. 5. Loeb Classical Library, 306. Cambridge, MA: Harvard University Press.

Bacon, Francis. 1908. *The Essays or Counsels Civil and Moral*. Edited by Fred Allison Howe. Boston: D. C. Heath & Co.

Bahulkar, S. S. 2004. "The Apocryphal (?) Hymn to Pratyaṅgirā in the Paippalāda Tradition." In Arlo Griffiths and Jan E. M. Houben, eds., *The Vedas. Texts, Language & Ritual. Proceedings of the Third International Vedic Workshop, Leiden 2002*, pp. 15–22. Groningen: Egbert Forsten.

Baldes, Richard W. 1975. "Democritus on Visual Perception: Two Theories or One?" *Phronesis* 2:93–105.

Baltrušaitis, Jurgis. 1993. *Le moyen-âge fantastique: Antiquités et exotismes dans l'art gothique*. Paris: Flammarion.

Banerjea, Jitendra Nath. 1938. "Some Folk Goddesses of Ancient and Medieval India." *Indian Historical Quarterly* 14:101–10.

———. 1941. *The Development of Hindu Iconography*. Calcutta: University of Calcutta.

Banks, S. E., and J. W. Binns, ed. and tr. 2002. *Gervase of Tilbury, "Otia Imperialia": Recreation for an Emperor*. Oxford: Oxford University Press.

Barbier de Meynard, Charles, and Pavet de Courteille, ed. and tr. 1863. *Maçoudi. Les prairies d'or*. Vol. 2. Paris: Imprimerie Impériale.

Baroja, Julio Caro. 1993. "Witchcraft and Catholic Theology." In Ankarloo and Henningsen, eds., *Early Modern European Witchcraft*, pp. 19–43.

Basil of Caesarea. *Homiliae*. In Migne, ed., *Patrologiae Cursus Completus*, Series Graeca, vol. 31. Online at https://archive.org/details/patrologiae_cursus_completus_gr_vol_031. Accessed March 22, 2018.

Baudouin de Gaiffier (Père). 1967. *Etudes critiques d'hagiographie et d'iconologie*. Brussels: Société des Bollandistes.

Baumbach, Sibylle. 2015. *Literature and Fascination*. New York: Palgrave Macmillan.

Baumgartner, Emmanuèle. 1988. "La fontaine au pin." In Jean Dufournet, ed., *Le chevalier au lion: Approches d'un chef-d'oeuvre*, pp. 31–46. Paris: Honoré Champion.

Beaujard, Philippe. 2017. "L'océan Indien, un éspace centrale du système-monde afro-eurasien avant le XVIe siècle." In Marcotte, ed., *Méditerranée et Océan Indien*, pp. 389–411.

Bentley, Jerry H. 2006. "Beyond Modernocentrism. Toward Fresh Visions of the Global Past." In Victor H. Mair, ed., *Contact and Exchange in the Ancient World*, pp. 17–29. Honolulu: University of Hawai'i Press.

Berglie, Per-Arne. 1982. "When the Corpses Rise: Some Tibetan Ro Langs Stories." *Indologica Taurenensia* 10:37–44.

Berthelot, Marcellin, ed. 1967. *La chimie au Moyen Âge*. Vol. 2, *L'Alchimie syriaque comprenant une introduction et plusieurs traités d'alchimie syriaques et arabes d'après les manuscrits du British Museum et de Cambridge. Texte et traduction avec notes, commentaires, reproductions des signes et des figures d'appareils, table analytique et index avec la collaboration de M. Rubens Duval*. Paris: Imprimerie Nationale, 1893; reprint Osnabrück and Amsterdam: Otto Zeller and Philo Press.

Berti, Daniela. 1999. "Un dieu maître-chanteur: La resolution d'un conflit villageois dans la vallée de Kullu (Himachal Pradesh)." In Assayag and Tarabout, eds., *La Possession en Asie du Sud*, pp. 61–97.

Bettini, Maurizio, and Cristiana Franco. 2010. *Il mito di Circe: Immagini e racconti dalla Grecia a oggi*. Rome: Einaudi.

Betz, Hans Dieter. 1992. *The Greek Magical Papyri in Translation, including the Demotic Spells*. 2nd ed. Chicago: University of Chicago Press.

Biedermann, Zoltán, and Alan Strathern, eds. 2017. *Sri Lanka at the Crossroads of History*. London: UCL Press.

Bitel, Lisa. 2018. "Secrets of the Síd: The Supernatural in Medieval Irish Texts." In Michael Ostling, ed., *Fairies, Demons, and Nature Spirits*, pp. 79–101. London: Palgrave MacMillan.

Bloch, Marc. 1928. "Pour une histoire comparée des sociétés européennes." *Revue de Synthèse Historique* 46 (Dec.): 15–50.

Blondel, Jean-François. 2011. *Guide des fontaines & chapelles guérisseuses*. Paris: Editions Trajectoire.

Bloomfield, Maurice, ed. 1972. *The Kauśika Sūtra of the Atharva Veda with extracts from the Commentaries of Dārila and Keśava*. New Haven, CT: American Oriental Society, 1889; Delhi: Motilal Banarsidass.

Böhtlingk, Otto, and Rudolf Roth. 1990. *Sanskrit-Wörterbuch*. 7 vols. St. Petersburg: Russian Imperial Academy of Sciences, 1855–75. First Indian edition: Delhi: Motilal Banarsidass.

Bollandus, Ioannes, and Godefridus Henschenius. 1658. *Acta Sanctorum*. Quotquot toto orbe coluntur, vel a Catholicis Scriptoribus celebrantur, Quæ ex Latinis & Græcis, aliarumque gentium antiquis monumentis collegerunt ac digesserunt. Seruata primigenia Scriptorum phrasi, & variis observationibus illustrarunt. Prodit nunc tribus Tomis Februarius, In quo MCCCX nominatorum Sanctorum &c. aliorum innumerabilium memoria vel res gestæ illustrantur, vol. 1 (complectens dies VI priores). Antwerp: Jacob Meursius. Online at http://acta.chadwyck.com.proxy.library.ucsb.edu:2048/all/fulltext?action=REGISTER&type=X&idref=BB010852&file=../session/1503611547_21201&SOURCE=indices.cfg#Page. Accessed July 31, 2020.

Bollard, John K. 1986. "Sovereignty and the Loathly Lady in English, Welsh, and Irish." *Leeds Studies in English*, n.s., 17:41–59.

Bolling, G. M. 1904. "The Çāntikalpa of the Atharva-veda." *Transactions and Proceedings of the American Philological Association* 35:77–127.

———. 1913. "The Çāntikalpa of the Atharvaveda." *Journal of the American Oriental Society* 33:265–78.

———. 1928. "Charms and Amulets (Vedic)." In Hastings et al., eds., *Encyclopædia of Religion and Ethics*, vol. 3, pp. 468–72.

Bolling, G. M., and J. von Negelein, eds. 1976. *The Pariśiṣṭas of the Atharvaveda*, with notes in Hindi by R. K. Rai. Varanasi: Chaukhambha Orientalia.

Bopearachchi, Osmund. 1999. "Sites portuaires et emporia de l'ancien Sri Lanka: nouvelles données archéologiques." *Arts Asiatiques* 54:5–23.

Bouckaert, Remco, et al. 2012. "Mapping the Origins and Expansion of the Indo-European Language Family." *Science* 337 (24 Aug.): 957–60.

Boudet, Jean-Patrice. 2006. *Entre science et nigromance: Astrologie, divination et magie dans l'Occident médiéval (XIIe–XVe siècle)*. Paris: Publications de la Sorbonne.

Boudreau, Abbé. 1976. "La fontaine St-Jean de Lamothe et 'Le culte des chiffons.'" *Bulletin de la Société Historique et Archéologique d'Arcachon* 7:17–19.

Bouillier, Véronique. 1989. "Des prêtres au pouvoir: Les Yogī et la fonction royale." In Véronique Bouillier and Gérard Toffin, eds., *Prêtrise, pouvoirs et autorité en Himalaya* (Puruṣārtha 12), pp. 193–213. Paris: Editions de l'EHESS.

———. 1991. "The King and His Yogī: Pṛthivīnārāyaṇ Śāh, Bhagavantanāth and the Unification of Nepal in the Eighteenth Century." In John P. Neelsen, ed., *Gender, Caste and Power in South Asia: Social Status and Mobility in a Transitional Society*, pp. 1–21. New Delhi: Manohar.

———. 2017. *Monastic Wanderers. Nāth Yogī Ascetics in Modern South Asia*. New Delhi: Manohar.

Bouillier, Véronique, and Dominique-Sila Khan. 2009. "Ḥājji Ratan or Bābā Ratan's Multiple Identities." *Journal of Indian Philosophy* 37:559–95.

Boulnois, Jean. 1989. *La caducée et la symbolique dravidienne indo-méditerranéenne de l'arbre, de la pierre, du serpent et de la déesse-mère*. Paris: Maisonneuve 1939; reprint Paris: Maisonneuve.

Bourgeaud, Philippe. 1983. "The Death of the Great Pan: The Problem of Interpretation." *History of Religions* 22, no. 3: 254–83.

Boussac, Marie-Françoise, Jean-François Salles, and Jean-Baptiste Yon, eds. 2016. *Ports of the Ancient Indian Ocean*. Delhi: Primus Books.

Boyce, Mary. 1986. "Apam Napāt." In Ehsan Yarshater, ed., *Encyclopædia Iranica*, vol. 2, fasc. 2, pp. 148–50. Online at http://www.iranicaonline.org/articles/apam-napat. Accessed August 11, 2015.

Boyce, Mary, and Ilya Gershevitch, eds. 1970. *W. B. Henning Memorial Volume*. London: Lund Humphries.

Boyer, Auguste M., E. J. Rapson, Émile Sénart, and Peter Scott Noble. 1997. *Kharoṣṭhī Inscriptions Discovered by Sir Aurel Stein in Chinese Turkestan*. Oxford: Oxford University Press, 1920–29; reprint New Delhi: Cosmo Publications.

Boyer, Régis. 1994. *La mort chez les anciens scandinaves*. Paris: Les Belles Lettres.

———. 2014. *Les Valkyries*. Paris: Les Belles Lettres.

Boyer, Régis, and Jean Renaud. 2012. *Sagas légendaires islandaises*. Toulouse: Anacharsis.

Bradbury, Nancy Mason. 2002. "Romance." In Lindahl, McNamara, and Lindow, eds., *Medieval Folklore*, pp. 346–50.

Braverman, Marcy Alison. 2003. "Possession, Immersion, and the Intoxicated Madness of Devotion in Hindu Traditions." PhD dissertation, University of California, Santa Barbara.

Brighenti, Francesco. 2016. "A 'Sulfurous' Śakti: The Worship of Goddess Hiṅgulā in Baluchistan." In Ferrari and Dähnhardt, eds., *Soulless Matter*, pp. 28–50.

Briquel, Dominique. 1981. "Sur un passage d'Hérodote: prise de Babylone et prise de Véies." *Bulletin de l'Association Guillaume Budé* 3 (Oct.): 293–306.

———. 1988. "La comparaison indo-européenne dans le domaine grec: l'exemple de Poséidon." In Charles-Marie Ternes, ed., *Actes du colloque international «Eliade-Dumézil», Luxembourg, avril 1988*, pp. 51–64. Luxembourg: Ministère de l'Éducation Nationale et de la Jeunesse.

Bromwich, Rachel. 1950. "Cantre't Gwaelod and Ker-Is." In Sir Cyril Fox and Bruce Dickins, eds., *The Early Cultures of North-West Europe (H. M. Chadwick Memorial Studies)*, pp. 215–41. Cambridge: Cambridge University Press.

———. 1960–61. "Celtic Dynastic Themes and the Breton Lays." *Etudes Celtiques* 9:439–74.

Brown, Arthur C. L. 1903. *Iwain: A Study in the Origins of Arthurian Romance*. Studies and Notes in Philology and Literature, 8. Boston: Ginn & Company.

Brunaux, Jean-Louis. 1993. "Les bois sacrés des Celtes et des Germains." In John Scheid, ed., *Les bois sacrés: Actes du Colloque International organisé par le Centre Jean Bérard et l'École Pratique des Hautes Études (Ve section)*, pp. 57–65. Naples: Centre Jean Bérard.

———. 2016. *Les religions gauloises (Ve–Ier siècles av. J.-C.)*. Paris: CNRS Editions.

Brunner, Hélène. 1974. "Un Tantra du Nord: Le *Netra Tantra*." *Bulletin de l'École française d'Extrême-Orient* 37:125–97.

———. 1975. "Le *sādhaka*, personnage oublié du Śivaïsme du sud." *Journal Asiatique* 63, nos. 3–4: 411–43.

Brunner, Hélène, Gerard Oberhammer, and André Padoux, eds. 2000. *Tāntrikābhidhānakośa I. A Dictionary of Technical Terms from Hindu Tantric Literature*. Beiträge zur Kultur- und Geistesgeschichte Asiens, no. 35. Vienna: Österreichischen Akademie de Wissenschaften.

———, eds. 2004. *Tāntrikābhidhānakośa II. A Dictionary of Technical Terms from Hindu Tantric Literature*. Beiträge zur Kultur- und Geistesgeschichte Asiens, no. 44. Vienna: Verlag der Österreichischen Akademie der Wissenschaften.

Bugge, John. 2004. "Fertility Myth and Female Sovereignty in 'The Weddynge of Sir Gawen and Dame Ragnell.'" *Chaucer Review* 39, no. 2: 198–208.

Buitenen, J. A. B. van, tr. 1975. *The Mahābhārata: Book 2, The Book of the Assembly Hall; Book 3, The Book of the Forest*. Chicago: University of Chicago Press.

Bullis, Douglas. 2012. *Mahavamsa: The Great Chronicle of Sri Lanka*. Fremont, CA: Asian Humanities Press.

Burchard of Worms. *Burchardi Wormaciensis ecclesiae episcopi Decretorum libri viginti*. In Migne, ed., *Patrologiae Cursus Completus*, Series Latina, vol. 140, cols. 537B–1058C.

Burchett, Patton E. 2019. *A Genealogy of Devotion: Bhakti, Tantra, Yoga and Sufism in North India*. New York: Columbia University Press.

Burgess, Glyn S., and Leslie C. Brook. 2016. *Twenty-Four Lays from the French Middle Ages*. Liverpool: Liverpool University Press.

Burjam, Friedrich Daniel Christian. 1917. *Den skandinaviska folktron om barnet under dess ömtålighetstillstånd i synnerhet före dopet.* Helsingfors: Arvingars Boktryckeri.

Burkert, Walter. 1979. *Structure and History in Greek Mythology and Ritual.* Berkeley: University of California Press.

———. 1985. *Greek Religion.* Translated by John Raffan. Cambridge, MA: Harvard University Press.

———. 1992. *The Orientalizing Revolution: Near Eastern Influence on Greek Culture in the Early Archaic Age.* Translated by Margaret E. Pinder and Walter Burkert. Cambridge, MA: Harvard University Press.

Burnouf, Émile. 1876. *Introduction à l'histoire du Buddhisme indien.* 2nd ed. Paris: Maisonneuve et Cie.

Burrow, Thomas E. 1935. "Iranian Words in the Kharoṣṭhi Documents from Chinese Turkestan, II." *Bulletin of the School of Oriental and African Studies* 7, no. 4: 779–80.

———. 1940. *A Translation of the Kharoṣṭhi Documents from Chinese Turkestan.* London: Royal Asiatic Society.

Bury, R. G. 1929. *Plato. Timaeus, Critias, Cleitophon, Menexenus, Epistles.* Loeb Classical Library, 234. Cambridge, MA: Harvard University Press.

Cairns, Douglas L. 2011. "Looks of Love and Loathing: Cultural Models of Vision and Emotion in Ancient Greek Culture." *Métis,* n.s., 9:37–50.

Caland, Wilhelm. 1900. *Altindisches Zauberritual. Probe einer Uebersetzung der wichtigsten Theile des Kauśika Sūtra.* Amsterdam, Johannes Müller.

Callaway, Ewen. 2015. "DNA Deluge Reveals Bronze Age Secrets." *Nature* 522 (June 11): 140–41.

Callieri, Pierfrancesco. 2001. "In the Land of the Magi. Demons and Magic in the Everyday Life of Pre-Islamic Iran." In Rika Gyselen, ed., *Démons et merveilles d'orient,* pp. 11–35. Res Orientales 13. Bures-sur-Yvette: Groupe pour l'Étude de la Civilisation du Moyen-Orient.

Campbell, J. Gabriel. 1976. *Saints and Householders: A Study of Hindu Ritual and Myth among the Kangra Rajputs.* Kathmandu: Ratna Pustak Bhandar.

Capdeville, Gerard, ed. 2004. *L'Eau et le feu dans les religions antiques.* Paris: De Boccard.

Caraka Saṃhitā. See Acharya 1992.

Carn Máil. See Gwynn 1924.

Carroll, Michael P. 1999. *Irish Pilgrimage: Holy Wells and Popular Devotion.* Baltimore: Johns Hopkins University Press.

Casanova, Angelo. 2012. "Plutarch as Apollo's Priest at Delphi." In Lautaro Roig Lanzillotta and Israel Muñoz Gallarte, eds., *Plutarch in the Religious and Philosophical Discourse of Late Antiquity,* pp. 151–57. Leiden: Brill.

Caulier, Brigitte. 1990. *L'eau et le sacré. Les culte thérapeutiques autour des fontaines en France.* Paris: Beauchesne.

Chakrabarti, Kunal. 2001. *Religious Process: The Purāṇas and the Making of a Regional Tradition.* Delhi: Oxford India.

Chakrabarty, Dipesh. 2000. *Provincializing Europe: Postcolonial Thought and Historical Difference.* Princeton, NJ: Princeton University Press.

Chalmers, Robert (Lord), tr. 1895. *The Jātaka or Stories of the Buddha's Former Births, translated from the Pāli by Various Hands under the editorship of E. B. Cowell.* Vol. 1. Cambridge: Cambridge University Press.

Chandra, Lokesh. 2003. "The Khotanese Mural of Hārītī in Shrine D II at Dandan-Uiliq." *Archiv Orientální, Quarterly Journal of Asian and African Studies* 71, no. 3 (Aug.): 293–302.

Chaucer, Geoffrey. "Wife of Bath's Tale." In Mann 2005.

Chaudhuri, Nanimadhab. 1935. "A Curious Cult in North Bengal." *Indian Culture* 2, no. 3: 565–71.

Chenu, Marie-Dominique. 1968. *Man, Nature and Society in the Twelfth Century: Essays on New Theological Perspectives in the Latin West, with a Preface by Etienne Gilson*. Selected, edited, and translated by Jerome Taylor and Lester K. Little. Chicago: University of Chicago Press.

Child, Francis James. 1965. *English and Scottish Popular Ballads*. Vol. 1. Boston: Houghton Mifflin & Co., 1882–84; New York: Dover Publications.

Chivers, C. J. 2015. "The Doomsday Scam." *New York Times Magazine*, November 22, pp. 36–39, 58.

Chrétien de Troyes. *Le chevalier au lion (Yvain)*. See Pierreville 2016; Kibler 1985.

Christensen, Arthur. 1941. "Essai sur la démonologie iranienne." *Det Kgl. Videnskabernes Selskab. Historisk-filologiske Meddelelser* 27, no. 1: 3–97.

Christopoulos, Lucas. 2012. "Hellenes and Romans in Ancient China (240 BC–1398 AD)." *Sino-Platonic Papers*, no. 230: 1–79. Online at http://www.sino-platonic.org/complete/spp230_hellenes_romans_in_china.pdf.

Clement, P. A., and H. B. Hoffleit, trs. 1969. *Plutarch. Moralia*. Vol. 8. Loeb Classical Library, 424. Cambridge, MA: Harvard University Press.

Cohen, Getzel M. 2013. *The Hellenistic Settlements in the East from Armenia and Mesopotamia to Bactria and India*. Berkeley: University of California Press.

Cohen, Richard S. 1998. "Naga, Yakṣiṇī, Buddha: Local Deities and Local Buddhism at Ajanta." *History of Religions* 37, no. 4: 360–400.

Cóir Anmann. See Stokes and Windisch 1891.

Constans, Léopold. 1890. *Le Roman de Thèbes, publié d'après tous les manuscrits*. 2 vols. Paris: Firmin Didot.

Coomaraswamy, Ananda Kentish. 1928. *Yakṣas. Part I*. Washington, DC: Smithsonian Institution.

———. 1931. *Yakṣas. Part II*. Washington, DC: Smithsonian Institution.

———. 1956. *Mediaeval Sinhalese Art, being a monograph on mediaeval Sinhalese arts and crafts, mainly as surviving in the eighteenth century, with an account of the structure of society and the status of the craftsmen*. 2nd ed. New York: Pantheon Books.

Cort, John. 1987. "Medieval Jaina Goddess Traditions." *Numen* 34, no. 2: 235–55.

———. 1997. "Tantra in Jainism: the Cult of Ghaṇṭakarṇ Mahāvīr, the Great Hero Bell-Ears." *Bulletin d'Études Indiennes* 15:115–33.

Couture, André, and Charlotte Schmid. 2001. "The *Harivaṃśa*, the Goddess Ekānaṃśā, and the Iconography of the Vṛṣṇi Triads." *Journal of the American Oriental Society* 121, no. 2 (Apr.–June): 173–92.

Cristofani, Mauro, ed. 1984. *Etruschi: Una nuova immagine*. Firenze: Giunti.

Crooke, William. 1908. "Notes on Homeric Folklore (Continued)." *Folklore* 19, no. 2: 153–89.

———. 1914. "Hinglāj." In Hastings et al., eds., *Encyclopædia of Religion and Ethics*, vol. 6, pp. 715–16.

———. 1928. "Charms and Amulets (Indian)." In Hastings et al., eds., *Encyclopædia of Religion and Ethics*, vol. 3, pp. 441–48.

———. 1968. *The Religion and Folklore of Northern India*. 2 vols. 2nd ed. Westminster: Archibald Constable & Co. 1896; 3rd reprint Delhi: Liberty Arts Press.

Ctesias. *Indika*. See Henry 1947.

Cun fuzhai wenji. See Zhu Derun 1997.

Cunliffe, Barry. 1969. *Roman Bath*. Report of the Research Committee of the Society of Antiquaries of London, no. XXIV. Oxford: Oxford University Press.

———. 2015. *By Steppe, Desert & Ocean: The Birth of Eurasia*. New York: Oxford University Press.

Cunningham, Alexander. 1885. *Report of a Tour in Eastern Rajputana in 1882–83*. Archaeological Survey of India, vol. 20. Calcutta: Office of the Superintendent of Government Printing, India.

Czarnowski, Stefan. 1919. *Le culte des héros et ses conditions sociales: Saint Patrick, héros national de l'Irlande*. Paris: Félix Alcan.

Dandekar, R. N., ed. 1971. *The Mahābhārata text as Constituted in Its Critical Edition*. Vol. 1. Poona: Bhandarkar Oriental Research Institute.

———. 1975. *The Mahābhārata Text as Constituted in Its Critical Edition*. Vol. 4. Poona: Bhandarkar Oriental Research Institute.

Daryaee, Touraj. 2009. *Sasanian Persia: The Rise and Fall of an Empire*. London: I. B. Taurus.

Dasa, Syamasundara. 1965–75. *Hindi Śabd Sāgar*. 9 vols. 2nd ed. Benares: Nagari Pracarini Sabha.

Dash, Bhagwan, and Lalitesh Kashyap. 1980. *Basic Principles of Āyurveda: Based on Āyurveda Saukhyam of Ṭoḍarānanda*. Delhi: Concept.

Davis, Edward. 2001. *Society and the Supernatural in Song China*. Honolulu: University of Hawai'i Press.

Daya, Dalpat Ram. 1990. *Demonology and Popular Superstitions of Gujarat*. Translated by Alexander Kinloch Forbes. Gurgaon: Vintage Books.

DeCaroli, Robert. 2004. *Haunting the Buddha: Indian Popular Religions and the Formation of Buddhism*. New York: Oxford University Press.

———. 2015. *Image Problems*. New York: Oxford University Press.

Delatte, Armand. 1927. *Anecdota Atheniensa, tome I. Textes grecs inédits relatifs à l'histoire des religions*. Paris: Édouard Champion.

———. 1932. *La catoptromancie grecque et ses dérivés*. Paris: E. Droz.

Delpech, François. 2010. "Saint Nectan: hagiographie, folklore, et mythologie comparée." In Gaël Hily et al., eds., *Deuogdonion. Mélanges offerts en l'honneur du Professeur Claude Sterckx*, pp. 133–55. Rennes: Tir.

De Mély, Fernand. 1895. "L'alchimie chez les chinois et l'alchimie grecque." *Journal Asiatique*, 9th series, 6 (Sept.–Oct.): 314–40.

Derrett, J. Duncan M. 1992. "Homer in India: The Birth of the Buddha." *Journal of the Royal Asiatic Society*, 3rd series, 2, no. 1: 47–57.

Derrida, Jacques. 1972. *Marges de la philosophie*. Paris: Editions de Minuit.

Deshpande, M. N. 1959. "The Rock-Cut Caves of Pitalkhora in the Deccan." *Ancient India* 15:66–99.

DesJardins, J. F. Marc. 2002. "Mahāmāyūrī: explorations sur la création d'une écriture prototantrique." PhD dissertation, McGill University, Montreal.

Desnier, Jean-Luc. 2004. "Le feu dans l'eau: Modes et fonctions: de Ninive à Veies, en passant par l'Irlande." in Capdeville, ed., *L'Eau et le feu*, pp. 291–302.

Dezső, Csaba. 2010. "Encounters with *Vetālas*: Studies on Fabulous Creatures I." *Acta Orientalia Academiae Scientiarum Hungaricae* 63, no. 4: 391–426.

Dharmaraja Adhvarindra. *Vedānta Paribhāṣā*. See Madhavananda 1942.

Dickie, Matthew W. 1991. "Heliodorus and Plutarch on the Evil Eye." *Classical Philology* 86, no. 1: 17–29.

Dietrich, Angela. 1998. *Tantric Healing in the Kathmandu Valley*. Delhi: Book Faith India.

Dietz, Siglinde. 1997. "The meaning of *kṛtya-kākhorda-mantra-vetāḍa*." In Bhikkhu Tampalawela Dhammaratana and Bhikkhu Pasadika, eds., *Dharmadūta. Mélanges offerts au Vénérable Thích Huyên-Vi à l'occasion de son soixante-dixième anniversaire*, pp. 86–94. Paris: Éditions You-Feng.

Dīgha-Nikaya. See Rhys Davids and Carpenter 1890.

Dimock, Edward Jr. 1989. *The Place of the Hidden Moon: Erotic Mysticism in the Vaiṣṇava-sahajiyā Cult of Bengal*. Chicago: University of Chicago Press.

Doulet, Jean-Michel. 2002. *Quand les démons enlevaient les enfants: Les changelins: étude d'une figure mythique*. Paris: Presses Universitaires de France.

Drescher, Karl, et al., eds. 1916. *D. Martin Luthers Tischreden 1531–46*. Vol. 4. Weimar: Hermann Böhlaus Nachfolger.

———. 1919. *D. Martin Luthers Tischreden 1531–46*. Vol. 5. Weimar: Hermann Böhlaus Nachfolger.

Dubuisson, Daniel. 1993. *Mythologies du XXè Siècle (Dumézil, Lévi-Strauss, Eliade)*. Lille: Presses Universitaires de Lille.

Duggan, Joseph J. 2001. *The Romances of Chrétien de Troyes*. New Haven, CT: Yale University Press.

Dumézil, Georges. 1963. "Le puits de Nechtan." *Celtica* 6:50–61.

———. 1981. *Mythe et épopée*. Vol. 3, *Histoires romaines*. 3rd ed. (*corrigé*). Paris: Gallimard (first ed. 1973).

———. 1983. *La courtisane et les seigneurs colorés: Esquisses de mythologie*. Paris: Gallimard.

———. 1986a. *Mythe et épopée*. Vol. 1, *L'idéologie des trois fonctions dans les épopées des peuples indo-européens*. 5th ed. Paris: Gallimard (first ed. 1968).

———. 1986b. *Mythe et épopée*. Vol. 2, *Types épiques indo-européens: un heros, un sorcier, un roi*. 4th ed. Paris: Gallimard (first ed. 1971).

Dundes, Alan, ed. 1992. *The Evil Eye: A Casebook*. Madison: University of Wisconsin Press.

Durkin-Meisterernst, Desmond. 2016. "Le rôle des acteurs de langues iraniennes." In Espagne et al., eds., *Asie Centrale*, pp. 155–65.

Dutt, Nalinaksa. 1984. *Gilgit Manuscripts*. Vol. 1. Bibliotheca Indo-Buddhica, 14. Srinagar: His Highness's Government, 1939; reprint New Delhi: Sri Satguru Publications.

Duval, Rubens. 1893. "Notes de lexicographie syriaque et arabe." *Journal Asiatique*, 9th series, 2 (Sept.–Oct.): 290–361.

Dwivedi, R. C., and Rastogi, N. 1987. *The Tantrāloka of Abhinavagupta with Commentary by Rājānaka Jayaratha*. 8 vols. 2nd ed. Allahabad: Indian Press, 1918–38; reprint: Delhi: Motilal Banarsidass.

Dyck, Andrew. 1981. "The Witch's Bed but Not Her Breakfast: An Odyssean Paradox." *Rheinisches Museum für Philologie* 124:196–98.

Dyson, R. W., ed. 1998. *Augustine, the City of God against the Pagans*. Cambridge: Cambridge University Press.

Eaton, Richard M. 2000. "(Re)imag(in)ing Other²ness: A Postmortem for the Postmodern in India." *Journal of World History* 11:57–78.

Edgerton, Franklin. 1953. *Buddhist Hybrid Sanskrit Grammar and Dictionary*. New Haven, CT: Yale University Press. Online at http://www.sanskrit-lexicon.uni-koeln.de/scans/BHSScan/2014/web/index.php.

Edwards, Cyril, ed. and tr. 2007. *German Romance: Volume III, Hartmann von Aue, Iwein or the Knight with the Lion. Edited from Manuscript B, Giesse, Universitätsbibliothek Codex Nr. 97*. Cambridge: D. S. Brewer.

Eichhorn-Mulligan, Amy C. 2006. "The Anatomy of Power and the Miracle of Kingship: The Female Body of Sovereignty in a Medieval Irish Kingship Tale." *Speculum* 81:1014–54.

Eliade, Mircea. 1969. *The Quest: History and Meaning in Religion*. Chicago: University of Chicago Press.

Elias, Jamal J. 2012. *Aisha's Cushion: Religious Art, Practice, and Perception in Islam*. Cambridge, MA: Harvard University Press.

Elliott, John H. 2016. *Beware the Evil Eye: The Evil Eye in the Bible and the Ancient World*. Vol. 2, Greece and Rome. Cambridge: James Clark Company, Ltd.

Elworthy, Frederick Thomas. 1895. *The Evil Eye: An Account of this Ancient & Widespread Superstition*. London: John Murray.

Emerson, Herbert William. 1920. *Punjab Gazetteers. Mandi State with Maps and Photographs. 1920*. Vol. XII-A. Lahore: Superintendent, Government Printing, Punjab.

Emlyn-Jones, Chris, and William Preddy. 2017. *Plato: Euthyphro, Apology, Crito, Phædo*. Loeb Classical Library, 36. Cambridge, MA: Harvard University Press.

Entwistle, A. W. 1990. "Māhātmya Sources on the Pilgrimage Circuit of Mathurā." In Hans Bakker, ed., *The History of Sacred Places in India as Reflected in Traditional Literature. Papers on Pilgrimage in South Asia*, pp. 5–32. Leiden: Brill.

Erndl, Kathleen. 1993. *Victory to the Mother: The Hindu Goddess of Northwest India in Myth, Ritual, and Symbol*. New York: Oxford University Press.

Ernout, A[lfred], and A[ntoine] Meillet. 1959. *Dictionnaire Étymologique de la Langue Latine. Histoire des mots*. 4th rev. ed. Paris: Klincksieck.

Escola, Marc, and Sophie Rabau. 2015. *Littérature seconde ou la bibliothèque de Circé*. Paris: Kimé.

Espagne, Michel. 1994. "Sur les limites du comparatisme en histoire culturelle." *Genèses* 17:112–21.

Espagne, Michel, et al., eds. 2016. *Asie Centrale: Transferts culturels le long de la Route de la Soie*. Paris: Vendémiaire.

Ewald, François. 1986. "Le messager des dieux." *Magazine Littéraire* 229 (Apr.): 16–21.

Falk, Harry. 2015. "Kushan Rule Granted by Nana: The Background of a Heavenly Legitimation." In Harry Falk, ed., *Kushan Histories. Literary Sources and Selected Papers from a Symposium at Berlin, December 5 to 7, 2013*, pp. 265–99. Bremen: Hempen Verlag.

Falk, Nancy E. 1973. "Wilderness and Kingship in Ancient South Asia." *History of Religions* 13, no. 1: 1–15.

Fallon, S. W. 1879. *A New Hindustani-English Dictionary, with Illustrations from Hindustani Literature and Folk-lore*. London: Trubner & Co.

Fausböll, Viggo, ed. 1877. *The Jātaka together with its commentary, being tales of the anterior births of Gotama Buddha. For the first time edited in the original Pāli*. Vol. 1. London: Pali Text Society.

———. 1879. *The Jātaka together with its commentary, being tales of the anterior births of Gotama Buddha. For the first time edited in the original Pāli*. Vol. 2. London: Pali Text Society.

Favret-Saada, Jeanne. 1985 (1977). *Les mots, les morts, les sorts*. Paris: Gallimard.

Feldhaus, Anne. 1995. *Water and Womanhood: Religious Meanings of Rivers in Maharashtra*. New York: Oxford University Press.

———. 1999. "Rivers and the Death of Children." In Elisabeth Schömbucher and Claus Peter Zoller, eds., *Ways of Dying. Death and Its Meanings in South Asia*, pp. 153–61. New Delhi: Mahohar.

Fercoq du Leslay, Gérard. 2017. *Ribemont-sur-Ancre: Hommes et dieux dans la Somme, il y a 2000 ans*. Amiens: Imprimerie du Conseil départemental de la Somme.

Ferrari, Fabrizio. 2015. *Religion, Devotion and Medicine in North India: The Healing Power of Śītalā*. London: Bloomsbury.

Ferrari, Fabrizio, and Thomas W. P. Dähnhardt, eds. 2016. *Soulless Matter, Seats of Energy: Metals, Gems and Minerals in South Asian Traditions*. Sheffield, UK: Equinox.

Filliozat, Jean. 1937. *Etude de démonologie indienne: Le Kumāratantra de Rāvaṇa et les textes parallèles indiens, tibétains, chinois, cambodgien et arabe*. Paris: Imprimerie Nationale.

Findly, Ellison Banks. 1979. "The 'Child of the Waters': A Revaluation of Vedic Apāṃ Napāt." *Numen* 26, no. 2: 164–84.

Fitzpatrick, Matthew P. 2011. "Provincializing Rome: The Indian Ocean Trade Network and Roman Imperialism." *Journal of World History* 22, no. 1 (Mar.): 27–54.

Flint, Valerie I. J. 1991. *The Rise of Magic in Early Medieval Europe*. Princeton, NJ: Princeton University Press.

———. 1999. "The Demonisation of Magic and Sorcery in Late Antiquity: Christian Redefinitions of Pagan Religions." In Ankarloo and Clark, eds., *Witchcraft and Magic in Europe*, pp. 277–348.

Folks, Cathalin B., and Carl Lindahl. 2002. "Loathly Lady." In Lindahl, McNamara, and Lindow, eds., *Medieval Folklore*, pp. 245–46.

Ford, Patrick K. 2008. *The Mabinogi and Other Medieval Welsh Tales*. Berkeley: University of California Press, 1977; second paperback printing.

Forrest, S. K. Mendoza. 2011. *Witches, Whores and Sorcerers: The Concept of Evil in Early Iran*. Foreword and other contributions by Prods Oktor Skjærvø. Austin: University of Texas Press.

Forster, George. 1808. *A Journey from Bengal to England, through the Northern Part of India, Kashmire, Afghanistan, and Persia, and into Russia by the Caspian-Sea*. Vol. 2. London: R. Faulder & Son.

Franke, Heike. 2010. "Akbar's *Kathāsaritsāgara*: The Translator and Illustrations of an Imperial Manuscript." *Muqarnas, an Annual on the Visual Cultures of the Islamic World* 27:313–56.

Frappier, Jean. 1969. *Étude sur Yvain ou le Chevalier au Lion de Chrétien de Troyes*. Paris: Société d'Édition d'Enseignement Supérieur.

Frasch, Tilman. 2017. "A Pāli Cosmopolis? Sri Lanka and the Theravāda Ecumene, c. 500–1500." In Zoltán Biedermann and Alan Strathern, eds., *Sri Lanka at the Crossroads of History*, pp. 66–76. London: UCL Press.

Frazer, James George (Sir), ed. and tr. 1898. *Pausanias's Description of Greece*. Vol. 3. Cambridge: Cambridge University Press.

———. 1959. *Ovid's Fasti with an English Translation*. Cambridge, MA: Harvard University Press, 1931; reprint.

———. 2002. *The Golden Bough: A Study in Religion and Magic*. Abridged ed. Mineola, NY: Dover Publications.

Frontisi-Ducroix, Françoise. 1995. *Du masque au visage: Aspects de l'identité en Grèce ancienne*. Paris: Flammarion.

Fuchs, Walter. 1958–59. "Ein Gesandtschaftsbericht über Fu-lin in chinesischer Wiedergabe aus den Jahren 1314–1320," *Oriens Extremus* 5/6:123–30.

Fuller, Christopher J. 1992. *The Camphor Flame: Popular Hinduism and Society in India*. New York, Viking.

Fynes, R. C. C., ed. and tr. 2005–6. *The Epitome of Queen Līlāvatī by Jinaratna*. 2 vols. New York: New York University Press and the JJC Foundation.

Gad, Tue. 1971. *Helgener. Legender fortalte i Norden*. København: Rhodos.

Gaidoz, Henri. 1883. "Deux parallèles: Rome et Congo." *Revue de l'Histoire des Religions* 7, pp. 5–16.

———. 1892. *Un vieux rite medical*. Paris: E. Rolland.

Gaignebet, Claude. 1986. *A plus hault sens. L'ésotérisme spiritual et charnel de Rabelais*. 2 vols. Paris: Maisonneuve.

Gail, Adalbert J. 1991–92. "OHþO: Bhūteśa—Śiva as Lord of the Demons in the Kuṣāṇa Realm." *Silk Road Art and Archaeology* 2:43–49.

Gallettier, Edouard, ed. and tr. 1952. *Panégyriques Latins*. Vol. 2, *Les panégyriques constantiniens (VI–X)*. Paris: Les Belles Lettres.

Gaselee, S., ed. and tr. 1969. *Achilles Tatius, with an English Translation*. Loeb Classical Library, 45. London: Heinemann, 1917; Cambridge, MA: Harvard University Press.

Gautama. *Nyāya Sūtra*. Online at http://gretil.sub.uni-goettingen.de/gretil/1_sanskr/6_sastra/3_phil/nyaya/gaunys_u.htm.

Geiger, Wilhelm, ed. 1908. *Mahāvamsa*. Pali Text Society, 63. London: H. Frowde.

Geiger, Wilhelm, and Mabel Haynes Bode, tr. 1912. *Mahāvaṃsa: the Great Chronicle of Ceylon*. London: Oxford University Press.

Gervase of Tilbury. *Otia Imperialia*. See Banks and Binns 2002; Pignatelli and Gerner 2006.

Geslani, Marko. 2018. *Rites of the God-King*. New York: Oxford University Press.

Gesta Romanorum. See Oesterley 1872.

Gharib, Badr az-Zaman. 1995. *Sogdian Dictionary. Sogdian-Persian-English*. Tehran: Farhangan Publications.

Giebel, Rolf W. 2016. "A Śaiva Text in Chinese Garb? An Annotated Translation of the *Suji liyan Moxishouluo tian shuo aweishe fa*." In Acri, ed., *Esoteric Buddhism*, pp. 381–88.

Gills, Barry K., and Andre Gunder Frank. 1992. "World System Cycles, Crises, and Hegemonial Shifts, 1700 BC to 1700 AD." *Review (Fernand Braudel Center)* 15, no. 4: 621–87.

Ginzburg, Carlo. 1984. *Les batailles nocturnes: Sorcellerie et rituels agraires aux XVIè et XVIIè siècles*. Paris: Flammarion.

———. 1992. *Le sabbat des sorcières*. Paris: Gallimard.

Gnoli, Raniero, tr. 1999. *Abhinavagupta: Luce dei Tantra, Tantraloka*. Milan: Adelphi.

Gold, Ann Grodzins. 1989. *Fruitful Journeys: The Ways of Rajasthani Pilgrims*. Berkeley: University of California Press, 1988; Delhi: Oxford India.

Gonda, Jan. 1937. "Altind. *pratisara-*, *sraj-* und Verwandtes." *Acta Orientalia* 15:311–28.

———. 1969. *Aspects of Early Visnuism*. Delhi: Motilal Banarsidass.

Goodall, Dominic, et al., ed. and tr. 2015. *The Niḥśvāsatattvasaṃhitā: The Earliest Surviving Śaiva Tantra*. Vol. 1, *A Critical Edition & Annotated Translation of the Mūlasūtra, Uttarasūtra & Nayasūtra*. Pondicherry: Institut Français de Pondichéry.

Goodall, Dominic, and Marion Rastelli, eds. 2013. *Tāntrikābhidhānakośa III. A Dictionary of Technical Terms from Hindu Tantric Literature*. Beiträge zur Kultur- und Geistesgeschichte Asiens, no. 76. Vienna: Verlag der Österreichischen Akademie der Wissenschaften.

Goold, G. P., ed. and tr. 1995. *Chariton. Callirhoe*. Loeb Classical Library, 481. Cambridge, MA: Harvard University Press.

Gordon, Richard. 1999. "Imagining Greek and Roman Magic." In Ankarloo and Clark, eds., *Witchcraft and Magic in Europe*, pp. 161–275.

Gotein, S. D., and Mordechai Akiva Friedman. 2008. *India Traders of the Middle Ages: Documents from the Cairo Geniza ('India Book')*. Leiden: Brill.

Gould, Stephen Jay. 1989. *Wonderful Life: The Burgess Shale and the Nature of History*. New York: Norton & Company.

Gower, John. *Confessio Amantis*. See Peck 2006.

Graça da Silva, Sara, and Jamshid J. Tehrani. 2016. "Comparative Phylogenetic Analyses Uncover the Ancient Roots of Indo-European folktales." *Royal Society Open Science* 3:150645, pp. 1–11. Online at http://dx.doi.org/10.1098/rsos.150645. Accessed August 5, 2018.

Graf, Fritz. 1997. *Magic in the Ancient World.* Cambridge, MA: Harvard University Press.

———. 2014. "Victimology; or, How to Deal with Untimely Death." In Stratton and Kalleres, eds., *Daughters of Hecate*, pp. 386–417.

Granoff, Phyllis. 2004. "Images and Their Ritual Use in Medieval India: Hesitations and Contradictions." In Phyllis Granoff and Koichi Shinohara, eds., *Images in Asian Religions: Texts and Contexts*, pp. 19–55. Vancouver: University of British Columbia Press.

Graus, Frantisek. 1965. *Volk, Herrscher und Heiliger im Reich der Merovinger: Studien zur Hagiographie des Merovingerzeit.* Prague: Nakladatelsvi Ceskoslovenske Academie.

Graves, Robert. 1973. *The Greek Myths.* Vol. 1. Reprint of 1957 rev. ed. Harmondsworth: Penguin.

———. 1990. *The Greek Myths.* Vol. 2. Reprint of 1957 rev. ed. Harmondsworth: Penguin.

Gray, David B. 2007. *The Cakrasamvara Tantra (The Discourse of Śrī Heruka) Śrīherukābhidhāna: A Study and Annotated Translation.* New York: American Institute of Buddhist Studies.

———. 2012. *The Cakrasamvara Tantra (The Discourse of Śrī Heruka). Editions of the Sanskrit and Tibetan Texts.* New York: American Institute of Buddhist Studies.

Gregory of Tours. *Liber in Gloria Confessorum.* In Migne, ed., *Patrologiae Cursus Completus*, Series Latina, vol. 79.

Grenet, Frantz. 1996. "Les marchands sogdiens dans les mers du Sud à l'époque préislamique." *Cahiers d'Asie Centrale* 1, no. 2: 65–84.

———. 2002. "Pour une nouvelle visite à la 'vision de Kerdīr.'" *Studia Asiatica* 3, nos. 1–2: 5–28.

———. 2006. "Iranian Gods in Hindu Garb: The Zoroastrian Pantheon of the Bactrians and Sogdians, Second-Eighth Centuries." *Bulletin of the Asia Institute*, n.s., 20:87–99.

———. 2011. "Quelques nouvelles notes sur Kerdīr et 'sa' vision." In R. Gyselen and Chr. Jullien, eds. *Rabbo l'olmyn. Florilège offert à Philippe Gignoux pour son 80ᵉ anniversaire*, pp. 123–39. Paris: Association pour l'Avancement des Etudes Iraniennes.

———. 2015. "Zoroastrianism among the Kushans." In Harry Falk, ed., *Kushan Histories: Literary Sources and Selected Papers from a Symposium at Berlin, December 5 to 7, 2013*, pp. 206–37. Bremen: Hempen Verlag.

———. 2016. "Transferts magiques et démoniaques de l'Orient romain à l'Asie central." In Espagne et al., eds., *Asie Centrale*, pp. 213–28.

Grether, Holly Jane. 2010. "Burning Demons and Sprinkling Mantras: A History of Fire Sacrifice in South and Central Asia." PhD dissertation, University of California, Santa Barbara.

Grimm, Jakob. 1999. *Teutonic Mythology.* Vol. 2. Translated by James Steven Stallybrass. London: George Bell & Sons, 1883; reprint Routledge/Thoemmes Press.

Gross, Charles G. 1999. "The Fire That Comes from the Eye." *The Neuroscientist* 5, no. 1: 58–64.

Guenzi, Caterina. 2013. *Les discours du destin: La pratique de l'astrologie à Bénarès.* Paris: CNRS Éditions.

Guha, Ramachandra. 1995. "Subaltern and Bhadralok Studies." *Economic and Political Weekly*, August 19, pp. 2056–58.

Guyénot, Laurent. 2011. *La mort féerique: Anthropologie du merveilleux, XIIᵉ–XVᵉ siècle.* Paris: Gallimard.

Guyonvarc'h, Christian-Joseph, tr. 1994. *La Razzia des vaches de Cooley.* Paris: Gallimard.

Gwynn, Edward. 1913. *The Metrical Dindshenchas*, III. Royal Irish Academy, Todd Lecture Series, vol. 10. Online at http://www.ucc.ie/celt/online/T106500C/. Accessed July 15, 2016.

———. 1924. *The Metrical Dindshenchas*, IV. Royal Irish Academy, Todd Lecture Series, vol. 11. Dublin: Hodges, Figgis, & Co.

Haak, Wolfgang, et al. 2015. "Massive Migration from the Steppe Was a Source for Indo-European Languages in Europe." *Nature* 512 (June 11): 207–20.

Haastrup, Ulla, and Robert Egevang, eds. 1985. *Danske Kalkmalerier: Gotik 1375–1475*. København: Nationalmuseet.

Hackett, William. 1861–62. "The Irish Bacach, or Professional Beggar." *Ulster Journal of Archaeology*, 1st series, 9:256–71.

Hahn, Thomas, ed. 1995. *Sir Gawain: Eleven Romances and Tales*. Kalamazoo: Medieval Institute Publications, Western Michigan University.

Hamilton, George L. 1911. "Storm-Making Springs: Rings of Invisibility and Protection—Studies on the Sources of the *Yvain* of Chretien de Troies." *Romantic Review* 2, no. 4 (Oct.–Dec.): 355–75.

Hanway, Jonas. 1753. *An Historical Account of the British Trade over the Caspian Sea: With a Journal of Travels from London through Russia into Persia; and back again through Russia, Germany, and Holland*. Vol. 1. London: Sold by Mr. Dodsley [etc.].

Harf-Lancner, Laurence. 1984. *Les fées au Moyen Âge: Morgane et Mélusine, la naissance des fées*. Paris: Honoré Champion.

———. 2003. *Le monde des fées dans l'occident médiéval*. Paris: Hachette.

———. 2005. "Des fées et des morts: La légende des fils de la Morte dans le *De nugis curialium* de Gautier Map." In Francis Gingras et al., eds., *"Furent les Merveilles Pruvees et les Aventures Truvees": Hommage à Francis Dubost*, pp. 320–31. Paris: Honoré Champion.

Harivaṃśa. See Vaidya 1969.

Harlé, Edouard. 1917. "Chiffons sur des buissons, au bord d'une source." *Bulletin de la Société préhistorique de France* 14, no. 9: 441–42.

———. 1919. "Chiffons au bord de sources et sous dans la main des morts." *Bulletin de la Société préhistorique de France* 16, no. 11: 369–71.

Hartland, E. Sidney. 1893. "Pin-Wells and Rag-Bushes." *Folklore* 4, no. 4: 451–70.

Hastings, James (Sir), et al., eds. 1908–27. *Encyclopædia of Religion and Ethics*. 13 vols. New York: Charles Scribner's Sons.

Hatt, Jean-Jacques. 1950. "La vision de Constantin au sanctuaire de Grand et l'origine celtique du labarum." *Latomus* 9, no. 4 (Oct.–Dec.): 427–36.

Heliodorus. *Aethiopica*. See Athenian Society 1897.

"Helmand River." 2003. In Ehsan Yarshater, ed., *Encyclopædia Iranica*, vol. 12, fasc. 2, pp. 170–76. Online at http://www.iranicaonline.org/articles/helmand-river. Accessed August 11, 2015.

Hemavijaya. *Kathāratnākara*. See Municandrasuri 1997.

Henken, Elissa R. 2002. "Owain (sixth century) [Owein, Owein ab Urien]." In Lindahl, McNamara, and Lindow, eds., *Medieval Folklore*, pp. 306–7.

Hennard Dutheil de la Rochère, Martine, and Véronique Dasen. 2011. "Des *Fata* aux fées: regards croisés de l'Antiquité à nos jours." *Études de Lettres* 289 (2011): 15–34.

Henning, W. B. 1947. "Two Manichæan Magical Texts with an Excursus on the Parthian ending -ēndēh." *Bulletin of the School of Oriental and African Studies* 12, no. 1: 39–66.

Henry, René, ed. and tr. 1947. *Ctésias, le Perse, l'Inde: Les sommaires de Photius*. Brussels: Lebegue.

Hesychius of Alexandria. *Lexikon*. See Schmidt 1868; Latte 1966.

Hett, W. S., tr. 1957. *Aristotle: On the Soul, Parva Naturalia, On Breath*. Loeb Classical Library, 288. Cambridge, MA: Harvard University Press.

Heubeck, Alfred, and Arie Hoekstra. 1989. *A Commentary on Homer's Odyssey*. Vol. 2. Oxford: Clarendon Press.

Hidas, Gergely. 2012. *Mahāpratisarā-Mahāvidyārājñī: The Great Amulet, Great Queen of Spells; Introduction, Critical Editions, and Annotated Translation*. New Delhi: Aditya Prakashan.

Hiltebeitel, Alf. 1976. *The Ritual of Battle: Krishna in the Mahābhārata*. Ithaca, NY: Cornell University Press.

Hintze, Almut. 1994. *Der Zamyād Yašt: Edition, Übersetzung, Kommentar*. Weisbaden: Dr. Ludwig Reichert Verlag.

———. 2014. "Yašts." In Ehsan Yarshater, ed., *Encyclopædia Iranica*. Online at http://www.iranicaonline.org/articles/yashts. Accessed February 20, 2017.

Hoernle, August Friedrich Rudolf. 1893–1912. *The Bower Manuscript; facsimile leaves, Nagari transcript, romanised transliteration and English translation with notes*. 3 vols. Calcutta: Archeological Survey of India. Online at http://gretil/sub.uni-goettingen.de/gretil/1_sanskr/6_sastra/7_ayur/bowermsu.htm (input by Klaus Wille). Accessed February 3, 2018.

Holt, John Clifford. 1996. *The Religious World of Kīrti Śrī. Buddhism, Art, and Politics in Late Medieval Sri Lanka*. New York: Oxford University Press.

———. 2004. "Sri Lanka." In Robert E. Buswell, Jr., et al., eds., *Encyclopedia of Buddhism*, vol. 1, pp. 795–99. New York: Macmillan Reference.

Homer. *Odyssey*. See Murray 1966.

Hooke, Della. 2013. "Christianity and the 'Sacred Tree.'" In Michael D. J. Bintley and Michael G. Shapland, eds., *Trees and Timber in the Anglo-Saxon World*, pp. 228–50. London: Oxford University Press.

Houdebert, Aurélie, and Pauline Lambert. 2017. *Chrétien de Troyes: Le Chevalier au lion*. Neuilly-sur-Seine: Atlantide.

Humbach, Helmut, and Pallan R. Ichaporia. 1998. *Zamyād Yasht: Yasht 19 of the Younger Avesta; Text, Translation, and Commentary*. Wiesbaden: Harrassowitz.

Hunt, Robert. 1908. *Popular Romances of the West of England, or the Drolls, Traditions and Superstitions of Old Cornwall*. London: Chatto & Windus.

Huntingford, G. W. B., tr. 1980. *The Periplus of the Erythraean Sea by an unknown author with some Extracts from Agatharkides 'On the Erythraean Sea.'* London: Hakluyt Society.

Husain, Mahdi. 1976. *Reḥla (India, Maldive Islands and Ceylon)*. Baroda: Oriental Institute.

Ibn Battuta. *Reḥla*. See Husain 1976.

Ideler, Julius Ludwig. 1841. *Physici et medici Graeci minores*. Vol. 1. Berlin: Reimeri. Online at https://archive.org/details/physicietmedicig01ideluoft. Accessed January 29, 2018.

Inglebert, Hervé. 2009. "Les relations entre le Daquin (l'empire romain) et le pays de Sères (l'empire chinois)." In Thierry Piel, ed., *Figures et expressions du pouvoir dans l'Antiquité*, pp. 127–41. Rennes: Presses Universitaires de Rennes. Online at https://books.openedition.org/pur/25883#text. Accessed April 28, 2019.

Jacobsen, Knut A., ed. 2012. *Yoga Powers: Extraordinary Capacities Attained Through Meditation and Concentration*. Leiden: Brill.

Jamison, Stephanie W. 2016. "Of Animals and (Wo)men: Traditional Philology and New Paradigms for Studying the Past." In Asko Parpola and Petteri Koskikallio, eds., *Vedic Investigations*, pp. 235–50. Delhi: Motilal Banarsidass.

Jamison, Stephanie W., and Joel P. Brereton. 2014. *The Rigveda: The Earliest Religious Poetry of India*. 3 vols. New York: Oxford University Press.

Jaski, Bart. 2000. *Early Irish Kingship and Succession*. Dublin: Four Courts Press.

Jātakas. See Fausböll 1877; Fausböll 1879; Chalmers 1895.

Jayakar, A. S. G., tr. 1908. *Ad-Damîrî's Ḥayât al-Ḥayawân (A Zoological Lexicon)*, vol. 2, part 1. London: Luzac & Co.; Bombay: D. B. Taraporevala Sons & Co.

Jayākhya Saṃhitā. See Krishnamacharya 1967.

Jayaratha. *Haracaritacintāmaṇi*. See Sivadatt and Parab 1983.

Jetly, J. S., and Vasant G. Parikh, eds. 1991. *Nyāyakandalī, being a commentary on Praśastapādabhāṣya, with three sub-commentaries*. Gaekwad's Oriental Series, no. 174. Baroda: Oriental Institute.

Jha, Ramchandra. 1991. *Pañcatantra*. 6th ed. Benares: Chowkhamba Vidyabhavan. Online at http://gretil.sub.uni-goettingen.de/gretil/1_sanskr/5_poetry/4_narr/vispancu.htm.

Jinaratna. *Līlāvatīsāra*. See Fynes 2005–6.

John of Salisbury. *Policraticus*. See Webb 1965; Boudet 2006.

Johnson, Janet H. 1992. "Introduction to the Demotic Magical Papyri." In Betz, *Greek Magical Papyri*, pp. lv–lviii.

Johnson, Steven. 2019. "Colleges Lose a 'Stunning' 651 Foreign-Language Programs in 3 Years." *Chronicle of Higher Education*, January 22. Online at https://www.chronicle.com/article/Colleges-Lose-a-Stunning-/245526.

Johnston, Sarah Iles. 1999. *Restless Dead: Encounters between the Living and the Dead in Ancient Greece*. Berkeley: University of California Press.

———. 2001. "Charming Children: The Use of the Child in Ancient Divination." *Arethusa* 34:97–117.

Jones, Christopher P., ed. and tr. 2005. *Philostratus, the Life of Apollonius of Tyana*. Vol. 1. Loeb Classical Library, 16. Cambridge, MA: Harvard University Press.

Jones, Frances. 1954. *The Holy Wells of Wales*. Cardiff: University of Wales Press.

Jones, W. H. S., tr. 1918. *Pausanias Description of Greece*. Vol. 1, books 1–2 (Attica and Corinth). Loeb Classical Library, 93. Cambridge, MA: Harvard University Press.

———, tr. 1933. *Pausanias Description of Greece*. Vol. 3, books 6–8.21 (Elis 2, Achaia, Arcadia). Loeb Classical Library, 272. Cambridge, MA: Harvard University Press.

Jørgensen, Marie-Louise, and Hugo Johannsen. 1981. "Undløse Kirke." In *Danmarks Kirker*, 4.1.5, pp. 357–97. København: Nationalmuseet.

———. 1983. "Skamstrup Kirke." In *Danmarks Kirker*, 4.2.9, pp. 809–46. København: Nationalmuseet.

Joshi, Damodar, ed. and tr. 2011. *Rasaprakāśa Sudhākara*. New Delhi: Indian National Science Academy.

Joshi, Prayag. 1977. "Kumāūnī lok-vārtāoṃ meṃ guru Gorakhnāth aur bārah nām vairāgī." In Gopinath Tiwari Ramlal, ed., *"Gorakh" Viśeṣāṅk*, pp. 242–47. Gorakhpur: Gorakhnath Mandir.

Kākacaṇḍīśvarakalpatantra. See Pandey 2003.

Kalhaṇa. *Rājataraṅgiṇī*. See Stein 1979; Pandey 1985.

Kalleres, Dayna S. 2015. *City of Demons. Violence, Ritual, and Christian Power in Late Antiquity*. Berkeley: University of California Press.

Kanga, M. F. 1987. "Astwihād." In Ehsan Yarshater, ed., *Encyclopædia Iranica*, vol. 2, fasc. 8, p. 873. Online at http://www.iranicaonline.org/articles/astwihad-av.

Kapferer, Bruce. 1991. *A Celebration of Demons. Exorcism, and the Aesthetics of Healing in Sri Lanka*. Washington, DC: Smithsonian Institution Press.

Karetzky, Patricia Eichenbaum. 2012. "The Image of the Winged Celestial and Its Travels along the Silk Road." *Sino-Platonic Papers*, no. 225. Online at http://sino-platonic.org/complete/spp225_winged_celestial_silk_road.pdf. Accessed August 27, 2018.

Kashikar, C. G., and N. S. Sontakke. 1936. *Ṛgveda-Saṃhitā with the Commentary of Sāyaṇācārya*. Vol. 2. Poona: Vaidika Samshodana Mandala.

Kāśyapa Saṃhitā. See Sharma 1998; Tewari 1996.

Kauśika Sūtra. See Bloomfield 1972.

Keḷadi Basava. *Śivatattvaratnākara*. See Rama Shastry 1969.

Kellens, Jean. 2016. *Cinq Cours sur les Yašts de l'Avesta*. Paris: Association pour l'Avancement des Études Iraniennes.

Kelly, Patricia. 1992. "The Táin as Literature." In Mallory, ed., *Aspects of the Táin*, pp. 69–102.

Kessler, Oliver. 2016. "Environment, Infrastructure and Nature of Ports in Ancient Sri Lanka: Archaeological Evidence from the Port, Monastery, Town and Shipwreck of Godavaya (*Godapavata Pattana*)." In Boussac, Salles, and Yon, eds., *Ports of the Ancient Indian Ocean*, pp. 435–58.

Ketelaar, James. 2006. "The Non-Modern Confronts the Modern: Dating the Buddha in Japan." *History and Theory* 45:62–79.

Khan, Shafaat Ahmad. 1927. *John Marshall in India: Notes and Observations in Bengal 1668–1672*. London: Oxford University Press.

Kibler, William W., ed. and tr. 1985. *Chrétien de Troyes. The Knight with the Lion, or Yvain (Le Chevalier au Lion)*. New York: Garland.

Kieckhefer, Richard. 1998. *Forbidden Rites: A Necromancer's Manual of the Fifteenth Century*. University Park: Pennsylvania State University Press.

Knipe, David M. 1989. "Night of the Growing Dead: A Cult of Vīrabhadra in Coastal Andhra." In Alf Hiltebeitel, ed., *Criminal Gods and Demon Devotees: Essays on the Guardians of Popular Hinduism*, pp. 123–56. Albany: State University of New York Press.

———. 1995. "Softening the Cruelty of God: Folklore, Ritual and the Planet Śani (Saturn) in Southeast India." In David Shulman, ed., *Syllables of Sky: Studies in South Indian Civilization in Honour of Velcheru Narayana Rao*, pp. 206–48. Delhi: Oxford University Press.

Krauskopff, Gisèle. 1989. *Maîtres et possédés: Les rites et l'ordre social chez les Tharu (Népal)*. Paris: Editions du CNRS.

Krishnamachariar, Madabhushi. 1937. *History of Classical Sanskrit Literature*. Delhi: Motilal Banarsidass.

Krishnamacharya, E., ed. 1967. *Jayākhya Saṃhitā of Pāñcarātra Āgama*. Baroda: Oriental Institute.

Kritzer, Robert. 2014a. *"Garbhāvakrāntisūtra": The Sūtra on Entry into the Womb*. Tokyo: International Institute for Buddhist Studies.

———. 2014b. "Affliction and Infestation in an Indian Buddhist Embryological Sutra." In Richard K. Payne, ed., *Scripture, Canon, Text, Context: Studies Honoring Lewis Lancaster*, pp. 181–202. Berkeley, CA: Institute of Buddhist Studies and BDK America, Inc.

Kriyākālaguṇottara. See Slouber 2017.

Kroonenberg, Salomon Bernard. 2013. *Why Hell Stinks of Sulfur: Mythology and Geology of the Underworld*. Chicago: University of Chicago Press/Reaktion Books.

Krusch, Bruno, and Wilhelm Levison. 1910. *Passiones Vitaeque Sanctorum Aevi Merovingici (Scriptorum Rerum Merovingicarum)*. Vol. 5. Monumenta Germaniae Historica. Hannover: Hahn.

Kumamoto, Hiroshi. 2005. "Paul Pelliot and the *Deśanā-parivarta* of the *Suvarṇaprabhāsa-sūtra*." *Bulletin of the Asia Institute, a Non-Profit Corporation*, n.s., 19:77–82.

Kumar, Pushpendra, ed. 1984. *The Matsya Mahāpurāṇa: Reprinted from the edition of Khemraj Shrikrishan, Dass*. New Delhi: Meharchand Lachhmandas.

Lam, Raymond. 2013. "Kuṣāṇa Emperors and Indian Buddhism: Political and Cultural Factors Responsible for the Spread of Buddhism through Eurasia." *South Asia: Journal of South Asian Studies* 36, no. 3: 434–48.

Lambert, Pierre-Yves. 2003. *La langue gauloise*. Paris: Errance.

Lambourne, Elizabeth. 2016. "'Describing a Lost Camel'—Clues for West Asian Mercantile Networks in South Asian Maritime Trade (Tenth–Twelfth Centuries AD)." In Boussac, Salles, and Yon, eds., *Ports of the Ancient Indian Ocean*, pp. 351–407.

Laṅkāvatārasūtra. See Vaidya 1963.

Larson, Jennifer. 2001. *Greek Nymphs: Myth, Cult, Lore*. New York: Oxford University Press.

Latte, Kurt. 1966. *Hesychii Alexandrini Lexicon. Recensuit et Emendavit*. Vol. 2. København: Einar Munksgaard.

Laurier, Sébastien. 2016. *Into ze Landes: Une quête de sources et de guérison*. Bordeaux: Elytis.

La Vaissière, Étienne de. 2002. *Histoire des marchands sogdiens*. Paris: Collège de France, Institut des Hautes Études Chinoises.

Lavaud, Patrick. 1986. "Rituels de guérison et fontaines thérapeutiques: L'exemple de la Grande-Lande." MA thesis, Université de Bordeaux II.

Law, Bimal Churn. 1933. *A History of Pāli Literature*. Vol. 1. London: Kegan Paul, Tranch, Trubner & Co., Ltd.

Le Borgne, Aude. 2002. "Clootie Wells and Water-Kelpies: An Ethnological Approach to the Fresh Water Traditions of Sacred Wells and Supernatural Horses in Scotland." PhD dissertation, University of Edinburgh.

Lecoy de la Marche, A. 1877. *Anecdotes Historiques: Légendes et Apologies tirés du recueil inédit d'Étienne de Bourbon, Dominicain du XIIIe siècle*. Paris: Renouard.

Lecuyot, Guy. 2007. "Ai Khanum Reconstructed." In Joe Cribb and Georgina Hermann, eds., *After Alexander: Central Asia before Islam*, pp. 155–62. Oxford: Oxford University Press.

Lefebvre, F.-A. (Abbé). 1888. *Sainte Godeleine: Son culte et ses reliques*. Arras: Sueur-Charruez.

Le Goff, Jacques. 1977. *Pour un autre Moyen-Âge: Temps, travail et culture en Occident*. Paris: Gallimard.

Legros, Elisée. 1952. "Trois récits de lutins et de fées dans le folklore wallon et le folklore comparé." *Enquêtes du Musée de la Vie Wallone* 6.65–68, pp. 129–227.

———. 1964. "Trois récits de lutins et de fées dans le folklore wallon et le folklore comparé." *Enquêtes du Musée de la Vie Wallone* 10.113–116, pp. 129–60.

———. 1967. "Trois récits de lutins et de fées dans le folklore wallon et le folklore comparé." *Enquêtes du Musée de la Vie Wallone* 11.125–128, pp. 129–59.

Lescarret, J.-P. 1980. "Fontaines consacrées et saints guérisseurs dans la Haute-Lande et ses régions limitrophes." In *Mélanges de mythologie française offerts au Président-Fondateur Henri Dontenville*, pp. 171–82. Paris: Maisonneuve et La Rose.

Le Strange, Guy, tr. 1919. *The Geographical Part of the "Nuzhat-al-Qulūb" Composed by Ḥamd-allāḥ Mustawfī of Qazwīn in 740 (1340)*. Leiden: Brill; London: Luzac & Co.

Leumann, Ernst. 1966. *Das Aupapâtika Sûtra, erstes Upânga der Jaina*. Part 1. Leipzig, 1883; reprint Nedeln, Lichtenstein: Kraus Reprint, Ltd.

Lévi, Sylvain. 1915. "Le catalogue géographique des yakṣa dans la Mahāmāyūrī." *Journal Asiatique*, 11th series, 5:19–138.

———. 1934. "Devaputra." *Journal Asiatique* 224 (Jan.–Mar.): 1–21.

Lewis, Todd. 1995. "Story of Siṃhala, the Caravan Leader." In Donald Lopez, Jr., ed., *Buddhism in Practice*, pp. 151–69. Princeton, NJ: Princeton University Press.

Liddell, Henry George, and Robert Scott. 1996. *A Greek-English Lexicon*. 9th ed., with a revised supplement. Oxford: Clarendon Press.

Lincoln, Bruce. 1985. "Notes toward a Theory of Religion and Revolution." In Bruce Lincoln, ed., *Religion, Rebellion, Revolution: An Interdisciplinary and Cross-Cultural Collection of Essays*, pp. 266–92. Basingstoke: Macmillan.

———. 1986. *Myth, Cosmos, and Society: Indo-European Themes of Creation and Destruction.* Cambridge, MA: Harvard University Press.

———. 1991. *Death, War, and Sacrifice: Studies in Ideology and Practice.* Chicago: University of Chicago Press.

———. 1994. *Authority: Construction and Corrosion.* Chicago: University of Chicago Press.

———. 1999. *Theorizing Myth: Narrative, Ideology, and Scholarship.* Chicago: University of Chicago Press.

———. 2012. *Gods and Demons, Priests and Scholars: Critical Explorations in the History of Religions.* Chicago: University of Chicago Press.

———. 2014. *Discourse and the Construction of Society: Comparative Studies of Myth, Ritual, and Classification.* 2nd ed. New York: Oxford University Press.

———. 2018. *Apples and Oranges: Explorations In, On, and With Comparison.* Chicago: University of Chicago Press.

Lindahl, Carl. 2002. "Folklore." In Lindahl, McNamara, and Lindow, eds., *Medieval Folklore,* pp. 142–48.

Lindahl, Carl, John McNamara, and John Lindow, eds. 2002. *Medieval Folklore: A Guide to Myths, Legends, Tales, Beliefs, and Customs.* New York: Oxford University Press.

Littleton, F. Scott, and Linda A. Malcor. 1994. *From Scythia to Camelot: A Radical Reassessment of the Legends of King Arthur, the Knights of the Round Table, and the Holy Grail.* New York: Garland.

Lockhart, Laurence. 1939. "Iranian Petroleum in Ancient and Medieval Times." *Journal of the Institute of Petroleum Technology* 25, no. 183: 1–18.

Lohuizen-de Leeuw, J. E. van. 1975. "The Contribution of Foreign Nomads to the Culture of the Indian Subcontinent." In Lawrence Saadia Leshnik and Günther-Dietz Sontheimer, eds., *Pastoralists and Nomads in South Asia,* pp. 16–29. Wiesbaden: Otto Harrassowitz.

Lord, Albert B. 1995. "Oral Composition and 'Oral Residue' in the Middle Ages." In Nicolaisen, ed., *Oral Tradition in the Middle Ages,* pp. 7–29.

Lorenzen, David N. 1972. *Kāpālikas and Kālāmukhas: Two Lost Śaivite Sects.* New Delhi: Thomson Press.

Luther, Martin. *Tischreden.* See Drescher et al. 1916, 1919.

Macdonnell, Arthur A. 1897. *Vedic Mythology.* Strassburg: Karl J. Trübner.

MacKenzie, D. N. 1971. *A Concise Pahlavi Dictionary.* London: Oxford University Press.

Mac Mathúna, Séamus. 2010. "Sacred Landscape and Water Mythology in Early Ireland and Ancient India." In Maxim Fomin, Séamus Mac Mathúna, and Victoria Vertogradova, eds., *Sacred Topology of Early Ireland and Ancient India.* Washington, DC: Institute for the Study of Man.

MacMullen, Ramsey. 1997. *Christianity and Paganism in the Fourth to Eighth Centuries.* New Haven, CT: Yale University Press.

Madhavananda, Swami. 1942. *Vedānta-Paribhāṣā of Dharmarāja Adhvarīndra.* Howrah: Ramakrishna Mission.

Mahābhārata. See Sukthankar et al. 1927–66; Dandekar 1971, 1975; Buitenen 1975; Smith 2009.

Mahāmāyūrīvidyārājñī. See Takubo 1972.

Mahānāma. *Mahāvaṃsa.* See Geiger 1908; Geiger and Bode 1912; Malalasekera 1977.

Mahāpratisarā-Mahāvidyārājñī. See Hidas 2012.

Mak, Bill M. 2013. "The Date and Nature of Sphujidhvaja's *Yavanajātaka* Reconsidered in the Light of Some Newly Discovered Materials." *History of Science in South Asia* 1:1–20.

Malalasekera, G. P., ed. 1977. *Vaṃsatthappakāsinī Commentary on the Mahāvaṃsa.* Vol. 1. London: Routledge & Kegan Paul, Ltd.

Malamoud, Charles. 1989. *Cuire le monde: Rite et pensée dans l'Inde ancienne*. Paris: Editions de la Découverte.

Malandra, William W. 2014. "Vāyu." In Ehsan Yarshater, ed., *Encyclopædia Iranica*. Online at http://www.iranicaonline.org/articles/vayu. Accessed January 2, 2018.

Mallārinābha. *Rasakautuka*. Anup Sanskrit Library, Bikaner, mss. 4203.

Mallory, J. P., ed. 1992. *Aspects of the Táin*. Belfast: December Publications.

Maloney, Clarence, ed. 1976. *The Evil Eye*. New York: Columbia University Press.

Mānava Gṛhya Sūtra. See Sastri 1926.

Mandelbaum, David. 1966. "Transcendental and Pragmatic Aspects of Religion." *American Anthropologist* 68, no. 1 (Oct.): 175–91.

Mann, Jill, ed. 2005. *The Canterbury Tales: Geoffrey Chaucer*. London: Penguin Classics.

Marchant, Annick. 2013. "Arbres à clous et arbres à loques." *Les Cahiers Nouveaux* 86:87–91. Online at http://lampspw.wallonie.be/dgo4/tinymvc/apps/cahiers/views/documents/flipping Book/CN86/CN86/assets/basic-html/index.html#1. Accessed June 29, 2018.

Marchetto, Monia, and Manuel Martin Hoefer. 2016. "Fron Iron to Sapphire: Indian Myths and Rituals about Saturn, the Implacable Lord of the Celestial Spheres." In Ferrari and Dähnhardt, eds., *Soulless Matter*, pp. 51–69.

Marcotte, Didier. 2016. "*Le Périple de la mer Érythrée* et les informateurs de Ptolémée." *Journal Asiatique* 304, no. 1: 33–46.

———, ed. 2017a. *Méditerranée et Océan Indien: Deux mondes en miroir. Topoi* Supplément 15. Lyon: Maison de l'Orient et de la Méditerranée Jean Pouilloux.

———. 2017b. "Avant-Propos." In Marcotte, ed., *Méditerranée et Océan Indien*, pp. 5–11.

Marliave, Olivier de. 2018. *Guide des Sources Guérisseuses des Landes de Gascogne*. Bordeaux: Éditions Sud-Ouest.

Marriott, McKim. 1976. "Hindu Transactions: Diversity without Dualism." In Bruce Kapferer, ed., *Transaction and Meaning: Directions in the Anthropology of Exchange and Symbolic Behavior*, pp. 109–42. Philadelphia: Institute for the Study of Human Issues.

Martianus Capella. *De Nuptiis Philologiae et Mercurii*. See Stahl and Johnson 1977.

Marx-Wolf, Heidi. 2016. *Spiritual Taxonomies and Ritual Authority. Platonists, Priests and Gnostics in the Third Century C.E.* Philadelphia: University of Pennsylvania Press.

Matsya Purāṇa. See Kumar 1984.

Maxwell-Stuart, P. G. 2000. *Martín del Rio: Investigations into Magic*. Manchester: Manchester University Press.

Mayaram, Shail. 1999. "Spirit Possession: Reframing Discourses of the Self and Other." In Assayag and Tarabout, eds., *La Possession en Asie du Sud*, pp. 101–31.

Maynadier, G. Howard. 1901. *The Wife of Bath's Tale: Its Sources and Analogues*. London: D. Nutt.

McCulloch, John Abnott. 1910. "Changeling." In Hastings et al., eds., *Encyclopædia of Religion and Ethics*, vol. 3, pp. 358–63.

McGregor, R. S. 1995. *The Oxford Hindi-English Dictionary*. Oxford: Oxford University Press.

Mees, Bernard. 2007. "Chamalières *sníeθθic* and 'binding' in Celtic." *Journal of Indo-European Studies* 35, nos. 1–2 (Spring–Summer): 9–30.

Meid, Wolfgang. 1994. *Gaulish Inscriptions. Their interpretation in the light of archaeological evidence and their value as a source of linguistic and sociological information*. 2nd, rev. ed. Budapest: Archaeolingua Alapítvány.

Menasce, Jean de, ed. 1973. *Le troisième livre du Dēnkart, Traduit du pehlevi*. Paris: Klincksieck.

Merutuṅga. *Prabandhacintāmaṇi*. See Tawney 1899; Sastri 1932.

Meulenbeld, G. Jan. 1999. *A History of Indian Medical Literature*. Vol. 2A. Groningen: Egbert Forsten.

———. 2000. *A History of Indian Medical Literature*. Vol. 1B. Groningen: Egbert Forsten.

Mevissen, Gerd J. R. 1991. "The Indian Connection: Images of Deified Spells in the Arts of Northern Buddhism, Part II." *Silk Road Art and Archaeology* 2:351–82.

———. 1999. "Images of Mahāpratisarā in Bengal: Their Iconographic Links with Javanese, Central Asian and East Asian Images." *Journal of Bengal Art* 4:99–129.

Michon, Daniel. 2015. *Archaeology and Religion in Early Northwest India: History, Theory, Practice*. London: Routledge.

Migne, Jean-Paul, ed. 1841–66. *Patrologiae Cursus Completus*. Series Latina. 221 vols. Paris: Imprimerie Catholique.

———, ed. 1857–64. *Patrologiae Cursus Completus*. Series Graeca. 161 vols. Paris: Imprimerie Catholique.

Minar, Edwin L., F. H. Sandbach, and W. C. Helmbold. 1961. *Plutarch. Moralia*. Vol. 9. Loeb Classical Library, 425. Cambridge, MA: Harvard University Press.

Minard, Antoine. 2002. "Breton Folk Narrative." PhD dissertation, University of California, Los Angeles.

Mines, Diane. 2005. *Fierce Gods: Inequality, Ritual, and the Politics of Dignity in a South Indian Village*. Bloomington: Indiana University Press.

Misra, Siddhinandan, ed. and Hindi tr. 1984. *Rasendracūḍāmaṇi of Somadeva*. Varanasi: Chowkhambha Orientalia.

Mitra, Kalipada. 1939. "Magic and Miracle in Jain Literature." *Indian Historical Quarterly* 15, no. 2: 175–82.

Mitterwallner, Gritli von. 1984. "Evolution of the Liṅga." In Michael Meister, ed., *Discourses on Śiva: Proceedings of a Symposium on the Nature of Religious Imagery*, pp. 12–31. Philadelphia: University of Pennsylvania Press.

Modak, B. R. 1993. *The Ancillary Literature of the Atharva-Veda: A Study with Special Reference to the Pariśiṣṭas*. New Delhi: Rashtriya Veda Vidya Pratishthan.

Mokhtarian, Jason Sion. 2015. *Rabbis, Sorcerers, Kings, and Priests: The Culture of the Talmud in Ancient Iran*. Berkeley: University of California Press.

Møller, J. S. 1940. *Moder og Barn I Dansk Folkeoverlevering, fra Svangerskab til Daab og Kirkegang*. København: Ejnar Munksgaard.

Monier-Williams, Sir Monier. 1976. *A Dictionary of English and Sanskrit*. 4th Indian edition. Delhi: Motilal Banarsidass.

———. 1984. *A Sanskrit-English Dictionary*. London: Oxford University Press, 1899; reprint Delhi: Motilal Banarsidass.

Morgan, Louise. 1909. "The Source of the Fountain-Story in the 'Ywain.'" *Modern Philology* 6, no. 3 (Jan.): 331–41.

Morris, T. E. 1893. "Sacred Wells in Wales." *Folklore* 4, no. 1: 55–79.

Mukherjee, Rila. 2017. "L'océan Indien, un éspace centrale du système-monde afro-eurasien avant le XVIe siècle." In Marcotte, ed., *Méditerranée et Océan Indien*, pp. 335–87.

Municandrasuri, Vijaya. 1997. *P[aṇḍit] Śrī Hemavijayagaṇiracitaḥ Kathāratnākara (258 Kathātmakaḥ)*. Parsvabhaktinagar: Omkarasahitya Nidhi Charitable Trust.

Murray, A. T. 1966. *Homer. The Odyssey*. Vol. 1. Cambridge, MA: Harvard University Press.

Murthy, S. R. 1979. "An Occurrence of Cinnabar in *Rasārṇavakalpa*." *Indian Journal of History of Science* 14, no. 2: 83–86.

Mus, Paul. 1934. *L'Inde vûe de l'Est: Cultes indiens et indigènes au Champa.* Hanoi: Imprimerie d'Extrême-Orient.

Mustawfī, Ḥamd-allāḥ. *Nuzhat-al-Qulūb.* See Le Strange 1919.

Nabokov, Isabelle. 2000. *Religion against the Self.* Berkeley: University of California Press.

Nagano, Yasuhiko, and Yasuke Ikari, eds. 1993. *From Vedic Altar to Village Shrine: Towards an Interface between Indology and Anthropology.* Senri Ethnological Studies, no. 36. Osaka: National Museum of Ethnology.

Nagy, Joseph Falaky. 2002. "Irish Tradition." In Lindahl, McNamara, and Lindow, eds., *Medieval Folklore*, pp. 212–17.

Natarajan, Kanchana. 2004. "'Divine Semen' and the Alchemical Conversion of Iramatevar." *Medieval History Journal* 7, no. 2: 255–78.

Needham, Joseph, Ho Ping-yu, Lu Gwei-djen, and Nathan Sivin. 2000. *Science and Civilisation in Ancient China.* Vol. 5, part 4. Cambridge: Cambridge University Press.

Netra Tantra. See Shastri 1926, 1939.

Nicolaisen, W. F. H. 1995a. "Introduction." In Nicolaisen, ed., *Oral Tradition in the Middle Ages*, pp. 1–6.

———, ed. 1995b. *Oral Tradition in the Middle Ages.* Binghamton, NY: Medieval & Renaissance Texts & Studies.

Nobel, Johannes. 1958. *Suvarṇaprabhāsottamasūtra, Das Goldglanz-Sūtra: ein Sanskrittext des Mahāyāna-Buddhismus. I-Tsing's chinesische Version und ihre tibetische Übersetzung.* Vol. 1, *I-Tsing's chinesische Version übersetzt, eingeleitet erläutert und mit einem photomechanischen Nachdruck des chinesischen Textes versehen.* Leiden: Brill.

Nooten, Barend A. van, and Gary B. Holland. 1994. *Rigveda: A Metrically Restored Text with Introduction and Notes.* Cambridge, MA: Harvard University Press.

Norman, K. R. 1983. *Pāli Literature: Including the Canonical Literature in Prakrit and Sanskrit of all the Hinayāna Schools of Buddhism.* A History of Indian Literature, vol. 7, fasc. 2. Wiesbaden: Harrassowitz.

Oberoi, Harjot. 1994. *The Construction of Religious Boundaries: Culture, Identity, and Diversity in the Sikh Tradition.* Chicago: University of Chicago Press.

Oesterley, Hermann, ed. 1872. *Gesta Romanorum.* Berlin: Weidmannsche Buchhandlung.

Oettinger, Norbert. 2009. "Zum Verhältnis von *Apąm Nāpat-* und X^{v}arənah- im Avesta." In Éric Pirart and Xavier Tremblay, eds., *Zarathustra entre l'Inde et l'Iran. Etudes indo-iraniennes et indo-européennes offertes à Jean Kellens à l'occasion de son 65ème anniversaire*, pp. 189–96. Wiesbaden: Reichert Verlag.

O'Flaherty, Wendy Doniger. 1980. *Women, Androgynes and Other Mythical Beasts.* Chicago: University of Chicago Press.

———. 1985. *Tales of Sex and Violence: Folklore, Sacrifice and Danger in the "Jaiminīya Brāhmaṇa."* Chicago: University of Chicago Press.

Ogden, Daniel. 1999. "Binding Spells: Curse Tablets and Voodoo Dolls in the Greek and Roman Worlds." In Ankarloo and Clark, *Witchcraft and Magic in Europe*, pp. 1–90.

———. 2012. "Secandar, Dragon-Slayer." In Stoneman, Erikson, and Netton, eds., *The Alexander Romance in Persia and the East*, pp. 277–94.

O'Grady, Standish H., ed. and tr. 1892. *Silva Gadelica (I.-XXXI.): A Collection of Tales in Irish with Extracts Illustrating Persons and Places.* 2 vols. London: Williams & Norgate.

Ó hUiginn, Ruairí. 1992. "The Background and Development of *Táin Bó Cúailnge.*" In Mallory, ed., *Aspects of the Táin*, pp. 29–67.

Oldenberg, Hermann. 1970. "Ṛgveda: Textkritische und exegetische Noten." 2 vols. In *Abhandlungen der Königlichen Gesellschaft der Wissenschaften zu Göttingen*, Philologische-Historische Klasse, n.s., vol. 11. Berlin: Weidmann, 1909; reprint Nendeln, Liechtenstein: Kraus Reprint.

Orofino, Giacomella. 1994. "Divination with Mirrors: Observations on a Simile Found in the Kālacakra Literature." In Per Kværne, ed., *Tibetan Studies*, vol. 2, pp. 612–28. Oslo: Institute for Comparative Research in Human Culture.

Osella, Caroline, and Filippo Osella. 1999. "Seepage of Divinized Power through Social, Spiritual and Bodily Boundaries: Some Aspects of Possession in Kerala." In Assayag and Tarabout, eds., *La Possession en Asie du Sud*, pp. 183–210.

Osto, Douglas. 2009. "'Proto-Tantric' elements in the *Gaṇḍavyūha-sūtra*." *Journal of Religious History* 33, no. 2: 165–77.

O'Sullivan, Daniel. 1853. *Irlande: Poésies des bardes, légendes, ballades, chants populaires*. Paris: Glashin.

Ottonelli, Sergio. 1994. "Un étranger dans le berceau." *Le Monde Alpin et Rhodanien* 22, no. 3: 125–36.

Overbye, Ryan Richard. 2016. "Vicissitudes of Text and Rite in the *Great Peahen Queen of Spells*." In David B. Gray and Ryan Richard Overbye, eds., *Tantric Traditions in Transmission and Translation*, pp. 257–83. New York: Oxford University Press.

Oxford English Dictionary. Online at http://www.oed.com.proxy.library.ucsb.edu:2048. Accessed August 17, 2018.

Paetz, Bernhard. 1970. *Kirke und Odysseus: Überlieferung und Deutung von Homer bis Calderón*. Berlin: Walter de Gruyter & Co.

Page, (Sir) Dennis L. 1973. *Folktales in Homer's Odyssey*. Cambridge, MA: Harvard University Press.

Pal, Pratapaditya. 2003. *Himalayas: An Aesthetic Adventure*. Chicago: Art Institute of Chicago in association with the University of California Press.

Pandey, Gyanendra, ed. 2003. *Kākacaṇḍīśvarakalpatantra*. Varanasi: Chowkhamba Sanskrit Series Office.

Pandey, Ramtej Shastri, ed. 1985. *Mahākavikalhaṇaviracita Rājataraṅgiṇī*. Delhi: Chaukhamba Sanskrit Pratishthan.

Panegyricus Constantino dictus. See Gallettier 1952.

Papas, Alexandre. 2016. "Le *Tugh* dans l'islam du Xinjiang." In Espagne et al., eds., *Asie Centrale*, pp. 343–50.

Parkin, David, and Ruth Barnes, eds. 2002. *Ships and the Development of Maritime Technology in the Indian Ocean*. London: Routledge Curzon.

Parpola, Asko. 2015. *The Roots of Hinduism: The Early Aryans and the Indus Civilization*. New York: Oxford University Press.

Pattelli, Giulia, et al. 2014. "Effects of the November 2012 Flood Event on the Mobilization of Hg from Mount Amiata Mining District to the Sediments of the Paglia River Basin." *Minerals* 4, no. 2: 241–56.

Pausanias. *Hellados Periēgēsis (Description of Greece)*. See Frazer 1898; Jones 1918; Jones 1933.

Peck, Russell L., ed. 2006. *John Gower. Confessio Amantis*, with Latin translations by Andrew Galloway. Vol. 1. Kalamazoo, MI: TEAMS Middle English Texts Series. Online at http://d.lib.rochester.edu/teams/publication/peck-confessio-amantis-volume-1.

Penzer, N. M., ed. 1926. *The Ocean of Story Being C. H. Tawney's Translation of Somadeva's Kathā Sarit Sāgara (Or Ocean of Streams of Story)*. Vol. 6. London: Chas. J. Sawyer Ltd.

Periplus of the Erythraean Sea. See Huntingford 1980.

Pharr, Clyde, tr. 2001. *The Theodosian Code and Novels and the Sirmondian Constitutions*. Union, NJ: Lawbook Exchange, Ltd.

Philostratus. *Life of Apollonius of Tyana*. See Jones 2005.

Picart, Bernard. 1728. *Cérémonies et coutumes religieuses de tous les peuples du monde, représentées par des figures dessinées de la main de Bernard Picart avec des explications historiques et des dissertations curieuses*. Vol. 3. Amsterdam: J. F. Bernard.

Pierreville, Corinne, ed. and tr. 2016. *Chrétien de Troyes: Le chevalier au lion*. Paris: Honoré Champion.

Pignatelli, Cinzia, and Dominique Gerner, eds. 2006. *Traductions françaises des "Otia Imperialia" de Gervais de Tilbury par Jean d'Antioche et Jean de Vignay. Edition de la troisième partie*. Geneva: Droz.

Pinch, William R. 1996. *Peasants and Monks in British India*. Berkeley: University of California Press.

Pingree, David. 1981. *Jyotiḥśāstra: Astral and Mathematical Literature*. Wiesbaden: Otto Harrassowitz.

Pirart, Eric. 2007. *Georges Dumézil face aux démons iraniens*. Paris: L'Harmattan.

Planke, Sverre, et al. 2003. "Mud and Fluid Migration in Active Mud Volcanoes in Azerbaijan." *Geo-Marine Letters* 23, nos. 3–4: 258–68.

Plato. *Phædo*. See Emlyn-Jones and Preddy 2017.

———. *Timaeus*. See Bury 1929.

Platts, John Thompson. 1884. *A Dictionary of Urdu, Classical Hindi, and English*. London: W. H. Allen & Co.

Pliny the Elder. *Natural History*. See Rackham 1975.

Plutarch. *Moralia*. See Babbitt 1936; Minar, Sandbach, and Helmbold 1961; Clement and Hoffleit 1969.

Pocock, David F. 1973. *Mind, Body, and Wealth: A Study of Belief and Practice in an Indian Village*. Oxford: Basil Blackwell.

Pokorny, Julius. 2007. *Indogermanisches Etymologisches Wörterbuch*. Bern and Munich: Francke, 1959. Revised and published by the Dnghu Association. Online at https://marciorenato.files.wordpress.com/2012/01/pokorny-julius-proto-indo-european-etymological-dictionary.pdf.

Pollard, Elizabeth Ann. 2013. "Indian Spices and Roman 'Magic' in Imperial and Late Antique Indomediterranea." *Journal of World History* 24, no. 1: 1–23.

Pollock, Sheldon. 2006. *The Language of the Gods in the World of Men: Sanskrit, Culture, and Power in Premodern India*. Berkeley: University of California Press.

Pradère, Onesime. 1872. *La Bretagne poétique*. Paris: Librairie Générale.

Primiano, Leonard. 1995. "Vernacular Religion and the Search for Method in Religious Folklife." *Western Folklore* 54, no. 1: 37–56.

Proferes, Theodore. 2007. *Vedic Ideals of Sovereignty and the Poetics of Power*. New Haven, CT: American Oriental Society.

Puhvel, Jaan. 1973. "Aquam Exstinguere." *Journal of Indo-European Studies* 1, no. 3 (Fall): 379–86.

———. 1987. *Comparative Mythology*. Baltimore: Johns Hopkins University Press.

Puttenham, George. 1936. *The Arte of English Poesie*. Edited by Gladys Doidge Wilcock and Alice Walker. Cambridge: Cambridge University Press.

Quinlan-McGrath, Mary. 2012. *Influences: Art, Optics, and Astrology in the Italian Renaissance*. Chicago: University of Chicago Press.

Quintanilla, Sonya Rhie. 2017. "Transformations of Identity and the Buddha's Infancy Narratives at Kanaganhalli." *Archives of Asian Art* 67, no. 1 (Apr.): 111–42.

Quintus Serenus Sammonicus. *Liber medicinalis*. Online at http://latin.packhum.org/loc/1515/1/0#0.

Rackham, Harris. 1975. *Pliny. Natural History, volume 8. Books 28–32*, second impression. Loeb Classical Library, 418. London: Heinemann, 1938. Cambridge MA: Harvard University Press.

Radhakrishna Sastri, S. V., ed. 1952. *Ānandakanda*. Tanjore: TMSSM Library.

Raffaelli, Enrico G. 2010. "L'Astrologie dans le Zoroastrisme d'epoque sassanide: L'exemple de la 5[e] section du *Bundahišn*." In Eugen Ciurtin and Mihaela Timus, eds., *Proceedings of the 6th EASR/IAHR Special Conference "Religious History of Europe and Asia," Bucarest, 20–23 September 2006 = Studia Asiatica* 11, nos. 1–2: 63–87.

Rakoczy, Thomas. 1996. *Böser Blick, Macht des Auges und Neid der Götter. Eine Untersuchung zur Kraft des Blickes in der griechischen Literatur*. Tübingen: Gunter Narr Verlag.

Rama Shastry, R., ed. 1969. *Śivatattvaratnākara*. 2 vols. Mysore: Oriental Research Institute.

Rasārṇava. See Ray and Kaviratna 1910.

Rastelli, Marion. 2003. "Maṇḍalas and Yantras in the Pāñcarātra Tradition." In Gudrun Bühnemann, ed., *Maṇḍalas and Yantras in the Hindu Tradition*, pp. 119–51. Leiden: Brill.

Raverty, Henry George. 1867. *A Dictionary of the Puk'hto, Pus'hti or Language of the Afghans: with remarks on the originality of the language, and its affinity to other oriental tongues*. 2nd, rev. ed. London: Williams & Norgate.

Ray, Prafulla Candra, and Hariscandra Kaviratna, eds. 1910. *Rasārṇava*. Calcutta: Baptist Mission Press.

Rees, Alwyn D., and Brinley Rees. 1961. *Celtic Heritage: Ancient Tradition in Ireland and Wales*. New York: Grove Press.

Ṛg Veda. See Kashikar and Sontakke 1936; Nooten and Holland 1994; Jamison and Brereton 2014.

Rhie, Marilyn M. 1988. *Interrelationships between the Buddhist Art of China and the Art of India and Central Asia from 618–755 A.D.* Supplement no. 54 to *Annali* 48, fasc. 1. Naples: Istituto Universitario Orientale.

Rhys, John. 1901. *Celtic Folklore: Welsh and Manx*. Vol. 1. Oxford: Clarendon Press.

Rhys Davids, Caroline. 1913. *Psalms of the Early Buddhists. II. Psalms of the Brethren*. London: Henry Frowde.

Rhys Davids, T. W., and J. E. Carpenter. 1890. *Dīgha-Nikaya of the Sūtta-Pīṭaka*. Vol. 1. London: Pali Text Society. Online at http://gretil.sub.uni-goettingen.de/2_pali/1_tipit/2_sut/1_digh/dighn1ou.htm (posted by the Dhammakaya Foundation, Thailand, 1989–96). Accessed February 6, 2018.

Roberts, John M. 1976. "Belief in the Evil Eye in World Perspective." In Clarence Maloney, ed., *The Evil Eye*, pp. 223–78. New York: Columbia University Press.

Robinson, F. N., ed. 1957. *The Works of Geoffrey Chaucer*. 2nd ed. Boston: Houghton Mifflin.

Roman de Thèbes. See Constans 1890.

Rose, H. A. 1990. *A Glossary of the Tribes and Castes of the Punjab and North-West Frontier Province*. 3 vols. Delhi: Asian Educational Services. (Orig. pub. 1914. Lahore: Superintendent, Government Printing, Punjab).

Ross, Anne. 1967. *Pagan Celtic Britain: Studies in Iconography and Tradition*. London: Routledge & Kegan Paul; New York: Columbia University Press.

Roth, Rudolph von, and William Dwight Whitney, eds. 1966. *Atharva Veda Saṃhitā*. 3rd ed. Bonn: Ferd. Dümmlers Verlag.

Russell, James R. 1987. *Zoroastrianism in Armenia*. Harvard Oriental Series, 5. Cambridge, MA: Harvard University Department of Near Eastern Languages and Civilizations and National Association for Armenian Studies and Research.

Russell, R. V., and H. Lal. 1993. *The Tribes and Castes of the Central Provinces of India.* 4 vols. London, Macmillan & Co. 1916; reprint New Delhi: Asian Educational Services.

Sachau, Edward, tr. 1983. *Alberuni's India.* 2 vols. London: Kegan Paul, Trench & Trubner, 1910; reprint Delhi: Munshiram Manoharlal.

Saint-Mars, Thomas de. 1817. "Fête de Saint-Estapin." *Mémoires de la Société Royale des Antiquaires de France* 1:427–32.

Saintyves, P. 1918. "Le transfert des maladies aux arbres et aux buissons." *Bulletin de la Société préhistorique de France* 15, no. 6: 296–300.

———. 1930. *En marge de la légende dorée: Songes miracles et survivances; Essai sur la formation de quelques thèmes hagiographiques.* Paris: Émile Noury.

Sakaria, Bhadri Prasad, and Bhupatiram Sakaria. 1982. *Rājasthānī-Hindī Śabd Koś.* 3 vols. Jaipur: Pancaship Prakashan.

Sakurzada, Ebrahim, and Mahmoud Omidsalar. 1998. "Čašm-zak̲m." In Ehsan Yarshater, ed., *Encyclopædia Iranica*, vol. 5, fasc. 1, pp. 44–47. Online at http://www.iranicaonline.org/articles/casm-zakm-lit. Accessed January 2, 2018.

Salem, Jean. 1996. *Démocrite: Grains de poussière dans un rayon de soleil.* Paris: J. Vrin.

Salles, Jean-François. 2017. "La baie de Bengale dans l'Antiquité: Une voie ouverte vers l'Est." In Marcotte, ed., *Méditerranée et Océan Indien*, pp. 45–82.

Sanderson, Alexis. 1986. "Maṇḍala and Āgamic Identity in the Trika of Kashmir." In André Padoux, ed., *Mantras et diagrammes rituels dans l'Hindouisme*, pp. 169–207. Paris: Editions du CNRS.

———. 2004. "Religion and the State: Śaiva Officiants in the Territory of the Brahmanical Royal Chaplain." *Indo-Iranian Journal* 47:229–300.

———. 2006. "The Lākulas: New Evidence of a System Intermediate between Pāñcārthika Pāśupatism and Āgamic Śaivism." *Indian Philosophical Annual* 24:143–217.

———. 2007. "Atharvavedins in Tantric Territory: The Āṅgirasakalpa Texts of the Oriya Paippalādins and Their Connection with the Trika and the Kālīkula, with critical editions of the Parājapavidhi, the Parāmantravidhi, and the *Bhadrakālī-mantravidhiprakaraṇa." In Arlo Griffiths and Annette Schmiedchen, eds., *The Atharvaveda and its Paippalāda Śākhā: Historical and Philological Papers on a Vedic Tradition*, pp. 195–311. Aachen: Shaker Verlag.

———. 2009. "The Śaiva Age—The Rise and Dominance of Śaivism during the Early Medieval Period." In Shingo Einoo, ed., *Genesis and Development of Tantra*, pp. 41–349. Tokyo: Institute of Oriental Culture, University of Tokyo.

Sanford, A. Whitney. 2005. "Shifting the Center: Yakṣas on the Margins of Contemporary Practice." *Journal of the American Academy of Religion* 73, no. 1: 89–110.

Śāntikalpa. See Bolling 1904, 1913.

Sarkar, Sumit. 2001. "The Decline of the Subaltern in *Subaltern Studies*." In David Ludden, ed., *Reading Subaltern Studies: Critical History, Contested Meaning, and the Globalization of South Asia*, pp. 400–429. London: Anthem Press.

Sarma, Sreeramula Rajeswara, and Yaduendra Sahai. 1995. "Gushing Mercury, Fleeing Maiden: A Rasaśāstra Motif in Mughal Painting." *Journal of the European Ayurveda Society* 4:149–62.

Sastri, Durgasankara K., ed. 1932. *Prabandhacintāmaṇi.* Mumbai: Harsiddhbhai Vajubhai Divatia.

Sastri, Jagadish Lal, ed. 1970. *Kathāsaritsāgaraḥ kaśmīrapradeśavāsinā Śrīrāmabhaṭṭanūdbhavena mahākavi Śrī Somadevabhaṭṭena viracitaḥ.* Delhi: Motilal Banarsidass.

Sastri, Ramakrishna Harshaji, ed. 1926. *Mānavagṛhyasūtra of the Mitrāyaṇīya Śākhā.* Gaekwad's Oriental Series, 35. Baroda: Central Library. Online at http://gretil.sub.uni-goettingen.de/gretil/1_sanskr/1_veda/5_vedang/2_grhya/manavgsu.htm.

Sax, William S. 2009. *God of Justice: Ritual Healing and Social Justice in the Central Himalayas*. New York: Oxford University Press.

Schäfer, Peter. 1990. "Jewish Magical Literature in Late Antiquity and Early Middle Ages." *Journal of Jewish Studies* 41, no. 1: 75–91.

Schaflechner, Jürgen. 2018. *Hinglaj Devi: Identity, Change, and Solidifaction at a Hindu Temple in Pakistan*. New York: Oxford University Press.

Scheid, John. 1993. "*Lucus, nemus*. Qu'est-ce qu'un bois sacré?" In John Scheid, ed., *Les bois sacrés*, Actes du Colloque International organisé par le Centre Jean Bérard et l'École Pratique des Hautes Études (Ve section), pp. 13–30. Naples: Centre Jean Bérard.

———. 2008. "Religion, institutions et société de la Rome antique." *Cours et travaux du Collège de France. Annuaire 108e année*, pp. 622–37. Paris: Collège de France. Online at https://www.college-de-france.fr/site/john-scheid/p1346267505254_content.htm. Accessed May 17, 2019.

Schmidt, Mauricius, ed. 1868. *Hesychii Alexandrini Lexicon*. Jena: Sumptibus F. Maukii.

Schmitt, Jean-Claude. 1979. *Le saint lévrier: Guinefort guérisseur d'enfants depuis le XIIe siècle*. Paris: Flammarion.

———. 1981. "Les traditions folkloriques dans la culture médiévale: Quelques réflexions de méthode." *Archives de sciences sociales des religions* 52, no. 1 (July–Sept.): 5–20.

———. 1983. *The Holy Greyhound: Guinefort, Healer of Children since the Thirteenth Century*. Translated by Martin Thom. Cambridge: Cambridge University Press.

———. 1988. "Les 'superstitions.'" In Jacques Le Goff and René Rémond, eds., *Histoire de la France religieuse*, vol. 1, *Des dieux de la Gaule à la papauté d'Avignon (des origines au XIVe siècle)*, pp. 417–551. Paris: Seuil.

———. 1994. *Les revenants: Les vivants et les morts dans la société médiévale*. Paris: Gallimard.

———. 2001. *Les corps, les rites, les rêves, le temps: Essais d'anthropologie médiévale*. Paris: Gallimard.

———. 2018. *Les rythmes au Moyen-Âge*. Paris: Gallimard.

Schömbucher, Elisabeth. 1999. "Death as the Beginning of a New Life: Hero-Worship among a South Indian Fishing Caste." In Elisabeth Schömbucher and Claus Peter Zoller, eds., *Ways of Dying: Death and Its Meanings in South Asia*, pp. 162–78. New Delhi: Manohar.

Schopen, Gregory. 1977. "Review of Edward Conze, *The Large Sutra on Perfect Wisdom with the Divisions of the Abhisamāyālaṃkāra*." *Indo-Iranian Journal* 19:135–52.

———. 1978. "The Bhaiṣajyaguru-Sūtra and the Buddhism of Gilgit." PhD dissertation, Australian National University, Canberra.

Schwartz, Martin. 1970. "Miscellanea Iranica." In Boyce and Gershevitch, eds., *W. B. Henning Memorial Volume*, pp. 385–94.

———. 2007. "Kirdēr's Clairvoyants: Extra-Iranian and Gathic Perspectives." In Maria Macuch, Mauro Maggi, and Werner Sundermann, eds., *Iranian Languages and Texts from Iran and Turan. Ronald E. Emmerick Memorial Volume*. Wiesbaden: Harrassowitz.

———. 2008. "On *Aiiehiiā*, Afflictress of Childbirth, and *Pairikā*: Two Avestan Demonesses (with an Appendix on the Indo-Iranian Shipwrecked Seaman)." *Bulletin of the Asia Institute*, n.s., 22: 95–103.

Schwartzberg, Joseph, ed. 1992. *A Historical Atlas of South Asia*. Chicago: University of Chicago Press, 1978; second impression, with additional material, New York: Oxford University Press.

Scobie, Alex. 1983. *Apuleius and Folklore*. London: Folklore Society.

Scott, David. 1993. "Śiva and the East Iranians of Bactria: Hindu cross-cultural expansion—I." *International Journal of Indian Studies* 3, no. 1: 87–106.

———. 1994. *Formations of Ritual. Colonial and Anthropological Discourses on the Sinhala "Yaktovil."* Minneapolis: University of Minnesota Press.

Sébillot, Paul. 1882. *Traditions et superstitions de la Haute-Bretagne*. Vol. 1. Paris: Maisonneuve & LaRose.

———. 1906. *Le folk-lore de France*. Vol. 3, *La faune et la flore*. Paris: Guilmoto.

Secunda, Shai. 2014. "The Fractious Eye: On the Evil Eye of Menstruants in Zoroastrian Tradition." *Numen* 61:83–108.

Sehgal, K. K. 1974. *Rajasthan District Gazetteer, Bhanswara*. Jaipur; Government Central Press.

Seligman, Sigfried. 1922. *Die Zauberkraft des Auges und des Berufen: Ein Kapitel aus der Geschichte des Aberglaubens*. Hamburg: L. Friederichsen & Co.

Sen, Sukumar. 1965. "On Dhāraṇī and Pratisarā." *Studies in Esoteric Buddhism and Tantrism: In Commemoration of the 1,150th Anniversary of the founding of Koyasan*, pp. 67–72. Koya: Koyasan University Press.

Sergent, Bernard. 2000. "Maponos: la malediction." In Alain Moreau and Jean-Claude Turpin, eds., *La magie, du monde babylonien au monde hellénistique*, vol. 1, pp. 197–218. Montpéllier: Université de Montpéllier.

———. 2002a. "Maponos et Nechtan." In Charles-Marie Ternes and Hartmut Zinser, eds., *Dieux des Celtes—Götter der Kelten—Gods of the Celts*, pp. 81–97. Luxembourg: Association européenne pour l'étude scientifique des religions.

———. 2002b. "Les Phéaciens avant l'Odyssée." In André Hurst and Françoise Létoublon, eds., *La mythologie et l'Odyssée: Hommage à Gabriel Germain*, pp. 199–222. Geneva: Droz.

———. 2004. *Le livre des dieux, Celtes et Grecs, II*. Paris: Payot.

Shakespear, John. 1834. *A dictionary, Hindustani and English: with copious index, fitting the work to serve, also, as a dictionary of English and Hindustani*. 3rd ed. London: J. L. Cox & Son.

Sharan, Vasudev. 1953. "Gāhā aur palhāyā." *Janapada* 1, no. 2: 70–74.

Sharma, Dharmananda, ed. 1962. *Rasaratnasamuccaya*. Varanasi: Motilal Banarsidass.

Sharma, Hemaraja, ed. 1998. *The Kāśyapa Saṃhitā (or Vṛddhajīvakīya Tantra) by Vṛddha Jīvaka revised by Vātsya with Sanskrit Introduction*. 5th ed. Benares: Chaukhambha Sanskrit Sansthan.

Shastri, Brahmshankar, ed. 1973. *Yogaratnākara Pūrvārdha*. Varanasi: Chowkhamba Sanskrit Series Office.

Shastri, Devadatt. 1978. *Āgneyatīrth Hiṅglāj*. Bombay: Lokalok Prakashan.

Shastri, Madhusudan Kaul, ed. 1926, 1939. *The Netra Tantram, with Commentary by Kshemarāja*. 2 vols. Bombay: Tattva-Vivechaka Press.

Shenkar, Michael. 2017. "The Religion and the Pantheon of the Sogdians (5th–8th centuries CE) in Light of Their Sociopolitical Structures." *Journal Asiatique* 305, no. 2: 191–209.

Sheth, Hargovind Das T. 1928. *Paia-Sadda-Mahaṇṇavo, a Comprehensive Prakrit Hindi Dictionary*. Calcutta: Gurjar Prabhat.

Shorter Oxford Economic Atlas of the World. 2nd ed. 1959. Prepared by the Economist Intelligence Unit. London: Oxford University Press.

Shorto, Russell. 2019. "Rembrandt in the Blood: An Obsessive Aristocrat, Rediscovered Paintings, and an Art-World Feud." *New York Times Magazine*, February 27. Online at https://www.nytimes.com/2019/02/27/magazine/rembrandt-jan-six.html?smid=nytcore-ios-share.

Shrivastava, C. M. 2001. *Śani kā prakop usse bacāo*. Delhi: Manoj Publications.

Silva, Roland. 1990. "Mantai, the Great Emporium of Cosmas Indicopleustes." *Ancient Ceylon* 14:1–14.

Simon, Gérard. 2004. "Eidôlon." In Barbara Cassin, ed., *Vocabulaire européen des philosophies: Dictionnaire des intraduisibles*, pp. 335–40. Paris: Éditions du Seuil.

Simpson, Jacqueline. 2002. "Evil Eye." In Lindahl, McNamara, and Lindow, eds., *Medieval Folklore*, p. 122.

Singh, Bhrigupati. 2012. "The Headless Horseman of Central India: Sovereignty at Varying Thresholds of Life." *Cultural Anthropology* 27, no. 2: 383–407.

Singh, Nag Sharan, ed. 1984. *The Skandamahāpurāṇa*. 3 vols. Delhi: Nag Publishers.

Sircar, Dinesh Candra. 1990. *Studies in the Geography of Ancient and Medieval India*. 2nd, rev. ed. Delhi: Motilal Banarsidass.

Sircar, Sanjay. 2018. *Fantasy Tales from the Bengal Renaissance*. New Delhi: Oxford India.

Sivadatt, Pandit, and Kasinath Pandurang Parab. 1983. *The Haracaritacintāmaṇi of Rajānaka Jayaratha*. Delhi: Bharatiya Vidya Prakashan.

Śivanātha. *Śivakalpadruma*. Anup Sanskrit Library, Bikaner, mss. 4349.

Skanda Purāṇa. See Singh 1984.

Skjærvø, Prods Oktor. 1995. "The Avesta as Source for the Early History of the Iranians." In George Erdosy, ed., *The Indo-Aryans of Ancient South Asia: Language, Material Culture and Ethnicity*, pp. 155–76. Berlin: Walter de Gruyter.

———. 2011. *The Spirit of Zoroastrianism*. New Haven, CT: Yale University Press.

Slouber, Michael. 2017. *Early Tantric Medicine: Snakebite, Mantras, and Healing in the Gāruḍa Tantras*. New York: Oxford University Press.

Slusser, Mary S. 1982. *Nepal Mandala: A Cultural Study of the Kathmandu Valley*. 2 vols. Princeton, NJ: Princeton University Press.

Smith, Frederick M. 2006. *The Self Possessed*. New York: Columbia University Press.

Smith, John D. 2009. *The Mahābhārata, an Abridged Translation*. London: Penguin Books.

Smith, Jonathan Z. 1971. "*Adde Parvum Parvo Magnus Acervus Erit*." *History of Religions* 11, no. 1: 67–90.

———. 1978a. *Map Is Not Territory: Studies in the History of Religions*. Chicago: University of Chicago Press.

———. 1978b. "Towards Interpreting Demonic Powers in Hellenistic and Roman Antiquity." In Hindegard Temporini and Wolfgang Haase, ed., *Aufstieg und Niedergang der römischen Welt. Geschichte und Kultur Roms im Spiegel der neueren Forschungen, II*, pp. 425–39. Berlin: Walter de Gruyter.

———. 1982. *Imagining Religion: From Babylon to Jonestown*. Chicago: University of Chicago Press.

———. 1987. *To Take Place: Toward Theory in Ritual*. Chicago: University of Chicago Press.

———. 1990. *Drudgery Divine: On the Comparison of Early Christianities and the Religions of Late Antiquity*. Chicago: University of Chicago Press.

Somadeva. *Kathāsaritsāgara*. See Sastri 1970; Penzer 1926.

Somadeva. *Rasendracūḍāmaṇi*. See Misra 1984.

Sommer, Marianne. 2007. *Bones and Ochre: The Curious Afterlife of the Red Lady of Paviland*. Cambridge, MA: Harvard University Press.

Sontheimer, Gunther-Dietz. 1989. *Pastoral Deities in Western India*. Delhi: Oxford University Press.

Sørensen, Henrik H. 2006. "The Spell of the Great, Golden Peacock Queen: The Origin, Practices, and Lore of an Early Esoteric Buddhist Tradition in China." *Pacific World*, 3rd series, 8:89–123.

Spivak, Gayatri. 1993. "Can the Subaltern Speak?" In Patrick Williams and Laura Chrisman, eds., *Colonial Discourse and Post-Colonial Theory*, pp. 66–111. New York: Columbia University

Press. Reprinted from Cary Nelson and Lawrence Grossberg, eds., *Marxism and the Interpretation of Cultures*, pp. 271–313. Basingstoke: Macmillan Education.

Śrīdhārāchārya. *Nyāyakandalī*. See Jetly and Parikh 1991.

Stahl, William Harris, and Richard Johnson, with E. L. Burge. 1977. *Martianus Capella and the Seven Liberal Arts*. Vol. 2. New York: Columbia University Press.

Stanziani, Alessandro. 2018. *Les entrelacements du monde: Histoire globale, pensée globale*. Paris: CNRS Éditions.

Stein, Sir Aurel. 1975. *Ancient Khotan: Detailed Report of Archaeological Explorations in Chinese Turkestan*. Oxford: Clarendon Press, 1907; reprint New York: Hacker Art Books.

———, tr. 1979. *Kalhaṇa's Rājataraṅgiṇī, Chronicle of the Kings of Kashmir*. 2 vols. London: Constable, 1900; reprint Delhi: Motilal Banarsidass.

Stephen of Bourbon. *Tractatus de diversis materiis prædicabilibus*. See Lecoy de la Marche 1877.

Sterckx, Claude. 1994. "Nûtons, Lûtons et dieux celtes." *Zeitschrift für Celtische Philologie* 46:39–79.

———. 2004. "Le feu dans l'eau de l'Apollon gaulois." In Capdeville, ed., *L'Eau et le feu*, pp. 303–19.

Stewart, C. E. 1897. "Account of the Hindu Fire-Temple at Baku, in the Trans-Caucusus Province of Russia." *Journal of the Royal Asiatic Society of Great Britain and Ireland* (Apr.): 311–18.

Stewart, Charles. 1991. *Demons and the Devil: Moral Imagination in Modern Greek Culture*. Princeton, NJ: Princeton University Press.

Stokes, Whitley. 1894. "The Prose Tales in the Rennes Dindshenchas." *Revue Celtique* 15:272–336, 418–84.

———. 1903. "The Death of Crimthann Son of Fidach, and the Adventures of the Sons of Eochaid Muigmedon." *Revue Celtique* 24:172–207.

Stokes, Whitley, and Ernst Windisch, ed. and tr. 1891. *Irische Texte mit Übersetzungen und Wörterbuch*, 3rd series, part 1. Leipzig: Hirzel.

Stoneman, Richard, Kyle Erikson, and Ian Netton, eds. 2012. *The Alexander Romance in Persia and the East*. Groningen: Barkhuis Publishing & Groningen University Library.

Stratton, Kimberly B., and Dayna S. Kalleres, eds. 2014. *Daughters of Hecate: Women & Magic in the Ancient World*. New York: Oxford University Press.

Strickmann, Michel. 1996. *Mantras et mandarins: Le bouddhisme tantrique en chine*. Paris: Gallimard.

———. 2002. *Chinese Magical Medicine*. Edited by Bernard Faure. Stanford, CA: Stanford University Press.

Subrahmanyam, Sanjay. 1997. "Connected Histories: Notes towards a Reconfiguration of Early Modern Eurasia." *Modern Asian Studies* 31, no. 3 (Special Issue: The Eurasian Context of the Early Modern History of Mainland South East Asia, 1400–1800): 735–62.

———. 2005. *Explorations in Connected History: From the Tagus to the Ganges*. New Delhi: Oxford University Press.

Sukthankar, Vishnu Sitaram, Shripad Krishna Velvalkar, P. L. Vaidya et al., eds. 1927–66. *Mahābhārata*. 21 vols. Poona: Bhandarkar Oriental Research Institute.

Sullivan, Karen. 2018. *The Danger of Romance: Truth, Fantasy, and Arthurian Fictions*. Chicago: University of Chicago Press.

Sullivan, Lucy Woods, and E. Sherman Oakley. 1905. *Holy Himalaya: The Religion, Traditions, and Scenery of a Himalayan Province (Kumaon and Garhwal)*. London: Oliphant Anderson & Ferrier.

Suśruta Saṃhitā. See Vaidya 1975.

Suttanipāta. See Andersen and Smith 1965.

Suvarṇaprabhāsottamasūtra. See Nobel 1958.

Tafazzoli, Ahmad. 2000. "Frāxkard." In Ehsan Yarshater, ed., *Encyclopædia Iranica*, vol. 10, fasc. 2, p. 201. Online at http://www.iranicaonline.org/articles/fraxkard-. Accessed August 11, 2015.

Takubo, Shuya, ed. 1972. *Ārya-Mahā-Māyūrī-Vidyā-Rājñī*. Tokyo: Sankibo. Online at http://gretil.sub.uni-goettingen.de/gretil/1_sanskr/4_rellit/buddh/mmayuvru.htm (input by Klaus Wille).

Taneja, Anand Vivek. 2018. *Jinnealogy: Time, Islam, and Ecological Thought in the Medieval Ruins of Delhi*. Stanford, CA: Stanford University Press.

Tarabout, Gilles. 1999. "Corps possédés et signatures territoriales au Kérala." In Assayag and Tarabout, eds., *La Possession en Asie du Sud*, pp. 315–55.

Taranatha, *Bka' babs bdun Ldan*. See Templeman 1983.

Tatia, Nathmal. 1973. *The Dhammapada-Aṭṭhakathā*. Vol. 1. Nalanda: Nava Nalanda Mahavihara.

Tawney, C. H. 1899. *Prabandhacintāmaṇi; or, Wishing-stone of Narratives*. Calcutta: Asiatic Society.

Templeman, David, ed. and tr. 1983. *Tāranātha's Bka' babs bdun Ldan; The Seven Instruction Lineages by Jonang Tāranātha*. Dharamsala: Library of Tibetan Works and Archives.

Tewari, Premvati. 1996. *Kāśyapa-saṃhitā or Vṛddhajīvakīya Tantra: Text with English Translation and Commentary*. Benares: Chaukhambha Visvabharati.

Therāgātha. See Rhys Davids 1913.

Tiwari, Jagdish Narain. 1985. *Goddess Cults in Ancient India [with special reference to the first seven centuries A.D.]*. With a preface by A. L. Basham. Delhi: Sundeep Prakashan.

Tomber, Roberta. 2008. *Indo-Roman Trade. From Pots to Pepper*. London: Duckworth.

Trachtenberg, Joshua. 2004. *Jewish Magic and Superstition: A Study in Folk Religion*. New York: Behrman's Jewish Book House, 1939; reprint Philadelphia: University of Pennsylvania Press.

Traill, George William. 1828. "Statistical Sketch of Kamaon." *Asiatic Researches* 16:138–234.

Tripathi, A. V., ed. 1968. *Bṛhatsaṃhitā by Varāhamihira with the commentary of Bhaṭṭotpala. Parts I–II*. Varanasi: Sarasvati Bhavan Granthamala.

Tulpule, Shankar Gopal, and Anne Feldhaus. 1999. *A Dictionary of Old Marathi*. Mumbai: Popular Prakashan.

Turner, (Sir) Ralph L. 1931. *A Comparative and Etymological Dictionary of the Nepali Language*. London: K. Paul, Trench, Trubner.

———. 1966. *A Comparative Dictionary of the Indo-Aryan Languages*. London: Oxford University Press.

Turnour, George. 1837. *The Maháwamso in Roman Characters with the Translation Subjoined and an Introductory Essay on Páli Buddhistical Literature*. Vol. 1. Kandy: Cotta Church Mission Press.

Turstig, Hans-Georg. 1985. "The Indian Sorcery Called Abhicāra." *Wiener Zeitschrift für die Kunde Südasiens und Archiv für indische Philosophie* 26:69–117.

Uhlig, Marion. 2018. *Le prince des clercs. "Barlaam et Josaphat" ou l'art du recueil*. Geneva: Droz.

Unbescheid, Günter. 1980. *Kānphaṭā. Untersuchungen zu Kult, Mythologie und Geschichte śivaitischer Tantriker in Nepal*. Wiesbaden: Franz Steiner Verlag.

Upadhyaya, Yadunandana, ed. 1992. *Śrīmad Vṛddhavāgbhaṭaviracita Aṣṭāṅgahṛdayam*. Varanasi: Chaukhambha Sanskrit Sansthan.

Uther, Hans-Jörg. 2004. *The Types of International Folktales: A Classification and Bibliography. Based on the System of Antti Aarne and Stith Thompson*. 3 vols. Folklore Fellows Communications nos. 284–86. Helsinki: Suomalainen Tiedeakatemia.

Vāgbhaṭa. *Aṣṭāṅgahṛdayam*. See Upadhyaya 1992.

Vāgbhaṭa. *Aṣṭāṅgasaṃgraha*. See Athavale 1980.

Vāgbhaṭṭa. *Rasaratnasamuccaya*. See Sharma 1962.

Vagnon, Emmanuelle. 2017. "La cartographie occidentale de l'océan Indien au Moyen-Âge et à la Renaissance: une evolution non-linéaire." In Marcotte, ed., *Méditerranée et Océan Indien*, pp. 183–205.

Vaidya, Lalcandraji, ed. 1975. *Suśruta Saṃhitā anuvāda Atrideva*. 5th ed. Delhi: Motilal Banarsidass.

Vaidya, Parasuram Lakshman, ed. 1963. *Saddharmalaṅkavatārasūtra*. Buddhist Sanskrit Texts, 3. Darbhanga: Mithila Institute. Online at http://gretil.sub.uni-goettingen.de/gretil/1_sanskr/4_rellit/buddh/bsu021_u.htm.

———, ed. 1969. *The Harivaṁśa being the Khila or supplement to the Mahābhārata*. Vol. 1. Poona: Bhandarkar Oriental Research Institute.

———, ed. 1971. *The Harivaṁśa being the Khila or supplement to the Mahābhārata*. Vol. 2 (appendixes). Poona: Bhandarkar Oriental Research Institute.

Varāhamihira. *Bṛhatsaṃhitā*. See Tripathi 1968.

Varma, Ramcandra, ed. 1981. *Saṃkṣipt Hindī Śabdsāgar*, 8th ed. Benares: Nagaripracarini Sabha.

Vasudeva, Somadeva. 2012. "Powers and Identities: Yoga Powers and the Tantric Śaiva Traditions." In Jacobsen, ed., *Yoga Powers*, pp. 265–302.

———. 2014. "*Prasenā, Prasīnā & Prasannā*: The Evidence of the *Niśvāsaguhya* and the *Tantrasadbhāva*." *Cracow Indological Studies* 16:369–90.

Vaudeville, Charlotte. 1999. *Myths, Saints, and Legends in Medieval India*. New Delhi: Oxford India.

Vayssière, Augustin. 1879. "Saint Guignefort, origine, forme et object du culte rendu à ce pretendu saint dans la paroisse de Romans (Ain)." *Annales de la société d'émulation (Agriculture, Lettres et Arts) de l'Ain* 12:94–108, 209–21.

Verardi, Giovanni. 1994. Homa *and Other Fire Rituals in Gandhāra*. Naples: Istituto Universitario Orientale.

Viennot, Odette. 1954. *Le culte de l'arbre dans l'Inde ancienne: Textes et monuments brâhmaniques et bouddhiques*. Paris: Presses Universitaires Françaises.

Villemarqué, Hersart de la. 1861. *Les romans de la Table ronde et les contes des anciens Bretons*. Paris: Didier et Compagnie.

Viṣṇudeva. *Rasasindhu*. Anup Sanskrit Library, Bikaner, mss. no. 4276.

Viṣṇuśarman. *Pañcatantra*. See Jha 1991.

Vita Amandi Episcopi. See Bollandus and Henschenius 1658.

Vries, Ranke de. 2012. *Two Texts on Loch nEchach: "De causis torchi Corc' Óche" and "Aided Echach maic Maireda."* London: Irish Texts Society.

Wagner, Heinrich. 1981. "Origins of the Pagan Irish Religion." *Zeitschrift für Celtische Philologie* 38:1–28.

Waldschmidt, Ernst, ed. 1965–2008. *Sanskrithandschriften aus den Turfanfunden*. Wiesbaden: Franz Steiner.

Wallerstein, Immanuel. 1974. *The Modern World-System*. New York: Academic Press.

Walter, Jonathan. 2000. "Buddhist History: The Sri Lankan Pali Vamsas and Their Community." In Ronald Inden, Jonathan Walters, Daud Ali, eds., *Querying the Medieval: Texts and the History of Practices in South Asia*. New York: Oxford University Press.

Walter, Michael. 2004. "Of Corpses and Gold: Materials for the Study of the Vetāla and the Rolangs." *Tibet Journal* 29, no. 2 (Summer): 13–46.

Warmuth, Vera, et al. 2012. "Reconstructing the Origin and Spread of Horse Domestication in the Eurasian Steppe." *Proceedings of the Academy of Sciences of the United States of America* 109, no. 21 (May 22): 8202–6.

Webb, Clemens C. I., ed. 1965. *Ioannis Saresberiensis Episcopi Carnotensis Policratici sive De Nugis Curialium et Vestigiis Philosophorum libri VIII*. Vol. 1. London, 1909; reprint Frankfurt am Main: Minerva.

Weber, Albrecht. 1873. *On the Râmâyaṇa by Albrecht Weber, Berlin*. Translated from the German by D. C. Boyd. Reprinted from "The Indian Antiquary," vol. 1. London: N. Trubner & Co.

Webster, Colin. 2014. "Technology and/as Theory: Material Thinking in Ancient Science and Medicine." PhD dissertation, Columbia University, New York.

Wedding of Sir Gawain and Dame Ragnelle. See Hahn 1995.

Weinberger-Thomas, Catherine. 1999. *Ashes of Immortality: Widow-Burning in India*. Translated by Jeffrey Mehlman and David [Gordon] White. Chicago: University of Chicago Press.

West, Emily. 2014. "Circe, Calypso, Hiḍimbā: The Odyssey and Graeco-Aryan Proto-Epic." *Journal of Indo-European Studies* 42, nos. 1–2 (Spring/Summer): 144–73.

Weststeijn, Thijs. 2010. "Seeing and the Transfer of Spirits in Early Modern Art Theory." In John Shannon Hendrix and Charles H. Carmen, eds., *Renaissance Theories of Vision*, pp. 149–69. Surrey, UK: Ashgate.

White, David Gordon. 1988. "The Other Gives Rise to Self: Dog-Men on the Borders of Medieval Europe, India, and China." PhD dissertation, University of Chicago.

———. 1991. *Myths of the Dog-Man*. Chicago: University of Chicago Press.

———. 1995. "The Ocean of Mercury: An Eleventh Century Alchemical Text." In Donald Lopez, Jr., ed., *Religions of India in Practice*, pp. 281–87. Princeton, NJ: Princeton University Press.

———. 1996. *The Alchemical Body: Siddha Traditions in Medieval India*. Chicago: University of Chicago Press.

———. 2003. *Kiss of the Yoginī. "Tantric Sex" in Its South Asian Contexts*. Chicago: University of Chicago Press.

———. 2006. "Digging Wells While Houses Burn? Writing Histories of Hinduism in a Time of Identity Politics." *History and Theory* 45:104–31.

———. 2009a. *Sinister Yogis*. Chicago: University of Chicago Press.

———. 2009b. "Bhairava." In *Encyclopedia of Hinduism*, vol. 1, pp. 485–90. Leiden: Brill.

———. 2009c. "Amulettes et lambeaux divines: «superstition», vraie «religion» et «science» pure à la lumière de la démonologie hindoue." In Ines G. Županov and Caterina Guenzi, eds., *Divins remèdes: Médecine et religion et Asie du Sud* (Puruṣārtha 27), pp. 135–62. Paris: Editions de l'EHESS.

———. 2010. "At the Mandala's Dark Fringe: Possession and Protection in Tantric Bhairava Cults." In David Haberman and Laurie Patton, eds., *Notes from a Mandala: Essays in Honor of Wendy Doniger*, pp. 200–223. Newark: University of Delaware Press.

———. 2011. "Tantra." In *Encyclopedia of Hinduism*, vol. 3, pp. 574–88. Leiden: Brill.

———. 2012. "*Netra Tantra* at the Crossroads of the Demonological Cosmopolis." *Journal of Hindu Studies* 5, no. 2: 145–71.

———. 2013. "Mercury & Immortality: The Hindu Alchemical Tradition." In Aaron Cheak, ed., *Alchemical Traditions: From Antiquity to the Avant-Garde*, pp. 207–28. Melbourne: Numen Books.

———. 2014. *The Yoga Sutra of Patanjali: A Biography*. Princeton, NJ: Princeton University Press.

———. 2017. "Variations on the Indo-European 'Fire and Water' Mytheme in Three Alchemical Accounts." *Journal of the American Oriental Society* 137, no. 4: 679–98.

———. 2020. "Were-Creatures of the Eurasian Ecumene: Variations on a Theme." *Journal Asiatique* 308, no. 1: 63–83.

White, Hayden. 1987. *The Content of the Form: Narrative Discourse and Historical Representation.* Baltimore: Johns Hopkins University Press.

Whitfield, Susan. 2004. *Aurel Stein on the Silk Road.* Chicago: Serindia Publications.

Whitney, William Dwight, and Charles R. Lanman. 1984. *Atharva Veda Saṃhitā.* 2 vols. Cambridge, MA: Harvard University Press, 1905; reprint Delhi: Motilal Banarsidass.

Wilford, Francis (Lieutenant). 1799. "A Dissertation on Semiramis, The Origin of Mecca &c from the Hindu Sacred Books." *Asiatic Researches* 4:363–84.

Williams Jackson, Abraham Valentine. 1911. *From Constantinople to the Home of Omar Khayyam: Travels in Transcaucasia and Northern Persia for Historic and Literary Research.* New York: Macmillan.

Wink, André. 1990. *Al-Hind. The Making of the Indo-Islamic World.* Vol. 1. Leiden: Brill, 1990; reprint Delhi: Oxford University Press.

Winternitz, Moritz. 1972. *A History of Indian Literature.* Vol. 2. Buddhist Literature and Jaina Literature. 2nd ed. Translated from the German by S. Ketkar and H. Kohn and revised by the author. Delhi: Oriental Books Reprint Corporation.

Wittkower, Rudolf. 1942. "Marvels of the East: A Study in the History of Monsters." *Journal of the Warburg and Courtauld Institutes* 5:159–97.

Witzel, Michael. 2001. "Autochthonous Aryans? The Evidence from Old Indian and Iranian Texts." *Electronic Journal of Vedic Studies* 7, no. 3: 1–93.

———. 2006. "Early Loan Words in Western Central Asia." In Victor Mair, ed., *Contact and Exchange in the Ancient World,* pp. 158–90. Honolulu: University of Hawai'i Press.

Wujastyk, Dominik. 2003. *The Roots of Āyurveda. Selections from Sanskrit Medical Writings.* 3rd ed. London: Penguin Books.

———. 2008. *Mathematics and Medicine in Sanskrit.* Delhi: Motilal Banarsidass.

Yarnall, Judith. 1994. *Transformations of Circe: The History of an Enchantress.* Urbana: University of Illinois Press.

Yaśodhara Bhaṭṭa. *Rasaprakāśasudhākara.* See Joshi 2011.

Yatromanolakis, Yoryis. 1988. "*Baskanos Eros*: Love and the Evil-Eye in Heliodorus' *Aethiopica*." In Roderick Beaton, ed., *The Greek Novel, AD 1–1985,* pp. 194–204. London: Croom Helm.

Yogaratnākara. See Shastri 1973.

Yule, Col. Henry, and A. C. Burnell. 1968. *Hobson-Jobson, a Glossary of Colloquial Anglo-Indian Words and Phrases, and of Kindred Terms, Etymological, Historical, Geographical, and Discursive.* 2nd ed. Edited by William Crooke. London: John Murray, 1886; reprint Delhi: Munshiram Manoharlal.

Zamyād Yašt. See Hintze 1994; Humbach and Ichaporia 1998.

Zhu Derun. 1997. *Cun fuzhai wenji.* 10 vols. Ji'nan: Qi Lu shushe.

Zuwiyya, David. 2012. "Umāra's *Qiṣṣa al-Iskandar* as a Model of the Arabic Alexander Romance." In Stoneman, Erikson, and Netton, eds., *The Alexander Romance in Persia and the East,* pp. 205–18.

Zysk, Kenneth. 1985. *Religious Healing in the Veda, with translations and annotations of medical hymns from the "Ṛgveda" and the "Atharvaveda" and renderings from the corresponding ritual texts.* Philadelphia: American Philosophical Association.

Index